Created and Directed by Hans Höfer

INSIGHT GUIDES
FLORIDA

Edited by Paul Zach
Updated by Joann Biondi
Managing Editor: Martha Ellen Zenfell

Editorial Director: Brian Bell

HOUGHTON MIFFLIN COMPANY

APA PUBLICATIONS

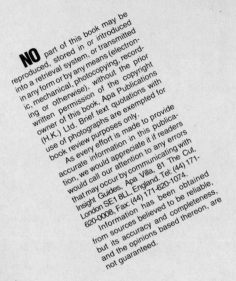
FLORIDA

Ninth Edition (Reprint)
© 1995 APA PUBLICATIONS (HK) LTD
All Rights Reserved
Printed in Singapore by Höfer Press Pte Ltd

Distributed in the United States by:	Distributed in Canada by:	Distributed in the UK & Ireland by:	Worldwide distribution enquiries:
Houghton Mifflin Company	**Thomas Allen & Son**	**GeoCenter International UK Ltd**	**Höfer Communications Pte Ltd**
222 Berkeley Street	390 Steelcase Road East	The Viables Center, Harrow Way	38 Joo Koon Road
Boston, Massachusetts 02116-3764	Markham, Ontario L3R 1G2	Basingstoke, Hampshire RG22 4BJ	Singapore 2262
ISBN: 0-395-68236-3	ISBN: 0-395-68236-3	ISBN: 9-62421-010-1	ISBN: 9-62421-010-1

ABOUT THIS BOOK

Florida, wrote Budd Schulberg in *American Panorama* some 30 years ago, "is to the United States today what the United States was to Europe a hundred years ago – a melting pot, a frontier, a place to improve your health or your luck." What was true then is even more so now, as the state of Florida grows in ever-leaping bounds towards new heights of prosperity and popularity.

The original edition of this Insight Guide to Florida, now comprehensively revised for the 1990s, was the brainchild of Apa founder **Hans Höfer** and freelance editor **Paul Zach**. Hofer's unique approach to travel literature, combining superb photography with insightful, colorful commentary, has won his 180-title Insight Guide series international acclaim and an enthusiastic audience around the world. Zach, who had covered Indonesia for several major US news organizations, gained his knowledge of Florida while a staff writer for the award-winning *Evening Independent* newspaper in St Petersburg.

An Exotic Land

Zach and co-editor **Leonard Leuras**, a native of New Mexico and an experienced Insight Guides contributor, approached Florida as an exotic land filled with Native Americans, Cubans and Crackers, pulsating with bizarre rites like Tampa's Gasparilla pirate invasion, and alive with alligators, flamingos and other wildlife.

This new edition of *Insight Guide: Florida* was prepared by contributing editor **Joann Biondi**, a Miami-based freelance writer who edited *Insight City Guide: Miami* and has written three Insight Pocket Guides. Her knowledge of the Sunshine State is formidable. Of her territory, she says: "It's easy for travelers to regard Florida as nothing more than a make-believe tourist trap. But those who take the time to dig a little deeper, and perhaps take the roads less traveled by the crowds, will find that the state does have authenticity and a unique sense of place."

Biondi was aided in her task by Apa's North American managing editor **Martha Ellen Zenfell**. Together they went through the original volume, tossing out the old and bringing in the new, in order to keep pace with Florida's ever-changing aspect. Zenfell, who hails from the American South, did the same with the pictures, providing a plethora of fresh, modern images.

Three top-notch, Cuban-born photographers added important visual components – **Ricardo Ferro**, a one-time Florida West Coast Press Photographers Association's Photographer of the Year; **José Azel**, a former *Miami Herald* staff photographer; and **Tony Arruza**, a West Palm Beach freelancer who produced the photos for the Insight Guides to Portugal, Lisbon, Barbados, and Miami.

Photographer **Bud Lee**, a native New Yorker who now lives in the rural Florida town of Plant City, has shot for numerous national publications including *Esquire*, *Holiday* Time-Life Books and *Life* magazine, which once awarded him the title "New Photographer of the Year." Some of the most stunning new images were contributed by **Catherine Karnow**, principal photographer on Insight Guides to France, Los Angeles and Washington DC. Karnow works overtime in setting up shots of people and places so the final result appears effortless. Thanks also to **Pat Canova** and to **Baron Wolmon**,

Zach

Leuras

Biondi

Zenfell

Ferro

a former chief photographer of *Rolling Stone*, who shot pictures for this book from the Pompano Beach-based Goodyear Blimp.

The brief for the locally based writers to this book was to go beyond the cartoon characters and pink plastic kitsch and put the state into a broader perspective. **Fred W. Wright, Jr**, who wrote the chapters on the East Coast, has been a writing resident of Florida for over 25 years. A former entertainment editor of the St Petersburg *Evening Independent*, he presently freelances from his St Petersburg home, specializing mostly in cinema and theater.

The chapters on Florida blacks, retirees, Crackers, and North Florida were written by husband-and-wife team **H. Taft Wireback** and **Deanna L. Thompson**. Thompson has received several awards from the Florida Society of Newspaper Editors for her stories.

Havana-born **Raul Ramirez**, a former *Miami Herald* reporter, joined the Cuban exodus to Miami in 1962. He drew upon his experiences as an immigrant in the Miami community to create the vivid portrait of Cubans in the "People" section. **Cindy Rose Stiff**, who contributed the chapters on South Florida, served as a news editor with the Associated Press Miami bureau, the Miami bureau of United Press International, and with the *Fort Lauderdale News/Sun-Sentinel*.

Pulitzer Prize-winning columnist **Dave Barry** added a light-hearted insider's view of a visit to Walt Disney World. Barry, the author of numerous humor books, including *Dave Barry's Only Travel Guide You'll Ever Need* (in which this essay was published), is one of America's most-read funny men.

Alice Klement, a journalist, lawyer and writing coach, says of her state: "When God said 'Let there be light,' (s)he must have had Florida in mind. The white-hot, brilliant light here must explain our lunacy. Welcome to the bin." Klement wrote the essays on food and festivals and also contributed to *Insight City Guide: Miami*.

The late **Jacques le Moyne** recorded early images of Florida in pen and ink. Le Moyne served as chief cartographer and artist on the 1562 French expedition to Florida led by explorer Jean Ribaut. Le Moyne's sketches, hand-colored by later artists, are the only known visual renderings of Florida's extinct aboriginal Indian tribes.

They Also Served

Thanks must also go to all the people who contributed to the first *Insight Guide: Florida,* whose work still filters through on these pages. A sun-drenched cheer, then, to **Tim Rosaforte**, **Paul Moran**, **Ray Holliman**, **John Anderson** and **Steve Shrader**.

Others who contributed in various ways were the Florida State Museum, NASA's photo department at the Kennedy Space Center; Kennedy Space Center Tours, TWA Services, Inc.; Circus World; the John and Mabel Ringling Museums, Sarasota; Everglades National Park; Weeki Wachee and United Press International.

In Insight Guides' London editorial office, **Jill Anderson** helped solve layout problems, inputted the massive amount of updated material and drove the task to completion, and **Dorothy Stannard** proofread, indexed and fine-tuned the final text.

Wright

Wireback

Thompson

Stiff

Klement

History

—by Paul Zach

People

Maps

TRAVEL TIPS

**For detailed information
see page 337**

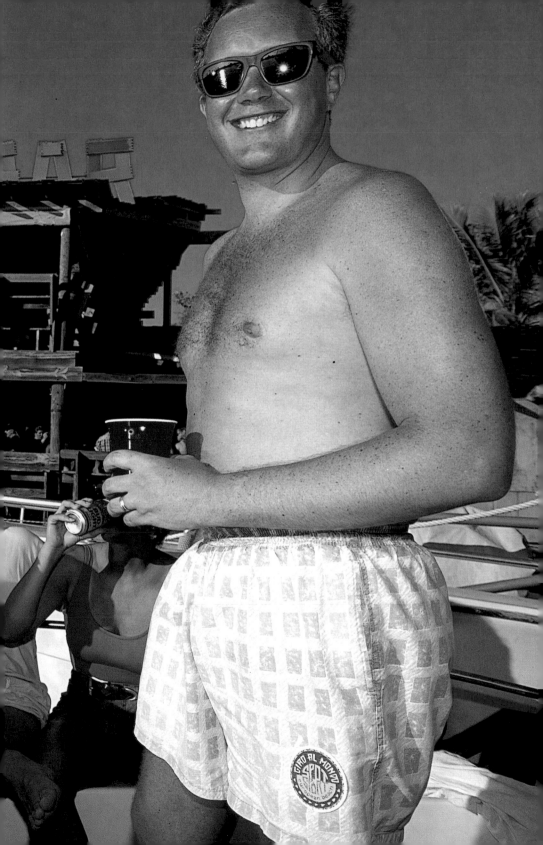

COME ONE! COME ALL!

Like an exuberant barker outside the Big Top, Florida beckons.

"Ladies and gentlemen, boys and girls. Step right up for the greatest show on earth. Guaranteed to assault your sensibilities. It's shocking! It's surprising! It's Florida!

"Meet the world's most celebrated mouse. Walk with weird and wondrous wildlife. Ride with a cowboy. Dance with an Indian. Swashbuckle with a pirate.

"Come one! Come all! To a superlative sideshow of sights, sounds and smells. A scintillating circus of sensations. A carousel

of curiosities. Right this way. Our clown will be your guide.

"Follow him on a search for the fabled Fountain of Youth. Follow him to saloons where Ernest Hemingway held court. To the Billion Dollar Sandbar that is now a fashion models' haven. Sail to northern reaches which look like the Deep South. Surf to southern resorts studded with pink palaces. Stroll through streets etched in Art Deco. See seaside playgrounds where the scorching sun affects people like the full moon. Indeed, even blast off for another planet.

"You've heard about her plastic flamingos. You've heard about her sequin-tailed mermaids. They're all here – and much, much more. It's decadent! It's delightful! It has kitsch! It has class! Ladies and gentlemen, boys and girls…"

Like a barker outside the Big Top, Florida beckons. And, every year, millions continue to come.

Preceding pages: pretty in pink; hats off to the sunshine state; lunchtime in the Keys; jumping in at the deep end; photo shoot, Miami Beach; Jules' Underwater Lodge, Key Largo. **Left**, our clown will be your guide. **Above**, welcome to Florida.

La Florida

Golfo Mexicano

Rio de flores

P.º de S. Ioan
naoidad.

P.ºbo.ª Andreo
baco.

Sinus Morguel.

Phondor de
Medaro.

Sinus Ioānis
Ponce

Rio Canotes.

Rio Pacis.

Aquatio

Arena Arena

Insulæ dictæ
Testudines

Calos.

CALOS

Scopuli dicti Martires

Cauana

Baya
honda

Xagua

Guanaguarico

Marienfis

Hauana

Portus
Matancas

S.XII. Cauana

CVBA INSVLA

Portus
princip.

S.Trinitatis

Jardines scopuli naui-
gantibus formidabiles

Albay hamo

C. d. Cruz

Atalia.

Seuilla

C. Cateche.

Inf. Pinorum

Merida.

Inf. Mulierum

Cypis anata

Hoc loco urina di sen

IAMAICA

Oriste

Comaiagua. Acula.

Sorrochos.

Barracou.

R. Sorrochas.

Iucayonoque fi

LVCAYA

Oathkaqua

Prom: Canaueral.

P. de Sant Hellenæ.

Mocossou.

La Emperadada

Bahama.

C. de Canareal.

Canalis Bahamæ versus
Septemtrionem semper fluit.

Bimini.

Ciquateo Guanima

Hæc Maris pars plena est Insulis,
scopulis breuibus et puluinis valde insidiosis.

Guanahani.

Caribds magna

Samana

Portus matris

Insula Arenarum Iumeto

Quibanaca

Maya guana.

Itinagua

Cuspis Mayaci

Portus Concepti onis

Inf. S. Tome.

Mons Chri-
sti.

Portus Baracoa

P. Na Gola

Natiuita Mos Cariuata Guanique Cibao

Hanc Insulam secunda N

et Hispaniol

Valli paradisi Xaragua

Portus Regius

Isabella

Cap franco.

HAYTI
SIVE SPANIOLA

Lago sal.

Port plan

C. Capris

Cayruli. Guanaba.

Lago dolce

C. Samana

Rio de Iuna

Caput de-
ceptionis
zachee

Bartico mos.

La Yaguana

Cega

SCIA Catana RA

Yaquina G. S. Iulian.

VA

Rio d'Ozama

S. Asua

S. Dominici Rio d'Azina

Yguey

ornica-
rum

Rio d'Or ama.

S. Catelina.

Saona

23

24

Florida flaunts its climate. There are so many warm, sunny days all year that the afternoon newspaper in the city of St Petersburg gives its street edition away free whenever the sun fails to shine. Life is easier, smoother. There are very few cold, somber days to cloud one's mind.

Lured by the laid-back lifestyle, 13 million people now call Florida their home, the fourth-largest state population in the country. That figure is expected to nearly double by the year 2000. Another 40 million tourists flock to Florida each year to spend a few weeks or months in this mellow, yellow land.

The same sunny features that continue to attract thousands of new residents each week undoubtedly proved a strong attraction to the peninsula's earliest inhabitants as well. Most scholars subscribe to the theory that hungry Asians crossed a land bridge linking Siberia to Alaska about 20,000 years ago, probably in search of warmer, fertile lands that had not been ravaged by the killer glaciers of the Ice Age. These first Americans pushed southward through Canada, across the Rocky Mountains and Great Plains to the Mississippi River Valley. Archaeologists believe some groups reached southern Georgia and the Florida Panhandle about 10,000 years ago.

A second theory comes from archaeologists who have unearthed evidence indicating cultural similarities between primitive Floridians and Central and South American tribes. This has led to a growing school of thought that North Americans may have been migrants from the south.

Florida's "paleo-Indian" culture, wherever it may have come from, arrived with its hunting skills and found a subtropical "promised land" teeming with prey – boar, opossum, bobcat, deer, woolly bison, squirrel, and now-extinct species like mastodon, sloth and mammoth. Quail, marsh hens, ducks, geese and coots fell victim to their primitive but deadly weapons.

Digs have uncovered fluted stones, called Clovis points or Suwannee points depending

Preceding pages: old map of Florida. Left, skeletons like this, from an Apalachee burial mound, are found throughout the state.

upon their age and the location in which they were found. These jagged-edged flints – discovered as far south as Fort Myers on the west coast and Vero Beach on the east – resemble the arrowheads of later Indians. Hunters probably lashed them to long sticks to make spears called *atlatl*. The oldest points have been found at Warm Springs outside Venice, about 60 feet underground.

Flanked by oceans of water, these ancient Floridians inevitably waded out into the rivers, bays and lakes and found another source of sustenance – seafood. They speared tasty grouper and flounder, gathered juicy clams and oysters, snared stone crab and spiny lobster. They filled their bellies and stayed.

Prehistoric trash: By 5000 BC, aboriginal cultures known simply as "pre-ceramic archaic" were taming the wilds of the peninsula. Primitive villages sprang up along the banks of the St Johns River. They were populated by huge, dark-skinned, straight-haired people. These early residents scraped the meat from clams, oysters and conchs, then used the shells as cooking vessels, or as tools for fashioning dugout canoes to explore and fish new waters. Discarded shells accumulated in garbage heaps, known by the more respectable-sounding archaeological term "middens." As the tribes died out or moved on to new locations, time buried their traces. New people with more advanced tools replaced them, and their trash in turn wound up in new middens.

Today, construction crews gouging foundations for new condominiums, and children digging along sand banks, occasionally rediscover these Indian mounds. They provide a layer-by-layer chronology of Florida's earliest inhabitants. From the ancient spearpoints of the "paleo-Indians" deep at the lowest levels, up through shards of pottery stamped with increasingly intricate designs, to the neck ornaments and smoking pipes of later civilizations, they relate a remarkable story.

A milestone occurred in the lives of Floridians about the year 2000 BC when the red clay of the earth was first used to create pottery. It was to be another 800 years before this clay began to appear in other parts of North America.

The earliest pieces were crude, shaped like boxes or washbowls, either smooth or with simple, checkerboard patterns. As the uses to which pottery was put became more diverse over the centuries, the designs became more artistic. The etchings provide some of the first evidence of a language which linguists believe was more closely related to one spoken in South America's Orinoco River delta than to other American Indian languages. By the year 850 AD, cultures of the Gulf Coast were producing fiber-tempered works of art. The late Florida anthropologist John M. Goggin said this pottery was "thought by many to be among the finest pottery in the United States…"

cooking corn. Radioactive Carbon 14 tests indicate charcoal from those backwoods barbecues may date to 1000 BC, much earlier than the introduction of corn in the Midwest. The grain may have been introduced from South America or Mexico.

Indian burial mounds: The most fascinating archaeological finds have been massive burial mounds that appear to have been influenced or introduced by the Hopewell cultures of Ohio and Illinois. From Matecumbe, way down in the Florida Keys, to Bear Lake in the Everglades, Malabar on the East Coast, Safety Harbor on the Gulf and dozens of sites in the Panhandle and near St Augustine and Jacksonville, the Indians created memorials

As the utensils for food preparation evolved, so did the means of obtaining the ingredients. The transition from chasing animals and fish and gathering shellfish, to planting the land and cultivating crops, occurred about 1000 BC. In digs near Lake Okeechobee, archaeologists have discovered early forms of irrigation ditches and garden plots laid on dikes above the wet savanna.

Some scientists theorize that maize, or corn, grew in South Florida before it sprouted anywhere else in the continental US. Mound excavations reveal the Indians burned lime from shells – and the only known use for lime in the preparation of food by Indians was in

to their chiefs and prominent tribesmen.

The lone skeletons of these nameless celebrities rest at the center of each mound in prone positions, facing towards the Florida sun. More skeletons, perhaps those of family members paying a last homage to their household head, rest in face-down positions above. The bones of others buried haphazardly, or in bits and pieces, are probably human sacrifices, testifying to the special position reserved for the carefully-entombed personage below. Distinctive ceramics and wooden effigies sculpted into human and bird forms, possibly prized possessions of the deceased or perhaps magic talismans to speed his ascent to heaven, also litter the burial mounds.

Florida's Indian mounds had become enormous earthworks by the time Christ began preaching his gospel in the Middle East. Canals and roadways connected some of the mounds in intricate patterns whose significance was known only to the Indians. Some scholars have remarked on similarities to the great temple-building civilizations of the Aztecs, Mayas and Incas in Central and South America. Mound-building led to empire-building by the time of the Christian era "Mississippian" culture. Located further north, this culture developed populous cities which were perched on top of pyramid-shaped mounds with flattened caps.

opers' bulldozers flatten 1 to 2 percent of them each year.

Vanishing tribes: The heterogenous groups of aboriginals eventually took on distinct unifying characteristics. Historians identify six major tribal groups. The largest, the Timucuans, inhabited most of northern Florida as far south as Cape Canaveral. A related but smaller tribe called the Tocobega lived in the Tampa Bay area. Other groups included the Calusas and Mayaimi near Lake Okeechobee and in southwest Florida below Tampa Bay; the Apalachee, a sizable group, who lived in the eastern part of the Panhandle and as far north as Georgia; the Pensacola, Apalachicola and Chtot in the western Pan-

Archaeologists have been engaged in a race against modern progress in their efforts to recover irreplaceable artifacts, and valuable information about their makers, from burial mounds around Florida. According to state archaeologist Calvin Jones, researchers at one time had recorded more than 14,000 such burial sites around the state, but devel-

Left, French artist Jacques le Moyne sketched a portfolio of Florida's extinct aboriginals in 1564. Here, ancient Indians offer a stag to the sun god. **Above**, Le Moyne sketched this vision of "Floridians crossing over to an island to take their pleasure."

handle; the Ais and Jeaga of the lower east coast's Saint Lucie River region; and the Tequesta, scattered along prime Gold Coast real estate that, many centuries later, would sprout cities like Palm Beach, Fort Lauderdale and Miami.

These Indian tribes – with their highly developed civilizations, artistic and agricultural talents, and engineering capabilities – owned Florida when the first white men stumbled upon its sun-washed shores shortly after Christopher Columbus changed the course of history. These same Indian tribes had vanished from the face of the earth less than three centuries after Columbus arrived.

JUAN PONCE DE LEON, SPANISH KNIGHT, DISCOVERER OF FLORIDA,
MARCH 27, 1513. AUTHENTIC PORTRAIT LOANED BY THE
ST. AUGUSTINE INSTITUTE OF SCIENCE AND HISTORICAL SOCIETY.

Ponce de León, a Spanish adventurer, was led by the fictions of a Carib girl... to explore the country in search of a fountain famed for renovating old age. (He was not the first, nor will he be the last old gentleman to be led up and down a bootless dance by the fascinations of the fair.)

—M.M. Cohen in Notices of Florida and the Campaigns, 1836

Credit for the European "discovery " of Florida usually goes to Spain's Don Juan Ponce de León. But an Italian with an anglicized name probably beat him here. The Genoa-born mapmaker and sea captain Giovanni Caboto, better known as John Cabot, made several voyages to Labrador and other northern points in the New World shortly after Christopher Columbus found it blocking his path to India in 1492. The voyages earned Cabot the praise of the English King Henry VII, who called him the man "who found the New Found Lands."

The king also commissioned Cabot to chart the land. So John and his son, Sebastian, quietly sailed into Spanish territory in 1498. Historians believe he skirted the coast of the peninsula as far south as Cape Florida, a promontory Cabot called the "Cape at the End of April," before turning north in May. Neither Cabot nor his son ever landed here – but shortly after their voyages, crude maps appeared in Europe depicting what appears to be the Florida peninsula.

De León first sailed to the New World with Columbus' second expedition. After he had established an outpost in Puerto Rico, King Ferdinand V rewarded him with the governorship of all Hispaniola. But Diego Columbus, Christopher's son, soon claimed that title. The king responded by giving de León the opportunity to become governor of a fabled island called Bimini, rumored to be a paradise flowing with waters that produced perpetual youth – if he could find it.

It was an appropriate undertaking for de León. The beginnings of his life remain

Left, Spain's Don Juan Ponce de León probably "discovered" Florida while searching for gold rather than a "fountain of youth."

shadowy; he may have been the illegitimate son of a nobleman of Seville. Some histories give 1460 as the year of de León's birth. That would have made him an old salt of 53 when he weighed anchor for fabled Bimini on March 3, 1513.

But it's unlikely that the prospect of taking a dip in a magic fountain – even one that could wash away some of those years – was the prime motivation for his trip. De León had better reasons for going. In addition to gaining administrative control over Bimini and any other places he might discover, the king had promised him virtual ownership of the lands, including any gold or other precious metals they might contain.

De León poked about in the Bahamas for about 25 days in the *Santa Maria de la Consolacion* and the *Santiago,* another ship. He found no trace of Bimini, but he did locate the Bahama Channel, a shortcut to the Caribbean from the Atlantic Ocean. De León and his crew celebrated *Pascua Florida,* the Feast of Flowers (also known as Easter), aboard ship. Six days later, on April 2, he sighted an unknown seashore.

He made landfall a few days later, somewhere between the site that would soon become the first permanent settlement in the continental United States – St Augustine – and a river now called St Johns. Some early histories say the discovery inspired de León to remark: "Thanks be to Thee, O Lord, Who hast permitted me to see something new." Then he christened the land in deference to the holiday season – *La Florida*. The name stuck, and was initially applied to all Spanish holdings on the North American continent.

Unfriendly natives: Further exploration led the expedition north to the St Johns River mouth, and south, where stops may have been made at Cape Canaveral and Biscayne Bay. Then the group sailed around the Florida Keys, which de León called *Los Martires* because the low rocky islands reminded him of a line of martyred men. That name has been forgotten, but his term for the dry patch of sand at the end of the Key stuck: *Tortugas,* the Spanish word for the sea turtles he found swarming along the beach.

After rounding the Keys, de León sailed

up the west coast, possibly as far as Pensacola Bay. Even if he never got that far, it had become apparent to him that he had found something more than a mythical island. He did make at least one more stop at Charlotte Harbor, once called Bahia Juan Ponce, near the modern city of Fort Myers. There, he encountered Florida's natives – tall, powerful and intensely hostile.

This initial hostile encounter has led historians to suspect that earlier contacts may have taken place between Europeans and the original Floridians. Some historians speculate that slave hunters from the Spanish settlements in the West Indies had hunted Florida Indians. Reports which maintain that Indians

scraped together two ships, 200 men, 50 horses, and all the equipment he needed. The king commissioned him and a contingent of missionary priests to settle the "island of Florida," but to treat the Indians well, "seeking in every possible way to convert them to our Holy Catholic faith."

De León again put ashore near Charlotte Harbor, an event Catholic scholars consider the first authenticated instance of priests landing on the soil of the future United States. Unfortunately for the ill-fated entourage, their collective prayers proved fruitless. While laying foundations for the first shelters of the settlement, the newcomers were surprised by a group of Calusas or

shouted Spanish words at astonished explorers lend credence to that theory.

Others believe Indians in colonized islands had somehow sent their Florida neighbors word of their own harsh treatment at Spanish hands. In fact, during the first eight years of the Spanish occupation of Puerto Rico and Haití alone, European settlers killed or enslaved more than a million of the native Caribs.

De León returned to Puerto Rico from that maiden voyage to plot his conquest of *La Florida*. But the king first ordered him to put down a Carib uprising in the Lesser Antilles; so it wasn't until 1521 that de León had

Mayaimis who attacked with a savage barrage of stones and arrows. De León vainly tried to lead a counterattack. He and his men fought pitched battles with daggers. Blood stained the newly-consecrated soil. By some accounts, the Spanish even set snarling greyhounds on their attackers.

The conquistadors: Despite heavy losses, the Indians never retreated. A primitive arrow hewn from swamp reed tore into the toughened flesh of de León. Six of his men also collapsed wounded around him. Survivors managed to get de León and the others into a boat. They reached Cuba, but there de León died. He was buried in Puerto Rico.

Instead of a fountain of youth, de León had stumbled into a pool of death.

Three major expeditions and several smaller ones followed de León into *La Florida* during the next 40 years, seeking to tame the hostile new land and its unfriendly inhabitants. All failed. About 2,000 Spaniards lost their lives in the process. Most had proudly brandished swords and donned armor to follow the battle-toughened leaders they called conquistadors.

Pánfilo de Narváez waded ashore at Tampa Bay with some 400 men on Good Friday, 1528. A red-bearded soldier, he had earned his reputation when he lost an argument and an eye to Hernando Cortéz in Mexico. He

firmly warned the Indians that if they did not obey him, and thus the King of Spain and the Pope, "I will take your goods, doing you all the evil and injury that I may be able… and I declare to you that the deaths and damages that arise therefrom, will be your fault and not that of His Majesty, nor mine, nor of these cavaliers who came with me." The Indians told de Narváez exactly what he

Left, Le Moyne's drawing, hand-colored by a later artist, depicted an early form of French foreign aid. Like Ponce de León, Spanish conquistador Hernando de Soto, <u>above</u>, failed in his attempts to tame Florida's hostile wilderness.

wanted to hear: there existed a land to the north called Apalachee, where they would find the treasure sought by every self-respecting conquistador – gold. De Narváez set out for Apalachee on foot, ordering his ships to rendezvous with him there. He found tall forests of longleaf pine, vast plains of cabbage palm, and sparkling springs and rivers, but no gold.

Occasional Indian raids and mosquito attacks took their toll. The dwindling party arrived in the Panhandle land of Apalachee exhausted and starving. Indian villagers offered them some small rations and they butchered their horses for meat. The ships never showed up. So de Narváez and his men built six makeshift vessels, crawled in and set off for Mexico.

De Narváez vanished along with the ships. Years later four survivors of the expedition turned up in Mexico. Led by Alvar Nunez Cabeza de Vaca, they had survived a shipwreck then wandered in the American Southwest for eight years before finding Mexico.

De Soto's cavaliers: Hernando de Soto, the star conquistador of his time, headed a more ambitious assault on Florida with only slightly better results than de Narváez. Cohen described the escapades of the handsome, adventurous 36-year-old member of Spain's *hidalgo* gentry as "poetry put in action; it was the knight errantry of the Old World carried into the depths of the American wilderness; …steelclad cavaliers, with lance and helm and prancing steed, glittering through the wilderness of Florida, Georgia, and the prairies of the Far West…"

De Soto landed at Tampa Bay in May 1539 with an impressive army of 1,000 knights and fortune hunters. They killed and enslaved Indians and penetrated the thick brush of Florida's interior, cutting their way past the present locations of Dade City, Lake City and Live Oak. Puzzled by the absence of gold and magnificent bejeweled cities such as those he had seen in Peru and Mexico, de Soto pushed on through the Panhandle to Georgia, North Carolina and the Smoky Mountains before turning west to Alabama to continue his search.

Three years and thousands of miles after his arrival in North America, de Soto died from fever. His men submerged his body in the Mississippi River. Most of the conquistadors returned to Spain empty-handed but

Saturiova

Saturiova Re della Florida nell'America Settentrionale
in atto di andare alla Guerra

with tales of the immense, changing landscapes of the New World.

Unfortunately, the precise details of de Soto's historic expedition died along with him. As Garcilasso Inca de la Vega, the son of a Spanish nobleman and a Peruvian Inca princess, wrote in his 1609 *History of the Conquest of Florida*, "the Spaniards did not think so much of learning the situation of places, as of hunting for gold and silver in Florida."

One lasting American legend came out of de Soto's trip, however. On Tampa Bay, the conquistadors curiously scrutinized one Indian who had greeted their arrival in fluent Spanish. Under his paint, the man turned out to be Juan Ortiz, a soldier who had landed with de Narváez and had survived capture by Timucuan Indians in a remarkable manner.

Garcilasso described Ortiz' ordeal at the hand of a Timucuan chief – or *cacique* – named Harriga: "They forced him to carry continually wood and water. He ate and slept very little, and was tormented… he began to run at sunrise, and did not stop till night; and even during the dining of the cacique they would not suffer him to interrupt his course, so that at the end of the day he was in a pitiable condition, extended upon the ground more dead than alive. The wife and daughters of Harriga, touched with compassion, then threw some clothes upon him, and assisted him so opportunely that they prevented him from dying."

Later, the *cacique* tried to roast Ortiz alive, but he was once again saved by the pleas of the chief's daughters: "Ortiz remained extended upon his griddle until the ladies, attracted by his cries, ran to his assistance… they took off the wretched Ortiz half burned, for the fire had already raised up on his body great blisters, of which some having broken covered him with blood… these merciful daughters had him carried to their house, where they treated him with herbs…"

Ortiz finally escaped with the aid of the chief's eldest daughter. Years later, upon reading of the adventures of Ortiz, a biographer of Captain John Smith "borrowed" the scenario for his own subject and an Indian girl named Pocahontas. Smith then perpetuated the plagiarism by putting it into his own history.

Tristan de Luna y Arellano, a wealthy Spanish nobleman, tried to conquer Florida next. He was undismayed by his predecessors' inglorious failures and undeterred by the murder of three Dominican missionaries by Indians at Tampa Bay in 1549. Ten years later, his party of more than 1,500 tried to establish a settlement on Pensacola Bay. Devastated by a hurricane, desperate for food and disillusioned by de Luna's quixotic leadership, the Spaniards abandoned the attempt in 1561.

A foothold in Florida: Pirates proved to be another thorn in Spain's flesh. French, Dutch and English sailors hoisted the Jolly Roger, cruised the Bahama Channel and coastal waters of the peninsula, and preyed upon Spanish treasure galleons plying trade routes between the homeland and the New World. Brash buccaneers – one-time cattlemen from Hispaniola who cured the beef over *boucans* – plundered doubloons, pieces of eight, gold and silver, sometimes burying their booty on Florida beaches or outlying islands where 20th-century treasure hunters dig for it. Hurricanes sank other treasure-laden ships off the Florida coast.

Emboldened by Spain's preoccupation with pirates and its inability to colonize *La Florida*, Jean Ribaut captained a French effort to establish a settlement on the St Johns River in 1562. Ribaut built an arrowhead-shaped fort, Caroline.

That move intensified Spain's own efforts. Their purpose now was not just to gain a foothold, but also to drive out the French trespassers, whom they considered tantamount to pirates. An enormous armada under the command of Pedro Menendez de Avilés established a site at a promising spot on the east coast, south of the French outpost, from which to mount its defense.

The day was August 28, 1565, the Feast of St Augustine. On September 8, Pedro Menendez formally broke ground for a settlement that to this day bears the name of that patron saint. It was the first permanent and is still the oldest continuous settlement on United States soil, founded more than a half-century before the Pilgrims clambered up Plymouth Rock in the north.

Well aware that Menendez planned to attack, Ribaut rushed back to Fort Caroline, assembled his forces, and tried to surprise the Spanish. But again nature played a role in molding Florida's destiny. A hurricane grounded the French warships before they reached St Augustine. Meanwhile, Menendez had marched up the coast and seized the French fort, killing all residents except Catholics, women and children. On the way back to St Augustine, he encountered remnants of Ribaut's assault party and had all but 16 of the 150 men executed, including Ribaut, who was beheaded. The French called the location of that bloody meeting *Matanzas*, the place of slaughter.

With the French out of the way, Menendez tried to guarantee Spain's Florida claims by befriending various Indian tribes, aiding Jesuit mission development, and trying to colonize other parts of the peninsula. Of the settlements, only St Augustine would survive, and somewhat shakily at that. England's Sir Francis Drake leveled the little city in 1585. Another killer hurricane flooded the rebuilt colony in 1599. But St Augustine has endured for more than 400 years.

Menendez died in 1574 in Spain, an ocean away from his beloved Florida. An epitaph on his grave, penned by José-Maria de Heredia, serves as a fitting tribute to him and the other conquistadors who found Florida their most formidable challenge:

Glory has grooved the furrows on thy brow,
And seamed thy cheek, illustrious cavalier;
The scars of wars and scorching suns appear
On that bold front that none could force to bow.

The end of the aboriginals: Ribaut and his mapmaker, Jacques le Moyne, provided future generations with a meticulous word-and-picture portrait of the Indian tribes they encountered. Ribaut wrote in a 1563 passage replete with language nuances: "The most parte of them cover their raynes and pryvie partes with faire hartes skins, paynted cunyngly with sondry collours, and the fore parte of there bodye and armes paynted with pretye devised workes of azure, redd, and black, so well and so properly don as the best paynter of Europe could not amend yt. The wemen have there bodies covered with a certen herbe like onto moste, whereof the cedertrees and all other trees be alwaies covered. The men for pleasure do alwayes tryme themselves therwith, after sundry fasshions. They be of tawny colour, hawke nosed and of a pleasaunt countenaunce. The women be well favored and modest and will not suffer that one approche them to nere, but we were not in theire howses, for we sawe none at that tyme."

In the pages of text that accompanied 42 revealing drawings, Le Moyne described some of the local customs. He indicated that the east coast groups generally seemed more curious and hospitable than their ferocious kinsmen on the west coast. He said they cultivated fields of beans, millet and maize which they stored in granaries; worshiped the sun; warred against other Florida tribes, scalping and mutilating their enemies, carrying the hair and limbs high on their spears in triumph; easily caught venereal disease;

sacrificed first-born children to their chiefs by clubbing the babies to death.

Le Moyne praised the Indians' success in hunting deer by disguising themselves in deer skins and antlers. "I do not believe that any European could do it as well," he wrote.

He vividly portrayed the heavily-tattooed chiefs and queens, who grew their fingernails long and sharpened them to points, and who painted the skin around their mouths blue. He said their gaudy attire included deer skin capes, belts made of Spanish moss, and earrings fashioned from oblong fish-bladders inflated and dyed red.

Le Moyne said that the Indians practiced a

form of primitive parliamentarianism: "The chief and his nobles are accustomed during certain days of the year to meet early every morning for this express purpose in a public place, in which a long bench is constructed, having at the middle of it a projecting part laid with nine round trunks of trees, for the chief's seat. On this he sits by himself, for distinction's sake; and here the rest come to salute him. Each, as he completes his salutation, takes his seat on the bench. If any question of importance is to be discussed, the chief calls upon his laüas (that is, his priests) and upon the elders, one at a time, to deliver their opinions. They decide upon nothing until they have held a number of councils

prayers or sacrifices," he reported. "However, they have temples, but they make use of them only to inter those who die, and to shut up their treasures. They erect also at the entrance of these temples, in the form of a trophy, the spoils of their enemies."

Contact with the Europeans eventually proved to be the fatal blow to the aboriginal cultures. Some fell victim to new diseases like chicken pox, measles and colds. Slave traders spirited away as many at 12,000 Indians. Many of those who resisted the European invasion died defending the lands their tribes had occupied for 10,000 years.

Coming of the Seminoles: By 1560, historians estimate the Indian population had

over it, and they deliberate very sagely before deciding."

Garcilasso also provided some insights into Indian life. He noted many similarities in customs to the Incas of Peru, particularly in their practice of putting their temples and the homes of their chiefs atop artificial mounds mounted by wooden stairways.

"The people of Florida are idolaters, and have the sun and moon for divinities, which they adore without offering them either

Left, Pedro Menendez de Avilés. **Above**, Le Moyne's drawing of the aboriginal Indians' unusual use of camouflage while stalking deer.

dwindled to less than one-fourth of its original size of about 25,000. Jesuit and Franciscan missionaries labored in Florida's humidity in their thick woolen robes, winning converts among north Florida aboriginals with a string of about 50 missions in the 17th century. But British raiders leveled all at the turn of the 18th century, driving the few remaining Timucuans and Apalachees further south. Spaniards took the last 200 aboriginals to Cuba with them when they handed Florida over to the British in 1763. By then, the Oconee Creeks had migrated into the peninsula from Georgia. In Florida, they would become known as Seminoles.

The tide of events that rippled through Florida after the arrival of the Europeans was as extraordinary as the shifts in the seas that gave the peninsula its unusual physical shape. Flags flying over St Augustine and Pensacola changed allegiance faster than semaphore signals. Nations fought to keep Florida, then bartered it away. Through it all, it remained a frontier wilder than the Old West would ever become.

Redcoat rule and revolution: Despite its long years of occupation, Spain had only managed to settle St Augustine and Pensacola, and man a small garrison at St Marks in the Panhandle. Great Britain eyed Florida from its burgeoning northern colonies, prompting Spain to build Castillo de San Marcos to defend St Augustine. The massive earthworks and cannon repelled repeated assaults by the British including a major attack by General James Edward Oglethorpe in 1742. But just 21 years later, England acquired Florida with pen rather than sword in the First Treaty of Paris. Britain had captured Cuba during the Seven Years' War and agreed to swap Havana back to Spain for Florida.

Remnants of the Spanish quickly evaporated. The Creek tribes of Alabama and Georgia, generally friendly with the British, accelerated their migration southward. Slicing the territory into East Florida (from the Atlantic Coast to the Apalachicola River) and West Florida (from there to the Mississippi River) made British administration easier and they virtually transformed the territory into their 14th and 15th colonies.

Under Redcoat rule, Florida for the first time experienced ties with the rest of the North American continent. Spain had always operated from its flourishing Havana base. New plantations of indigo, rice and citrus, a subsequent increase in the slave trade from Africa and the West Indies, and a wave of new immigrants with Cork and Cockney accents also marked British rule in frontier Florida.

The revolutionary rumblings in Britain's

original 13 colonies never reached Florida. British subjects in Florida remained loyal to London when rebellious American colonists turned their backs on King George III on July 4, 1776. Angry St Augustine residents even strung up effigies of American revolutionary leaders John Hancock and John Adams and burned them.

Capitalizing on Britain's preoccupation with fighting the American Revolution, Spain recaptured Pensacola and regained control of all West Florida. East Florida remained

Tory territory, its citizens donning red woolen coats and brandishing muskets to beat back three attempted incursions by American Whigs from the North.

But in the Second Treaty of Paris in 1783, only 20 years after acquiring Florida, the British gave it back to Spain. The fact that the territory had refused to fall into the American column was small consolation.

Rogues and refugees: Florida's reputation as a magnet for the homeless, the displaced and the runaway predates recent influxes of "boat people" from Cuba and Haiti. At the time of the American Revolution, Florida already sheltered a cross-section of the

Left, General US Grant steams up the Oklawaha River in this 19th-century view of Florida. **Right**, Seminole Chief Billy Bowlegs.

world's populations – Africans, West Indians, English, Spanish, Germans, Greeks, Sicilians, Minorcans, Creek and Choctaw Indians. All put down roots that would flourish in the subtropical sunshine. The races inevitably mixed. Blond haired, blue-eyed Creek Indians appeared. Others became as dark-skinned as the slaves. It was no surprise then that the society produced men like Alexander McGillivray, William Augustus Bowles and Zephaniah Kingsley.

The son of a Scottish trader and a woman with Creek and French blood, McGillivray was a diplomatic marvel. He cultivated a working relationship between the Spanish governors of Florida, English traders, the

driven them off Indian land. His colorful adventures included an attack on the St Marks garrison, before Spain captured him and imprisoned him in Havana, where he died.

Kingsley was a flamboyant Scotsman with a hunchback and a flair for the slave trade. He imported thousands from Africa and the West Indies, trained them in the servile arts, then resold them for a handsome profit. He became a Florida legend by staunchly defending the slave system, even marrying one of his own servants and raising the half-caste children to be his heirs.

US acquisition: The second Spanish occupation of Florida fared little better than the first. British, black and Indian refugees from

United States Army, and a confederation he organized among 45,000 Indians of various tribes. This impossible alliance endured until his death in 1793. The confidence and self-respect with which he imbued the Indians never diminished.

Bowles, on the other hand, had no Indian blood, but he lived among the Creeks and married the daughter of a chief after emigrating from England. When the Spanish returned to power, he made several attempts to re-establish himself in Florida. He even contacted McGillivray and offered to supply the Creeks with weapons and ammunition to wage war against the Georgians, who had

the newly formed United States continued to trickle into the state. Georgians stirred up trouble along the northern border, forcing Spain to withdraw to the 31st parallel, the modern Florida-Georgia boundary.

In 1800, Spain ceded the Louisiana Territory to France, which in turn sold the territory to the US – foreshadowing imminent acquisition of the Florida peninsula by the Americans. The US extended its claim in 1813 to Mobile (Alabama), Florida's present western boundary. Americans in West Florida instigated a movement for independence. So in another unusual twist, the British, to whom the Spanish were allied in the War of 1812,

sent troops to Pensacola reputedly to rein-
force Spain's claim. This sparked concern
about the return of Redcoats.

Tennessee's Andrew Jackson, nicknamed
"Old Hickory" because of his stern reputation, took it upon himself to prevent the
British from rebuilding their forces in Florida.
He used a Creek Indian uprising in Alabama
as a pretext for advancing toward Florida. He
defeated the Indians at the Battle of Horseshoe Bend, then marched on Pensacola and
drove out the British.

A subsequent skirmish between Americans and Indians sparked the First Seminole
War of 1817–18. Spain then accepted an
offer by the US to cancel $5 million in debts
to Washington in exchange for the ownership of the Florida peninsula. Andrew Jackson
returned to Pensacola in 1821, the first
American governor of Florida.

Blood stains the Green Swamp: Andrew
Jackson remained only three months as governor of Florida before returning to Washington – where he would soon exercise influence over the new territory directly from the
White House. The officials he left behind
quickly realized that the distance between
Pensacola and St Augustine was too great to
manage the territory effectively, so they con-
solidated government in a village of Talasi
Indians, and Tallahassee became Florida's
capital in 1823.

White settlers elbowed the Indians aside
when founding Tallahassee, as they so often
had when seizing land for farming or carving
out a highway. The migration of tribes, mostly
associated with the Creek confederation, had
continued steadily as the aboriginals disap-
peared from Florida. They took over the
deserted farmlands and game-filled forests.
These Indians collectively came to be known
as Se-mi-no-lee, a Creek word meaning "wild
ones" or "runaways." Some spoke variations
of the Hitchiti language, others Nuskogee.

As Whites and Indians trickled into the
new territory, Florida's population nearly
doubled from 34,370 in 1830 to 66,500 in
1845. Jackson's initial clash with the
Seminoles proved to be only a taste of bloodier
days ahead. Pressure mounted for the gov-

Left, forts like this one situated on Tampa Bay
were built to protect settlements from Seminole
Indian attacks. **Right**, General Andrew "Old
Hickory" Jackson.

ernment to remove Florida's Indians to reservations in the West.

In 1823, Seminole tribes massed at
Moultrie Creek near St Augustine. Led by
Neamathla, chief of a group called Miccosukees, the Indians agreed to a compromise
with the American government. Thirty-two
chiefs signed a treaty calling for them to
move their people and their black slaves to a
4 million-acre reserve in west central Florida,
in return for payment for abandoned lands
and financial aid to help them live on the new
lands. Neither side abided by the provisions
of the agreement. The Seminoles found the
land unsuitable for agriculture and migrated
there slowly, if at all. Drought aggravated

food shortages on the reservation. The US
government reneged on payments. In 1830,
Congress passed a removal act requiring all
Indians in the east to be sent west.

The two sides met again at Payne's Landing on the Oklawaha River running through
the rugged Green Swamp of Central Florida.
This time, US officials managed to coax only
seven chiefs into signing a new agreement,
which canceled the Moultrie Creek Treaty
and required the Seminoles to move to reservations in the Arkansas Territory (part of
present-day Oklahoma). Most of the Seminole nation reacted angrily when the seven
chiefs returned from a visit to the new reser-

vations and reported that they had been co-erced into agreeing to the move. But President Jackson issued an edict to the Seminoles in which he warned: "I tell you that you must go and that you will go."

Flanked by 10 companies of soldiers, General Duncan L. Clinch ordered Seminole chiefs at Fort King, near modern Ocala, to sign away their Florida lands. He managed to get the "X" of Micanopy, the timid chief of the nation, but few others. Florida tradition holds that an indignant young brave named Osceola plunged his knife into the document and cried, "The only treaty I will ever make is this!"

With that act, Osceola became an American hero. Though his great grandfather was a Scotsman, he publicly disavowed any white ancestry and fervently pursued the Creek culture. Historian Marjory Stoneman Douglas considered Osceola "unquestionably the greatest Floridian of his day."

Inspired by Osceola's act of defiance at Fort King, the Seminoles rebelled. A party of warriors ambushed Major Francis Langhorne Dade while he was en route from Fort Brooke (on Tampa Bay) to Fort King. The Indians killed Dade with their first bullet and massacred all but three of his 111 men.

The capture of Osceola: The incident touched off the Second Seminole War, a bloody 7-year struggle in which the outmanned Seminoles fought the better-armed white soldiers to a stalemate. They used the wilds of the Green Swamp to their advantage, striking at American settlements, then melting back into the marshes. The waters of the Withlacoochee and Oklawaha ran red with the white man's blood. The war cost the United States $40 million and nearly 1,500 dead. To protect themselves, the settlers built defensive forts like Lauderdale, Jupiter, Myers and Pierce.

Deception contributed to the defeat of the Seminoles. In 1837, Osceola rode into St Augustine under a white flag of truce sent him by General Thomas S. Jessup. Jessup violated his own flag by arresting Osceola. He imprisoned the great warrior, his wives, children and 116 others at Fort Moultrie in Charleston.

An army surgeon, Jacob R. Motte, de-scribed Osceola in his journal of the war years: "He was at the time of his capture about thirty five years old; and his person, rather below than above the common height, was elegantly formed, with hands and feet effeminately small. He had a countenance expressive of much thought and cunning, and though when captured evidently sad and care-worn, the fire of his flashing eyes was unsubdued.

"His forehead was tolerably high, and cast in an intellectual mold – the upper portion which was generally concealed by his hair being worn low and hanging out in front expressed dignity and firmness, while the full arched brow indicated a man who thought

much and intensely. His eyes were black and piercing; and when animated were full of dark fire, but when in repose they were softer than the soft eye of woman. His mouth, when relieved by a smile, wore an expression of great sweetness; and his lips were chiselled with the accuracy of sculpture."

That proud face suffered a gruesome fate. The despondent Osceola died a year after his capture, of malaria and a broken spirit. The attending doctor cut off his head, retribution for an incident in which Osceola had severed his brother-in-law's head early in the war. The great granddaughter of the doctor later recalled that he used to hang Osceola's head

<u>Left</u>, Seminole hero Osceola. <u>Right</u>, portrait of a Seminole brave in front of a *chickee*.

on a bedpost in the room of his three little boys if they misbehaved. The doctor also exhibited the head in circus side shows.

Osceola's capture broke the spirit of the Seminoles. Jessup continued his trickery, capturing another 400 Indians and Chief Alligator after promising to meet with them for truce discussions. General Zachary Taylor didn't pull any underhanded punches, however, when he defeated a party of Seminole braves on the Kissimmee River in the last major battle of the war. The army rounded up Seminole men, women and children and in 1842 shipped 3,000 of them west of the Mississippi River.

Some Seminoles managed to avoid depor-rivers of the Everglades and, thus, in safety.

The Seminoles were really never defeated. As Coacoochee so eloquently stated in a speech to his people during the war: "The white men are as thick as the leaves in the hammock; they come upon us thicker every year. They may shoot us, drive our women and children night and day; they may chain our hands and feet, but the red man's heart will always be free."

From Statehood to Civil War: After two decades of successful politicking by forces which saw benefits in joining the Union, Florida became an American state on March 3, 1845. But the romance ended just 16 years later. A man's wealth in Florida was measured by the

HUNTING INDIANS IN FLORIDA WITH BLOOD HOUNDS.

tation by disappearing deep into the Ever-glades and Big Cypress swamps. There, under Chief Billy Bowlegs, they regrouped – and in 1855 massacred a camp of surveyors whom they considered trespassers. That ignited the Third (and final) Seminole War. Soldiers and settlers hunted the Seminoles like dogs for the next three years.

They offered huge rewards for the capture of Indians. Chief Bowlegs surrendered with a group of warriors in 1858 and was sent west. Others stubbornly refused to leave and evaded capture. Floridians eventually gave up the search, enabling about 300 Seminoles to remain beyond the impenetrable saw grass number of slaves he owned. Influential plant-ers and landowners opposed the abolition of slavery and convinced their legislators to secede from the Union on January 10, 1861. Florida joined forces with the renegade Confederate States and went, with some zeal, to war against the North.

The Civil War proved particularly disas-trous to Florida. The new state had only barely recovered from the tragic Seminole Wars which had stunted its growth for decades. Agriculture had just begun making an impact with multiplying acres of cotton, indigo, rice, sugar and tobacco. Dr John Gorrie had put the little town of Apalachicola on the map in 1848 when he invented an ice-machine, the forerunner of modern refrigerators and air conditioners. The rugged interior of the state had begun to open by 1861 when a railroad sliced through the forests of scrub and pine and linked Tallahassee to Cedar Key on the Gulf Coast.

The Civil War halted such modest progress in its tracks. Florida mustered its minuscule population and its even smaller budget to wage war. Its participation was brief and limited, but devastating.

Union forces invaded the bustling port of Jacksonville four times. They seized most of Florida's forts. Fernandina Beach, once a haven for slave-smuggling after the US held their ground. They stopped the advance of the Union army, which suffered twice as many casualties.

The "Cradle and Grave Company," consisting of fresh-faced teenagers and old men, later fell to a Union brigade in another Panhandle confrontation. But the "Baby Corp," mainly school boys, bravely turned back Union soldiers wearing hats inscribed "To Tallahassee or Hell" at a natural bridge over the St Marks River on March 5, 1865. Union soldiers never did reach Florida's capital city. But this was a hollow triumph for the Floridians. Only a month after the Natural Bridge battle, General Robert E. Lee surrendered on behalf of Florida and the rest of the

banned the practice, fell to the Union.

Inspired by the daring exploits of Captain J. J. Dickison, however, Florida's Confederate soldiers fought back valiantly. Their biggest battle occurred on February 20, 1864, when 10,000 blue and gray-clad soldiers clashed at Olustee near Lake City. The Floridians had nearly 100 men killed and more than 800 wounded, but the survivors

Left, stunned by the bold Seminole resistance, US troops resorted to hunting Indians with bloodhounds. **Above**, Florida's Confederate troops fought off the Union Army at the Battle of Olustee in 1864.

Confederacy at Appomattox.

The war cost Florida about 5,000 lives and $20 million in damage to its smoldering cities. The slaves were freed only in principle. The presence of Harriet Beecher Stowe (whose *Uncle Tom's Cabin* inspired abolitionists) at her cottage in Mandarin near Jacksonville notwithstanding, hooded Ku Klux Klansmen and gun-toting "regulators" continued to keep blacks down. In fact, until the Civil Rights Act of 1964, blacks in many parts of Florida still rode in the backs of buses and used segregated "public" drinking facilities and washrooms.

The American flag flew over the Florida

capital again on May 30, 1865. Political and economic reconstruction lurched to a hesitant start. Florida remained a wild frontier where the strong and the armed prevailed, fostering a violent streak in the state that persists today. Yellow fever, malaria and cholera also slowed settlers. Still, the sun lured Northerners. Florida's population ballooned from 140,000 in 1860 to 270,000 by 1880. Among the immigrants were developers, entrepreneurs, inventors and writers.

Hamilton Disston drained the Kissimmee and Caloosahatchee valleys, clearing the rivers for navigation and making soggy South Florida solid enough for settlement and farming. Cubans followed Vincente Martinez

Ybor to Tampa in the 1880s to roll tobacco into cheroots and stogies, helping to make the name of the city synonymous with cigars.

On the East Coast, a Chinese immigrant named Lue Gim Gong developed a frostproof orange that began to flourish in groves along the Indian River, laying the basis for the state's citrus industry.

Railroads and tourists: The far-sightedness of two men of that era in particular laid the groundwork for the boom of the 20th century. They were Henry Morrison Flagler and Henry Plant. The latter constructed the Atlantic Coastline Railroad that linked Richmond, Virginia, with Tampa. At the end of

the line, Plant built the ostentatious but luxurious Tampa Bay Hotel, with Moorish minarets that still dominate the city's skyline. And the tourists began to come.

Flagler's Florida East Coast Railroad had an even bigger impact on the growth of the state. Beginning in 1885, he sank about $50 million into a series of hotels at locations connected by his railroad line, from the posh Ponce de León in St Augustine to the Ormond north of Daytona. In 1894, his rail line abruptly ended on a desolate slip of land by the sea. Flagler dubbed it Palm Beach, built the venerable Breakers Hotel, and created a haughty haunt for the extremely wealthy.

A freeze nearly wiped out the state's infant citrus industry in the winter of 1894–95. Mrs Julia D. Tuttle, a rich refugee from Cleveland, convinced Flagler to extend his railroad further south to a strip of scrub on Biscayne Bay in 1896. Miami was born. Flagler laid tracks to Homestead in 1903, then to Key West in 1912, the year before he died. More hotels followed. So did more immigrants and tourists.

The words of a growing colony of writers also fueled the move to Florida. Harriet Beecher Stowe turned from attacking slavery to extolling the virtues of the state's sunshine, crystal springs and green, fragrant forests. *Chicago Times* correspondent George M. Barbour, impressed by a visit to the state with General Ulysses S. Grant in 1879, wrote *Florida for Tourists, Invalids and Settlers*. The prose of poet Sidney Lanier in his 1875 work, *Florida: Its Scenery, Climate and History*, makes it easy to understand why the trickle of Florida immigrants swelled quickly to a flood.

Lanier was moved to write: "The Question of Florida is a question of an indefinite enlargement of many people's pleasures and of many people's existences as against that universal killing ague of modern life – the fever of the unrest of trade throbbing through the long chill of a seven-months' winter… Here one has an instinct that it is one's duty to repose broad-faced, upwards, like fields in the fall, and to lie fallow under suns and airs that shed unspeakable fertilizations upon body and spirit."

Left, Florida railroad barons pose in front of a locomotive. **Right**, 19th-century *Harper's Weekly* sketches of tourist sites in Key West.

The Naval Depot.

A Venerable Hack.

A Residence.

Green Turtle Soup.

The Custom House
(and Fort in Distance).

The Milk-man
on his Rounds.

A Key West Yacht.

Preparing Sponges for the Market.

45

The 19th century ended with the boom of cannons so familiar to Florida's war-weary residents. But the sound of nearby battles quickly gave way to the welcome "boom-chunk" of piledrivers. Up and down the East and West Coasts, cities sprang up along the railroad tracks laid by Plant and Flagler.

Unlike previous conflicts, the Spanish-American War stimulated Florida's growth instead of stunting it. Florida's role in the war grew out of the cigar factories and Spanish cafés of the community founded by Ybor

in Tampa. The Cuban immigrants vicariously, if not actively, cheered on efforts by compatriots back in the homeland to free Cuba from Spanish control. Rebel leader José Marti rallied huge crowds in Tampa, pleading for contributions to the Cuban cause. The cause was so popular that a rising political star with the commanding name of Napoleon Bonaparte Broward – soon to become one of the state's most progressive governors – staked a claim to fame by surreptitiously supplying arms and ammunition to Cuban rebels before the US officially entered the war.

The suspicious sinking of the US battle-ship *Maine* in Havana Harbor in 1898 gave America an excuse to join the revolutionaries in the war against Spain. Troops poured into Florida, setting up tent cities while waiting to sail to Cuba. The army turned Tampa into a command post. Theodore Roosevelt rode into town with his Rough Riders, en route to glory at San Juan Hill. Red Cross founder Clara Barton established hospital headquarters there. A young journalist named Winston Churchill checked into the majestic Tampa Bay Hotel and had a glorious story to report. Spain was driven out of the New World at the very place it had begun its conquest four centuries earlier.

The boom begins: The victorious Americans returned to their northern homes with stories of their exciting exploits – and with glittering tales of Tampa, Miami, Key West and other Florida ports. Some returned home only long enough to gather up their belongings, family and friends before heading back to Florida. By 1920, Florida's first major boom was well under way.

Many of the characters who wheeled-and-dealed in real estate plundered Florida much as the Spanish and British had done earlier, interested only in fast fortunes. Others came, made money, stayed and formed the first solid core of state leaders.

Walter Fuller carved up St Petersburg, a sun-kissed Gulf Coast city founded by Russian railroad czar Peter Demens. In his book, *This Was Florida's Boom*, Fuller tells how he paid $50,000 for some land that he later resold for $270,000.

Glib-lipped salesmen took to wearing white bow ties and knickers as they auctioned off swampy-looking lots. Even the golden-tongued William Jennings Bryan, whose verbal skills earned him Democratic presidential nominations and the Secretary of State's job, sold real estate. Bryan's eloquence sold keys to luxury living in George Merrick's Coral Gables, the country's first planned community. It boasted regal entrance gates, pools, hotels, golf courses, zoned business districts, and alluring lots on palm-lined boulevards and canals.

Nearby, Carl Fisher dredged sand from the bottom of Biscayne Bay and transformed tangles of mangroves off the coast of Miami into a beach. In 1925 alone, 481 hotels and apartment buildings rose in Miami Beach. Over on the West Coast, circus tycoon John Ringling created Sarasota, and Dave Davis dredged up islands that became enclaves for Tampa's elite.

Overnight paupers: In 1926, a cold winter slowed spiraling prices. Then a hurricane whipped the peninsula, killing hundreds and bulldozing some of the flimsy housing developments. That brought the madness temporarily to an end, but it was nothing compared to the stock market crash and Great Depression of 1929. Davis, Fuller and dozens of other millionaires were turned into paupers overnight. Still, the groundwork had been laid for resumed growth after the effects of the Depression wore off.

ing increasingly urban. By 1940, more than 55 percent of the people were living in towns and cities – compared to 37 percent in 1920. Tampa attracted more industry, Miami more sun-worshippers. More hotel rooms were built in greater Miami between 1945 and 1954 than in the rest of the state combined.

In addition to the tourist dollars, parimutuel betting on greyhounds and horses was legalized in 1931, bringing additional money to the state's coffers – and organized crime to the streets of its big cities. Members

Between 1920 and 1940, Florida's population doubled to nearly 2 million. By the start of World War II, 2½ million tourists visited annually. The population was grow-

Left, railroad and hotel baron Henry Morrison Flagler. Above, idyllic postcard images of Florida helped spark this century's tourist explosion.

of the syndicate shuttled between profitable rackets in Miami. Mobster Al Capone found the location so convenient he moved into a fortified estate in Miami Beach.

New architectural marvels helped add dramatic dimensions to Florida's flatness. After a hurricane shredded Flagler's railroad through the Keys in 1935, engineers decided to transform the remnants into an Overseas Highway that included the Seven Mile Bridge, which sits on 544 pilings. The first span of the magnificent 11-mile Sunshine Skyway over Tampa Bay opened in 1954 – only to collapse after being hit by a freighter on its 25th anniversary in a tragic accident

HURRICANE ANDREW

I t was South Florida's worst nightmare. Just before dawn on August 24, 1992, a storm packing 160-mph winds and a 12-foot tidal wave slammed into the southern tier of the state leaving in its wake a surreal scene of devastation.

Hurricane Andrew, the worst natural disaster ever to hit the US, destroyed over 60,000 homes and left 150,000 people — 10 percent of Dade County — homeless. The category five hurricane, so rare that only one or two occur every century, left a 20 to 35-mile wide swath of damage estimated at $20 billion. Over 35 people died in storm-related deaths.

Hardest hit were the rural and suburban areas about 20 miles south of downtown Miami — Homestead, Florida City, Kendall — most of which were totally destroyed. South Miami and parts of Coconut Grove and Coral Gables were also badly damaged. Along with piles of debris that once were houses, Andrew left a battlefield of wounds: schools, shopping centers, gas stations and churches demolished; cars smashed and overturned; boats damaged and blown ashore; crumpled airplanes; and a severely scarred landscape of uprooted trees.

In the days and weeks that followed, thousands of civilian volunteers from around the country, along with the American Red Cross, poured in to help. The president deployed over 20,000 US troops to the area to help deter looting, clean up the debris, and build temporary tent cities. The soldiers, many of whom had served in the war-torn areas of Lebanon and Kuwait, said that they had never seen such massive destruction. But locals complained that state and national officials, caught in a bureaucratic confusion with no one in charge, took too long before mobilizing government assistance — tens of thousands of people went for days without food, water, medical care or shelter in the 95° heat before help arrived. So desperate was the situation, that Florida City police officials hijacked a water truck that was headed for nearby Homestead.

Along with the human suffering, animals also fell victim to the storm. Thousands of dogs and cats, not allowed into the pre- or post-storm shelters, were left on the streets to fend for themselves. One Coconut Grove homeowner woke up to find a shark, washed over in the storm, floating in his swimming pool; others found fish in their television sets. Over 2,000 monkeys and baboons, used by the University of Miami and a private scientific foundation for medical research, escaped when their cages were destroyed. A nasty rumor — that the animals carried the AIDS virus and should be shot on sight — quickly spread throughout the county. Hundreds of the animals were gunned down by police and frightened, armed residents.

When the images of the hurricane hit the news media, foreign aid flowed in from around the world as if Dade County — one of the most cosmopolitan counties in the US — were suddenly a Third World country. Canada, Japan and Taiwan all sent relief. Even President Boris Yeltsin offered to send Russian workers and machinery to help with the clean-up. Despite these offers of help, the rebuilding will likely take years.

Hurricane Andrew, however, did leave Dade County, an area often beleaguered by ethnic and racial conflicts, a more cohesive community. Residents, whether white, black, Cuban, Haitian, Guatemalan or all-American, worked together. "As one we will rebuild" was the spirit.

And, fortunately for the county's vital tourism industry, the damage wrought by Andrew to most tourist areas was minimal. Miami Beach suffered only broken windows and fallen trees; downtown Miami the same. Had the hurricane's eye hit just a few miles to the north, Miami would likely have been wiped out. Hurricane Andrew, the awesome force of nature, could have been worse. ∎

that killed 35 motorists. Construction of Florida Southern College, based on architect Frank Lloyd Wright's designs, began in 1938 in Lakeland.

Florida's greatest contribution to the future began taking shape shortly after World War II, when the War Department began testing missiles at Cape Canaveral. Florida hosted the world's first scheduled airline service, a short hop between St Petersburg and Tampa, and in 1959 inaugurated the first domestic jet flights in the US. By that time, Cape Canaveral was well on its way to becoming the site of Kennedy Space Center. The last steps Neil Armstrong took on Mother Earth before his "giant step" on the moon in

Castro's 1959 coup in Cuba sent a massive wave of Spanish-speaking peoples into the state throughout the 1960s. During the 1970s a slow but steady exodus continued, and in 1980 another massive wave – 125,000 Cubans – landed on Key West's shores. Most of those 125,000 eventually made their way to the Miami area where an intricate immigrant network was already in place. The 1980s also brought about 75,000 Nicaraguan refugees to South Florida who fled the communist government of their country, and about 125,000 Haitians who made the perilous journey in home-made wooden boats in order to escape the dire poverty of their Caribbean homeland.

1969 were on the sandy soil of Florida.

Two of the more colorful characters who made headlines in Florida during the 1960s included Jackie Gleason, whose television show crowned Miami Beach as the "sun and fun capital of the world," and Pulitzer Prize-winning playwright Tennessee Williams of *A Streetcar Named Desire* fame. Williams made Key West his winter home until his death in 1983.

The new Floridians: Florida's reputation as a haven for refugees has never faltered. Fidel

Left, Hurricane Andrew's havoc. **Above**, Gandy Bridge across Tampa Bay.

In addition, the '80s brought population explosions to Palm Beach County, the Orlando area, and the West Coast as hundreds of thousands of Northerners continued to stream into the state in search of Sun Belt prosperity. Many major US companies moved their headquarters to Florida, and the international banking industry blossomed. In 1988, there were so many requests for new telephone lines that the state's telephone company created a new area code. For Florida, it was an invigorating period of solid, steady growth, both economic and demographic.

But that growth also came from many people seeking prosperity in less than legal ways. With money from dealing in illegal drugs, the so-called Cocaine Cowboys left their mark on South Florida along with a trail of violence. Buying luxury homes and fancy sports cars with suitcases full of cash, drug-smuggling cowboys pumped billions of dollars into the state's economy.

Along with the influx of immigrants and relocated Northerners, the 1980s brought both good times and bad times for the southern regions of the state. In 1983 the Bulgarian artist who calls himself Christo burst onto the scene with one of his eccentric landscape-as-art experiments. By wrapping 11 uninhabited islands in Miami's Biscayne Bay with flamingo-pink plastic, Christo

turned the city's otherwise pastoral waters into an outrageous spectacle of shimmering artistry – the world watched in awe. In 1984, the slick, action-packed television series *Miami Vice* premiered and the international image of Miami changed overnight – from retirement haven to sexy and sleek pastel paradise. Syndicted in 136 countries around the world, *Miami Vice* glamorized Miami's crime-ridden reputation and made mayhem in the tropics a fashionable trend.

And then there were the bad times. Fueled by economic hardships and ethnic tensions, Miami's black community erupted with violence. First in the neighborhood of Liberty City in 1980, and again in Overtown in 1982. Combined, the two riots left millions of dollars worth of damage, and forced the city to address its urban problems.

Into the 1990s: As the 1990s began, the state was still growing rapidly. This time around the influx of people included Europeans, South Americans, and Japanese who saw Florida as one great sunny investment opportunity. In addition to winter homes, they invested in hotels, restaurants, and businesses throughout the state.

Tourism, the golden egg for the state's economy, continued to grow at staggering rates. The number of tourists visiting Orlando mushroomed, as did the numbers visiting Tampa, Key West, and Miami. The Art Deco District of South Miami Beach underwent a renaissance that can only be described as spectacular. Fashion models, photographers, foreign tourists and America's trendsetters elbowed each other for table space at Miami Beach's outdoor, Ocean Drive cafés. Pop music star Madonna bought a waterfront winter home in Miami. Jewelry designer Paloma Picasso did the same.

Hurricane Andrew's four-hour trip through Florida in the summer of 1992 left the southern half of Dade County in a sad state of shambles, but even that didn't stop tourists from coming. And yes, the influx of immigrants continued. In 1993, a rusty old freighter packed with Haitian refugees on its way to Miami sank off the coast of Florida, drowning about 400 people. Florida officials saw it as a sign of things to come. With the quality of life in Haiti getting worse instead of better, and the communist government in Cuba facing its most difficult crisis ever, the state grappled with the possibility of another influx of immigrants. But even if that happens, Florida will persevere by virtue of its miraculous ability to absorb armies of newcomers, and its hospitable policy that always tries to make room for more.

Mix moon-bound adventurers, real estate tycoons, lazy alligators, hungry pelicans and a mix of nationalities and races; flavor it with Key limes and conch chowder; spread it on a bed of orange blossoms; add the scent of magnolias; baste in azure seas and broil under pastel skies. That's 20-century Florida.

Left, stars of *Miami Vice*. **Right**, peninsula or pool, Florida is surrounded by water.

MANGOS
2 for $1.29
or
69¢ ea.

A settler in Florida – whether he comes as a capitalist, as a farmer, or as a laborer – can live with more ease and personal comfort, can live more cheaply, can enjoy more genuine luxuries, can obtain a greater income from a smaller investment and by less labor, and can sooner secure a competency, than in any other accessible portion of North America.

—George M. Barbour in *Florida for Tourists, Invalids, and Settlers*, 1896

Barbour probably did not realize his enthusiastic guide book would help touch off an exodus to Florida unmatched since New York newspaper man Horace Greeley said "Go West, young man" several decades earlier. One thing most racial and ethnic groups seem to share is a predilection for sampling paradise.

Nearly a century later, much of Barbour's assessment still holds true – and untold multitudes continue to flock to Florida. This in-migration has turned the peninsula not into a melting pot of people, but into a veritable sea of faces and faiths.

Several immigrant groups have had a particularly profound influence on Florida's development: Seminole Indians, who proudly balk at making peace with a government that drove them from their lands and who stoically carry on the legal fight to win back their property; Cubans who, like Ponce de León and his boatload of Spaniards, come from Havana in search of a dream; landed Crackers with roots dating back to 19th-century settlers; millions of Yankees newly uprooted from unpleasant northern regions; blacks, whose ancestors fled slavery; and retirees of all races and ethnic backgrounds, who comprise an entire subculture, seeking a place in the sun before it sets on their lives.

Other groups deserve mention: the Greeks of Tarpon Springs, the Minorcans of New Smyrna, the Japanese of Delray Beach, the Jews of Miami Beach, the Conchs of Key West. Vietnamese trickled in from Air Force bases around the state and country after their 1975 exodus from communism to Florida. There are even the carnival people of Gibsonton. This medley of people, and others, have made Florida sing with vitality. Indeed, this fresco of faces gives Florida's flat and monotonous landscapes shape, color and character.

Preceding pages: mango stand, Florida; walking to school, Ocala. **Left**, retiring in the sun.

The Florida Indians trace their roots back to around 300 people who were led into the Everglades by Chief Billy Bowlegs (or Mr William B. Legs as the US Government called him) following the Seminole Wars in the 1850s. They melted into the marshes and refused to budge, and the US Government eventually gave up.

True to the name Seminole, from the Creek word for "wild" or "ones apart," they kept to themselves, living off corn, cane and pumpkins; trading alligator skins, deer hides and bird feathers, oblivious to Florida's headlong rush into the 20th century. Miccosukees congregated around the Calusa mounds near Chokoloskee, while others grouped around Pine Island near Fort Lauderdale, the Miami River, Big Cypress and the Ten Thousand Islands area. They mingled with the white man only out of necessity and without trust.

Some Seminoles turned to construction of the Tamiami Trail in the 1920s – and proved to be the hardiest workers. The road was a mixed blessing, bringing tourists and money, but eroding their traditions. The establishment of Everglades National Park in 1947 also had its good and bad points. It was in keeping with the Seminoles' love of the land, but it took their land out from under them.

Tribal rights: Today, about 1,500 Seminoles live and work mainly on the 42,278-acre Big Cypress reservation, north of the Miccosukee land; the 35,805-acre Brighton reservation, northwest of Lake Okeechobee; and on a small plot in Hollywood.

Like many other Floridians in the area around Brighton, the Seminoles raise cattle on primordial-looking land that could easily pass for an African veldt or western prairie. The Indians look more like cowboys as they chase a stray bull on horseback, then rope it in with ease. They wear Levis, thick belt buckles and western hats or truckers' caps. Only signs along State Road 721, sometimes scrawled with graffiti plugging "Indian Power," tip you off that you're on Seminole property.

Left, a smile from George Storm, the Miccosukee's tribal storyteller. **Right**, an elderly woman ponders the present.

The Miccosukee branch of Florida's Seminole Indians number around 550. Most still live close to their roots on the Tamiami Trail and Alligator Alley reservations, although some have turned their backs on the past in favor of Miami's suburbs. One of the places to meet them is the Miccosukee Indian Village and Culture Center, set up on a 5-mile long by 500-ft wide strip of the Tamiami Trail.

The village/culture center features several uniquely Florida Seminole attractions. There are refreshment stands and a restaurant where young waitresses wear blue denim jackets over their traditional Seminole skirts. There is also an interesting model of the kind of homestead the Indians once lived in when they encamped in hammock "islands" in the Everglades harsh swamplands. The homestead is composed of a cooking *chickee*, a sleeping *chickee* and other all-purpose *chickees* where leather-faced old women string beads and sew jackets and skirts.

The biggest ethnic action, however, takes place at a nearby alligator pit. Visitors can watch as an Indian guide pokes a pile of snoozing gators into a hissing wakefulness. He nonchalantly drags one of the alligators into a sand pit where he pries its jaws apart and clamps the alligator's snout shut between his chest and chin, then rubs its throat – "to put it to sleep."

The souvenir stand and shop shelves are filled with items long handcrafted by Seminoles – assorted bracelets and necklaces, palmetto fiber dolls, baskets and painted wooden tomahawks. But a closer look reveals something more, a part of the renaissance that has gripped the tribe in recent years. One chickee contains brilliantly colored paintings. The artist's work combines the hues and patterns historically associated with Seminole crafts in modern themes that dramatize the dual nature of the tribe's

primary historical differences between these Seminoles and the Miccosukee branch in the south. The latter speak a form of Hitchiti, the others the more common Creek tongue called Muskogee. Both groups are making efforts to put them into written forms.

Unfortunately, with the Muskogee language, many of the sounds are different from those in English, and there is a dwindling numbers of Indian children who speak their ancestral tongue. The Miccosukees have had slightly better luck. Children learn it along with English in the reservation school. The tribe's efforts to preserve and promote their heritage in such forms as a public arts festival every winter and an annual Everglades

D35--SEMINOLE INDIAN WOMEN AND THEIR CHILDREN IN THE EVERGLADES

present-day existence – its struggle to come to grips with a changing world.

West of the model village, this struggle manifests itself in a modern school for Indian children, air-conditioned offices, cars and trucks bearing Miccosukee Indian license plates, and even a police department. Homes with the Everglades in the backyard combine a kind of Gothic chickee architecture with Florida functional. Most have television antennas sticking out of the thatch roofs.

The Hollywood-headquartered Seminoles and the Miami-area Miccosukees maintain separate existences as well as separate tribal organizations. Language has been one of the

Music Festival have also helped keep the native language alive.

Despite the obstacles to maintaining these languages where English – and Spanish – prevail, their impact on Florida is strong. Place names like Chassahowitzka (hanging pumpkins), Chattahoochee (marked rocks), Okaloacoochee (little bad water), Oklawaha (crooked river), Halputtlockee (alligator eats), Panasoffkee (deep ravine), Wacasassa (some cows there) and Thonotasassa (place of flints) come from the Seminole tongues. Names like Miami, usually interpreted as "great water," and Pensacola, meaning "the place where the bearded people live," date back to the languages of Indians who lived here before the Seminoles.

One important link with the past that all Seminoles cling to is the annual Green Corn Dance. The late medicine man Sam Jones told *National Geographic* magazine in an interview years ago that if the dance is not held every few years, "the medicine die – and then no more Indians."

It's a ritual the Seminoles still guard jealously, rarely inviting outsiders and usually prohibiting photography. Medicine men conduct the centuries-old rites over the course of a week. Hundreds of songs are sung and chanted in the native language to the sound of rattles. Boys become men when they en-

friends in government has grown, and the Indian issue has become an important one. The Brighton, Big Cypress and Hollywood Creeks fortified their political clout by organizing into the Seminole Tribe of Florida and a five-member council in 1957. The Miccosukees followed suit by forming a separate body in 1962.

Each tribe subsequently intensified its battles with the US Government over land and money. The Indian Claims Commission awarded $16 million to the Seminoles in 1970 as compensation for land seized under early treaties, but there has been a long-running disagreement about how to split the money between Seminoles in Oklahoma and

dure deep scratches from sharp needles.

Even more important to the Seminoles is their view of the universe as a wheel spinning slowly like the circle of logs in their ceremonial fires. It has come to symbolize their will to survive on their own terms, to bounce back from poverty and adversity and re-emerge even stronger to carry on a long and hard-fought battle for their rightful part in Florida's heritage.

Over the years, the number of sympathetic

Left, the rainbow-colored fashions of the Seminoles brighten up an old postcard. **Above**, a Miccosukee Indian woman sewing dresses.

those in Florida. The Miccosukees have declined any stake in that settlement, demanding the return of land instead. They filed suit claiming most of Southwest Florida, including the cities of Fort Myers and Naples, acreage granted them by President James Polk in a treaty in 1845.

In a tentative agreement, the Miccosukees may drop that claim in return for about $1 million in cash from the state, a perpetual lease on 192,000 acres of land in Dade and Broward counties that must remain in its natural state, and the right to subsistence hunting and fishing and commercial frogging without license on certain lands.

During the 19th century, long before it became fashionable in other social circles, blacks began migrating south to Florida. They didn't come for the sunshine or the beaches; they came to escape slavery. They crept under cover of darkness down the coast of Florida to a swampland inhabited by alligators and Indians. Even today, the image of Florida as a promised land for blacks lingers, despite the century of segregation, rebellion, integration and demonstrations that followed the heady days of emancipation.

"Florida blacks are told that Florida is a wonderful place," said Dr Victoria Warner, head of the sociology department of Florida A&M University (which has been the state's predominant black university since 1887).

"We have to tell our graduates, 'Pack your bags and go where the opportunities are'," said Warner. "We practically have to shove them out of the state."

Like northern whites, many black Floridians have bought the image of Florida as a land of waving palm trees, success and the good life, Warner said.

One reason for the state's popularity is geography. Not much of Florida was even settled during the confining days of slavery. Only the northern tier was dotted by cotton and tobacco plantations. Then, too, there were the governors. Leroy Collins began his term in the late 1950s as a moderate segregationist, but later gained national attention as a new, more liberal Southern governor who at least talked favorably about the rights of blacks. Reubin Askew is credited by many historians with being the first governor to follow up talk with action by bringing blacks into government at all levels.

This isn't to say that Florida blacks have had an easy time. The state was indeed part of the old plantation South, if only in its most northern reaches. In the 1860 census, 61,475 slaves were counted on the plantations of North Florida. Well into this century restaurants, buses, hotels, public buildings and

schools were segregated. In a May 1956 state-conducted survey, 60 percent of the parents of white high school seniors said that black youths should not be admitted to the white universities of Florida under any circumstances.

For years, blacks truly lived on the "wrong side of the tracks," along the eastern coast from Jacksonville to Miami. Whites lived to the east of the railroad tracks, where the ocean was; the blacks inland to the west. But now, as elsewhere in the South, outward

manifestations of segregation and discrimination have faded.

Lifestyles and locations have changed, too. The number of blacks in the state more than doubled in 30 years, from about 600,000 to 1.3 million, making Florida sixth in the US in total black population. Most inhabit urban areas – Jacksonville, Fort Lauderdale-Miami, Orlando and St Petersburg-Tampa. Sixty years ago the majority lived in rural areas.

Panhandle power: Unlike their urban counterparts who escaped the last vestiges of the plantation system by leaving, many rural blacks still find themselves tied financially and politically to the paternalism of whites.

<u>Left</u>, a young Florida woman asserts her African heritage through her traditional dress and jewelry. <u>Right</u>, much-loved North Florida civil rights leader, the late C.J. Steele.

Until the late 1960s, Gadsden County in the Panhandle – nearly 60 percent black – remained tied to the era when shade tobacco was the main crop and blacks were the work force that harvested it. But one town within Gadsden has changed – Gretna, where 88 percent of the 1,448 residents are black. A white minority ruled the town until 1971. Ten years later, the mayor, all five city commissioners, the city administrator and the city clerk were black.

Gretna isn't the oldest or even the most famous of Florida's black-run towns. Eatonville in Central Florida holds that distinction. When the town was incorporated in 1888, it may well have been the first almost

The first black in recorded history to visit Florida is known only as "Little Steven." He accompanied Pánfilo de Narváez on his 1527 expedition to Florida. Virtually every Spanish expedition into Florida included black soldiers. Historians agree that under Spanish rule Florida had a reputation as a place where blacks could get ahead largely unhampered by the restraints evident elsewhere in America. Both Pensacola and St Augustine had a heritage of intermarriage. Many blacks there became skilled artisans, learning crafts reserved elsewhere for white men.

Runaway slaves who sought refuge in Florida also found the Seminole Indians and their swampy Florida existence a better way

fully black community in the United States.

In fact, all South Florida might have been a black community had a plan of the post-Civil War's Freedmen's Bureau worked out. The bureau, responsible for helping blacks adjust to emancipation, devised several plans for deeding land to former slaves. One suggested that the bottom half of the Florida peninsula, then virtually uninhabited, be set aside for homesteaders. The plan called for 50,000 former slaves from Virginia to be relocated on 500,000 acres of federal land in South Florida. The scheme never materialized, but a limited homesteading program was approved.

of life than the plantations. In 1838, 1,400 blacks were living with the Seminoles, only 200 of them as slaves. The Seminoles demanded little of their slaves; an annual tithe of corn to the owner was often the only requirement.

The most famous runaway, Abraham, began his life with the Seminoles as a slave, but proved such an invaluable asset that they freed him. He served as a translator and advisor to Chief Micanopy and became a leader in the Second Seminole War.

When the American Civil War broke out, 1,200 blacks from Florida joined the Union Army. But more than 60,000 slaves remained on plantations. In the years of reconstruction that followed, local blacks enjoyed the fruits of a new liberalism. At one point as many as 19 freedmen served in the state legislature. More significant was the appointment of Jonathan C. Gibbs as Florida's secretrary of state in 1988, and later, as superintendent of public instruction. Gibbs was known widely as a great orator, but after only 18 months in office he died of a seizure. Some suspected poisoning. The man had so many enemies he slept in his attic with a brace of pistols for protection.

The next several decades were not to be so lucrative in terms of public office. Blacks made strides toward political office only as

relations were quiet until 1980, when blacks in a Miami ghetto called Liberty City rioted and killed to avenge the death of another black, insurance man Arthur McDuffie. Eighteen whites and blacks died in the devastating violence.

Some viewed the eruption in Miami as not just a race riot, but an economic protest. The small group of blacks who rioted were fed up with a system that not only – in their view – led to the death of a black man at police hands but allowed them to be beaten out of their bread-and-butter jobs by Cuban immigrants willing to take lower-than-low wages. The acquittal of four white police officers in McDuffie's death may have been the match

late as the 1970s. At that time, Governor Reubin Askew appointed blacks to the Cabinet, the state Supreme Court, the university system's Board of Regents and to important positions in other government departments.

Those appointments were major victories for Floridians, who had demonstrated along with the rest of the South's activists in a 1956 bus boycott in Tallahassee, and in Daytona Beach, Jacksonville and St Augustine in the 1960s. After the civil rights era passed, race

Left, Florida blacks still celebrate religion in traditional ways like this river baptism. **Above**, sharecropping tobacco, Quincey, the Panhandle.

that sparked the violence, but economic frustrations were the kindling. There is good as well as tragedy in the incident, however. Blacks' insistence that they should not have to accept less than a minimum wage reflected a new pride.

In the 1990s, black Floridians have a number of encouraging role models. In addition to Florida A&M University, students can see blacks heading state departments, working in middle-level management in the state bureaucracy and performing other highly visible jobs. A good example is Carrie Meek, a black woman from South Florida who was elected to the US Congress in 1992.

Since 1959, Cuban refugees have descended on South Florida in waves as regular as weather fronts. They have arrived aboard commercial flights, private planes and hijacked aircraft, and as stowaways on merchant vessels. With alarming frequency, they've made the crossing on virtually anything that would float long enough to carry them through the treacherous Gulf currents separating Cuba from the Florida Keys: boats, rafts, auto inner tubes, coconuts wrapped in nets, even palm leaves.

Tens of thousands of Puerto Ricans and Central and South Americans have also settled in the Greater Miami area, but the story of Hispanic Florida today is mainly a Cuban tale. Their record in South Florida has been one of remarkable achievement in spite of continuing hardship and poverty among recent arrivals, most of whom reached Florida's shores destitute.

Impact: Nowhere is the Cuban impact more visible than in the section of southwestern Miami called Little Havana. Once a decaying neighborhood dotted by dimly-lit apartment houses perennially fronted by "For Rent" signs, Little Havana is now a busy, noisy hub that revolves around Flagler Street and *Calle Ocho*, the Hispanic name for Miami's Southwest 8th Street.

The peeling facades and boarded-up storefronts that greeted the first waves of refugees to southwest Miami are now shiny showcase windows, busy mini-shopping centers, religious goods stores, toy shops, coffee shops and restaurants. Street signs, as in many other parts of Miami, require drivers not only to "Stop" but also to "*Parar*" at intersections. Triangular yellow signs advise motorists to "Yield" and "*Ceder.*"

Neon and painted signs invite visitors to savor aromatic Cuban coffee and taste guava pastries; to buy elaborately mounted photos of John F. Kennedy, or Cuban patriot José Marti; to pause for a sugar-cane juice drink, sample *moros y cristianos* (black beans and rice) and nibble on banana chips or Cuban sandwiches; and to view the latest Mexican or Spanish film (shown with English subtitles, of course).

Cuban music – the cha cha, rhumba and mambo precursors of today's salsa – reflects the people's zeal for life, movement and color. The lesser known *boleros* – slow dance music with lyrics pegged to love themes – speak to traditional and hopelessly romantic values. This eagerness to live fast and to communicate in more than surface words is mirrored in the Cuban dialect. Cuban Span-

ish is staccato and distinct from the language spoken by other Latinos. Esses and even entire syllables are chopped off, leaving phrases to flow together ever faster. The people's demeanor – expressive eyes and faces, hands darting about in rapid, sweeping movements – make Cuban enclaves loud, hectic, indomitable, immensely human and alive places.

The biggest of all Cuban celebrations is a gigantic block party 2 miles long along *Calle Ocho*, in the heart of Little Havana. All of Miami is invited to this mixture of cultural and religious celebration and old-fashioned Havana-style carnival, complete with strut-

Left, Cubans still blend fine tobaccos by hand to create the cigars that made Tampa famous. **Right**, daughter of a Cuban immigrant.

ting conga lines and Cuban dancers in full costumed regalia.

Flights to freedom: Events like the *Calle Ocho* celebrations bring out the wide range of people that constitute the Cuban experience. Beginning in 1959, when a small group of political and military henchmen of the deposed dictator Fulgencio Batista Zaldivar first arrived in the area, the Cuban influx into Miami has been anything but homogeneous. Almost every year has brought another new wave of refugees representing a new segment of Cuba's social, economic, political and racial strata disillusioned with Castro's communist experiment.

The 1959 influx of Latin American political émigrés seeking refuge in Miami was

were the first to depart, followed soon after by wealthier Cubans frightened by Castro's socialist drift. A brain drain of professionals – doctors, lawyers, civil servants, journalists and old-style politicians – had begun by 1960. By 1962, middle-class technocrats, skilled workers and virtually every class of Cuban joined the exodus. By 1990, about 1 million Cubans had left Cuba. Over half were settled in South Florida.

For many Cubans the shock of exile, combined with language barriers and obsolete professional skills, has forced them to accept only a small share of the community's extraordinary success. Even today, the dishwasher in a Miami Beach restaurant or the

cal émigrés seeking refuge in Miami was hardly unusual, except in the huge numbers of people. Always a vacation land for Latin America's rich, the city also has long been a popular regrouping spot for Caribbean and Latin American revolutionaries and politicos waiting out interregnums in their rule or struggle for power. Even Fidel Castro stopped in South Florida to ponder his options before going home to overthrow Batista's bloody, US-backed dictatorship.

Castro's leftward drift, spurred by US hostility to his revolutionary regime, ironically coaxed hundreds of thousands of Cubans to flee to the US. Batista's discredited lackeys

man cleaning the rest room at a southwest Miami service station may once have been a promising lawyer. A great many Cubans, especially those who turned to exile in their middle years, have not totally abandoned the dream of someday returning to a different Cuba. The lingering hopes and continuing attachment of large numbers of Cubans to the old land is reflected in the existence of social, cultural and political organizations pegged to old Cuban institutions.

But the battle that most South Florida Cubans have joined is the one to conquer the almighty dollar. From a penniless lot, the exiled community has become an economic success story. Initially, they got back on their feet with the help of US agencies. But, Cubans proudly point out, the doubling up of work shifts by middle-aged men and women and the relentless drive to improve their lot – often just to be able to take pictures of the new house or car and send it back to Cuba – may well account for the Cubans' success.

By the 1980s, the South Florida Cuban population had moved from ethnic-enclave status to one of powerful political and economic clout. Of all US metropolitan areas, Miami's Dade County has the largest number, per capita, of Hispanic owned businesses, with most of them being Cuban owned. Along with their presence in the private profes-

were many mentally ill and criminally prone young men. US officials saw Castro's decision to include the problem men among the departing masses as a clever way of converting embarrassment into a convenient mechanism for jettisoning some of his problems into the hands of the US – and Miami.

Though comprising a minority among those who fled in the dramatic upsurge in refugees, many of these young men proved to be too unskilled and emotionally unstable to find employment or even proper housing. Lumped together as Marielitos, because they left Cuba from the port of Mariel, these people have been ostracized even by Miami's Cubans and are believed to have been involved in a

sional sector, Cubans are also prominent in the public sector. In 1985 Miami elected its first Cuban-born mayor, and many other Cubans hold key positions throughout the government bureaucracies.

Although the Cubans in South Florida have a proven success record, they remain haunted by an unwelcome wave of immigrants that arrived in 1980. Among the 125,000 refugees who fled Cuba in a mass exodus during that year's "freedom flotilla"

Left, grocery store in Miami's Little Havana. **Above**, Cuban refugees arrive at Key West during the 1980 "freedom flotilla."

disproportionate share of violent crimes.

Life has never been easy for the Miami Cubans, though. Some black civil rights leaders see them as a barrier to the training and job opportunities that might improve the economic lot of native-born blacks, and in white areas, such as the large middle-class Jewish enclaves throughout Dade County, complaints about the Cuban presence led to a successful drive to reject a referendum designating Miami as an officially bilingual city. Hostility from elements in both the black and white communities has existed all along, however, and has not hindered the Cuban success story.

Crackers represent the state's link with its past, as well as its rural heritage of plantation politics and small-scale sharecropping. Yankees are indicative of a changing Florida, of high-density suburbs, crowded beaches and burgeoning metropolises.

Depending on how loosely you define the two terms, Crackers and Yankees account for between 50 and 70 percent of the state's population. Cultural distinctions separate them. They live in different parts of the state, eat different foods, speak differently, and pursue their occupations and leisure activities in different ways.

The term "Yankee" began as British slang for colonists living in New England in the days before the United States won its independence, but in Florida a Yankee is anyone who hails from the northeastern or midwestern regions of the United States.

A Cracker, on the other hand, is someone with strong roots in the South, someone hailing only from the extreme southeastern part of that region, or a very exclusive group of those born and bred in the Sunshine State, depending on which definition you choose.

Then there are the purists, like Florida writer Ernest Lyons in his essay, A Florida Cracker Came Into His Own. "Your dyed-in-the-wool, honest-to-God, genuine Florida Cracker traces his family back to the Indian wars," Lyons wrote. "Their folks were here when Colonel Zachary Taylor and his troops fought chiefs Wildcat, Alligator and Sam Jones at the battle of Okeechobee in 1837.

"The Florida Cracker is as closely rooted to his pine and palmetto ranchland as the Tennessee mountaineer to his blue hills. A Cracker may rise to be a supreme court justice or a governor but his heart stays at the ranch with his cows, catch-dogs and rattlesnakes. His ancestors made their own salt from the sea, their own homespun from patches of cotton, ran wild hogs and wild cattle, lived off the land."

Lyons got even more specific. He said the truly genuine Florida Cracker has a surname

Left, a native north Florida farmer relaxes atop his peanut pile. **Right**, another prize winner at the Florida State Fair.

like Platt, Carlton, Rowell, Hendry, Bass, Cash, Alderman and Whiddon.

Visitors should be careful when they use the term "Cracker," however, because it has been interpreted in some quarters to mean "poor, white trash." Understandably, some native Floridians are antagonistic that this is implied. Florida author Allen Morris advised his readers that it was wise to use the nickname with a quick smile.

Still, Florida scholar Angus McKenzie Laird said social and political philosophy

has a lot to do with the acceptance and even willingness to be known as a Cracker.

"The proud Crackers think of themselves as the common people, opposed to privilege and special interests," he explained.

One of the first recorded usages of the word was in *The Life and Death of King John*, a 1590 play by William Shakespeare. "What Cracker is this same that deafs our ears with this abundance of superfluous breath?" asks the Duke of Austria in the play. In those days, a Cracker was a storyteller of considerable accomplishment. And that apparently is why the nickname was originally bestowed on the roughhewn ancestors of present-day Platts, Carltons, and Cashes.

Other theories on how the nickname evolved relate to corn and cowboys. The vegetable theory says the nickname was bestowed on native Floridians because they cracked their corn to make grits. Another theory is that Crackers received their title because Florida ranchers had a habit of making loud snaps with their cattle whips.

"Cowboys on horses shouting at the tops of their lungs and whips cracking like pistol shots," said Laird, telling of one such cattle drive he saw during his youth in North Florida. "It was a sight to see and hear, and those Crackers were something."

Whatever the source, the nickname stuck.

Flagler, who built the railroads that sparked a land and building boom.

During that boom, many Northerners got their first peek at the state. Called Tin Can Tourists, they came by train or auto, stayed in impromptu tent cities and ate from tins. Many liked what they saw and adopted a vision of Florida that eventually emerged as its most popular image – a sunny playland where the lifestyle was more pleasant than back home.

World War II marked the watershed. Hundreds of thousands of Yankees were assigned to military bases near Jacksonville, Pensacola, Tampa and other Florida cities. Many servicemen returned to Florida after

Its early recipients carved a bountiful lumber, farming and ranching domain out of the semi-tropical jungle that once was inland Florida. Today, some of their descendants live in those same inland enclaves on land passed down directly from those ancestors, often working at agricultural enterprises begun by their forefathers.

Yankee Doodle Dandy: The mass influx of Yankees from the North changed the face of Florida from predominantly rural and sparsely populated to urban and industrialized. Much of the groundwork for the population surge was laid by a pair of Connecticut Yankees, Henry B. Plant and Henry M.

the war, fueling an 81.5 percent growth rate during the 1940s.

This set the stage for the massive growth of the next few decades. Now, 30 percent of the state's population hails from the Northeast or the Midwest, while only 22 percent come from southern states other than Florida. The Northerners tend to concentrate in the Atlantic or Gulf coasts of the peninsula. This trend has produced crowded neighborhoods, crowded streets, crowded restaurants and crowded beaches. The top states feeding Florida's ongoing population boom are New York, New Jersey, Ohio, Michigan and Illinois. Yankees have remade South Florida in the image of the overpopulated Northeast.

If the newcomers are a polyglot of ethnic origins, they do share one important ideal – that vision of Florida implanted in the national consciousness during the land boom of the 1920s. "I thought the whole state would be like one of those picture postcards of Miami Beach," said one woman who relocated from the North in the mid-1970s. "I was pleased to discover that wasn't true, but I think some small part of me still sees the state in those terms."

Despite the crowding, Yankees remember why they came to the Sunshine State. "I'll never go back," said Russ Chilcoat, a native of landlocked Pennsylvania. "I like living

Florida Cracker shows signs of feeling threatened by the newcomers.

"It seems like they are a completely different kind of people," said one county official in the Panhandle. "I think their way of operation and their background is totally different. It's a faster lifestyle, and I kind of like things the way they used to be."

Subtle differences: So there are some tensions between the Yankees and Crackers. Crackers feel that the changes are happening too quickly and are not necessarily for the better. Yankees feel that Crackers are too wedded to the traditions of another place and time. Friction between the two groups is rare, but it sometimes shows in small ways.

near the water, the sand, the surf."

Native Floridians are harder to pin down on the subject of what they love about their state. "It's my home," said one lifelong Florida resident. "I was born and raised here and it's just my home and I love it."

"I don't like that there are tall buildings on the beach where I grew up," said Pat Hendry, a native of Daytona Beach. "We used to have just cottages there."

Often the product of a small town, the

"There is an obvious sense of pride among natives," wrote Florida publisher and editor Harris Mullins. "They usually refrain from throwing their distinction verbally in the face of non-natives. They inject it subtly by reference."

Somewhat tongue in cheek, Mullins outlined basic differences between the two groups by noting that natives never go swimming after Labor Day, dislike Miami Beach, live within 12 minutes of the office, dislike crowded beaches, real estate taxes, crisply cooked vegetables and lamb, but love pork, cool days, politics, and doing business with their old friends.

Left, a *Harper's Weekly* illustration of "Florida Crackers Going to Church." **Above**, Plant City citizens mimic portraits in a John Briggs' mural.

The post-war baby boom made big news in US demographics in the 1950s. But Florida experienced another kind of population surge, a mass migration of retirees to the Sunshine State. This is a trend that began more than 60 years ago and continues today.

This in-migration of senior citizens has reshaped Florida, transforming former villages like Clearwater and Fort Myers into overnight metropolises, creating a demand for dozens of service industries, and making retirement payment checks one of the state's major sources of cold cash. It also has given Florida the nation's highest concentration of elderly residents. That distinction, when combined with the influx of honeymooners, has earned Florida a dubious reputation as a "land of the newlywed and the nearly dead."

Seniority: Of the state's 13 million residents, nearly 2 million are 65 years old or more. That means nearly one in every six Floridians is a senior citizen.

In 15 of Florida's 67 counties, more than a third of the populace is over 60. Senior citizens number more than 40 percent of the residents in five of those counties; in Charlotte County on the state's southern Gulf Coast, retirees account for fully 52.5 percent of the population.

And the trend shows no signs of abating. If anything, it is gathering steam. The retire-to-Florida syndrome has become part of the national mythology, particularly in the Northeast and Midwest; it's a final installment of an American Dream. For millions of working Americans, Florida is their deserved reward for decades of labor in the landlocked and seasonally cold northern states. Retirement here is what they promise themselves on all those snowy winter mornings when the car refuses to start, and during those endless business meetings when the boss refuses to listen. It has been that way ever since the 1930s, when Florida began to attract its first influx of retirees.

There are also strong and pressing finan-

cial reasons for Florida's popularity among retirees. It is one of the most favorable of US states in terms of tax conditions. Many people come for the financial reasons alone; the sunshine is merely a bonus.

In the early years, the bulk of retirees settled in Miami Beach and St Petersburg. But, in the last two decades, retirees have grouped throughout South Florida, particularly along the Gulf and South Atlantic coasts. Each section of Florida seems to draw its senior citizens from a different socio-eco-

nomic strata and a distinct area of the US. So, retirees from the Midwest flock to the central Gulf Coast, from Tampa Bay south to Fort Myers. Often, these people are middle class, with secure pensions and conservative political bents.

Retirees from the urban Northeast usually go to extreme South Florida, the Fort Lauderdale and Miami areas. Their politics are usually more liberal than their Midwestern counterparts. A sizable number of them are Jewish, and many are workers and trade-union members.

But where does the wealthy retiree go, the person who couldn't care less whether the

Left, a senior swinger swats a hit in St Petersburg's unretiring Kids and Kubs baseball league. **Right**, Florida's senior citizens like to ride motorcycles in their spare time.

Social Security check arrives on time, who buys General Motors stock but who drives about – or is chauffeured – in a Rolls? That person retires to Palm Beach. Jacksonville is popular with black retirees. It is also preferred by retired military personnel, a distinction it shares with the Pensacola area.

Retired life in Florida varies according to individual tastes, and the money available to pursue those tastes. Some buy homes in neighborhoods specifically oriented toward the elderly. Others rent apartments, or mobile homes in a trailer park catering to older people. Purchasing a condominium apartment is another popular option. The standard condominium is a tall apartment building

exercise. Others are lawn bowling, and shuffleboard courts. Most cities with sizable retirement populations have acres of them. Both sports involve little strain or exertion and allow ample opportunity to socialize.

Seniors clubs and "adults only" neighborhoods are also prevalent. The former are social organizations restricted to people 55 or older. Big band music of yesteryear is featured at weekly dances; card games and fashion shows fill other free time. "Adults only" enclaves cater to elderly people who want to escape noisy children and the changing proclivities of the modern world.

Silver-haired politicians: Political activity is another important aspect of Florida's retirees.

with dozens of one or two-bedroom units. Residents own their apartments and pay a monthly fee for the upkeep of common grounds, which give them freedom from maintenance worries.

Not all of Florida's retirees are full-time residents. Some come during the winter, and return North in the spring. Their migratory habits have earned them the nickname "snowbirds," because they follow northern fowl that fly south for the winter.

There are several traditional symbols of retirement communities. One is a tricycle, popular because it handles more easily than a two-wheeler, while still providing ample

Many find local politics a hobby and go on to become mayors and councilmen in their communities. This syndrome has helped mold the elderly into a potent state-wide political force. You can write off the candidate for Florida governor who does not court the senior citizen vote.

The Silver-Haired Legislature, a collection of over-60 seniors elected by their peers, gathers annually in the state capital. It doesn't have the power to pass laws, but it does make influential recommendations to the real legislature regarding ways of improving laws affecting Florida's senior citizens.

Many retirees have the money to back up

their political convictions, but pockets of destitute old men and women do, of course, exist. St Petersburg's downtown area has become known as "The Battle Zone" because those who inhabit its cheap tenement homes are easy prey for muggers, robbers and thieves. These impoverished retirees are the exception, however. Retirement income pumps $12 billion annually into the state, and nearly a third of Florida's lucrative real estate transactions involve the elderly. More than 75 percent of the homes headed by retirees are owned by them.

So, with money, political clout and leisure activities aimed at their age group, retirement in Florida is the perfect answer for

rent accommodation or travel in Florida for a year until they decide if it's right for them. Experts also advocate that the elderly pursue some project or leisure interest that will keep life meaningful.

Virgil Connor, for instance, used his freedom from the work-a-day world to renew a college career he abandoned several decades ago. He obtained his master's degree in history from Florida State University, and then, at the age of 92, became the oldest man in state history to earn a doctorate.

"I was 80 when my son suggested that our business could do just as well without me as with me, and I wasn't sure what the future held for me,' Conner said. "Going back to

everyone approaching the sunset years. Right? Wrong. Many ultimately find that Florida just isn't for them. They get depressed by the self-imposed segregation of hundreds of thousands of old people. They miss their home towns and the opportunity to mingle with the young and vigorous.

"Retirement to Florida sometimes produces a lemon instead of a juicy orange," wrote essayist Ernest Lyons.

Lyons and other experts advise retirees to

Left, Sunday morning strollers on a St Petersburg street corner. **Right**, strolling in the shade on Miami Beach.

school was the best thing I ever did."

Some retirees turn to sports they never had the time to conquer in their youth. St Petersburg's Kids and Kubs play in a unique baseball league where the aged, not the young, have the edge in spring tryouts. You must be at least 75 years old to qualify for a team. One player was still swinging at age 95.

Many older people do find happiness here, that pot of golden sunshine at the end of the rainbow. As a result, there's one sight common to Florida that is more moving than any sunset or spectacular seascape. It's that of an elderly couple, obviously content, holding hands and strolling along the beach.

On Guavaween, a Halloween-style event celebrated by Hispanics, the mythical Mama Guava heads the city of Tampa's Stumble Parade. Her mission? To take the "bore" out of historic Ybor City (pronounced *Ee-bore*). How? With festival flair: rock and reggae; food and festivities, plus tweaks at the politically correct and Holy Rollers on roller skates.

Floridians find any excuse to celebrate. In fact, in this state, community camaraderie is a historic mandate. Two hundred years ago, Seminoles met each harvest time for a Corn Dance. Today, festivals promote everything – food, music, art history, folklore – for the really party-hearty.

Admittedly, festivals in Florida are loosely defined. San Antonio puts a bounty on rattlesnakes, and hunters bring them in by the sackful, dead or alive, during an October round-up. Each March, Miami offers a Carnaval that rounds up a million revelers for a 23-block-long party on Little Havana's Calle Ocho.

Every six months, state tourist officials list such festivals, though they can never say for sure how many there are or how big they will be. But certainly, national holidays grab attention. Fireworks pop and sizzle on Independence Day each July, whether at Gainesville's "Fanfare and Fireworks," Marathon's "Star-spangled Event" or Fernandina Beach's "Red, White & Blue Parade." This is America.

Having said that, regional quirks are preserved. The Florida Keys and coasts honor the sea – they cavort, race and catch and eat fish. Inland, cattle and citrus take over. And the boys – good ol' Cracker boys and cowboys – honor themselves with such fanfare as Fort Myers' Cracker Festival in March, or Okeechobee's rodeo parade in September.

Some small towns say this partying puts them on the map. Others complain that traditions run amok. In the mid-1980s, Fort Lauderdale, hyped in the film *Where the Boys Are*, claimed back the beaches for its residents. So, each March, college students

on Spring Break now take beer blasts, cruising, and considerable dollars, not to Fort Lauderdale, but north to Daytona Beach.

Ethnic Glory: When newcomers landed on Florida's shores – explorers and colonizers from Europe, refugees from the Caribbean and the frozen American north – they brought play along with the hopes and hard work. Each year, festivals revisit history. St Augustine salutes Christopher Columbus with a parade, and Miami stages a weekend regatta. Jensen Beach counters with a Viking wel-

come to that other European colonizer, Leif Ericson. Who's first? Who cares!

In January, on Epiphany, descendants of Greek sponge divers pursue a gold cross tossed in the water. Then they carry their *baklava* coast to coast, in parties stretching from Boca Raton in March to Tallahassee in November. Minorcans claim a day in St Augustine; Italian-Americans, one in Venice, and Puerto Ricans, one in Orlando. Hollywood salutes Canadian snowbirds (winter vacationers from the North) in February.

At Dunedin, Scottish clans gather in March for Highland Games of piping, a military tattoo, and a ceilidh variety show. German brews, brods, and bands add oompah-pah music to Oktoberfests in Cape Coral, Titusville and Naples. Brooksville gets the jump with Septemberfest.

Bahamas Goombay festivals add Caribbean rhythms and limbo lines to Key West in October and Coconut Grove in June, the latter the largest African-American heritage festival in the United States.

Wet and wild: Florida revelers adrift on a peninsula, never far from water, ask two quintessential questions: Will it float? Is it fast? The answers turn into celebrations.

Rafts skitter along rivers in Melbourne, near Titusville and outside Port St Lucie in spring and fall. In April, a boating jamboree

early sprinters at Ormond Beach in November by swapping tips and parts. Derby darlings hit the soapbox circuit at Naples.

Men and Myths: Florida history brims with conquistadors, pirates, military battles, and regular changes of national flag. From June to August, St Augustine stages the official version of its founding in 1565 as the nation's oldest permanent city. Pensacola and Fernandina Beach honor flag-bearers in May and June, respectively.

Some cities declare loyalty to particular rogues. Fort Walton Beach touts the one-legged scoundrel, William Augustus Bowles, who besieged the coast in 1778. With his name corrupted to Bowlegs, his spirit returns

dominates Kissimmee's chain of lakes while Marathon runners dash over the water in the Seven-Mile Bridge Run in the Keys.

Compared with water frolics, sand is serious. Sand sculptors compete from Sarasota in February to Fort Myers in November, and in between. The best sand castles – gigantic displays with towers and moats – win awards for artistry, originality, and structural integrity.

Hot-air balloon buffs top trees at Tallahassee in March. Aviators "fly-in" to Lakeland or watch spins and rolls in spring at Punta Gorda and New Smyrna Beach in fall. Owners of seriously pre-owned cars honor

for the Billy Bowlegs festival in June. In February, Tampa honors José Gaspar. Bloodthirsty pirates board a schooner, invade a parade downtown, kidnap the mayor, and trigger a week of merry-making.

Florida likes to adopt heroes. Key West honors a favorite son, author Ernest Hemingway, with literary workshops, a short story competition, a Papa Look-alike Contest and macho musts such as billfish tournaments. Fort Myers celebrates inventor Thomas Edison with a Pageant of Light birthday party each February.

Every year, time lines contract; history becomes the present. In April, never-say-die

Key West secedes from the state of Florida, declaring independence as the "Conch Republic." The town of Micanopy hops through the centuries – from Pedro Menendez's 1656 arrival, to botanist William Bartram's 1774 travels, to Seminole hunting parties and Confederate cavalry. Milton Town celebrates with a Scratch-Ankle fund-raiser in March honoring the thick briars that once kept outsiders out.

Florida offers cowboys and Indians, real and staged. Professional cowboys, the real thing, ride into Central Florida for calf ropin', bronco-bustin' and even square dancin' on horseback. Kissimmee holds a Silver Spurs Rodeo, among the nation's top 20 and the

tribal artists from throughout the hemisphere.

For re-enactments, try Pioneer Days in High Springs, and Frontier Days in Naples. Choose horseback or covered wagon for a week-long trek across Osceola County, or Can Can at Pensacola's October round-up, shoot-outs available.

Homesteaders, then and now, offer down-home county fairs, with agricultural exhibits, livestock judging, and country music. Held in early fall or late winter, they feature marching bands, parades, and prizes. Tampa's two-week state fair in February sets the pace, with red ribbons for the jammiest jam or squealingest pig.

National artists and craft artisans circulate

state's oldest rodeo, each February and July. For the Florida twist, visit Marathon's lobster rodeo in August.

Native American rodeos, strong in South Florida, are now paired with pow wows ("big gatherings") that offer tempting prize money in frenetic dance competitions. Seminoles hold several each winter, including an annual tribal fair in Hollywood. Look for wrestling – arm and alligator. Near the Everglades, Miccosukees host an Indian-only art festival each December, drawing

Left, doing the Highland Fling at Dunedin. **Above**, parade in Key West.

on warm breezes through a state-wide circuit of outdoor shows. In Miami, more than 300 artists and a million visitors meet at the Coconut Grove Arts Festival in February. Already 30-something years old, it's one of the largest art shows in the US and Florida's most popular. Fairs in Winter Haven, Mount Dora and elsewhere are gaining in popularity, too.

During Art Deco Weekend in January, Miami Beach honors preserved pastel architecture with outdoor dances and Big Band tunes. Even movie lovers prefer outdoors in Florida, so the Miami Film Festival in February and the Greater Fort Lauderdale Film

Festival in November offer open-air forums and street dances where stars and star-gazers can meet.

Music festivals – free extravaganzas of national and international acclaim – are also held throughout the state. For jazz, head to Pensacola or West Palm Beach in spring, and Jacksonville, Clearwater, and Sanibel Island in fall. Bluegrass flourishes – fiddle, dulcimer, banjo, blues guitar, even diddley bow – on the banks of the Suwannee River at Live Oak in April and at Kissimmee in March. In spring, Cajun music heads down to Destin, while arias drift through Seaside, and in fall, marching bands strut in St Petersburg.

Some open-air parties are decidedly dif-

ferent. Shell blowers compete in Key West's conch contest in March. In June, on Big Pine Key, boaters coast near the reef, hook up speakers, and offer divers and beachcombers a four-hour, commercial-free underwater music festival.

Food Feasts: Everywhere pays homage to the stomach. Florida's favorite citrus, the orange, gets a regatta in Lakeland in April and a squeeze-off in Winter Haven in February. The Orange Bowl, the largest post-season football game in the US, spills off the field when a jamboree invades Miami streets on New Year's Eve. Citrus Bowl football and parades engulf Orlando in January.

Seafood festivals dot the coast. Among the oldest is Apalachicola's salute to oysters, but other cities promote their favorites, too. In May, Pensacola celebrates lobster; Panacea, blue crab; and Amelia Island, shrimp. Fellsmere pulls its frogs' legs. The Boggy Bayou Festival at Niceville honors mullet – smoked, fried, or gumbo-ed. Not to be outdone, each March, Bonita Springs celebrates fruit and fish at its Tomato-to-Snook tournament.

Just preparing food prompts a party. At Green Cove Springs, teams compete in "ham jams." West Palm Beach stages a clambake. Pensacola plots a barbecue rib burn-off; Sandestin offers a gumbo cook-off. Tallahassee folks grind the cane and distill the syrup at an 1880s homestead, while Land O Lakes touts the flapjacks and Naples crowns champions of chili.

Even inedible plants get recognition. The first bud of the new year is honored at Delray Beach's bonsai festival. Sarasota flaunts orchids; Winter Haven, chrysanthemums. At Caryville, they aren't afraid to get dirty, thump, thump, thumping sticks into moist soil to lure earthworms at an international gathering of worm-fiddlers. Is the melody enticing – or the vibrations just excruciating?

Traditions Floridiana: On occasion, Floridians roll down their sleeves and fasten the top button to respect tradition – Florida-style. At Easter, a bishop blesses boats in St Augustine, and Daytona Beach plans a jog on its hard-packed, white sand. At Christmas, glittery regattas wind along coastal waterways almost everywhere in the state. In January, Pensacola slates a Pola Bear Dip and manufactures flakes for Snowfest contestants who build sandmen and snowmen.

Even spoofs are delivered fun-in-cheek. For Key West's Halloween each October, owners and pets parade in costumes during Fantasy Fest's twilight parade. The King Mango Strut, the outcasts' answer to Orange Bowl organizers, parades through Coconut Grove in December, thumbing a collective nose at stuffy tradition and rigid ritual.

Too tame? Visit Wausau on its official Fun Day in August. Race bullfrogs, auction off possums, call a hog, climb a greased pole, enter a corn pone bake-off. Florida certifies your fun.

Left, Plant City celebrates itself. Right, sun-gazing in feathers.

In Florida, a simple combination such as chicken and rice will allow you to eat your way through the state's history and diverse ethnic cultures.

In the northeast, descendants of Minorcans spice *pilau* with fiery, homegrown datil peppers, plus any seafood available locally. Inland, a more Southern version prevails, simple, and spiked with black pepper from Africa and garnished with chopped, hard-boiled eggs. In Miami and Tampa, Cuban immigrants go gaudy – tinting *arroz con pollo* golden with saffron, adding garlic and onions galore, and topping it all with red peppers and green peas. Backwoods Crackers deep fry the chicken and substitute grits for rice.

As food lovers discover, such variety has been shaped by newcomers lured to Florida by the land, legends and tropical lushness. Many of the foodstuffs, too – even the native orange – come from someplace else. Spanish missionaries introduced European cooking. Portuguese and Greek seafarers tossed in other Mediterranean touches. French Huguenots brought muscadine grapes for vineyards. Blacks accompanying the conquistadors brought Africa's yams, eggplant and okra.

North Americans added seeds and hybrids, turning cooking into cuisine. British loyalists and Bahamians added steamed pudding and conch salad. Pre-colonial refugees promoted a Southern taste for biscuits and gravy. Colonial descendants contributed more rice and hot breads. Creole cooking – gumbos and jambalaya – edged eastward from Louisiana into the Panhandle.

This century, Palm Beach socialites imported chefs and continental cuisine. Jewish sun-worshipers, en route to Miami Beach, brought kosher delicatessens and gorged on heaping platefuls of "early bird specials." Fast-food entrepreneurs pumped the national craving for anything-and-fries: almost 2,000 eateries, many with elaborate themes, blossomed in Orlando.

Even Kennedy Space Center astronauts affected the packaging of food: making it

Preceding pages: juicy fruit stand.<u>Left</u>,a chef's touch can make all the difference. <u>Right</u>, pork on a stick.

bite-sized, freeze-dried, squeeze-tubed and thermo-stabilized. Recently, adventurous cooks discovered Florida's constants – fresh seafood and exotic fruits. Now, with New World cuisine rejuvenating Florida's appeal to health seekers, papaya salsa competes hard on the heels with grits and greens.

Meaty Treats: Florida's earliest explorers were treated to venison, boar, and even bear. Seminoles and Miccosukees often bartered these with the settlers. The tribes also simmered morsels of turtle, duck eggs, frog legs,

eels, alligator, and tasty herbs. Some of these early dishes, seasoned with bacon drippings, are still available at the Miccosukee Indian Village outside Miami.

In *Cross Creek Cookery*, popular author Marjorie Kinnan Rawlins admitted she enjoyed bear meat "thoroughly," but would "happily settle for a stupid steer." It's that not-so-exotic staple – choice prime beef – that now dominates diets everywhere.

Some traditions, such as earth roasts for venison favored in the Panhandle, admittedly still hold. But today's legacy is steak on the barbecue. Rattlesnake meat and tasty gatortail can be found, not in Seminole stewpots, but on toothpicks. These are delicate hors d'oeuvres served with cocktails.

Still, beef has its backers. When Cubans arrived in Tampa in the mid-19th century, and then in Miami post-1959, they added more dishes dominated by beef: *bolichi* (beef stuffed with boiled eggs), *alcaporado* (beef stew with olives and raisins), and *palomilla* (thin, breaded steak spiced with lime).

In inexpensive eateries, Cubans also supply generous portions of roast pork and chicken, fried plantains, and black beans and white rice, cooked separately as *arroz con frijoles negros*, or cooked together as *moros y cristianos*.

Other staples are spreading throughout the

state from Florida's urban centers: Cuban bread, its crust crispy and its top flattened, stretched to two feet; Cuban coffee, gulped black, strong and sweet (café Cubano) or doused with steamed milk (café con leche); and Cuban sandwiches, bread sliced to eight inches and stuffed with pork, ham, salami, cheese, pickle, and topped with yellow mustard. You can eat it pressed – with pork drippings, flattened, and grilled, or plain.

In recent years, this heavy diet has been tempered by nuevo Cubano and Caribbean tastes – from Jamaica, Haiti and the Bahamas and parts of Latin America. Nicaraguans brag, with justification, about their

beef flank *churrasco* with *chimichurri* sauce.

Sea bounty: From river banks, ocean depths, freshwater lakes, saltwater lagoons and off-urban bridges, Floridians angle for fish – for sport or for supper.

With 700 species of fish, and 60 available commercially, Florida leads the nation in catering for lovers of seafood. Perched on a peninsula never far from water, this kind of dining can always be close to the source.

Key West offers perhaps the widest temptations: conch fritters, turtle steak, deviled crabs, baked kingfish, broiled stone crabs, fresh ceviche, conch chowder, curried lobster, crawfish bisque. Its Conchs (Key West natives) always eat seafood seasoned with a few drops of Old Sour, a lime juice concoction that mellows with age.

Inland havens such as Okeechobee produce bass, bluegill, speckled perch and catfish, ready for pan frying. Scampi is touted as the best freshwater fish, whether fried, sautéed, or broiled.

Big-game ocean catches include tarpon, marlin, swordfish, sailfish, barracuda, and dolphin (the fish, not the friendly mammals). Smaller saltwater game include snook, bluefish, bonefish, mackerel, and speckled trout. The sea also yields bounty beyond fish. Tons of shrimp – available fresh at the docks from short-run shrimpers – pour into Gulf ports, clearly the catch much in demand both locally and up the coast.

Among half a dozen distinctive crabs, stone crabs offer a rare treat. Eat them boiled, then iced and served with tart mayonnaise, mustard sauce, drawn butter, or fresh lemon. Fishermen remove only one claw in season (mid-October to mid-May), allowing crabs to regenerate up to four more.

Key West crawfish, known as Florida lobster, are caught in coral reef waters and shipped alive or frozen to markets along the east Atlantic Coast. Among turtles, the common alligator cooter, named for its ridged shell, has the whitest, sweetest meat. Other turtles, like greens and loggerheads, can make tasty meat for soup.

Tiny pompano clams come on summer tides to the Gulf's saltwater beaches. Oysters gathered at nearby Apalachicola Bay, the major bed in the southern US, are cited as aphrodisiacs. The hammered flesh of the Queen conch, housed in an iridescent shell, is light and flavorful. Served raw in salad or stewed in chowders, it's always drenched with lime juice.

Off-season, purists do without seafood; others settle on frozen. But aqua culture – fish farming for table delicacies – is gaining popularity. Early harvests supply freshwater crawfish, catfish, striped bass and eels.

Topping the fish fry menu is mullet or grouper on the West Coast, and mullet or snapper on the East. But re-educated palates are forsaking frying to make way for grilling, broiling, poaching and blackening. In fact, smoked seafood like mullet, mackerel or shrimp, are prized on both coasts.

Local holdout: Only Southern cooking – "good ol' Cracker cookin'" with saltmeat, a Bible story, a wash pot full of swamp cabbage (hearts of palm) stew, and sweet potato pie."

The truly hungry could also ask for side dishes of squirrel, coon, grits (whole grains of white corn treated with lye and boiled) gopher (land tortoise), or hush puppies (fried corn meal dough). Or Hoppin' John (black-eyed peas and hog jowls), which promises good luck on New Year's Day.

Until recently, this was country fare for family reunions, church suppers, or maybe a funeral dinner. Today, it's available in city restaurants, along with imported wines. Ask for the watermelon chilled – and plugged a day earlier with corn liquor.

cornmeal and molasses – has been relatively untouched by migrations. A carryover of the "poor white" diet in the antebellum South, this is the staple of Florida's north and back-woods areas. As old-timers are quick to point out, this is different to the soul food basic to the black South, which tends to be more seasoned and greasy.

A dinner suggested by Ernest Matthew Mickler, author of the classic *White Trash Cooking*, might include "fried chitlins, a mess of turnip greens, enough hoe cakes for

Left, selling Cuban sandwiches at the Calle Ocho festival. **Above**, Caribbean crawfish.

Fresh pickin's: Since the turn of the century, Florida has picked, washed, sorted, graded, packed and shipped fruits and vegetables to markets throughout the US. Homesteaders, who survived hurricanes and freezes, turned the land into major producers. Sweet, juicy, rich Florida citrus comes in at least 10 varieties of orange, plus four of grapefruit, two each of tangerines, lemons and limes. Riding a vitamin C high, Florida produces about two-thirds of the nation's oranges. Different varieties ripen at different times, so fresh oranges are available year-round.

Legend has it that Columbus brought oranges from European groves, and the abundant grapefruit were seeded in Cuba. Hybrids like tangelos (tangerine and grapefruit), tangors (tangerine and orange) and ugli fruit (grapefruit and orange) – have come from imaginative research closer to home.

In the mid-1940s, the concentration process brought Florida orange juice to the world, infinitely extending the sweet oranges' season. But it still disturbs purists to discover that chilled juice dispensed at Florida's welcome centers is concentrate, not freshly squeezed or even frozen.

South Dade county produces almost all of the country's limes, an import from Asia, though perhaps not Tahiti or Persia as named. Limes make thirst-quenching drinks, good

topping for fish, nice nuances for vegetables and desserts or garnishes for black bean soup and consommé.

The tangy Key lime is a Florida Keys trademark, and the main ingredient of its pungent pie: a creamy yellow concoction, topped with meringue, with plenty of fresh egg yolks, condensed milk and a big wallop of the same juice. Green coloring, corn starch, whipped cream, or prepared pudding mixes irk the loyalists.

Other than citrus, the subtropical south produces pineapples, coconut, banana, even sugar cane, plus grove and backyard treats such as:

● Mangoes, with gorgeous gold, scarlet, purple and green skin. Its sweet flavor is hard to pin down, so judge for yourself. Peel the skin and duck. Sploosh! Or cut, slice, dice and eat – preferably in a bathtub.

● Guavas, white or light pink or red, with a sweet flavor, aromatic when ripe. Eat as paste, marmalade, sauce or right off the tree.

● Papayas, sweet and musky, a mass of black spots when ripe. Peeled, cubed, chilled, sweetened or not, the flavor is mild enough to need a boost from lime or lemon juice.

● Avocados, in season between January and July. Mash and snack. Imported from Mexico in the early 1800s, avocados are Florida's largest non-citrus crop.

For berry lovers, strawberries ripen December to June in the state's Hillsborough County – the world's winter strawberry capital. Florida jellies, preserves, marmalades, chutneys, even ice-cream reach way beyond basic berries to kumquat, mayhaw, roselle, gooseberry and passion fruit.

Lake Okeechobee and Everglades muck are a paradise for winter vegetables, with rows of radishes, eggplant, peppers, celery, and lettuce. Florida's vast vegetable bin brims with beans (bush, pole, limas) and peas (southern, black-eyes, conch, field, table, cowpea, zippers) plus a major crop and major treat: sweet corn.

Most fruits and vegetables are available in winter months, with some late fruit available in June and July. Load up at U-pick fields, specialty shops, farmer's markets, roadside stands, or even from hawkers at crowded city intersections.

Such roadside signs are classic Floridiana. During the Depression, one researcher for the Federal Writers' Project noted: "Nearly everywhere gastronomy and distance are combined in directional markers that announce '11 miles to Guava Paste' or '13 miles to Tupelo Honey'."

Nowadays, in northern Florida, look for roadside pointers to "boiled peanuts" in steaming paper sacks. Near Fernandina Beach and Apalachicola Bay, bumper stickers proclaim: "Eat Oysters Love Longer." In the southwest, discover a café tucked in a swamp that boldly advertises "Eat Here and Get Gas and Worms." Can you resist?

Left, Palm Beach Yacht Club. Right, wearing o' the green at Universal Studios.

Sports widows (and widowers) beware! If whacking a golf ball, riding a wave and swimming with dolphins were not enough to keep sports lovers satisfied in Florida, die-hard fans can be seduced into added athletic diversions in the form of any number of spectator sports.

Florida can be a very dangerous place for sports-junkie gamblers. But if you admit that you're hooked, and just can't say no, give in to one of the three big vices, and promise you'll quit in the morning.

Speed demons: On a crisp February day in 1959, they held a race at Daytona International Speedway, and the world of stock car racing changed forever.

Since then, headlines in newspapers world-wide have chronicled racing in Florida, but no story every approached that first race at Daytona in significance. It was the contest of all contests that took Florida stock car racing out of the proverbial backwoods and brought with it a following that had previously been reserved for classic American race cities like Indianapolis.

Not that stock car racing was anything new here. William H.G. "Bill" France, seeking his fortune in the South years before, trans-formed a group of grease-covered speed demons into the National Association for Stock Car Auto Racing, now internationally known as NASCAR. If the popular open-wheel cars could have a showplace like the Indianapolis Speedway, France speculated, why couldn't stock cars have a similar starry showplace?

Daytona International Speedway made its debut on that February day in 1959. Its "D"-shaped speedway and ultra-high banking turns were designed for blazing speeds, and first-day fans were left enthralled – stock car racing, born in the North Florida hill country decades before, had been born again in Daytona. Soon after, the entire nation grew curious about the doings of "those crazy rednecks down South."

Today, spectators are still enthralled by

Preceding pages: Harley lovers, Daytona Beach. **Left**, Indy-style and rubber-burning speed, Daytona. **Right**, a hydroplane roars past Miami.

the course and even more enthralled by the speeds. The patch of land in suburban Daytona Beach has since become the second most famous racecourse in the nation, next to Indianapolis. Names like Richard Petty, A.J. Foyte and Mario Andretti have established Daytona as one of the greatest fuel-guzzling, engine-blasting, high excitement speedways in the world. And Daytona has become the end of racing's greasy rainbow for aspiring stock drivers, most of whom never get to make the 40-car starting lineup determined

by two 125-mile qualifying races.

Although officials never release attendance figures, it is estimated that between 100,000 and 150,000 fans jam the speedway each February for the Daytona 500, its premier race. And those who make the annual pilgrimage are not only hard-core speed vo-yeurs, but a rip-roaring bunch of beer-drinking, snakepit-screaming, stay-up-all-night-and-party kind of guys – and gals. So much so, that the entire Daytona Beach community is turned upside down by the crowds, noise and crazed commotion that envelops the city each year.

Not long after participants in the Daytona

500 head home, they return for the famous 12 Hours of Sebring in March. In the days of racing prototypes, when red Ferraris and blue Porsches dueled for the manufacturers' championships, the races of Sebring were unsurpassed in popularity.

Even though the prototypes are now gone, Sebring remains a major stop for sports car drivers. The course is laid out in steamy Central Florida over the old Sebring Airport runways and taxiways. Known for its less-than-smooth speedway with patches of crumbling concrete, drivers relish the rough and rugged conditions.

For the 35,000 or so spectators who converge on this small Florida town each March,

Stadium near Key Biscayne. Inboards, outboards and offshore power-boats also ply Miami's waters in major events each year. Speed boat races also take place in St Petersberg, Stuart and Cocoa.

Taking a gamble: If the incessant roar of engines is still not enough to sate a craving for a sports-induced high, Florida offers the intoxicating thrill of legalized gambling. While casino gambling has been considered by Florida residents, it has yet to win statewide voting approval. But don't despair, Florida is a haven for those who love the excitement of pari-mutuel betting.

Over 15 million people a year wage over $1.6 billion on jai-alai and horse racing in

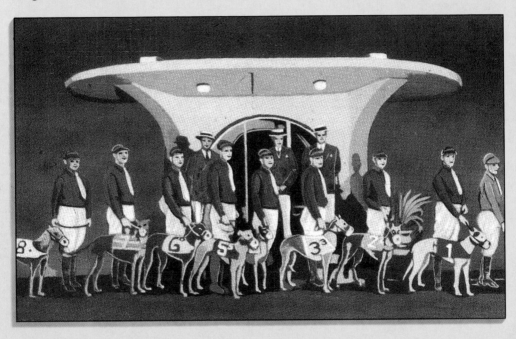

the 12 Hours – like the Daytona 500 – is a good excuse to throw a party. The land surrounding the course turns into a huge campground and during the race it looks like a giant cook-out. Fans often get rowdy in some sections as drugs and alcohol take their combined effect.

The other speed sport popular and particularly suited to watery Florida is boat racing. Every kind of craft from tiny speed boats to enormously powerful cigarette boats and hydroplanes churn through its bays, lakes, rivers and seas in an endless quest for aquatic supremacy.

The sport's focal point is Miami Marine

Florida. Generally, pari-mutuel sports attract two distinct types of fans – the serious player who approaches his or her gamble of choice with a steadfast dedication and desire to win, and the second type, vacationers or residents betting for fun rather than for profit.

Thoroughbred racing dominates the state's gambling industry. Horse-racing's tradition of glamor, high-society, and heroes is known throughout the world and earned it the sobriquet the "Sport of Kings." The Miami area has been a winter mecca for the nation's best horses and jockeys for over 60 years, and in a routine winter season, every important thoroughbred in training east of the Mississippi River is likely to be stabled somewhere in South Florida.

Years ago, prominent sports, entertainment and political figures made South Florida's horse tracks a place to see and be seen. These days, those memories still have a ghostly hold over some of the more elaborate tracks – Hialeah and Gulfstream – but for the most part the crowds are more pedestrian than genteel. Hialeah remains the Grand Dame of thoroughbred racing in Florida with its manicured gardens, flocks of flamingos, and Mediterranean architecture. Gulfstream, north of Miami Beach, is now more urban modern and sits in the middle of a high-rise condominium community. Together, the two

men to Florida. Virtually all of the sport's superstars ship their stables to Pompano for winter racing. They also prepare young horses being developed for the next summer's races in the North.

Along with horses, Florida's greyhound racing industry is without peer. The state is, by far, the most important greyhound area in the nation if for no other reason than sheer volume. Annual paid attendance statewide is about 8 million people who wager, with zeal, over $900 million.

All major metropolitan areas have at least one track nearby where the sleek canines can be watched as they are lured by an artificial rabbit around the track to the cheer of anx-

tracks compose the proving grounds for the best 3-year-old thoroughbreds in the country, those bound for northern Triple Crown sweepstakes. Pompano and Tampa also have first-rate tracks.

Between October and April, South Florida is also the focal point of the nation's harness racing. The opening of Pompano Park in Pompano Beach over 25 years ago served as the catalyst for what has become an annual southern migration of big name harness horse-

Left, "Greyhounds on parade," an old-postcard look at Miami racing. **Above**, on towards the winning post at a Florida night race.

ious bettors. The modern version of greyhound racing is believed to have evolved from a coursing meet held in 1904 near Hot Springs, North Dakota. Anthropologists claim that Cleopatra fancied greyhounds, a trait she shared with most Egyptian royalty. And in England, the sport reached its great popularity during the reign of Queen Elizabeth I, who inspired the slogan the "Sport of Queens."

As if horses and dogs did not represent sufficient opportunities to gamble, Florida is also one of the few states where you can wager on human beings – provided they are playing the ancient Basque game called *jai-*

alai (joyous festival). And once again, Florida takes first place in this sport; there are more jai-alai *frontons* (arenas) here than in any other state.

The wagering concepts common to other pari-mutuel sports hold for jai-alai. Win, place, show, quinela, perfecta, trifecta – all apply to these helmeted men with baskets attached to their hands who play a version of handball on an oversize court. Jai-alai vernacular is a blend of Spanish and Basque. The player is a *pelotari*, the ball a *pelota*, the basket a *cesta*. Each pelotari wears a red sash called a *faja* and a helmet, the *casca*.

Although it might sound like a simple game, jai-alai is in reality a super-fast phe-

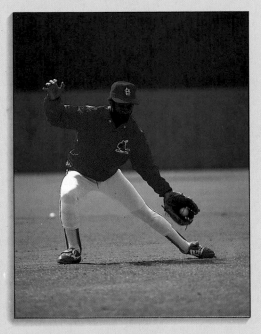

nomenon that appears to the eyes as a lightening-quick blur.

Baseball boys: Another spectacular spectator sport that lures fans by the droves to Florida is the all-American, apple-pie institution of baseball.

Careers are reborn every spring in Florida as baseball busts out all over the state when 17 out of 26 Major League teams head to Florida for training. Like polar bears awakening from a winter hibernation, the boys of baseball stretch and yawn and try to get in shape. Umpires squat and wave their arms, and batters get blisters on their fingers. Stiff pitching arms are loosened and catchers'

hands burn at the first pop of a 96-mile an hour fastball.

It begins in early March, when most of the US is still scraping ice off their driveways, and lasts for two months. The skies are their azure clearest and the temperature seems locked in at 70°-plus. Author Pat Jordan wrote: "Spring training is like a big summer picnic, where everyone's playing softball and eating barbecue. It's like a big country fair with people all around the ballpark."

And even though nothing counts for real, the multi-million dollar star players attract tens of thousands of baseball fans from across the country who eat mediocre hot dogs, drink warm beer, and scream and shout with excitement at the thought of scoring a foul ball tossed over a chain link fence or an autographed baseball cap.

There's something about getting a baseball player's autograph that dates back to the childhood rush of getting close enough to touch and talk to someone who never before seemed real.

Although ballpark seats are not free, they cost considerably less than a real world major-league series game.

Hard-core baseball fans follow teams across the state. These teams can easily match city counterparts: Orlando – the Minnesota Twins, Winter Haven – the Boston Red Sox, Sarasota – the Chicago White Sox, Lakeland – the Detroit Tigers, West Palm Beach – the Atlanta Braves, Fort Lauderdale – the New York Yankees. Even the Los Angeles Dodgers, blessed with their own glorious weather, make a pilgrimage to Vero Beach to train each spring. And each geographic area becomes a magnet for each city's baseball fans.

Along with being fun to watch, spring training is also big business; loads of money is spent. Television crews and news organizations from around the country and the world are dispatched as a national spotlight shines on Florida.

Hotels fill up, rates get higher, restaurants require reservations. A spring training camp can mean as much as $30 million to a local economy and several city mayors have gone so far as to try to lure teams away from another city to procure their own 2-month joy ride. Who says it's just a game?

Left, a Cardinal catch. **Right**, New York Mets batting practice during spring training.

The coins were relics of the annual currents of trade that once pulsed through the great Portobello fair, the port of Cartagena, and the entrepôt of Havana. Here were the surrogates for the hopes, lusts, fears and savings of private persons, the risks taken by long-dead merchants, and the once-coveted revenues of half-forgotten kings. Yes, here was death – the dissolution of men's hopes, the fatal decline of empire, the passing of an epoch. But the coins also spoke of life: the culture and commerce of colonial Spain. And we were privileged, as we sat among the heaps of coins, to touch all this.

—Eugene Lyon in
The Search for the Atocha

A uniformed guard, shotgun propped on hip, stood in front of the two-story Key West Conch House. Guests checked in on the ground floor, where they received a name tag and clearance to proceed to the second floor. A room at the top of the stairs contained more guards and displays of what looked like museum pieces – broken bowls, pottery shards, old cannon balls, muskets. Most people then gravitated to an adjoining room. There, jaws fell to chests the way the unhinged mouths of puppets would.

Amid the guards were several long cases lined with electric blue material. Inside, absorbing the glint of spotlights until it glowed richly, was *gold*. Bars, chains, plates, coins, ingots, bullion and solid chunks of pure gold. Not ounces, but pounds of gold. In one squat case alone was $10 million worth of long, thick gold chains. The total value of the treasure in those two rooms well exceeded $20 million.

"Here, feel it," a man said. He plopped a lump of yellow rock into a visitor's hand. An armed guard trained his eyes on the exchange. "You're holding a quarter million dollars."

The visitor needed two hands to hold it. It was more than a heavy piece of precious

Preceding pages: underwater treasure. **Left**, treasure-hunting king Mel Fisher brandishes a gold chain and an ancient kris from the *Atocha*. **Right**, a diver brings up more booty.

metal, more than a king's ransom. Here was something that had the most romantic of histories, something that had lain on the bottom of the sea for nearly 400 years. Indeed, it and all the treasure on display had been recovered from the worm-eaten, barnacle-encrusted hulls of two legendary Spanish galleons that sank in 1622 – the *Nuestra Señora de Atocha* and the *Santa Margarita*.

The exhibit was a routine affair in Key West held at the offices of Treasure Salvors, Inc. Company founder Mel Fisher has be-

come as much of a legend here as the fabulous treasures he has found. A strong, imposing figure, he bears no resemblance to those comic book characters who follow "x-marks-the-spot" maps to buried treasure chests. Fisher has made treasure-hunting a legitimate business. And he's helped make Florida a magnet for other dreamers hoping to find their fortune.

Sunken bounties: During the 16th and 17th centuries, Spanish ships listed with loads of gold, silver, precious commodities and other goods from their New World colonies in South America and the West Indies. These galleons plied routes that skirted Florida's southern coasts and keys. They made prime targets for marauding bands of pirates who darted from behind mangrove islands in swift, small ships, butchered passengers and crew, and made off with anything of value. Sometimes the buccaneers stashed the loot in island hideaways where it remains undiscovered today. Just as deadly as pirates were the forces of nature – violent thunderstorms, tricky currents, and sea-shaking hurricanes.

Two powerful war galleons, the *Atocha* and *Santa Margarita*, left Havana on September 4, 1622, in a Spanish fleet brimming with consignments of royal and private treasure. A hurricane devastated the fleet in the Straits of Florida the next day. The violent

storm shredded eight ships, killing 550 people and swallowing a fortune in gold, silver, indigo, copper and tobacco. The *Atocha* and *Margarita* were among the missing vessels.

Legends grew around the ships and their immense treasures, as usually happens. But no one seriously investigated the story or pursued the ships until Mel Fisher vowed to find them in the mid-1960s. Encouraged by efforts in recovering doubloons and pieces of eight from the wreck of a 1715 Spanish Plate Fleet off the coast of Vero Beach, Fisher began his new quest in the Keys.

The story of his search for the *Atocha* has all the ingredients of a best-selling novel. Suspenseful hunts through yellowing, old documents in archives in Spain; and years of cruising treacherous seas. Fisher's own son and daughter-in-law, as well as a crew member's son, were killed in boating accidents. And still he raced to beat other treasure hunters to the *Atocha* and to find it before he went broke. Tragedy and intrigue at last climaxed in triumph in June 1971.

Fisher demonstrated he had indeed found the *Atocha* with his typical flare for the dramatic. A silver bar he found in the wreck, with the number 4584 carved on it, had been listed on a 17th-century manifest which documented items loaded on the *Atocha* in Havana Harbor. All that remained was to weigh his bar and see if it matched the weight of the one listed on the manifest – 63.6 pounds. Before a crowd of newsmen, photographers and friends in Key West, Fisher adjusted a scale to 63.6 pounds. Then he put silver bar number 4584 on the scale. The balance beam hesitated for a moment and stopped in the middle. The weights matched. After proving himself right with the *Atocha*, Fisher went on to collect the bounties of the *Santa Margarita*, valued at about $20 million.

After several years of salvaging, Fisher and his crew were able to bring up the remaining treasures from the *Atocha* in 1985. The mother lode, or "Big Pile" as it was called, was worth more than anyone ever imagined and represented the largest recovered shipwreck treasure in the world, estimated at about $4 billion.

A booming industry: Since then, Fisher changed the name of his enterprise to the Mel Fisher Maritime Heritage Society and moved his operation, which includes an impressive museum, into a large stone building at 200 Greene Street in Key West. The museum's Treasure Exhibit includes gold bars, chains, precious stones, cannon balls and pottery found in the *Atocha* and *Margarita* wrecks. Fisher himself has become an international hero, his face gracing the cover of dozens of magazines and his story the focus of many television documentaries. Amid all the acclaim he remains a modest man, and can often be found wandering around his museum wearing red suspenders and a massive gold chain around his neck.

But it remains uncertain how much money Fisher, his employees and investors will reap from all of this. The US government and the

State of Florida have both battled in court for the rights to the treasure. So far, Fisher has won and the bulk of the riches remain in his hands. But legal challenges continue to arise. Florida officials and state archaeologists argue that an uncontrolled treasure-hunting industry here could damage other wrecks and the historical value of their cargoes. Marine conservationists argue that treasure-hunters are damaging the natural reefs and marine life in the waters. The National Oceanographic and Atmospheric Administration placed a federal injunction against Fisher in the late 1980s in order to stop his endeavors in the Keys, and in 1992, the Florida Keys National Marine Sanctuary placed a general six-month ban on treasure-hunting in the Keys to assess the situation. Fisher contends that the US and State governments are greedy, have already received a great deal of money from him in taxes, and are merely trying to cash in on his good fortune.

Fisher's exploits have indeed helped make Florida a mecca for treasure-hunters. Competitors discovered another old galleon off the coast of Brevard County just 1,000 feet from shore. It's believed to contain 20,000 to 50,000 silver coins. Further south, near Elliott Key in Biscayne National Park, a diver stumbled upon a Spanish-era wreck while spearfishing – and surfaced with old cutlasses and pottery instead of dinner.

Further afield, Florida-based Burt Webber, an old foe of Fisher's, discovered the sunken hull of the *Concepcion* off the coast of the Dominican Republic after a 15-year search. His operation, Seaquest International, has salvaged about $40 million in booty. Doubloon Salvage has been working wrecks near Fort Pierce thought to be more of the 1715 Spanish Plate Fleet, and Soul Treasures of Florida has been exploring the potentially lucrative waters around St Augustine Harbor.

Men like Fisher and Webber have turned treasure-hunting into businesses, utilizing sophisticated equipment and investing hundreds of thousands of dollars in searches. But the simple man who goes out to the woods or beaches with pick, shovel and some sketchy information is more common.

Tips for beginners: St Petersburg's L. Frank Hudson claims to be the authority on treasure along Florida's West Coast, although in his

Left and right, samples of old *Atocha* gold.

various publications he never admits to unearthing any pirate chests. In his *Lost Treasure of Florida's Gulf Coast*, he diagrams "pirate tree markings" and advises amateur hunters to keep their shovels sharp. He also obligingly provides the general locations of dozens of "treasures," some of which he says may be worth as much as $200 million.

Among some of the choice spots identified by Hudson are Naples Beach, where gold doubloons have washed ashore after high tides or storms; Cockroach Island in lower Tampa Bay; Indian Rocks Beach and Ross Island near St Petersburg's archaeologically rich Weedon Island. Cara Pelau Island near the mouth of Charlotte Harbor reputedly

served as headquarters – and therefore personal bank vault – for José Gaspar, one of the most famous of Florida pirates. There is, in fact, some doubt whether the West Coast ever attracted many pirates because Spanish shipping lanes were near the Keys and the southeast coast of the state – where most real treasures have been discovered to date.

Yet neither the doubts nor the unlikelihood of striking it rich deter the determined. Many can be seen solemnly scouring Florida's beaches, waving metal detectors around like divining rods, listening intently for the "bleep" in their headphones, while keeping sand scoops and sifters poised in their belts.

An appalling, unearthly report followed instantly, such as can be compared to nothing whatever, not even to the roar of thunder or the blast of volcanic explosions! No words can convey the slightest idea of the terrific sound! An immense spout of fire shot up from the bowels of the earth as from a crater...

At the moment when that pyramid of fire rose to a prodigious height into the air the glare of the flame lit up the whole of Florida; and for a moment day superseded night over a vast expanse of the country. This immense canopy of fire was perceived at a distance of 100 miles out at sea and more than one ship's captain entered in his log the appearance of this gigantic meteor.

The discharge of the Columbiad *was accompanied by an earthquake. Florida was shaken to its very depths.*
—Jules Verne in *From the Earth to the Moon*, 1863.

Thus did visionary author Jules Verne describe the launch of a mid-19th century space shuttle. With uncanny prescience, he named today's spacecraft and identified its launch site more than a century before the actual event occurred. Indeed, Verne's spirit may well have been at the Kennedy Space Center on April 12, 1981, almost 118 years after his vivid launch.

That morning, a blast of light burned the eyes, as if a photographer had just snapped your picture with a flash gun. The *Columbia*'s flash outshone the rising sun. Then, smoke bathed the horizon. Suddenly, incredibly, an enormous flying machine eased up out of its self-made cloud, hesitated, and accelerated atop a tail of angelic white smoke.

It was then you heard the rumble – faint at first, but rapidly building to a solid roar that astonished Florida's flatlands with its tremble and rippled through nearby human bodies. It turned into a staccato jackhammer beat as a vapor column vanished above. The sound finally faded away, but the quickened beat of hearts left earthlings in a state of exhilaration

long after the *Columbia* ripped itself from the earth's gravity. Florida was indeed "shaken to its very depths."

Seeing, hearing and feeling the launch of a vehicle bound for the future from the Kennedy Space Center is the highlight of a trip to Florida for many people. Even memories of a hot pink sun melting into the Gulf of Mexico at dusk recede when the countdown reaches "t minus one second."

Unlike many of Florida's fanciful attractions, which bend nature and technology into

mediums aimed at making people believe they are somewhere they aren't, the Kennedy Space Center is real. It is functioning technology in the midst of a natural wonderland, transporting human beings into the vacuums of a place far more mysterious than the plastic paradise of Walt Disney World or the manicured veldts of Busch Garden's Dark Continent.

Of course, seating aboard its space shuttles is still, with a couple of exceptions, limited to trained astronauts and scientists. But viewing the start of a voyage into space, and wandering among the "ancient" rocket graveyards of Cape Canaveral, at least pro-

Preceding pages: Florida's space shuttle launch pad. Left, the first shuttle launch. Right, weightless in a weighty industry.

pels one's brain waves into the ozone.

Flourishing wildlife: The Space Center sprawls across the ecological Eden of the Merritt Island National Wildlife Refuge and Canaveral National Seashore, 220 square miles of primitive swamp, savanna, hammock, marsh and windswept beaches. Flocks of egrets, ibis, herons and ducks appear unruffled about sharing this kingdom with monstrous birds that occasionally rocket past them with deafening roars. (According to one study, some of the local birds have indeed lost their hearing.)

More than 280 species of avifauna have been observed in the refuge, including endangered or threatened marvels like the

refuge offers the Oak Hammock hiking trail. There are also two wildlife driving tours, one along Max Hoeck Creek and the other along Black Point.

Only about 7 percent of the 140,000 acres owned by the National Aeronautics and Space Administration (NASA) has sprouted launch pads, industrial complexes, base-support facilities and roads. Most of the miles of grassy scrub, palmetto and brackish waters remain much as they must have looked when Europeans first set foot in the New World.

"We protect not only the wildlife but the habitats it needs to survive. We have demonstrated that high technology, natural landscapes and wildlife can coexist successfully,"

Southern bald eagle, the brown pelican and the rare Arctic peregrine falcon.

Other inhabitants include about 200 affectionate but imperiled West Indian manatees or "sea cows" and about 5,000 alligators, many of which can be seen lolling on the banks of canals that run along the main roads of the Space Center.

Guides warn against wearing white tennis shoes while venturing near bodies of water because the local gators have become addicted to tourist-tossed treats, particularly marshmallows. Colored foot-wear is suggested for those wishing to take in a little flora and fauna with their technology: the

explains the Space Center's director, Richard G. Smith.

It is fitting that America's first explorers – men who walked on lands that would become the continental United States – first stepped off their ships not far from this cape, which has served as the port of embarkation for ships carrying the first explorers to walk on the moon.

Ponce de León first sighted the sandy cape that juts into the Atlantic Ocean in 1513 and named it *Corrientes*, a Spanish reference to its turbulent currents. The name did not last. A word used by the Ais Indians who peopled the wilderness, persevered instead. *Canave-*

ral, meaning canebearer, is thought to have appeared on maps of the cape after 1520, following a battle in which a slave-ship captain named Francisco Gordillo lost many of his men to laser-sharp Ais arrows made from canes or reeds. Except for a brief identity crisis in the 1960s when it became Cape Kennedy, it has been named Cape Canaveral ever since.

It has also remained wilderness through most of its existence. Few, with the exception of the Ais Indians, have braved its mosquito-infested brush. The Ais left behind their burial mounds and shell middens, which today stand side-by-side with the bunkers and block-houses of the space program.

created NASA nine months later. On May 5, 1961, it put the first American, Alan Shepard, into space in a Mercury capsule atop a Redstone rocket.

NASA originally established its offices and laboratories on the cape itself, but in 1964 shifted most operations west across the Banana River to Merritt Island. The two-man Gemini missions followed. Scientists, engineers, technicians – and their money – flooding in. Contractors followed, putting up housing developments faster than NASA could send up rockets. Employment peaked at about 26,000 in 1968.

By then, NASA was shooting three men into space at a crack as part of its Apollo

Missiles began flights to the heavens from Cape Canaveral about 1947. The War Department chose the site that year because it provided miles of uninhabited buffer zone to catch stray projectiles, as well as offshore islands for tracking stations. The first satellite launched by the United States, *Explorer I*, left Cape Canaveral on January 31, 1958, in a belated attempt to match the feat of the Soviet Union's *Sputnik*. The government

Left, from footsteps in Florida sand to imprints in moondust: astronaut James B. Irwin of *Apollo 15* salutes, 1971. **Above**, the lunar module *Intrepid* during a 1969 mission by *Apollo 12*.

program. That culminated in Neil Armstrong's historic footfall on the Moon on July 20, 1969. The kind of monstrous Saturn V rocket that took man to the Moon lies on display in front of the Vehicle Assembly Building (VAB).

Enter Kennedy Space Center's Spaceport USA from State Road 405, which runs into NASA Parkway. Whether you enter here through Gate 3, or take State Road 3 from the Cocoa Beach area through Gate 2, just follow the signs to Spaceport USA. A row of rockets pointing starward identifies the Visitors' Center on the south side of the parkway. Facilities include a Gallery of Space Flight which traces the chronology of the space program's achievements.

Spaceport USA includes a huge IMAX movie. *The Dream Is Alive*, shown on a 5½-story-high screen. There's a nominal charge for the film, and another for a guided tour of the site.

A tour of the launch site: Drivers are not permitted to tour the grounds of Kennedy Space Center unescorted. The best way to see the Saturn, the VAB and other sites is aboard one of the inexpensive, NASA-sanctioned bus tours.

The boarding station for these buses, which take you on a 2-hour tour of the premises, is here at Spaceport USA. Enthusiastic guides continue by Complex 39, from which the Apollo Moon missions, Skylabs and the space shuttles left the earth; and past the rusting remnants of abandoned complexes. Guides take visitors through the Astronaut Training Building, where a recreated Launch Control Center, and the Lunar Excursion Model (LEM) used for the Apollo XI moon mission, are on permanent display.

Enthusiasm returns: With the end of the Apollo program in the mid-'70s, NASA's activities at Kennedy Space Center wound down. Rows of "astro-bars" closed as NASA laid off aerospace workers, who left Florida and took their severance checks with them. Interest in the space program flagged.

provide a lively, running commentary, answering questions which range from how astronauts use the bathroom to how they eat.

Barring schedule changes because of launches or other activity, the buses usually stop at the imposing Vehicle Assembly Building. At 525 feet tall, 716 feet long and 588 feet wide, the VAB is one of the world's largest buildings with a total volume of 129.5 million cubic feet. The entire Empire State Building in New York, if chopped into sections, could be stored inside the VAB.

The buses take you past the monstrous crawler-transporter that carries spaceships to the launch pads at a snail's speed. They

All that changed dramatically, probably permanently, on April 12, 1981. Early that morning, more than a million people lined the banks of the Indian and Banana rivers to experience the beginning of a new era in space – the launch of the space shuttle *Columbia*. In its maiden voyage, *Columbia* became the first vehicle to be shot into orbit on the spine of a rocket and return to earth under its own power by landing like an airplane. The space-craft was flown from its landing site in California back to Florida aboard a Boeing 747, and it may make more than 100 similar flights.

More than 5,000 newsmen from around

the world gathered to witness that momentous launch. Even veteran launch-goers admitted the shuttle lift-off was the most spectacular they had ever observed. The whir of the shutters of thousands of cameras and the whoops of spectators were smothered by the earthquaking sound of that launch, which has reverberated throughout Florida's Space Coast. Employment at Kennedy has steadied at 20,000. The astronauts are back, and with them legions of new space fans.

Since the first historic mission, NASA's ambitious space shuttle program has successfully carried out numerous tests and experiments with each successive launch. *Columbia* flew four additional missions. It was

visitors to plan a trip around a shuttle mission. Interest has grown so rapidly that Spaceport USA receives more than 3 million visitors a year.

Blast off: Information about shuttle launches is available by telephone (*for more details see the Travel Tips section*). Or write NASA well in advance of a scheduled launch and ask for a car pass. This will get you through the gate on a launch day and allow you to park your car along the Indian River, which is approximately 5 miles from the pad. A good set of binoculars or a camera with a telephoto lens can aid in viewing, although just using the naked eye will provide an equally inspiring sight.

followed by *Challenger* which carried the first women astronaut, Sally K. Ride, into space in 1983. But a dark cloud passed over the Center in 1986 when a tragic accident occured. Minutes after take-off, the *Challenger* shuttle malfunctioned and exploded in front of thousands of spectators. Six crew members were killed as was Christa McAuliffe, a school teacher who was chosen to be the first civilian to join a NASA crew.

The routine flights should make it easy for

Left, a view of Saturn as seen by *Voyager 1* in its 1980 flight past the planet. **Above**, *Apollo 10's* glimpse of Mother Earth.

Failing those options, you can park anywhere outside the Space Center where you see cars gathering for a glimpse of a launch. There are choice spots along US Highway 1 in Titusville and along State Road 402 north of Complex 39. If you approach the area from Orlando, take the Bee-Line Expressway until it turns into the Bennett Causeway, another choice viewing spot. Jetty Park, at the end of the causeway near Cape Canaveral city, and beaches north to Ponce's Inlet, also offer a good view.

The Kennedy Space Center has made the state of Florida the closest place to the stars a visitor can get to – on earth.

THE BATTLE OF THE THEME PARKS

Once upon a time, before there was Disney, a Florida vacation meant mom-and-pop motels, catfish and hush puppies, and downhome diversions, small, offbeat tourist attractions that didn't charge outrageous admission fees for a family of four.

In 1971, all of that changed. Mickey Mouse made his debut, and Disney World's self-contained environment of fantasy fun became the standard by which a Florida vacation was rated. In just a few years, the theme park industry became so lucrative that corporate giants swooped on Florida in droves in a frenzied attempt to get a piece of the great big tourism pie. Following the Disney model, a string of mega theme parks now dominates the landscape. In fierce competition with one another, they battle for the almighty tourist dollar.

Orlando overdrive: For even in these hard economic times, when consumer spending is down, tourism seems to thrive. Each year the state of Florida attracts 40 million visitors, who bring in more than $30 billion in revenue. Almost $8 million a year is spent on promotion and advertising, to lure them to Florida in the first place. Much of this activity centers around Mickey Mouse's town of Orlando, which has the highest concentration of hotel rooms in the United States (77,000) and the highest occupancy rate (nearly 80 percent). The number of tourists arriving at Orlando International Airport has risen by 300 percent in the past decade, a figure that is expected to double in just a couple of years.

Perhaps theme parks – fairy-tale worlds where even the trash bins seem to glisten like gold – are just what a tired workforce needs to escape from hard, humdrum life. Immaculate, orderly, and flawless, they emit a grand illusion of perfection that stimulates the senses while putting the intellect to one side. As holy shrines to leisure, minus the beggars, foul smells, and hassles, theme parks are meant to entertain rather than enlighten.

Although it may appear as one happy car-

Preceding pages: waving to the crowds. **Left**, around and around at Busch Gardens. **Right**, gorilla power.

toon-character party, the theme park business is a cut-throat industry where attractions copy and imitate ideas, disguising their corporate greed in a veneer of all-American fun. Advertising campaigns and public relations gimmicks feed the industry, and confuse the consumer. That's not surprising when you consider what is at stake: according to an article published in the *Wall Street Journal*, it cost $80 million to build just one of Disney World's attractions, the popular Splash Mountain ride. Universal Studios cost

$650 million to build. The stakes are high, and the money is real.

Over 20 major and dozens of minor theme parks now dot the state. And it's not just Central Florida that has fallen prey to this philosophy. Miami, Tampa and even old Key West have encouraged theme park development while also adopting a glitz and hype approach to tourism promotion. Hotel and restaurant chains have joined forces with the theme parks by creating a complex system of inclusive packaging that insures their own piece of the pie.

The theme parks' self-contained approach serves them well. By creating walled-in cities full of maze-like paths, they manage to hold people, and their spending money, hostage for an entire day. At most major theme parks you can exchange currencies, rent baby carriages and wheel chairs, buy food, drinks, film, cameras, sun hats, and even a new pair of shoes for tired feet.

The Mickey model: If Walter Elias Disney were alive today, even he would be amazed at the phenomenal success of his industry. His dream child, Walt Disney World, plays host to more tourists than any other commercial attraction in the world, and is surpassed in numbers only by Kyoto, Mecca and the Vatican. Because of Disney World there are direct flights to Orlando from Tokyo, Paris, try, the sole purpose of visit for 60 percent of its sun-seeking tourists.

Disney employees must conform to a corporate code of dress and behavior. Company rules require workers to pick up litter whenever they see it, smile all day – and night – long, and always speak favorably of their founding father, Walt Disney. Executives from around the world have come to Florida to study Disney's effective management style, and anthropologists have come to examine its cultural impact on society.

Disney has set the tone for the theme park industry, and although challenged by other theme-park giants, it reigns as king. Even airlines have been influenced by the big

London, and Rio. And, because of Disney World, the Orlando area now draws four times the number of visitors than in pre-Mickey 1970.

The power and influence of Disney World cannot be ignored. It has sovereign status and functions as an independent political entity similar to that of Vatican City. It has its own building codes, fire department and taxation authority. It is also vastly important to the city of Orlando. According to *Time* magazine, Disney World is the largest employer (33,000 workers), the largest taxpayer ($23 million a year), and the single largest contributor to Florida's tourist indus- mouse. Every few years in a heated competition they vie for favored status as Disney World's "official carrier."

The competition: Although Tampa's Busch Gardens was in operation for 12 years before Disney World opened its gates, it was because of the Disney success story that the African zoo and theme park expanded into the major attraction that it is today. Post-Disney, Busch Gardens' management realized that it had to enlarge and improve, and throw in a little pizzaz. In order to compete in the tourist marketplace, it added thrilling roller coasters, waterfall and white water rides, a Moroccan palace, and dozens more wildlife exhibits. The Tampa tourism bureau works hard to promote Busch Gardens and lure tourists away from the Orlando area, even if just for a day.

Gatorland, Weeki Wachee, and Cypress Gardens, three of the oldest tourist attractions in the state, have also undergone major facelifts to keep in with the big-name competition around them.

Sea World, a landlocked extravaganza that pays tribute to the life of the sea, is one of Disney's strongest competitors (4.1 million visitors annually). Although more tranquil than most theme parks, it takes an aggressive marketing stance. So much so, that in the past few years rumors have spread that the

Restaurants have also adopted the theme park mentality. Rarely can a dinner out be just a dinner out. These days, dinner means being bombarded by a glitter and tinsel floor show while trying to eat a six-course meal. Theme restaurants like Medieval Times, King Henry's Feast, Arabian Nights, and Mardi Gras all offer spectacular productions in a fabricated fantasy backdrop similar to the scenarios at Disney World.

Enter King Kong: When the Disney corporation, expanding its empire still further, opened its Disney-MGM Studios in 1989, it thought it had the movie theme park market cornered. Along with being a working film and television studio, Disney-MGM Studios

powers that be at Disney are considering building their own marine world attraction some time in the late 1990s.

Water theme parks – with make-believe rivers, lakes, waterfalls, wave pools, and slides – are another post-Disney outgrowth. Like wild mushrooms, they have sprung up almost overnight and now exist in most major urban areas. Places like Wet 'n' Wild, Watermania, Atlantis, and Wild Waters all insist that they have the best, the biggest, and the wildest water rides in the world.

Left, watching the elephants having fun. **Above**, pausing for a snack, Universal Studios.

would offer movie-lovers a chance to walk on real sets and watch special-effects and stunts in the making.

But one year after it opened, Disney-MGM Studios had to contend with a new kid on the block: Universal Studios Florida. The largest working film studio outside Hollywood, California, Universal Studios gave the guys at Disney a run for their money, attracting 6.7 million tourists in one year alone. In what the local media tagged "King Kong tackles Mickey Mouse," the two studios entered a zealous can-you-top-this battle. Disney heralded its Catastrophe Canyon; Universal countered with its Earthquake experience.

Teenage Mutant Ninja Turtles tried to outshine *E.T.* and *Jaws*.

Ships and rockets: The cruise industry, which pumps $14 billion a year into the American economy, has also been swayed by the theme park approach. Once synonymous with Old World elegance and classic European style, in the past 10 years the cruise industry has taken on a flashy, flamboyant persona.

Although a few classic beauties with varnished teak, mahogany railings, and antique maps remain, a new breed of "Disneyfied" ship has sailed into the market. Their interiors are juxtaposed prisms of deep purples, shocking pinks, and electric blues. Neon racing stripes, twinkling ceiling stars and mosaic

carpeting. And themes, themes, themes. With names like *Fantasy*, *Ecstasy* and *Sensation*, their interior design themes range from Egyptian tombs to bright city lights.

Today's ships have become floating theme parks with non-stop activities and glitz galore. The cruise ship industry, with the bulk of its business based in Florida, is in direct competition with Disney World and other theme park based vacations. Premier, the "official cruise line of Walt Disney World," has a distinct advantage. It sets sail with a chorus of Disney characters on board.

Not wanting to be left out, the Florida-based space program has taken on some of the theme park attitude. During the 1970s, the Kennedy Space Center felt like an educational trade show that attracted about 500,000 people a year. In 1982 the space program transformed its small visitor's center into Spaceport USA, a high-tech, multi-media show with big-screen movies, narrated bus tours, and a space-age cafeteria. The center's *Star Wars* decor now attracts almost 3 million visitors a year.

The big daddy of the industry has not taken all of this in its stride. Walt Disney World has continuously expanded, remodeled, and opened more theme park attractions in order to maintain its number one status. The Disney corporation is notoriously cagey about releasing figures of any sort, and those that do surface do not necessarily tally with others. Nevertheless, in a report published by the International Amusement Parks and Attractions Association, more than 30 million people a year visit Disney World. Not bad for a little guy with big ears.

Blatant disasters: What all this means to Florida, and the people who live here, is that their state has been transformed into an endless array of "worlds." Flea World, Orange World, Shoe World, Shell World, Christmas World. Ordinary businesses believing that being a "world" will invoke that wonderful Disney aura and make shopping a theme-park experience rather than an ordinary chore.

Real estate prices, especially in the Orlando area, have skyrocketed since Disney came to town. So valuable has local property become, that land that sold for $200 an acre in the late 1960s, is worth $100,000 an acre in the 1990s. Many farmers and citrus growers have sold their land to theme park developers.

The theme park industry has, however, had its share of failures. Some developers had great plans, but financial problems, zoning disputes, or poor management skills ruined several grandiose endeavors. A few of the more blatant disasters include Bible World, a panoramic journey into Christiandom; Hurricane World, a glorified wind tunnel that would take tourists into a simulated eye of a storm; Winter Wonderland, a Central Florida, working ski resort; and Little England, a "Disneyfied" recreation of a historic British village.

Left, Sea World. **Right**, riding the wild surf in fun-land Florida.

YOU WILL HAVE FUN!

Dave Barry, the Florida-based Pulitzer Prize-winning journalist and author, offers some advice on surviving a Florida vacation.

I'm an expert on visiting Disney World, because we live only four hours away, and according to my records we spend about three-fourths of our after-taxes income there. Not that I'm complaining. You can't have a bad time at Disney World. It's not allowed. They have hidden electronic surveillance cameras everywhere, and if they catch you

failing to laugh with childlike wonder, they lock you inside a costume representing a beloved Disney character such as Goofy and make you walk around in the Florida heat getting grabbed and leaped on by violently excited children until you have learned your lesson. Yes, Disney World is a "dream vacation," and here are some tips to help make it "come true" for you.

When to Go: The best time to go, if you want to avoid huge crowds, is 1962. How to Get There: It's possible to fly, but if you want the total Disney World experience, you should drive there with a minimum of four hostile children via the longest possible route.

Once you get to Florida, you can't miss Disney World, because the Disney corporation owns the entire center of the state. Just get on any major highway, and eventually it will dead-end in a Disney parking area large enough to have its own climate, populated by large nomadic families who have been trying to find their cars since 1979. Be sure to note carefully where you leave your car, because later on you may want to sell it so you can pay for your admission tickets.

But never mind the price; the point is that now you're finally there, in the ultimate vacation fantasy paradise, ready to have fun! Well, okay, you're not exactly there yet. First you have to wait for the parking-lot tram, which is driven by cheerful uniformed Disney employees, to come around and pick you up and give you a helpful lecture about basic tram safety rules such as never fall out of the tram without coming to a full and complete stop.

But now the tram ride is over and it's time for fun. Right? Don't be an idiot. It's time to wait in line and buy admission tickets. Most experts recommend that you go with the 47-day pass, which will give you a chance, if you never eat or sleep, to visit all of the Disney themed attractions, including The City of the Future, The Land of Yesterday, The Dull Suburban Residential Community of Sometime Next Month, Wet Adventure, Farms on Mars, The World of Furniture, Sponge Encounter, the Nuclear Flute Orchestra, Appliance Island, and the Great Underwater Robot Hairdresser Adventure, to name just a few.

Okay, you've taken out a second mortgage and purchased your tickets. Now, finally, it's time to... wait in line again! This time, it's for the monorail, a modern, futuristic transportation system that whisks you to the Magic Kingdom at nearly half the speed of a lawn tractor. Along the way cheerful uniformed Disney World employees will offer you some helpful monorail safety tips such as never set fire to the monorail without first removing your personal belongings.

And now, at last, you're at the entrance to the Magic Kingdom itself. No more waiting in line for transportation! It's time to wait in line to get in! There are tour groups here with names like "Entire Population of New York." There sure must be some great attractions inside these gates!

And now you've inched your way to the front of the line, and the cheerful uniformed Disney employee is stamping your hand with a special invisible chemical that penetrates your nervous system and causes you to acquire the personality of a cow. "Moo!" you shout as you surge forward with the rest of the herd.

home, and by God you're going to take him on it, no matter how long the... My God! Can this be the line for Space Mountain? This line is so long that there are Cro-Magnon families at the front. Perhaps if you explain to little Jason that he could be a deceased old man by the time he gets on the actual ride, he'll agree to skip it and... NO! Don't scream, little Jason. We'll just purchase some official Mickey Mouse sleeping bags, and we'll stay in line as long as it takes. To hell with school next year. We'll just stand here and chew our

And now, unbelievably, you're actually inside the Magic Kingdom! At last! Mecca! You crane your head to see over the crowd around you, and with innocent childlike wonder you behold: a much larger crowd. Ha Ha! You are having some kind of fun now!

And now you are pushing your way forward, thrusting other vacationers aside, knocking over their baby carriages if necessary, because little Jason wants to ride on Space Mountain. Little Jason has been talking about Space Mountain ever since you left

Left, humorist Dave Barry. Above, a pregnant gorilla settles in for a snooze.

cuds. Mooooo!

Speaking of education, you should be sure to visit EPCOT Center, which features exhibits sponsored by large corporations showing you how various challenges facing the human race are being met and overcome thanks to the selfless efforts of large corporations. EPCOT Center also features pavilions built by various foreign nations, where you can experience an extremely realistic simulation of what life in these nations would be like if they consisted almost entirely of restaurants and souvenir stores.

One memorable EPCOT night my family and I ate at the German restaurant, where I had several large beers and a traditional German delicacy called "Bloatwurst," which is a sausage that can either be eaten or used as a tackling dummy. When we got out I felt like one of those snakes that eat a cow whole and then just lie around and digest it for a couple of months. But my son was determined to go on a new educational EPCOT ride called "The Body," wherein you sit in a compartment that simulates what it would be like if you got inside a spaceship-like vehicle and got shrunk down to the size of a gnat and got injected inside a person's body.

I'll tell you what it's like: awful. You're looking at a screen showing an extremely vivid animated simulation of the human in-

proportional to how horrible it is. There's hardly ever a line for nice, relaxing rides like the merry-go-round. But there will always be a huge crowd, mainly consisting of teenagers, waiting to go on a ride with a name like "The Dicer," where they strap people into what is essentially a giant food processor and turn it on and then phone the paramedics.

So my idea is to open up a theme park called "Dave World," which will have a ride called "The Fall of Death." This will basically be a 250-ft tower. The way it will work is, you climb to the top, a trapdoor opens up, and you splat onto the ground below like a bushel of late-summer tomatoes.

Obviously, for legal reason, I couldn't let

terior, which is not the most appealing way to look at a human unless you're attracted to white blood cells the size of motor homes. Meanwhile the entire compartment is bouncing you around violently, especially when you go through the aorta. "Never go through the aorta after eating German food," that is my new travel motto.

What gets me is, I waited in line for an hour to do this. I could have experienced essentially the same level of enjoyment merely by sticking my finger down my throat. Which brings me to my idea for getting rich. No doubt you have noted that, in most amusement parks, the popularity of a ride is directly

anybody actually go on this ride. There would be a big sign that said:

WARNING!

NOBODY CAN GO ON THIS RIDE.

THIS RIDE IS INVARIABLY FATAL.

THANK YOU.

But this would only make The Fall of Death more popular. Every teenager in the immediate vicinity would come to Dave World just to stand in the line for it.

Dave World would also have an attraction called "ParentLand," which would have a sign outside that said: "Sorry, Kids! This Attraction Is for Mom 'n' Dad Only!" Inside would be a bar. For younger children, there would be a "Soil Fantasy," a themed play area consisting of dirt or, as a special "rainy-day" bonus, mud.

I frankly can't see how Dave World could fail to become a huge financial success that would make me rich and enable me to spend the rest of my days traveling the world with my family. So the hell with it.

Other attractions: You must be very careful here. You must sneak out of Disney World in the dead of night, because the Disney people do not want you leaving the compound and spending money elsewhere. If they discover that you're gone, cheerful uniformed employees led by Mickey Mouse's lovable dog Pluto, who will sniff the ground in a comical

I am also not making up Gatorland, which is next door. After entering Gatorland through a giant pair of pretend alligator jaws, you find yourself on walkways over a series of murky pools in which are floating a large number of alligators that appear to be recovering from severe hangovers, in the sense that they hardly ever move. You can purchase fish to feed them, but the typical Gatorland alligator will ignore a fish even if it lands directly on its head. Sometimes you'll see an alligator, looking bored, wearing three or four rotting, fly-encrusted fish, like some kind of high swamp fashion headgear.

This is very entertaining, of course, but the real action at Gatorland, the event that brings

manner, will track you down. And when they catch you, it's into the Goofy suit.

So we're talking about a major risk, but it's worth it for some of the attractions around Disney World. The two best ones, as it happens, are right next to each other near a town called Kissimmee. One of them is the world headquarters of the Tupperware plastic food container company, where you can take a tour that includes a Historic Food Containers Museum. I am not making this up.

Left, Mardi Gras comes to Orlando in a variety of shades and forms. **Above**, a little souvenir to take home after a hard day.

even the alligators to life, is the Assault on the Dead Chickens, which is technically known as the Gator Jumparoo. I am also not making this up. The way it works is, a large crowd of tourists gathers around a central pool, over which, suspended from wires, are dangling a number of plucked headless chicken carcasses.

As the crowd, encouraged by the Gatorland announcer, cheers wildly, the alligators lunge out of the water and rip the chicken carcasses down with their jaws. Once you've witnessed this impressive event, you will never again wonder how America got to be the country that it is today.

133

PLACES

There's just too much to see waiting in front of me,
And I know that I just can't go wrong
With these changes in latitudes, changes in attitudes.
—Jimmy Buffett

With those words, Florida-based balladeer Buffett put his guitar-pickin' finger on a fundamental reason for Florida's popularity as a retreat for routine-weary Americans. No other place in the continental United States lies in more southern latitudes. Some folks have become so addicted to the tranquilizing effects of Florida's balmy climes, they return year after year for another dose. It's the national sedative.

Nature laid the groundwork for this annual people invasion by providing the beaches and forests. Then man added hotel and amusement complexes. Now, it's a rare corner of Florida that doesn't have at least a gator farm or orange juice stand within jogging distance.

Yet Florida is much too big, much too diverse to swallow in one gulp. The following pages have been designed to give you Florida in smaller sips.

The state has been subdivided into six sections.

● **South Florida** is anchored by Metropolitan Miami (whose urban tentacles stretch to Art Deco South Beach and all the way to Fort Pierce), but is bounded by acres of rural lands and towns like Homestead in the south and Palmdale to the west.

● The **Everglades** includes the Big Cypress Swamp, and the **Florida Keys** are crowned by their uncommon capital, Key West.

● The **East Coast** strip stretches from Melbourne to Jacksonville, and includes NASA and Daytona Beach.

● The **Central Florida** tourism hub revolves around Orlando and Walt Disney World but extends as far south as Sebring, north to the Ocala National Forest and west to Lakeland.

● **North Florida** encompasses the Pensacola to Tallahassee Panhandle region as well as the "pan" – Gainesville, Cross Creek and the rugged Big Bend country.

● The beach-fringed **West Coast** has Tampa-St Petersburg as its nucleus, Marco Island as its southern end and Cedar Key at its northern tip.

Florida, a tasty blend of spices and sultry tropical charm, is guaranteed to whet your appetite for more.

Preceding pages: Miami's Deco District skyline; Fort Jefferson in the Keys; Everglades sunset. **Left**, head over heels in Florida.

CAPT. TONY'S
SALOON

The First and Original SLOPPY JOE'S 1933-1937

SOUTH FLORIDA

The area known as South Florida – the state's lower east coast region – is a microcosm of the entire state. There are cowboys and Indians, Crackers and Yankees, Cubans and Haitians. The varied landscape features superhighways and dirt lanes; rows of mobile homes and fields of sugar cane; skyscrapers and swamps. From metropolitan Miami, full of designers, Art Deco and models, to peaceful Vero Beach and Lake Okeechobee, South Florida has it all.

The region also includes the Everglades – 1.4 million acres, or most of Florida's southern tip – an alligator-inhabited area larger than the state of Delaware. The Everglades' somewhat unglamorous waters cloak a fascinating blend of tropical and temperate environments, a laboratory where nature can experiment with the ever-changing cycles of life and death.

In keeping with the many idiosyncrasies that set Florida apart from other states in the country, its southern boundary doesn't just come to an abrupt end, but trickles gently away in a splash of coral and limestone islands known as keys ("key" being an anglicization of *cayo,* the Spanish word for "little island"). They stretch 180 miles from Miami's Biscayne Bay to the Dry Tortugas, just 86 miles north of Havana, Cuba. Forty-three of the islands hang like freshly-washed linen on a clothesline: the 113-mile-long US Highway 1, "the Overseas Highway," stretching over 43 bridges along the way.

From the scuba culture of Key Largo to the Bohemian counterculture of Key West, each island maintains its own distinct identity and even the people are different from one key to the next: disillusioned Gold coasters populate the upper islands, while natives of the lower Keys proudly call themselves Conchs. But they are even more different from Florida mainlanders. Out here in the islands, it's just not normal to get wrapped up in a hustle-bustle lifestyle, or even to be on time for appointments.

Mañanaland, Margaritaville, the American Riviera – the Keys have been called many things. Whatever the appellation, they are a place to take off your watch and kick back. Get up early and watch the sun rise over the Atlantic Ocean. At night, stroll to the other side of your island to catch the sunset into the Gulf of Mexico. Conchs will tell you that's the only way to tell time.

Miami. Palm Beach. Swamps and tranquil islands. Welcome to South Florida.

Preceding pages: artist Christo's *Surrounded Islands*, Biscayne Bay, 1983. **Left**, passing the time in Key West.

METROPOLITAN MIAMI

Miami and its famous sister city, Miami Beach, have shared a meteoric transition from mosquito-infested swamp and palmetto scrubland to subtropical megalopolis. From an aircraft approaching Miami International Airport, you can look down at the Everglades and glimpse the past – a soundless sea of saw grass. Now look again and gaze upon the fast-pulsed cacophony of the present – a white-washed, high-rise skyline, set starkly against the aquamarine of Biscayne Bay.

Your first encounter echoes the accolades of travel brochures. Here are wall-to-wall beaches, balmy weather and around-the-clock nightlife. Even Hurricane Andrew, which in 1992 ripped through the suburbs of Coconut Grove and Coral Gables, could not puncture the dream. But under the banks of cauliflower clouds, you will also find a major international finance center and growing commercial complex, buoyed by the Latin-flavored cultural diversity of Greater Miami and the Art Deco success story of Miami Beach.

Fishing to phenomenon: Problems have in the past tarnished Miami's sparkle. Fickle northern tourists years ago began spending their vacation dollars in other parts of Florida. Some $15 million in beach restoration counter the erosion of storms and tides. Rampant urban growth has consumed farms. An outbreak of racial violence has rocked a city once smug in its desegregation process. And an uncontrolled influx of Cuban and Haitian refugees has in the past also taxed Miami's stability.

Nevertheless, the history of Miami remains an American Cinderella story. Miami was only a fishing village on the edge of a vast wilderness when it was incorporated as a city in 1896. Railroad magnate Henry M. Flagler even voiced doubts about the city's future when his first train chugged into town. But his Florida East Coast Railroad triggered phenomenal growth all along the Gold Coast. In gratitude, the major street bi-

secting Miami now bears his name. So does a dog-racing track and a savings-and-loan company. A marker in Bicentennial Park on Biscayne Boulevard honors Flagler at the site of the original port of Miami, built to service early steamships.

The history of surrounding Dade County predates Flagler's appearance, however. The first white man believed to have lived in the area was a shipwrecked Spanish sailor enslaved by Tequesta Indians living at the mouth of the Miami River.

In his memoirs, the sailor wrote about a place the Indians called the "Lake of Mayaime." Historians speculate that the name meant "very large" and was a reference to Lake Okeechobee, northwest of modern Miami. Somehow, the word Mayaime evolved into Miami, the Tequesta word for "sweet water."

Later, many of the settlers who manned Fort Dallas to keep Seminole Indians at bay early in the 19th century stayed on in the area. The site of the fort became the exclusive address of Julia

ft and right,
ami's
nTrust
wer
anges color
command.

Tuttle, one of the first Yankees to flee cold Cleveland winters for Florida's warmth. She convinced Flagler to extend his railroad to the banks of Biscayne Bay, sending him orange blossoms in the middle of winter when a freeze caused citrus losses upstate.

Tuttle's former home site is now a parking lot fronting the DuPont Plaza Hotel at the southern terminus of Biscayne Boulevard in downtown Miami. The city moved the barracks of **Fort Dallas**, stone by stone, to Lummus Park on North River Drive on the Miami River in 1924.

Biscayne Boulevard spills into **Brickell Avenue**, named for Mary and William Brickell. In the 1870s, they owned all the bayfront land from the Miami River south to Coconut Grove. During the boom that followed Flagler's railroad down the East Coast, the wealthy constructed handsome homes here along the bay.

Today, searching for the past among the concrete offices and condominiums of burgeoning Brickell Avenue is like trying to find a mountain in South Florida. But there is a 14-room stone house in the 1,500 block patterned after the 14th-century Priory St Julienne in Duoy, France. It has three towers, wrought-iron gates and dormer windows. Isolated mansions such as this one, trapped among the modern highrises, hint at the grace that was Brickell Avenue at the turn of the century when the woods were so dense, timid residents refused to venture out after dark.

Only one small public section remains of wooded **Brickell Hammock** in **Alice C. Wainwright Park**, a block south of the Rickenbacker Causeway intersection. Pirates once camped in the area, but today the park hosts weekend weddings. It even sports a "hill." Some 100,000 years ago, when Miami was covered by a shallow sea, fast currents rolled up little balls of limestone. This limestone rock now crops out in a 2-mile ridge parallel to the bayshore. Geology books call it Miami oolite.

Also near Wainwright Park is **Villa Serena**, former residence of famed ora-

The *Fantasy* leaves the largest cruis[e] port in the world.

146

tor and politician William Jennings Bryan. The two-story, Spanish-style home, built in 1915 at 3115 Brickell Avenue, is not open to the public.

The growth and prosperity spawned by the railroad also breathed life into the mangrove islands and scrublands surrounding the city's core. Miami Beach, Hialeah, Opa-locka, Coral Gables and other suburbs flourished. Land promotion turned into speculation. Property changed hands several times, sometimes the same day and always at higher prices. But a combination of the 1926 hurricane and the Great Depression ended Miami's first growth phase.

Gradual improvement in the economy and the establishment of new business opportunities kicked off Miami's modern period of expansion in the 1930s. Commercial aviation transformed the city into an international destination. Modern **Miami International Airport**, connected to the city center via a pair of fast expressways, offers air routes to most corners of the world.

Thousands of servicemen trained in Miami Beach during World War II, housed in hotels-turned-barracks and beaches that doubled as drill fields and rifle ranges. Many of these servicemen returned with their families after the war. Some used the GI Bill to attend the **University of Miami**. Founded in 1925, the school floundered when the crash came but rebounded with the injection of military blood. Located in Coral Gables, the University is noted for its medical school, marine science department and the **Lowe Art Museum**.

The coming of the Cubans: Miami hogged national headlines in the 1950s during the US Senate Committee hearings on organized crime. The city had once attracted mobsters like Al Capone, whose home still stands at 93 Palm Island, north of the MacArthur Causeway. He bought the house during the Roaring '20s from Clarence M. Busch of the beer family, and died in it in 1947.

By the 1960s, both **Biscayne Bay** and the **Miami River** suffered from the scars of rapid growth. The area was panned nationally as a "polluted paradise." En-

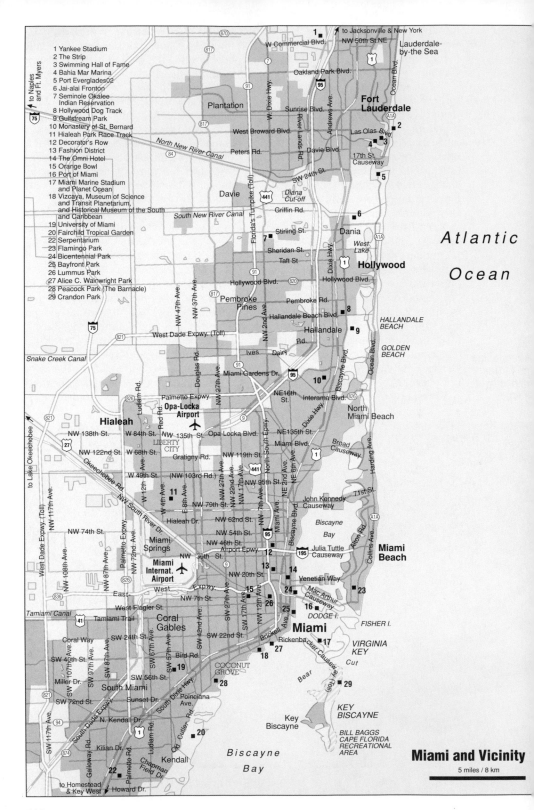

Miami and Vicinity

1 Yankee Stadium
2 The Strip
3 Swimming Hall of Fame
4 Bahia Mar Marina
5 Port Everglades02
6 Jai-alai Fronton
7 Seminole Okalee
  Indian Reservation
8 Hollywood Dog Track
9 Gulfstream Park
10 Monastery of St. Bernard
11 Hialeah Park Race Track
12 Decorator's Row
13 Fashion District
14 The Omni Hotel
15 Orange Bowl
16 Port of Miami
17 Miami Marine Stadium
   and Planet Ocean
18 Vizcaya, Museum of Science
   and Transit Planetarium,
   and Historical Museum of the South
   and Caribbean
19 University of Miami
20 Fairchild Tropical Garden
22 Serpentarium
23 Flamingo Park
24 Bicentennial Park
25 Bayfront Park
26 Lummus Park
27 Alice C. Wainwright Park
28 Peacock Park (The Barnacle)
29 Crandon Park

to Jacksonville & New York
NW 50th St.NE
Lauderdale-by-the Sea

to Naples
and Ft. Myers

W Commercial Blvd.
Oakland Park Blvd.

Fort Lauderdale

Plantation

Sunrise Blvd.
West Broward Blvd.
Las Olas Blvd.
Peters Rd.
Davie Blvd.
17th St. Causeway
SW 24th St.

Davie

Diana Cut-off
Griffin Rd.

South New River Canal
North New River Canal

Stirling St.
Sheridan St.
Taft St.

Dania
West Lake

Hollywood
Hollywood Blvd.

Pembroke Pines
Pembroke Rd.
Hallandale Beach Blvd.

Hallandale

HALLANDALE BEACH
GOLDEN BEACH

Snake Creek Canal

West Dade Expwy. (Toll)

Ives Dairy Rd.

Miami Gardens Dr.

NE16th St.
Interama Blvd.

North Miami Beach

Opa-Locka Airport

Hialeah

NW 138th St.
NW 122nd St.
W 84th St.
W 68th St.
Opa-Locka Blvd.
NE135th St.

LIBERTY CITY

Gratigny Rd.
NW 119th St.

NW 49th St. (NW 103rd Rd.)
NW 95th St.

Miami Blvd.
Broad Causeway

NW 74th St.

Hialeah Dr.
NW 79th St.
NW 62nd St.
NW 54th St.

John Kennedy Causeway

Miami Springs

Biscayne Bay

NW 46th St.
Airport Epwy.
NW 36th St.

Julia Tuttle Causeway

Miami Beach

Miami International Airport

NW 20th St.

Venetian Way
Mac Arthur Causeway

West Flagler St.

West Expwy.
NW 7th St.

Coral Gables

Tamiami Canal
Tamiami Trail

DODGE I.
FISHER I.

Miami

Rickenbacker Causeway

VIRGINIA KEY

Coral Way
SW 24th St.
Bird Rd.

SW 40th St.
SW 22nd St.

Poinciana Ave.

COCONUT GROVE

SW 56th St.

South Miami
Sunset Dr.

KEY BISCAYNE

N. Kendall Dr.

Kilian Dr.

Kendall

Chapman Field Dr.

to Homestead
& Key West
Howard Dr.

Key Biscayne

BILL BAGGS CAPE FLORIDA RECREATIONAL AREA

Biscayne Bay

Atlantic Ocean

Miami and Vicinity

5 miles / 8 km

148

vironmentalists attracted community interest toward cleaning up the waters and blocked location of new industrial plants. Government planning was centralized in a Metro body with countywide powers to improve control over unrestricted development and pollution.

Following the pattern of other metropolitan areas, established white residents fanned out into the suburbs while the inner city, already heavily black, attracted hundreds of thousands of refugees who fled Cuba after Fidel Castro seized power in 1959. The influx dissolved some racial barriers, but the poverty of black ghettoes worsened and black resentment deepened while the Cubans prospered. The economic schism contributed to an eruption of violence in Liberty City, a predominantly black area of northwest Miami, while the Republican National Convention camped out at Miami Beach in 1968.

Trouble peaked in 1980 when 18 people died in riots that caused $200 million damage. Another influx of Cuban "boat people" that year had added to Miami's problems, particularly since many of the 125,000 refugees unleashed by Castro came from Havana's prisons. Jobless and penniless, some returned to their old criminal habits, adding another unwanted face to Miami's mural of urban unrest. In 1980, 243 homicides made Miami's murder rate the highest per capita in the United States.

For all its warts, Miami is a cosmopolitan mix of Americans, Canadians and Europeans who contribute to a cultural exchange rivaling that of New York City. The unprecedented rise of Miami Beach as a style capital and mecca for bright young things put Miami back on the map. Designers and other artistic visitors flocked to the beach.

Hurricane Andrew, which gave a devastating blow to the beautiful homes and swaying palms of Coconut Grove and Coral Gables, miraculously left most of the beach area unscathed. Miami, always a refuge for forward-thinking people, is back with a vengeance.

Downtown Miami: A black monolith called the **Omni** and a brightly lit edifice called the **International Place** stand in stark contrast as centers of Miami's renaissance. The International Place, with its 47 floors, stands as one of the tallest office buildings south of New York and lights up the Miami night sky. The 20-story Omni hotel draws a healthy share of free-spending South and Central Americans and the 150-plus stores in its two-level mall give them plenty of opportunity to part with their money.

East of the Omni are the offices of the *Miami Herald*, one of the country's largest newspapers. South of it, below the Interstate 395 bridge, is **Bicentennial Park**, a good vantage point from which to watch and photograph cruise ships docking or leaving their terminals on **Dodge Island**. Access to the island is further south on Biscayne Boulevard. Here you will find the **Port of Miami**, the world's leading cruise-passenger facility. It caters to enormous pleasure craft with names like *Fantasy* and *Sovereign of the Seas*.

South of the Port Boulevard entrance lies **Bayfront Park**, a brief respite from

ight, owntown Miami seen om the Miami River.

the hustle of downtown Miami. Here is the **John F. Kennedy Memorial Torch of Friendship**, symbolizing friendly relations between Miami and Latin America with an 18-foot shaft topped by a perpetual flame. Other monuments in the park honor Christopher Columbus; José Martí, liberator of Cuba; José Cecello del Valle, who wrote the federal constitution of Honduras; and Ruben Dario, Nicaraguan poet. There's also a monument, near a brand-new amphitheater, to the 1986 Challenger shuttle disaster. In addition, a $100 million **Bayside Marketplace**, featuring entertainment and waterfront shopping, has been added in recent years.

Construction of new buildings and multi-million-dollar entertainment complexes are changing the look and energy of downtown Miami. In addition to the **Metro-Dade Cultural Center**, a Mediterranean-style complex that houses the **Center for Fine Arts**, the **Historical Museum of Southern Florida** and the main public library, there is the **Gusman Theater for the Performing Arts**. Designed in rococo style, this ornate center features high-class entertainment – opera, ballet, symphony – as well as top headliners.

The **Miami Arena** also features entertainment in the form of professional basketball as well as pop music and rock concerts and special events, such as touring circuses and ice shows. The Arena is sited in Overtown, north of the core of the downtown sector.

Havana dreaming: Across from the park, a line of hotels borders the busy commercial district. If you can manage to pick your way through the crowds of Latin American tourists in the lobby of the rejuvenated **Everglades Hotel**, ride the elevator to the pool and sun deck area on the roof for a panoramic view of the city.

Other downtown sites include the blue-delft-tiled mosaic on the **Bacardi Art Gallery** building, from the same people who bring you rum, in the 2,100 block of Biscayne Boulevard. The brass onion-shaped dome of the **Assumption Ukrainian Catholic Church** at 58 N.W. 57th Avenue lends a touch of the East to

the city. There's also a bit of the Mideast in the bakeries, shops, churches and restaurants of Lebanese, Syrians, Greeks and Palestinians along SW Third Avenue in the vicinity of the Rickenbacker Causeway exit from Interstate 95.

For all its diversity, the heart that has kept Miami healthy during the past 20 years is a Hispanic one. Old Havana didn't disappear when Castro took Cuba in 1959. It just moved, lock, stock and barrel to Florida. Don't be surprised if the bellboy at your hotel addresses you in Spanish before trying English. Gas station attendants will often only smile if you speak to them in any language *but* Spanish. Shopkeepers hang signs advising potential customers "English Spoken." A trip to Miami is like vacationing in a foreign port.

Hialeah and Coral Gables have both become Spanish-speaking enclaves, but **Little Havana** remains the core of the community. Wedged between downtown Miami on the east and Coral Gables on the west, and roughly bounded by W Flagler Street on the north, and

Neighborhoo
shrine in
Little Havana

SW 22nd Street on the south, Little Havana promotes itself as a chic Latin quarter with cosmopolitan airs.

SW Eighth Street, here known as **Calle Ocho**, is Little Havana's main street. It is alive with cigar-chomping men in crisp, white *guayaberas* (the cotton shirt of the tropics), quaint fruit stands, unique boutiques and factories where employees still roll cigars by hand. If you want to try strong, aromatic Cuban coffee, stop at one of the many sidewalk coffee counters. They also sell *churros* – long spirals of sweet dough, deep-fried. Watch them being made, then sprinkle with sugar, dip in a cup of Cuban chocolate, and devour.

An ideal way to visit Calle Ocho is to drive its 30-blocks, picking out sections you find interesting. Then park and stroll. Bear in mind, it's a one-way street where traffic flows to the east, so if you are coming from downtown, drive west on SW Seventh Street before cutting back. Older Cubans enjoy company, so don't be afraid to strike up a conversation. They have fascinating stories to tell about their escapes from a Communist homeland. In **Maximo Gomez Park**, you'll find men, and sometimes women, intent on games of dominoes. Bus stop benches in Little Havana are tiled, and lamp posts are Spanish-style.

Several restaurants along Calle Ocho operate as retail fish markets and seafood restaurants, and offer fresh selections from a retail case cooked to order. **La Mar Pescaderia** features *ceviche*, an appetizer of raw fish that actually "cooks" in a special lemon juice marinade. **Centro Vasco**, a gathering spot for established, upscale Cubans, features *paella* and *sopa marinero*, which has become so popular it could qualify as Miami's version of the traditional *bouillabaisse* of Marseille.

Other than seafood, you can try **La Esquina de Tejas**, **Islas Canarias**, or **El Pub** for a Cuban hamburger or *frita* served with pencil-thin French fries inside a bun, or a variety of hearty, garlic-flavored Cuban dishes. The **Versailles** offers about the best Cuban sandwich in Little Havana, although **Casablanca** is

heated
ame of
ominoes.

also popular. The ingredients aren't special – crispy Cuban bread; boneless, processed ham cured in boiling sweet water and baked in sugar; slow-boiled pork; imported Gruyère cheese; pickles and butter. But there's an art to putting the sandwich together to get the right blend of tastes. For Peruvian food try **El Inka**, for Colombian, there's **Restaurante Monserrate**. And for dessert, stop in at the Perezsosa Bakery next to Maximo Gomez Park.

Of shrines and gas stations: A popular way for Cubans to show their devotion to a particular saint is by erecting shrines in their front yards and even at their businesses. You'll find many on the lawns of neat houses if you venture into the side streets bordering Eighth Street. The most revered patron is Saint Lazarus, a hero to the Cubans because of his ability to endure poverty and pain.

One shrine incongruously decorates a corner of Armando Tundidor's gas station at 1599 W Flagler Street. **La Virgen de la Caridad del Cobre** sits on a revolving pedestal in a wrought-iron

cage right under the Phillips 66 sign. **Almacenes Gonzalez**, near 27th Avenue, sells a full line of religious statues for a wide range of prices.

A shrine particularly important to the Cuban exiles is **Ermita de La Caridad** near a Catholic high school on Miami Avenue. Inside a cone resembling a spaceship, a Spanish-language tape explains that the shrine's shape symbolizes the Virgin of Charity's mantle and the six columns stand for the six provinces of Cuba. The hectagonal cement block beneath the altar was made with rock, water and dirt from Cuba. The priest's chair is carved from a Cuban palm tree and the church faces the old country across the seas. "Pray for Cuba," pleads the voice.

A more blunt reminder of the homeland is the Bay of Pigs monument at the **Cuban Memorial Plaza** on 13th Avenue, the site of many commemorative ceremonies. Each March all of Miami is invited to a block party called Carnaval Miami, a sort of Cuban Mardi Gras. Another important celebration is the Three Kings Parade on the first or second Sunday of January, which includes nearly 100 floats and marching units, some with flamenco dancers.

Within the overwhelming Cuban community, close inspection will also turn up a Little Buenos Aires, a Little Managua, a Little Bogotá, a Little Quito and a Little Caracas. These myriad quarters have shaped Miami into a melting pot of Central and South American cultures.

The design district: To the north of Little Havana is the area known as **Director's Row**, a hidden shopping area frequented by wealthy customers. Centered between 35th and 40th streets, and N. Miami Avenue and N.E. Second Avenue, the area is worth a look even if you only want to window shop. The displays will update you on the latest trends in the furniture and accessories for the home and office. Most showrooms are open to the public, but some have signs reading "to the trade only." That means a designer must refer or accompany you, but only the haughtiest storekeepers will turn you away if you arrange a call from an architect, or pro-

Haitian shop along 59th Street.

duce a card of introduction from a major furniture store or designer.

Caribbean colors: Further to the north again is the neighborhood of **Little Haiti**, an enclave of recent immigrants with houses and storefronts painted the Caribbean colors of vibrant reds, blues, yellows, and greens. The heart of Little Haiti lies along N.E. Second Avenue between 54th and 79th streets. Here you will find Haitian grocery stores selling goat heads, dried fish, hot spices, and tropical fruits. You will also find "botanicas" that sell spiritual goods pertaining to the religion of Voodoo, and record shops specializing in Haitian music. The **Caribbean Marketplace**, a massive, open-air market styled after the one in Port-au-Prince, sells Haitian paintings, wood-carvings and other crafts. Although the beautiful market is a showpiece for the neighborhood, it, like the Haitian community itself, is always battling a financial crisis.

Visiting Vizcaya: You can visit Miami's southern reaches via Brickell Avenue. Unfortunately, this area was slammed by Hurricane Andrew's 160-mph winds, demolishing most of the trees. As Brickell veers toward Federal Highway, take a left into S Miami Avenue. On the bayside is the grand gateway to **Vizcaya**, an Italian Renaissance villa and gardens built by International Harvester magnate James Deering in 1916. A winding road through an exotic jungle leads to the edifice *National Geographic* magazine once described as "a triumph in recalling the Golden Age of art and architecture… a repository of Italian decorative art, unexcelled in America."

In addition to the palatial home filled with fine period furniture, textiles and sculpture, Vizcaya (Basque for "elevated place") has 10 acres of formal gardens that, pre-hurricane, closely resembled the European original. In Biscayne Bay opposite the gardens, Deering anchored a sculptured stone barge. It was used as a clandestine dock for unloading shipments of illegal liquor.

Across Miami Avenue from Vizcaya is the **Museum of Science** and **Space**

The villa and gardens at Vizcaya.

Transit Planetarium. The Planetarium has an entertaining laser show which uses light beams, color imagery and music to take you on a trip through a black hole.

Continue down South Miami Avenue until it becomes Bayshore Drive and you wind up in **Coconut Grove**. The oldest settlement in the area, "the Grove" developed a reputation as a winter resort for northerners as early as the turn of the century. For years, its Peacock Inn was the only hotel in town. Built in 1880, it overlooked Biscayne Bay from the rock ridge above modern day **Peacock Park** on McFarlane Road near South Bayshore Drive. A marker in the park commemorates the hotel.

The catalyst for settlement of the Grove was naval architect and photographer Ralph Middleton Munroe. He built a house called **The Barnacle**, now a historical museum at 3485 Main Highway. The Barnacle was originally a one-story building of materials salvaged from shipwrecks. Instead of constructing a new home to accommodate his growing

family, Munroe jacked the entire house up on stilts and built a new first floor underneath in 1895.

Meanwhile, a colony of blacks moved in and inspired the Bahamian-Key West-style "gingerbread" architecture of the area. You can still admire these early homes on **Charles Avenue**. At the west end of the street, the gravestones of pioneers dot the **Charlotte Jane Stirrup Memorial Cemetery**. The character of the area is changing to upscale, however, with the modern-looking **CocoWalk** pavilion now serving as a focal point for the Grove. CocoWalk includes several shops, restaurants, bars and movie theaters.

Goombay in the Grove: All kinds of colorful characters cruise the sidewalks of the Grove on roller skates, bicycles, skateboards, even feet. The Goombay Festival each June, where musicians prefer to play the horse conch and kazoo to the guitar, is a prime time to visit.

A well-marked bike path can be used for touring the Grove. Pedal past ice-cream parlors, a Christian Science reading room and boutiques to Main Highway. The shops give way to churches and schools.

Off Main Highway is the **Plymouth Congregational Church**, built in 1897 to resemble a Spanish mission. The area's first schoolhouse is also located here, at 3429 Devon Road, built by early settlers from the wood of wrecked ships. Continue south on the bike path, then turn left on dead-end St Gaudens Road. You are now officially in **Coral Gables**, a city built by dreamers.

George Edgar Merrick planned this remarkable community which sprang up almost overnight during the first Florida boom. He would still be pleased today at its refined cultural atmosphere. The city derives its name from Merrick's own gabled mansion of coral.

Florida writer Rex Beach sized up Merrick: "At heart, he was a writer, a poet, an artist. But fate with a curious perversity decreed that he should write in wood and steel and stone, and paint his pictures upon a canvas of spacious fields, cool groves and smiling waterways..."

Coconut Grove's Commodore Plaza.

Merrick's stately plan, only slightly amended, still controls the arrangement of the winding, often confusing streets and the architecture of the houses. He dictated that Coral Gables' homes should have a Mediterranean flair, later adding a dash of France, Holland, South Africa and China – although he had never been outside of the United States. A tour of Coral Gables, therefore, can turn out to be a trip around the world. Book a visit on a tour bus, or lead yourself with a self-guiding pamphlet available at City Hall on the western end of the shoppers' street called **Miracle Mile**.

Merrick paid William Jennings Bryan a salary of $50,000 a year to promote his city from a floating platform in the **Venetian Pool** at Almeria Avenue and Toledo Street. Once a stone quarry, the pool is now a tropical paradise of islands, caves, rock towers, cascades and arched bridges open to the public.

The main entrance to Coral Gables is **La Puerta del Sol** ("The Sun Portal") at Douglas Road and 8th Street. Merrick designed its water tower, town clock and belfry to mimic a Mediterranean town square. Coral rock gates adorn other entrances to the city. A resort hotel Merrick built for $10 million flanks the western edge of the city: the **Biltmore** has a tower patterned after the Cathedral of Seville, but it fell into disrepair during the Depression. It has been totally renovated and is once again a luxurious hideaway.

To Key Biscayne: Only one road leads to the island community of Key Biscayne. The **Rickenbacker Causeway**, surrounded by water on both sides, can on weekends be jammed with traffic. Along the route, you'll find the **Miami Marine Stadium** where you can watch pop concerts at twilight from the grandstand overlooking the lagoon, or from a boat. Flipper, the porpoise, and Lolita, the killer whale, are the lures of the **Seaquarium**.

Two of hundreds of islands that surround the southern tip of Florida, Key Biscayne and Virginia Key are sedimentary barrier islands, strung north to south, parallel to the South Florida main-

Coral Gables' Venetian Pool.

land. They began as sandbars, millions of years ago. As ocean waves and winds piled limestone and quartz on top of hard coral rock, islands emerged, a barrier between the Atlantic Ocean and the mainland for that same water and wind.

Its topographical quirks are hidden. East along the island's sandy northern shore, for example, lies a small reef, obvious at low tide but at high tide barely awash.

Crandon Boulevard runs into Key Biscayne, which was the site of the Florida White House during the Nixon Administration. The most popular spot is the lighthouse in **Bill Baggs Cape Florida State Park**. In 1836, Seminole Indians trapped the keeper and his aide in this tower, then tried to burn them out. A keg of gunpowder hurled from the top put an explosive end to the Indians' efforts: a patrolling ship heard the discharge and came to the rescue.

The five-room keeper's home has been restored to its original form. Unfortunately, much of the natural beauty of Bill Baggs – miles of wild Australian pine trees – was badly destroyed by Hurricane Andrew in 1992. Park officials say it will take decades for the trees to grow back.

Developers have discovered Key Biscayne, but a quiet tempo still prevails. Shops are more retro than trendy, delivering the basics with old-fashioned service; the hardware store will still sell you one nail or one screw. There are few traffic lights on Key Biscayne, and even fewer traffic jams.

Readily accessible from Key Biscayne by boat are the **Spoil Islands**. Fourteen dot Biscayne Bay, providing peaceful settings for camping, fishing or lazing in the sun. They were formed from rock and sand pumped from the bay bottom to deepen ship channels.

Miami Beach developer Carl Fisher enlarged one, **Monument Island**, to honor Henry Flagler, and installed a column similar to the Washington Monument, flanked by four statues symbolizing prosperity, industry, education and pioneers.

Nightlife is scattered from one end of Miami to the other, from the venerable **Crazy Horse Saloon** in North Miami Beach where men take it all off, to **Les Violins Supper Club** downtown, where strolling violinists are followed by a Cuban floor show. Or the smoke-filled blues and jazz club **Tobacco Road**, the oldest – and some say the best – bar in Miami.

Talk to the animals: To the south of the city is the **Miami Metrozoo**, a sprawling 290-acre cageless zoo considered to be one of the best in the country. Dedicated to tropical life, it has more than 100 species living in island sites surrounded by moats, including koala bears, elephants, and rare Bengal tigers. But like many natural attractions in South Dade County, Metrozoo suffered a massive loss during Hurricane Andrew. Although much of the lush landscape was destroyed, the zoo remains a favorite with animal lovers young and old.

Another interesting attraction includes the **Monastery of St Bernard**, south of the park near Snake Creek. Moorish, Jewish and Christian slaves carved its stones from hills near Zamora, Spain. You can still see the symbols in the rock – stars of David, crescents and crosses. The bulk of the structure was built in the 12th century. Newspaper magnate William Randolph Hearst bought it from Spain and planned to reassemble it at his San Simeon castle in California. Instead, he sold it to a group who rebuilt the monastery here.

Miami's major annual sporting event is the **Orange Bowl** football game when major college teams clash under the light of the moon around New Year's Day. The **Joe Robbie Stadium** is the home of the Miami Dolphins National Football League team.

Greater Miami has more to offer than most resort areas – from mad metropolitan nights to mellow mornings on the beach. Despite previous negative publicity, the city continues to thrive and boom. A multi-million dollar Miami Free Trade Zone, similar to zones at Port Everglades and Orlando, solidified its position as the American capital of Latin American business. Further development of Watson Island is promised, once municipal minds can agree.

MIAMI BEACH

Since Carl Fisher shaped it out of a rattlesnake and rodent-infested sandspur and cut Lincoln Road through dense mangrove using circus elephants in 1915, golden days in Miami Beach have come, gone and come again. Once the dream-vacation mecca of every red-blooded American, it fell into disrepair as families spurned it for central Florida and Walt Disney World during the 1970s. Now, like a dowager snoozing on the porch of a South Beach hotel, the city has awakened to the voices of a new generation of visitors, including young American families and tourists from Europe and South America.

Dredging ships have already put the beach back where it belongs behind the solid wall of overblown hotels along Collins Avenue. Preservationists campaigned for restoration of the Beach's unmatched collection of F. Scott Fitzgerald-era Art Deco hotels, with remarkable success. Parks have been cleaned up and improved. South Beach is now the place to be – and be seen. Nowhere more so than on South Beach are the boundaries between trendy and tacky so blurred. Tacky is trendy here: kitsch is cool. And the beach beckons all year round.

"Miami Beach," as one observer put it, "has had more comebacks than Peggy Lee." And here it is again, with a vengeance and a bang, this time driving a souped-up retro convertible and sipping a pale pink cocktail.

Gateway to the beach: Several causeways span Biscayne Bay between the mainland and Miami Beach. Interstate 195 crosses the Julia Tuttle Causeway, then runs into Arthur Godfrey Road. Venetian Way links the islands of the same name before turning into Dade Boulevard. But the most entertaining route is over the MacArthur Causeway.

First stop is **Watson Island Park**, named after three-time Mayor James Watson, who came to Miami in 1898. Here, you'll find a helicopter base offering air tours of the city. The oldest airline in the world, **Chalk's International Airlines**, makes trips to the Bahamas aboard amphibious planes.

Watson Island also offers landlocked tourists a stunning view of the coming and going cruise ships that use the port across the bay. These liners, large and small, draw a steady stream of onlookers. And city-ward, the view of Miami from Watson Island offers a big-city skyline of high-rise condos mixed with a few surviving palm trees.

MacArthur Causeway enters the city at Fifth Street, an inauspicious introduction to the beach. Fortunately, the revitalization plans did not take away such landmarks as the **Fifth Street Gym**, where Muhammad Ali trained for early championship bouts, and **Joe's Stone Crab Restaurant** on Biscayne Steet, a local institution where in season you can dine on delectable claws some people consider tastier than lobster.

You'll notice a proliferation of Stars of David painted on Jewish synagogues in the area. The beach has always attracted Jewish retirees who choose to

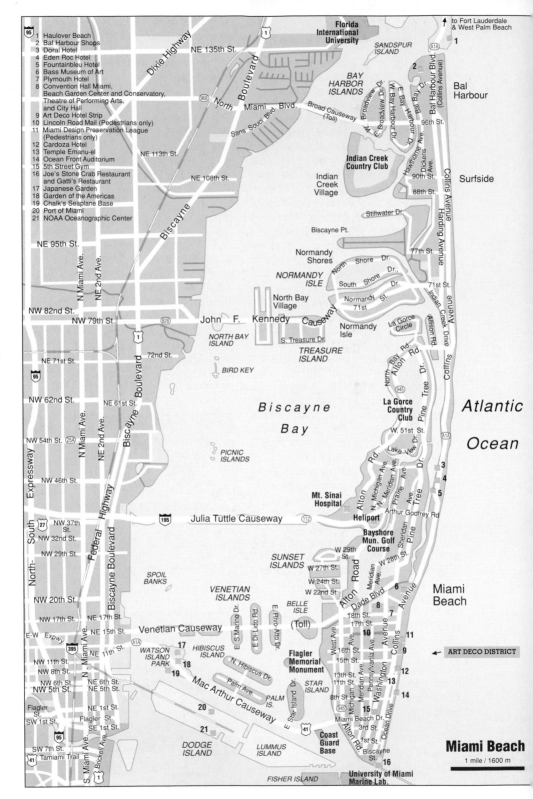

1 Haulover Beach
2 Bal Harbour Shops
3 Doral Hotel
4 Eden Roc Hotel
5 Fountainbleu Hotel
6 Bass Museum of Art
7 Plymouth Hotel
8 Convention Hall Miami,
  Beach Garden Center and Conservatory,
  Theatre of Performing Arts,
  and City Hall
9 Art Deco Hotel Strip
10 Lincoln Road Mall (Pedestrians only)
11 Miami Design Preservation League
  (Pedestrians only)
12 Cardoza Hotel
13 Temple Emanu-el
14 Ocean Front Auditorium
15 5th Street Gym
16 Joe's Stone Crab Restaurant
  and Gatti's Restaurant
17 Japanese Garden
18 Garden of the Americas
19 Chalk's Seaplane Base
20 Port of Miami
21 NOAA Oceanographic Center

to Fort Lauderdale & West Palm Beach

Florida International University

SANDSPUR ISLAND

BAY HARBOR ISLANDS

Bal Harbour

Broad Causeway (Toll)

Indian Creek Country Club

Indian Creek Village

Surfside

Biscayne Pt.

Stillwater Dr.

Normandy Shores

NORMANDY ISLE

North Bay Village

Normandy Isle

La Gorce Circle

Biscayne Bay

NORTH BAY ISLAND

S. Treasure Dr.

TREASURE ISLAND

John F. Kennedy Causeway

BIRD KEY

PICNIC ISLANDS

La Gorce Country Club

Atlantic Ocean

Mt. Sinai Hospital

Heliwport

Arthur Godfrey Rd.

Julia Tuttle Causeway

Bayshore Mun. Golf Course

SPOIL BANKS

SUNSET ISLANDS

VENETIAN ISLANDS

BELLE ISLE

(Toll)

Miami Beach

ART DECO DISTRICT

Venetian Causeway

WATSON ISLAND PARK

HIBISCUS ISLAND

Flagler Memorial Monument

STAR ISLAND

Mac Arthur Causeway

PALM IS.

DODGE ISLAND

LUMMUS ISLAND

Coast Guard Base

University of Miami Marine Lab.

FISHER ISLAND

Miami Beach

1 mile / 1600 m

while away their last years with fellow spirits in front of the old hotels and rooming houses.

Art Deco dreaming: North of Fifth Street lies the **Art Deco District**, more than 80 blocks and 800 buildings surrounding **Flamingo Park**. These were the first 20th-century structures to be listed on the National Register of Historic Places. At first, you may see them as a collection of pastel hotels and apartment houses that have seen better days. If that is the case, drop by the **Miami Design Preservation League** headquarters at 1244 Ocean Drive. Someone there will be happy to open your eyes to the streamlined racing stripes, porthole windows, glass-block construction, pipe railings, ribbon windows, and bands of pastel pinks, oranges, limes, blues and yellows that give these creations of the 1930s a funky, contemporary style. And if you are particularly interested in Art Deco, someone from the League may be available to take you on a walking tour of the District.

For a sample of what this group has saved from the savage wrecking ball, take a long stroll down Ocean Drive. Visit the **Cardozo Hotel** at 13th Street, or the nearby **Leslie**, **Cavalier**, and **Park Central** hotels. All were among the earliest to have undergone Deco facelifts and are now in impeccable shape. Don't neglect to explore the interiors of these magnificent old structures. You'll find murals of flamingos, etched glass windows with sea nymphs, mermaids and tropical birds. They all have views across the street of **Lummus Park**, a wide expanse of white sand dotted with pink Deco lifeguard stations.

Significant structures in Art Deco motif, also called Streamline Moderne, are too numerous to list. Notables include the Ocean Drive stretch highlighted by the **Avalon**, the **Edison**, the **Clevelander**, the **Adrian** and **Royal Palm** hotels; the curvilinear corner architecture of the **Warsaw Ballroom**; the Middle Eastern eclectic dome of **Temple Emanuel** on Washington Avenue; and the **Spanish Village** on Española Way, whose Moorish arcades and hidden courtyards served as the setting for many episodes of *Miami Vice*. Part of the Spanish Village is now the **Miami Beach International Youth Hostel**, also called the Clay Hotel. The hostel is a favorite gathering place for European tourists.

Hot spots and greasy spoons: With the rekindled love affair that tourists are having with the Art Deco District these days, dozens of fine restaurants and cafés have blossomed on the beach. Some of the more popular spots known to attract European photographers, fashion models, and other in-the-know characters, include the **News Café**, **Stuart's** and **Café des Arts** – all on Ocean Drive.

For a non-touristy look at Miami Beach and a chat with some locals, stop in at the **Irish House** bar on Alton Road, a neighborhood hang-out with a large juke box and greasy food. Or try **Club Duce** on 14th Street where the clientele ranges from motorcycle tough guys to aging transvestites.

The **Lincoln Road Mall**, a pedestrian-only street at the intersection of Collins Avenue and 16th Street, is an-

ART DECO

Sliding across the rainbow from erotic pink to lizard green, the Art Deco structures on Miami Beach were built to uplift the spirits of America and to offer a distraction from the Great Depression. Over 60 years later, preservationists say they are some of the most architecturally significant structures in America. For Miami's tourism industry, they represent the ultimate pink flamingo.

The roots of Art Deco go back to 1901 when the Société des Artistes Decorateurs was formed in Paris with the goal of merging the mass production of industrial technology with the decorative arts. It borrowed styles from Bauhaus, Cubism and Constructivism and eventually spread its aesthetics from architecture and furniture to ceramics and jewelry.

It was proudly introduced to the world in 1925 at the Paris Exposition Internationale des Arts Decoratifs et Industriels Modernes. The nickname Art Deco came about in 1966 at a retrospective of the 1925 Paris show.

Typical characteristics of Art Deco architecture and the Art Moderne which followed it are streamline designs using rounded corners, geometric forms, flat roofs, racing stripes and porthole windows. The structures copied the aerodynamic designs of the sleek ocean liners and cars of the period. Strong vertical lines, thick glass blocks and, for the first time, neon lights were used. In celebration of the discovery of Tutankhamun's tomb in the 1920s, occasional Egyptian details were thrown in.

Between the two world wars, over 500 Art Deco structures were built in the southern part of Miami Beach. They developed a unique personality and became known as Tropical Deco, Florida style. The stark, white stucco exteriors lent themselves well to the outrageous tropical colors, as did the bright sunny skies and brisk ocean breezes that cooled the verandas.

The etched-glass panels common in Art Deco structures used mermaids, sea horses and waves to evoke the nautical. Flamingos, egrets, pelicans and palm trees became popular. Eyebrows – overhanging canopies above porthole windows – were introduced to create shade from the South Florida sun.

For the next few decades the Art Deco hotels continued to enjoy prosperity and served as a welcome refuge for Americans escaping the brutal cold of northern winters. But by the 1960s they had begun to decay. The many layers of paint cracked and peeled and several of the once-glamorous hotels became low-rent housing for the elderly.

In 1976, the Miami Design Preservation League was formed to stop the demolition of the Art Deco buildings and to encourage the restoration of the structures without disrupting the elderly community they housed. In 1979, what is now called the Art Deco District – approximately 125 blocks running from 6th to 23rd Streets along the Atlantic Ocean and west to Alton Road – was placed on the National Register of Historic Places, the only 20th-century structures ever granted such a distinction.

Many South Beach Art Deco hotels have been restored to their original condition. A few have been treated to some extra helpings of cartoon colors and now scream peach, lavender and turquoise. Miami Beach's buildings represent the largest concentration of Art Deco architecture in the world. ■

other rejuvenated area. Although it still has a fair share of tacky souvenir shops, the mall is a mecca for the arts scene with several art galleries, restaurants, and theaters. The mall also serves as the home base for the **Miami City Ballet** and Miami's **New World Symphony**. At the entrance to the mall is the world's only Art Deco Burger King. Nearby is the **Colony Theater**, a former movie house, now a performing arts center that hosts both big name and offbeat acts. The **Bass Museum of Art** on Collins Avenue is a small but interesting museum. Its diverse collection includes European paintings and 16th-century Flemish tapestries.

Into the 1950s and beyond: Driving north on Collins Avenue is like taking a time trip through 20th-century architectural periods. You go from the colorful 1930s to the drabber, but occasionally ostentatious and always monstrous, constructions of the 1950s. The granddaddy of that era is the **Fontainebleau**, now enjoying new popularity under Hilton management after a $25-million facelift.

Its pool has an island in the middle with eight palm trees, and waterfalls that cascade over the heads of swimmers. Bars and restaurants lurk around every bend of the tropically-landscaped grounds. Even if you're not staying in one of the hotel's 1,224 rooms, you can park at **Indian Beach** and stroll over for a look.

Next door, the **Eden Roc** has also been spruced up. So have the **Sans Souci**, the **Seville** and the **Versailles**. Collins Avenue eventually caves into a canyon of concrete: condos on the west, and hotels on the Atlantic. This is typical of the 1960s method of cramming the maximum number of people into waterfront compartments.

To view the rich in their natural habitat, swerve over to **North Bay Road**. Its developer, Carl Fisher, memorialized in **Fisher Park**, set aside this corner of Miami Beach for the wealthy and lived at 5020 North Bay Road. Celebrities like Gloria Estefan and Barry Gibb (of the Bee Gees) now live in this area.

Many of these show places went up

lishing up the hotel at sparked e Art Deco storation.

between 1922 and 1924 and incorporate the lavish details of that period. They sport balconies, Corinthian columns, and stucco reliefs with vegetable motifs. Number 4750 has a brick lookout tower and wishing well. Others have servant quarters built over the entrance gates. If you pedal into the area on a bicycle, don't let the guard at the gatehouse put you off. The public is legally entitled to ride through.

Collins Avenue continues north through **Surfside**, passing **North Shore Ocean Park** – an oasis of sea grapes and roofed pavilions with a boardwalk for pedestrians and cyclists. **Bal Harbour** encompasses the most modern hotels as well as an exclusive shopping center with expensive retailers, such as Neiman Marcus, Saks Fifth Avenue, Gucci and Cartier.

Across the bridge over Baker's Haulover Cut is **Haulover Beach Park** with 2 miles of beach, sightseeing cruises, helicopter rides, surfing, golf and deepsea fishing.

Before leaving Miami Beach, visit

one of its many delicatessens for a bowl of matzoh ball soup, blintzes or pastrami on rye. **Wolfies, Pumperniks** and the **Rascal House** are landmarks. Kosher restaurants, butcher shops and Torah treasure stores with Hebrew religious books are other evidence of the Jewish influence here.

In addition to the retirees, Miami Beach includes recent arrivals from Russia, plus many Israelis and even Cuban Jews. The religious observances of these immigrants range widely: some of the newcomers are completely passive, while the ultra-orthodox can be recognised by their beards, black hats and prayer shawls.

A detour south: Few visitors realize that south of the close-packed resorts and residents of Metropolitan Miami lie rich agricultural fields that put Dade County among the top 100 producing counties in the United States. Many farms encourage people to "pick-your-own" during the growing season, especially in the area known as "The Redland" south of Miami.

It takes a good deal of fertilizer to enrich the clay-like soil, but off US 1 near **Homestead** and **Florida City** is the nation's "winter vegetable basket" laden with potatoes, tomatoes, lush strawberries, peas, cucumbers, limes and avocados.

But unfortunately it was here, in the prosperous agricultural areas of South Dade County, that most of the destruction and damage caused by Hurricane Andrew in August, 1992, occurred. Slowly, some of these important agricultural lands are being restored, but for the most part Florida City and Homestead will be undergoing major rebuilding and replanting for years to come.

One of the few post-Andrew points of interest that remain, not surprisingly, is a sturdy, whimsical place called **Coral Castle**. Located on US 1, better known as Dixie Highway, just north of Homestead, Coral Castle was built by a 97-pound Latvian immigrant named Edward Leedskalnin between 1925 and 1940. This bizarre castle contains rock furniture, a sundial and a finely-balanced 9-ton swinging gate.

Left, towerin dreams. **Right**, Ocear Drive, Miam Beach.

FORT LAUDERDALE AND POINTS NORTH

There are three basic ways to drive north from Miami. Interstate 95 is fast and free. The Florida Turnpike is fast but expensive. Neither of those superhighways make for a particularly interesting drive. Highway A1A, on the other hand, takes forever to drive as it skirts the East Coast. It's occasionally scenic, occasionally overwhelmed by the highrise condominiums and hotels which blot out views of the Atlantic Ocean, and it's always crowded – but it's rarely boring. You'll have to cut back inland to US 1, wherever A1A runs into unbridged inlets. But the reward for enduring the traffic lights and detours will be some memorable rides through seaside resorts which beg for long stops.

A sophisticated fort: When you see the sophisticated beauty of the beaches and resorts of **Fort Lauderdale**, it will seem inconceivable that it was a dismal swamp, unfit for habitation, less than a century ago. A wooden fort built here during the Seminole Wars, and named after Tennessee volunteer Major William Lauderdale, rotted for two decades after troops left in 1857 before significant development occurred – construction of a House of Refuge for shipwrecked sailors. For the most part, it remained a mangrove swamp that hid runaway slaves and desperate army deserters. Henry Flagler's railroad again changed that. In 1911, the city was incorporated.

Its swampy coast kept construction off the famous beach until men were farsighted enough to keep the sands open to the public, and situated hotels and businesses on the far side of A1A. Today, a drive along that beach highway stirs the senses. The 6½ miles of open beach are undoubtedly the city's primary attraction.

To transform the mangrove swamp into prime real estate, Charles Green Rodes resorted to "finger-islanding" – dredging up a series of parallel canals and using the fill to create long peninsulas between them. It was the same system used in a certain Italian city, and it earned Fort Lauderdale the nickname, "Venice of America." The town boasts more than 350 miles of natural and artificial canals, inlets, rivers and bays bordered by lovely homes.

Downtown Fort Lauderdale is neat and clean, brandishing a new skyline of modern high-rise office buildings. Some of the city's more prominent atttractions include the **Broward Center for the Performing Arts**, a 2,700-seat theater that features major cultural events; the **Fort Lauderdale Museum of Art**, home to an extensive collection of CoBrA paintings, sculptures and prints; and the newly opened **Museum of Discovery and Science**, the largest science museum in South Florida featuring hands-on educational exhibits that include video games, an indoor citrus grove, and bubble-making experiments. All of these are connected by the city's palm-lined **Riverwalk**, a 28-acre series of parks and walkways that border the **New River**.

On the east side of the Riverwalk is **Stranahan House**, the restored 1913 home of Fort Lauderdale pioneer Frank Stranahan that is now a museum and gift shop. Across the tunnel from Stranahan House is **Las Olas Boulevard**. One of the prettiest streets in all of South Florida, Las Olas is a brick-paved boulevard decorated with old-fashioned gas lights and dotted with numerous fine quality shops, restaurants and art galleries.

Where the boys are: The east end of Las Olas runs into the honky-tonk area simply called "The Strip." The 1960 beach-party movie and song *Where the Boys Are* romanticized this beachfront stretch as the magnet for college students on spring break. Throughout the 1970s, the boys kept coming, and so did the girls, and The Strip became one big drunken beach party just like the movie. But during the 1980s, local officials and city residents grew intolerant of the noise, trash, and violent brawls created by the college kids and began curtailing their behavior. New bars that were not part of hotels were banned, as was public consumptin of alcohol. Arrests for violations were common. By 1990, the

eft, gone shin'.

word reached college campuses across the country and many of the students moved their spring break antics north to Daytona Beach where city officials were more tolerant. Kids still come for a glimpse of The Strip, but their numbers are smaller and their behavior has been tempered. The once-notorious **Elbo Room** bar, made famous in the movie, is still open, but even the bartenders admit that it's just not what it used to be.

The forerunner of "spring break migration" was the Collegiate Aquatic Forum, a unique winter attraction when it started in 1935 at the city-owned casino and pool. College students came first in a trickle then in waves. The city replaced the old pool in 1965 with the **Swimming Hall of Fame**. Completely updated and remodeled in 1993, the Hall of Fame located just west of A1A is now one of Fort Lauderdale's most popular attractions. It includes four swimming pools, a reference library, art gallery, and 10,000 sq-foot exhibition hall housing trophies and mementos of athletes past and present.

Although toned down a bit, Fort Lauderdale still has a lively bar scene. About 35,000 people drop into Broward County bars on a typical weeknight. Recently, much of the action has moved to **Commercial Boulevard** and the banks of the **Intracoastal Waterway**. A few of the more festive bars are **Confetti**, a high energy dance club where bartenders blow flames and perform tricks; **Shooters**, a waterfront saloon that is popular among the speed-boat crowd, and **Coconuts**, where live music draws huge crowds on weekends. A few of the more subdued, elegant and long-standing are **Stan's**, the **Down Under**, and **Casa Vecchia**. An offbeat favorite of families and tourists since 1956 has been **Bob Thornton's Mai Kai**, where imported Polynesian dancers perform while you sip a banana daquiri in a tropical garden setting.

Where the boats are: Fort Lauderdale claims to berth more pleasure craft than any other Florida city. Many tie up at Bahia Mar, a marina full of magnificent yachts. The area had a House of Refuge

Student stomping grounds, the corner of Las Olas and A1A

and Coast Guard station before being transformed into a luxury marina in 1949. Picking up on the theme, the **Yankee Clipper** hotel nearby closely resembles a cruise ship.

The real things sail from **Port Everglades**, at the eastern end of State Road 84 in the southern part of the city. Once a shallow landlocked lake, the port was opened to the Atlantic when a channel was blasted in 1928.

Other Lauderdale sites include **Ocean World**, another of Florida's myriad fish shows, next to the Marriott Hotel on East 17th; a **Seminole Indian Village** on State Road 7 at Stirling Road; and the *Jungle Queen*, a paddleboat that navigates the New River, setting out from the Bahia Mar Yacht basin, and where passengers can enjoy dinner or evening cruises on the water.

At the north end of Fort Lauderdale Beach, behind a row of markers that read "Private Beach Between Signs," is a curiosity that takes some explaining. The signs bracket the quarter mile of private property known as **Bonnet**

House. Hidden behind a patch of seagrape trees, Bonnet House is the winter home of artist Evelyn Bartlett, who is now over 100 years old. Mrs Bartlett is the widow of an esteemed painter, and the home that they once shared together is a lyrical mansion of artistic whimsy. Decorated with unusual antiques and a bizarre collection of nicknacks, the home is open to the public from May through November.

The town of **Davie**, to the southwest, offers airboat rides into the fringes of the Everglades from **Sawgrass Recreation Area**, which is close to Alligator Alley and US 27.

Dania and **Hollywood** are smaller towns with lovely beaches that you hit before reaching Fort Lauderdale en route from Miami. Dania Beach Boulevard harkens back to the days when mangroves grew by the roadside and still had plenty of room to flourish and multiply. It leads to a beach and to the **Dania Fishing Pier**. Just north is **John U. Lloyd Beach Recreation Area**, 244 acres of barrier island.

Windsurfing along the coast.

Hollywood was founded by a Californian, but bears no resemblance to its West Coast namesake. The major draw is the oceanfront boardwalk which is graced at the southern end by the **Hollywood Beach Hotel** and its adjoining **Oceanwalk**, a multi-level, entertainment complex of restaurants, bars, boutiques and cinemas. Recently Hollywood Beach has become the favorite winter vacation spot for tens of thousands of French Canadians, transforming it into a bilingual community.

Up the coast on A1A: The beach drive north from Fort Lauderdale is particularly rewarding. Each resort seems to melt into the next until you hit **Pompano Beach**. For the next 25 miles the road brushes the shoreline and butts against the Intracoastal Waterway.

Although it has grown rapidly as a resort and condo community, Pompano is still a major agricultural center with one of Florida's largest wholesale vegetable markets. Long before the sun rises each morning during the winter growing season, the **Pompano Beach Farmers' Market** buzzes with growers, vegetable brokers and homemakers bartering for the best prices.

The Pompano Beach Air Park is home to the Goodyear Blimp, which you may see but not touch, or go up in.

The **Deerfield Island Park**, one of 288 parks in Broward County, can be reached only by boat and offers a nature trail, tennis and 55½ acres of solitude.

The area's premier restaurant is **Cap's Place** in **Lighthouse Point**. Follow N.E. 24th Street and Yacht Club signs from Federal Highway to Cap's Dock. The *S.S. Dramamine* will take you to the island restaurant and bar. If it's not docked, blink your car lights and wait until it arrives. Cap Knight, a Spanish-American war veteran and occasional rum-runner, opened the Club Unique here in the 1920s on some beached barges and a derelict dredge. Guests boated to the hideout to gamble and defy Prohibition. Notable guests included the Duke of Windsor, Franklin D. Roosevelt, Jack Dempsey and Winston Churchill. The ramshackle atmosphere remains.

Bill Stewart's Riverview Restaurant, under the causeway bridge on Hillsboro Boulevard, has a similar history and atmosphere. It was converted from packing house to casino in the 1930s. Gangsters sometimes frequented the place and Al Capone had begun transactions to buy the triangular island across the way – until he was busted for income-tax evasion. The island, now a pristine park that can be visited by boat, still bears Capone's name.

Continuing north past the miles of towering dwellings that edge A1A, **Boca Raton** is soon reached. Eccentric architect Addison Mizner envisioned a fleet of gondolas romantically plying a man-made canal through town. But the waterway was never completed and the only gondola shipped from Italy disintegrated during the Depression. The filled-in ditch became one of Florida's most attractive streets, **Camino Real**, whose tall palms grace the route to the **Boca Raton Hotel**.

Originally known as the Cloister Inn, the hotel is considered one of Mizner's greatest achievements. The loggias, archways, tiled patios and sculptured fountains of the original section convey the opulence of the 1920s. Boca Raton grew up around the hotel, acting as its service village for many years. Boca Raton's posh veneer even surpasses that of Palm Beach in one respect: it fields a better polo team. Only Prince Philip's dashing British group and the expert horsemen of Argentina are thought to be better. The action occurs every Sunday from January through April.

Delray Beach is a pleasant, inexpensive alternative to the plush resort cities to the north and south. Its **Morikami Park Museum** offers changing exhibits dealing with Japanese art and a *bonsai* display of dwarf trees.

One of the world's largest circulation, but least influential, newspapers has put **Lantana** on the map. It's the headquarters for the lucrative *National Enquirer*, the scandal sheet that dishes up soapy stories about celebrities.

Lantana is linked with its northern neighbor, **Lake Worth**, which straddles a lake of the same name and is actually a salt-water lagoon.

Right, primed for polo at Boca Raton.

PALM BEACH

Enclave of enormous wealth and power. The poshest of the posh. A haven for the idle rich. These are some of the things that have been said about South Florida's most fabled city, **Palm Beach**.

If you are not extremely wealthy, you may not like the vibrations that emanate from this island. You can practically smell money growing here. Its residents may, in turn, look upon you with disdain. Tourists are tolerated, although not exactly welcomed. But if you keep a low profile and keep your eyes from bulging out of your head at the displays of excessive wealth, it's a fascinating side trip.

A few words of caution: leave your camera in the car, don't stare at the regulars at Petite Marmite, don't try to ogle mansions over the ficus hedges, and don't ask the prices of the diamond necklaces on Worth Avenue. The cost probably exceeds your mortgage. And remember, it's against the law to park most anywhere, to own a kangaroo or any other exotic animal, or to hang a clothesline.

Born millionaires: In his enlightening literary portrait, *Palm Beach*, author-resident John Ney told the story of a young Junior Chamber of Commerce type bragging at a Palm Beach party. "I'm one of those under-40 millionaires!" the man boasted, startling an established resident of Palm Beach who involuntarily replied, "I was a millionaire before I was born!"

The moral of the story is that it's impossible to ride into Palm Beach and blend in with the surroundings, so don't even try.

Unless you prefer to gape at empty mansions undergoing beauty treatments and garden manicures, visit during the "social season" – an indeterminate period of time that falls somewhere between Thanksgiving and Easter. That's when you'll see the pretty people who, yes, actually live in – or at least decorate – the palatial dwellings.

The annual migration of money ig-nites a round of galas, teas, charity balls and political cocktail parties in election years. People willing to pay up to $1,000 a plate can get invited to some of the prestigious, glittering balls. But it may take a larger donation to get into one of the exclusive political gatherings.

Appropriately, a boatload of Spanish sailors with 100 cases of wine aboard stumbled upon the barren strand in 1878. They sold their cargo, including 20,000 coconuts, to a shrewd islander for $20. The islander sold two coconuts for a nickel to his neighbors. They planted them in the sand and, *voilà*, the beach got its palms. Not long afterward, Henry Flagler and his railroad rolled into town. He liked it, built a home and transformed Palm Beach into a personal playground for himself and his wealthy, fun-loving friends. Addison Mizner added his ostentatious architectural touches, his Spanish spires, courtyards, plazas and arcades.

Astors, Goulds, Vanderbilts, dukes and duchesses followed Flagler into town. They stayed at the Royal Poin-

eft, Palm 2ach's 4latial Mar-Lago. ght, watery 2pths.

ciana, one of the largest wooden buildings ever constructed and the largest resort hotel of its time. Black men pedaled them around the grounds aboard "Afromobiles," and a feature attraction was Cakewalk Night, where black dancers competed for a big white cake, then entertained richly-dressed guests with spirituals. The hotel has long since been dismantled, but its ghost lingers.

Opulence unlimited: You can leave Florida – and enter Palm Beach – by proceeding north on Highway A1A. You can't miss it. The garish strings of shopping centers and neon hotel signs vanish. Clean, uncluttered streets of class take over. The structures behind the high walls of concrete and ficus are not museums, just second homes to Palm Beachers. If you suddenly feel conspicuous among the Mercedes and Jaguars in your battered Ford or rented Honda Civic, visit Classic Motor Tours on Poinciana Plaza. They'll ride you through this monied maze in a 1958 Rolls-Royce Silver Shadow.

South Ocean Boulevard runs right past the Moorish estate of the late cereal heiress, Marjorie Merriweather Post. It's called Mar-A-Lago, and is now owned by entrepreneur Donald Trump. You can see its highest tower north of the Southern Boulevard Bridge. Its 17 acres, complete with nine-hole golf course and 117 rooms, has been valued at a cool $20 million, minimum. At 702 South Ocean Boulevard is a home formerly owned by the late Beatle, John Lennon. Next door is a mansion that once belonged to Woolworth Donahue, heir to the dime store fortune.

Turn left into Worth Avenue. It has been likened to London's Bond Street, Rome's Via Condotti and Paris' Faubourg St Honoré. Here Courrèges, Hermes, Gucci and other shops open onto courtyards and winding vistas. Try not to exhibit astonishment.

Show up at least a half-hour before noon to get a table at **Petite Marmite**, where you can eat shoulder-to-shoulder with celebrities if you don't mind paying dinner prices for lunch. The photo case has a picture of John Lennon hav-

An opulent bathroom fit for a sheik.

ing dinner there with his wife, Yoko Ono, and actor Peter Boyle. Younger heirs gravitate to **Chuck and Harold's** on Royal Poinciana Way with its Parisian-style sidewalk café.

The Esplanade is a two-story klatch of shops surrounding a courtyard with another popular lunch spot, **Café l'Europe**. To find out who partied where and with whom, pick up a copy of *The Palm Beach Daily News.* (It may be all you can afford to buy here.) Note that it is printed on paper especially treated to prevent ink from smudging expensive hands or outfits.

Most of the exotic-looking animals heeling like military cadets at their masters' sides are probably dogs. John Ney once wrote: "It is correct to have any sort of dog, *comme il faut* to have a small dog like a corgi or pug, and *de rigueur* in certain circles to have a toy poodle. The poodle is such an important demonstration of conspicuous consumption that many people who have no money at all haul poodles around in their cars as the easiest and cheapest way of pretending

that they are really loaded, but it rarely works."

Royal families: Flagler's old home, built in 1901, is now a museum to one of Florida's prime movers. He and his third wife lived in it for only four years. The rooms and most original furnishing have been restored, and one of Flagler's railroad cars is on display in the museum's backyard.

Another memorial to Flagler regally sprawls across the street. **The Breakers** has weathered booms, busts and even two fires, but remains one of the nation's first-class resorts. Stately Venetian arches lead into the lobby, comfortable sofas and Persian carpets line the rambling hallways, and the Circle Dining Room has an immense circular skylight, cathedral windows and bronze chandelier. Another cavernous old hotel, **The Biltmore** (north of Royal Poinciana Way), is now a condominium.

The northern reaches of Palm Beach have more of the same. Just beyond 1075 N. Ocean Boulevard is the compound of the Kennedys. Here, a young

aking a cket.

Senator John Kennedy wrote his best-selling *Profiles in Courage* after a stint in World War II. He later wintered in Palm Beach after becoming President, but John Ney wrote of a local prejudice against this neighboring "royal family."

It was also here, in 1992, that Kennedy's nephew, William Kennedy Smith, was charged with raping a young woman he had met in a Palm Beach bar. After a grueling, nationally televised trial, Smith was found not guilty.

During the 1980s Palm Beach enjoyed a renaissance fueled by an influx of wealthy scions from abroad. Prominent newcomers included French tycoon Robert de Balkany and his wife, Princess Maria Gabriella of Savoy, the Duke of Doudeauville, and Prince Yuka Troubetskoy, who long dominated the French Riviera social scene. Amid all this royalty, the men of Palm Beach won an eight-year battle in the late 1980s when they were finally granted the right to jog through the streets of the city, topless.

If you keep driving north on Ocean Boulevard you will eventually run out of road. Park in a metered space, if you can find one, and take the short hike to the wooden clock on the Palm Beach Inlet. If you make it early enough you'll witness a sunrise all the money around you can't buy.

With champagne and cold duck hawked from a canopied cart instead of hot dogs and beer, it's obvious that polo is not akin to a Sunday afternoon baseball game. Palm Beach's pet sport is played at nearby **Palm Beach Polo and Country Club** and Boca Raton's **Royal Palm Polo Club**. Here, some of the top matches in the world have attracted players as illustrious as Great Britain's Prince Charles. You must be either rich or an expert with a wealthy sponsor to participate. But it costs little to watch from your car or camper. More than 20 area polo fields host matches from October to July.

The other Palm Beach: West Palm Beach, across Lake Worth, was conceived as an asterisk by its rich patron Flagler. It was reserved for servants, gardeners and other peons who toiled to

Cornelius Vanderbilt (far right) and friends at the Royal Poinciana, 1896.

keep Palm Beach from crumbling while their employers partied, shopped, played polo, and made more money. In fact, Palm Beach still parks its garbage trucks around here.

The drab downtown has no pretensions, but may prove a refreshing change from the rarefied air of Palm Beach. And it has things the beach hasn't – including a new **Palm Hotel**, with convention facilities and international-standard service, at Okeechobee and Australian boulevards.

Nearby **Belle Glade** and **Clewiston** have come into their own as commercial centers for the forests of sugar cane that dominate much of Palm Beach County. They produce enough sugar to supply more than 15 million Americans for an entire year. Try sucking the delicious sap right out of the cane.

Construction, real estate and banking are other major Palm Beach County industries. **Palm Beach Gardens** is headquarters for the Professional Golfers Association (PGA), which has given its initials to one of that town's main thoroughfares. The PGA operates a housing development with four championship golf courses and a **Gold Hall of Fame**. Palm Beach Gardens is also home of the National Croquet Association, which holds international tournaments each year.

Fifteen miles west of downtown is **Lion Country Safari**. The well-fed lions have grown lazy, but it's thrilling to watch one lead a parade of cars or see a giraffe peering in your window. Keep your windows closed, though.

You can stop off and pick your own oranges at **Anthony Groves** on State Road 7. Some 17,000 citrus trees bloom here in the winter months. **Knollwood Groves** south of Lake Worth offers wagon train rides.

Planets and movie stars: Highway A1A curves back to the beach over Blue Heron Boulevard. You can follow it through the high-rises of **Singer Island** all the way to **Jupiter**. Although considerably south of Kennedy Space Center, this town once was a terminal for the Celestial Railroad, which took

alm Beach's
ve-star
reakers
otel.

its name from the stations it served – Juno, Neptune, Mars and Venus, as well as Jupiter. Flagler bypassed this peninsula with his railroad, so it has remained less developed. A monument in Jupiter marks the site of the abandoned Celestial track.

A red brick lighthouse juts from a mound at Jupiter Inlet. Climb it for a view of the Gulf Stream – a veritable river in the Atlantic Ocean – then quench your thirst at **Harpoon Louie's** across the water. Barefoot mailmen once began their long trek from here to Miami. Visit the home of Harry DuBois on the shell mound for insights into those days.

Jupiter is famous as the hometown of actor Burt Reynolds. His dad once served as the town sheriff and still operates the **Burt Reynolds Ranch Tack and Feed Store** on Jupiter Farms Road off Indiantown Road.

Burt and his wife Lonnie Anderson are frequently seen in the area. The **Jupiter Theater**, formerly the Burt Reynolds Theater, stages top plays with stars like Sally Fields, Farrah Fawcett, Carol Burnett, Martin Sheen and occasionally, Burt himself.

The mansions of **Jupiter Island** house millionaires who don't like Palm Beach. But the owners are equally wary of tourists. You will find no hotels, convenience stores or gas stations here. Police pull over any vehicles that stray off public roads into narrow, private drives. Photo-electric beams along the roadways tell police the direction of a vehicle at night. Still, it's worth a look. Turn off US 1 to State Road 707 through an archway of overhanging trees.

Australian pines, tall palms and bushy fuchsia hide most homes. Expensive yachts huddle along the shore. In 1961 a circuit court judge upheld restrictive zoning laws here when he said Jupiter Island "was cut from one mold and its counterpart cannot be found elsewhere. Many people would consider it dead – but it is very much alive with genteel living, friendship and compatibility. The town doesn't want what many others have, but many others would be better off if they had more of what this town

Palm Beach and the Roya Poinciana Bridge.

has and wants to keep – seclusion, solitude and tranquility."

Rivers, turtles and rocks: In Martin County, to the north off US 1, **Jonathan Dickinson State Park** preserves the last wild river in southeast Florida. You can paddle your canoe along the upper Loxahatchee River past alligators half-submerged in the water, and rarities like the bald eagle. **Trapper Nelson's camp** upriver can be reached by canoe or via the *Loxahatchee Queen* river cruise. Trapper was a folk hero who opened a zoo here where he wrestled alligators and devoured raw possum. His property made him a millionaire, but health officials closed the zoo and he retreated into isolation, discouraging visitors with his shotgun. When police found him dead with a bullet in his head, some suspected foul play because he had been holding up an important multi-million dollar land deal.

Dickinson Park rolls through tall sand dunes that peak at **Hobe Mountain**, an 86-foot sand pile with a 22-foot observation deck. It is the highest point above sea level in South Florida. Jonathan Dickinson was shipwrecked here in 1696. Indians stripped him, but he escaped to St Augustine.

The **St Lucie River** splits into two forks at **Stuart**. This stream and the **Caloosahatchee River** form the **Okeechobee Waterway**, used by thousands of craft annually. The *MV East Chop*, run by **Hyline Cruises** of Stuart, takes you into wilderness on the St Lucie Canal locks, through orange and lemon groves to Lake Okeechobee, and back.

Turtles attract tourists to **Jensen Beach**. Large loggerheads and green sea turtles crawl out of the ocean at night each May to lay eggs in the sand.

Hutchinson Island has rocky cliffs where the **House of Refuge Museum** can be visited. High on stilts on Highway A1A, it is the only one still standing of six lifesaving stations for sailors built more than 100 years ago. Locals call the outcroppings along this beach, unusual for Florida, "worm rocks."

Look for Florida's largest Chinese vegetable plantation, the **Sang Yick**

Farm, west of **Hobe Sound**. It does no retail business but you'll find exotics like bok choy, woo, okra and long beans growing here.

The inn that drifted in: Fort Pierce concentrated on the shipping and processing of Indian River citrus products for decades, but it now also draws its share of tourists to resorts and luxury campgrounds. Within the city's limits is the **Savannahs Wilderness Area**, akin to the Everglades. The drives up State Road 707 or Highway A1A to the city are particularly scenic.

Vero Beach's landmark is a rickety-looking complex called the **Driftwood Inn**. Eccentric entrepreneur Waldo Sexton fashioned it from just that. Its newer additions have gone condo, but visitors can snack in its dining room or stroll through this impromptu architectural jumble perched like a shipwreck on the tideline. So improbable is the construction, it looks as if a simple tug might bring the whole thing down. Yet it has withstood high waves and fierce hurricanes ever since the 1930s.

Each bedroom in the original section is unique. An assortment of unmatched windows on one side adds to the odd appearance. Cannons from Spanish ships sunk offshore, hand-painted ceramic tiles, ornate church windows, rusting iron chains, and bells, bells, bells hang in the halls and rooms. Sexton loved bells. Appropriately, a statue of Miguel de Cervantes, author of *Don Quixote*, greets you at the main entrance. It's carved from a single piece of walnut.

Another Sexton creation, the **Ocean Grill**, serves dinner a stroll away up the beach. Its bar extends over the beach where windows mist with sea spray. Also in Vero Beach, the **Indian River Island Sanctuary** can be reached by a footbridge at the end of Dahlia Lane.

Thirteen miles north of the city near **Sebastian** in the Indian River is **Pelican Island**, the nation's oldest wildlife sanctuary. Established in 1905, the 7,000-acre refuge is the breeding place for that awkwardly built bird that flies so gracefully. Rent a boat for a close look, but obey signs warning: "Stay Off the Island."

Sebastian Inlet Park on the ocean is considered excellent for fishing. **McLarty State Museum** is on the site of an old Spanish salvage camp. Archaeologists believe an Indian mound near the inlet may contain the skeletal remains of some of the first European settlers of Florida. Researchers think shipwreck survivors may have lived with the Ais tribe at least three years before the founding of St Augustine. Documents in Spanish archives indicate that two men picked up by a French ship testified to their capture by the barbaric tribe in 1562. Researchers say a large cross of conch shells found over the grave of a chief of the extinct tribe indicates someone had introduced the Indians to Christianity.

Florida's best, and virtually only, surfing action is on the East Coast's Atlantic waves. The implacable Gulf of Mexico provides little surf (except during hurricanes) and caters to windsurfers instead. Most non-wind enthusiasts "hang ten" in the wavey regions from Sebastian Inlet to Daytona Beach.

Left, Palm Beach is known for its golf. Right, balloon cruises are one way to see Florida.

INLAND SOUTH FLORIDA

Inland southern Florida revolves around enormous **Lake Okeechobee**. This is Florida Cracker country, as lazy and laid back as other sparsely settled spots in the United States. Cowboys and Indians raise cattle and sugar cane, fish and hunt. Migrant workers come and go. Travel the main routes like US 27 up through the Everglades and cane fields from Miami, US 441 or 90 from West Palm Beach. You'll find ghost towns and wisps of towns. Veer off onto some of the smaller roads, if you can find any. You might see a Seminole roping a calf or a Jamaican immigrant cutting cane.

The "Big Water": Lake Okeechobee's name comes from an Indian word meaning "big water." Okeechobee is 750 square miles of crystal waters, Florida's largest lake and the second largest freshwater body within the boundaries of a single state. It has been both a blessing and a curse to the people who live nearby.

Early settlers to **LaBelle** and **Clewiston** watched two hurricanes spin flood waters from the lake over their fields and homes. More than 1,800 persons died during the destruction, but an exact body count proved impossible.

A system of dikes, pumping stations, spillways and canals has tamed Okeechobee and helped turn some surrounding mucklands into an agricultural paradise of vegetables and sugar cane. Fish camps and resorts punctuate the lake's perimeter. Okeechobee is the centerpiece of a water-control district stretching from Orlando to Miami. The US Army Corps of Engineers controls the level of water; some environmentalists contend it is to the detriment of the Everglades. Both the Everglades and South Florida's cities have been threatened with drought in recent years by the dwindling water level of the lake. Excessive pumping for the booming population growth along the Gold Coast have been sucking it dry.

You won't see mighty Okeechobee from US 27 as you drive from Belle Glade to Clewiston. The 35-foot-high Hoover Dike, which took 40 years to build, obscures the view.

Clewiston is headquarters for the US Sugar Corporation, the south's largest sugar mill. The **Clewiston Inn** is a homey hotel you would expect to find in such a city. City promoters like to call Clewiston "the sweetest town in America." Be prepared for an interminable procession of signs along western US 27 imploring you to eat at the **Old South Bar-B-Q Ranch**. The annual Swamp Cabbage Festival here brings out country-western bands and cloggers, who take part in an energetic, arm-waving, stomping dance from the mountains that has become popular here.

Moore Haven, on the Caloosahatchee River, caters to truckers and bass fishermen. Here, a lock allows access from the lake to Fort Myers, 50 miles west. This is the final link in a chain of waterways connecting the Atlantic Ocean to the Gulf of Mexico.

Up State Road 78 toward the town of **Okeechobee**, you'll pass by the **Calusa**

Tractor-pull contest.

Lodge, a resort for hunters and fishermen whose trophies adorn its restaurant walls. Even the wild boars were bagged nearby. Seminole Indians often lunch here, not far from the **Brighton Indian Reservation**. These early Florida inhabitants have used their land for cattle farming and turned it into big business.

Okeechobee is the largest town on the north shore of the lake, another center for vegetables grown on thousands of acres of drained muckland. The city holds a Speckled Perch Festival on the second Saturday of March, drawing thousands to a fish fry. Labor Day brings in the Cattlemen's Association Rodeo. The Rodeo Bowl itself is east of the lake near **Indiantown**.

Sucking sap from a cypress knee: West of Lake Okeechobee, US 27 travels to two old-time attractions that entertained early tourists. **Gatorland** will allow the kids a close-up look at snakes and other reptiles, peacocks and raccoons. You may well be the only customers, so prepare to enjoy a personalized visit.

A line of tree limbs beg you to stop at Tom Gaskins' **Cypress Knee Museum**, just north of Fisheating Creek in **Palmdale**. Gaskins began collecting knees, the gnarled roots that poke from the ground around the trees, in 1934 when he noticed their natural shapes resembled dolphins, insects, bears, people and even famous faces. Customers began buying them as souvenirs of Florida's wilder side. Gaskins will show you how he peels and preserves the knees, how you can make a meal from them by sucking on the nutritious sap, and how they grow along the catwalk he himself built through an oak and cabbage hammock and a cypress swamp (now drying up) adjoining his workshop and showroom. Across US 27 he has preserved some of his favorite finds in a museum. There you will find the "Mona Lisa," "FDR," "Joseph Stalin," and several "Madonnas."

Instead of the standard Mickey Mouse ears or bushel of oranges, you may wish to take home a cypress knee, a glass-top tree table, a turkey call or some driftwood from Gaskins' place.

rop-dusting
gar cane
ear the
ighty
keechobee.

Bird
Observation Area

THE EVERGLADES

If the founding forefathers' foresight had inspired them to preserve natural treasures when they drew up the Constitution, they might have roped off Florida's northern boundary and declared the entire state a national park. Fortunately, latter-day leaders stepped in before all was lost to the plow and bulldozer. In 1947 they established **Everglades National Park** encompassing 1.4 million acres, or most of Florida's southern tip – an area larger than the state of Delaware.

Unlike the Grand Canyon, Niagara Falls, Yellowstone and other national jewels, the Everglades does not overwhelm the casual visitor with majestic vistas. On the contrary, the seas of sawgrass that stretch in all directions, embellished only by island hammocks of hardwood trees, sparse stands of cypress and slash pines and clumps of mangroves, may strike many as boring.

But don't let this dull facade deter you from dipping down the Florida peninsula to the Everglades. It's just a clever disguise that cloaks a fascinating blend of earthy and watery environments, tropical and temperate species of plant and animal life and a laboratory where Nature experiments with her cycles of life and death.

Everglades National Park actually represents only a fraction of a slow-flowing river called *Pa-hay-okee* – "the grassy waters" – by Indians. An English surveyor dubbed it the "River Glades," but later English maps corrupted "river" to "ever" and the present name that seems so perfect came into common use during the 19th century.

To find the source of this "River of Grass," look north to the lakes of Central Florida's Kissimmee Valley which feed the mighty Lake Okeechobee, which in turn supplies the Everglades.

The beauty of the Everglades must be sampled slowly. Treat it like you would a bottle of good wine. Inhale its fragrance, sip its essence, swirl it on your palate, eye its color and texture. That's the only way to appreciate the subtleties of its splendors.

A fragile environment: The Glades flow for 200 miles, bulging up to 70 miles in width, at an average depth of only 6 inches that rise and fall during rainy and dry seasons. It oozes down a gradual incline in Florida's surface that drops only 15 feet over hundreds of miles. Above ground waters move southwest to the Gulf of Mexico and, underground, they seep through porous limestone foundations east to the Atlantic Coastal Ridge that stretches from Fort Lauderdale to Long Pine Key. Its fresh water finally mixes with salt seas.

The Everglades is unique. Nearly 300 varieties of birds, 600 kinds of fish and countless mammals call it home. It even has 45 indigenous species of plants found nowhere else. Geologists and geographers say there is nothing quite like the Everglades anywhere else in the world. Unfortunately, there may soon be nothing at all like it in the world.

Some experts believe it is only a matter of a few decades before man's as-

Preceding pages: see *Travel Tips* for identification of birds. Left, wading into the Glades. Below, airboat cruise.

sault on South Florida irreversibly alters the fragile environment of the Everglades. Dikes and 1,500 miles of canals carved out of the landscape by man crisscross the once free-flowing river and impede its normal fluctuations in water levels. In fact, the Army Corps of Engineers has reversed these natural cycles, opening watergates and flooding fields in winter when the Glades should be dry, and curbing the flow in summer when South Florida should be submerged in water from torrential thunderstorms. The rich marl or muck built up from hundreds of centuries of rotting sawgrass has been plowed and seeded and has sprouted into sugar cane and vegetable farms, further upsetting the delicate ecological balance of the region. And populous cities of the Gold Coast and lower West Coast have plugged into its aquifer like leeches, draining precious reserves for their washing machines, swimming pools and toilets. The Glades is so dry during some springtimes that fires regularly rage out of control, consuming sawgrass

and hardwoods and robbing wildlife of its traditional habitats.

Shark Valley area park ranger Bill Wise warns that the Everglades may cease to exist within 20 years. "It's such a fragile environment. There's got to be water and there's got to be cycles and right now man has screwed up the water levels and screwed up the cycles. The park tries to exist on what water we get after the people in town get it."

Man's mistakes: Wise likens the Everglades environment to a tapestry in which every thread depends upon another for its survival. "If the water levels continually stay low, everything's going to die. If you don't have naturally fluctuating water levels, you won't have periphyton (algae) matter that little critters feed on. So the little critters will die and the bigger critters that depend on them for survival have nothing to eat. The food chain collapses."

The Everglades evolved during 6 million years or so of shifting sea action and limestone build up. But it has come to the brink of extinction in less than a

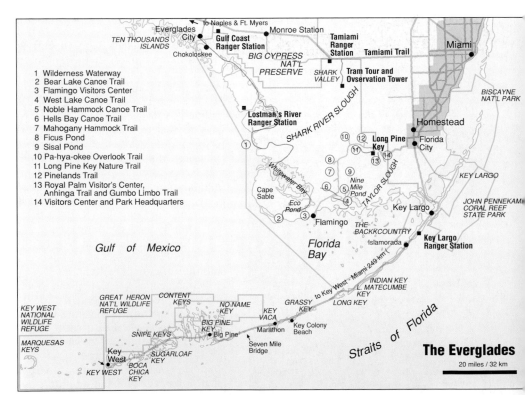

1 Wilderness Waterway
2 Bear Lake Canoe Trail
3 Flamingo Visitors Center
4 West Lake Canoe Trail
5 Noble Hammock Canoe Trail
6 Hells Bay Canoe Trail
7 Mahogany Hammock Trail
8 Ficus Pond
9 Sisal Pond
10 Pa-hya-okee Overlook Trail
11 Long Pine Key Nature Trail
12 Pinelands Trail
13 Royal Palm Visitor's Center, Anhinga Trail and Gumbo Limbo Trail
14 Visitors Center and Park Headquarters

The Everglades

20 miles / 32 km

century. Its chief enemy, man, first infiltrated its hammocks about 2,000 years ago with the arrival of early Indians. But the Calusas more often than not lived in harmony with the Glades.

The first white man to roam the Everglades appears to have been Hernando Escalante de Fontaneda, a Spaniard who washed up in the Keys after a shipwreck and lived among Indians for 17 years. He penned a vivid account of how the Calusas, Tequestas and Mayaimis lived throughout the Glades and South Florida. But it wasn't until the 1880s that man began efforts to drain what was simply considered useless swampland. Governor Napoleon Bonaparte Broward threw the government into the efforts and, by 1909, the Miami Canal that connects Lake Okeechobee to Miami became the main conduit in a network of waterways through the Everglades. The hurricanes of 1926 and 1928 that dumped Lake Okeechobee onto the heads of thousands of South Florida settlers sparked the involvement of the Army Corps of Engineers. It promptly ringed the lake, the core of the Everglades, with Hoover Dike in 1930.

Ironically, another 1947 hurricane that flooded Dade County dramatized the chaos caused by the uncontrolled dike and canal construction in the Everglades. It led to creation of the predecessor of the present-day South Florida Water Management District that has come to be known as Swiftmud. Meanwhile, efforts by the Audubon Society (to control the ruthless slaughter of birds for plumes), the Florida Federation of Women's Clubs and the Tropical Everglades National Park Commission culminated in dedication of the area as a National Park by Harry S. Truman in 1947. After realizing the Everglades system also depended on the survival of surrounding systems, the adjacent Big Cypress National Preserve was established in 1974.

But the summer of 1992 brought a devastating blow to the Glades when Hurricane Andrew ripped through the park leaving a 35-mile swath of destruction behind. As the hurricane's winds buzzsawed through, the Glades' vast ecosystem was swept into a violent turmoil. Dense forests of mangroves, pines and palms were sucked out by the roots and carried away. Thousands of birds either flew or were blown away. Thousands of animals, reptiles and fish were killed; many more were left homeless when their natural habitat was ravished.

The developed tourist areas of the park, like Shark Valley and the main entrance visitor center near Florida City, crumbled like matchsticks. Damages to the park grounds, ranger stations, walkways, observations decks, marinas, campsites, and information centers was estimated at over $25 million. It took several months after the storm to clean up the mess before visitors were allowed back in. Many of the park's amenities and tourist centers have been rebuilt, others are still awaiting reconstruction.

Ecologists don't know for sure how severely the plant and wildlife will be affected in the decades to come because this is the first time they have experienced such a large area of destruction.

Some, more pragmatic than others, regarded Hurricane Andrew's damage as Mother Nature's way of cleaning house. They say that it was meant to be, and that with time, the ecosystem will rejuvenate itself.

A Glades glossary: The Everglades possesses a variety of ecosystems essential to its maintenance. Among them:

● **Hardwood Hammock**, a big "island" likened by ranger Wise to a castle with a moat around it. These high and dry mounds of dead plant matter provide ground for the growth of cabbage palms, strangler figs, West Indian mahogany, gumbo limbo trees and satin leaf hardwoods. During high-water seasons, bob-cats, deer, otters, raccoons and opossums find refuge here.

● **Heads**, smaller shallower islands where the cocoplum, red bay, sweet bay and magnolia wax myrtle grow. They do not have the limestone mound base of the hardwood hammocks.

● **Willows**, the light green tails of vegetation that fill the deep water surrounding some hammocks. They are the home of the Everglades' most renowned inhabitant, the alligator. Seen from above, willows look like doughnuts with the nucleus of water in the middle called a solution hole or gator hole. Here, alligators soak, feed once every few weeks, and sink down out of the sun.

● **Saw grass prairie**, that fabled expanse of thin spiny-edged vegetation that seems to dominate the Everglades.

● **Fresh water sloughs** (pronounced "slews"), channels of fresh water, like the major one in the Shark River Valley, that act as reservoirs and supply routes. They help plants and animals survive during the dry season.

● **Pinelands**, found in elevated areas of bare limestone outcroppings. Fire is necessary to their existence, because it cleans out competing vegetation.

● **Cypress eco-systems**, which contain bald and stunted varieties of this cousin of California's redwoods. Dripping with Spanish moss, they give the Glades its swampy reputation.

● **Coastal prairies**, containing salt-tolerant plants like cactus, yucca and prickly pear. A home to marsh rabbits.

● **Mangrove estuary** rims the southwest edge of the Glades, acting as a coastal barrier against high storm surges. The leaf of the mangrove provides food for microscopic animals, that are, in turn, eaten by larger animals.

For a crash course in identifying these critical features of the Everglades, and your best introduction to the "River of Grass," begin your expedition at the **Visitor Center** at the national park's main entrance on State Road 9336.

Bring the bug spray: The National Park Service had the presence of mind to lay a single paved road into the heart of the Everglades and attach side roads to trails and boardwalks. But that is as far as the park service has gone in tampering with nature for the convenience of man. So, pack a pint of insect repellent. Mosquitoes, deer flies and other biting bugs can be vicious, particularly during the wet summer season.

The Visitor Center sells repellent and provides maps, brochures and displays to help you fully appreciate your visit; it also has a brief film worth viewing.

A purple gallinule.

State Road 9336 is the main road into, and out of, Everglades National Park. It is about 38 miles to its southwest deadend at **Flamingo**. But even if you are wedded to your car, make sure you detour to at least a few of the other visitor centers, trails and observation decks along the way.

The **Royal Palm Visitor Center**, the first stop just 2 miles from the park entrance, has an easy trail through a typical hardwood hammock, named for the gumbo limbo tree, a common sight along the path. Here, you will find ferns, air plants and a cool, rain forest-type-environment. Carefully examine tree limbs for the dazzling *Liguus* snail found only on these hammocks and in Cuba and Hispaniola. There's also the **Anhinga Trail** boardwalk into a willow head at the tip of **Taylor Slough**. Yes, the lumps you see in the water are the eyes of live alligators.

Long Pine Key features a 7-mile nature trail that winds through a typical pinelands ecosystem. There are also campgrounds and picnic areas. You will

drive over **Rock Reef Pass**, all of 3 feet above sea level to **Pa-hay-okee Overlook**, an observation tower in a hardwood hammock edged with cypress stands and a fresh water slough. There are about 100 species of grass in the Everglades and most can be observed from the boardwalk, although you may find it impossible to distinguish between beard-grass, coinwort, marsh fleabane, love-vine, creeping Charlie and ludwigia. Saw grass, ironically, is not a true grass, but a sedge.

Mahogany Hammock Trail winds under some of the largest mahogany trees in the continental United States. Rare paurotis palms, stretching 12 to 30 feet high, flank **Paurotis Pond** and its plethora of wildlife. The **Nine Mile Pond** sits in freshwater marl prairie and a mangrove estuary.

Paddlers are faced with a choice further down the road. **The Noble Hammock Canoe Trail**, named after a legendary Everglades bootlegger, traverses a 2½-mile loop through mangrove clusters. **The Hell's Bay Trail**, as its name

The great blue heron.

implies, is for prepared and experienced canoeists. It leads 5 miles deep into uncharted parts of the Everglades referred to as the backcountry and can take an entire day to paddle. The **West Lake** footpath wriggles through sawgrass and cattails. Pink shrimp feed and reproduce among the mangroves in places like this before maturing and migrating to the Gulf of Mexico.

Winging it in Flamingo: Once an isolated fishing village accessible only by boat, **Flamingo** now exists mainly as an isolated colony catering to tourism in Everglades National Park. There are 235 motor campsites, 60 tent plots, and, for the less hardy and traditional, 120 motel rooms at the Flamingo Lodge. During the high winter and spring book a room well in advance.

Check with the ranger station or Lodge office for a schedule of activities. If you have brought your own boat or hiking gear, be sure to file float or walk plans with the ranger station before disappearing into the backcountry. Even skilled sportsmen and locals have been known to vanish into the maze of mangroves, rivers and bays – for good. Otherwise, you can rent a boat or whatever equipment you need. You can even move into a fully-equipped houseboat and cruise the waterways in comfort.

The **Flamingo Marina** is the southern terminus of the 100-mile **Wilderness Waterway** which begins way up at the Everglades City end of the park. It proceeds south through such alluring niches as **Chokoloskee Island**, the **Lopez River**, **Sunday Bay**, **Alligator Bay**, **Big Lostman's Bay**, **Cabbage Island**, the **Wood River**, and the **Shark River**. At **Canepatch** you will find wild sugar cane growing among wild limes, banana and papaya, evidence of Calusa and Seminole Indian settlements that survived until 1928.

Shark River is one of the park's most popular fishing areas, featuring 45 species, including snook, redfish, sea trout, the silvery tarpon, grouper and snapper. **Gunboat Island**, named for its unusal shape. Enormous **Whitewater Bay** pours into **Buttonwood Canal** which

Look before you leap.

carries you to the Flamingo Marina.

Of course, Flamingo offers shorter cruises and walks. Tour boats will take you to the white sand shores of **Cape Sable**, the southernmost point in the continental US. Or you can boat around the clusters of keys in **Florida Bay**. The park boundaries extend to the **Intracoastal Waterway** just a few miles north of the Florida Keys. Primitive camping is permitted on **North Nest Key**, the **Rabbit Keys** and **North Sandy Keys**.

Ask directions to the **Eco-pond**, a short walk from the Flamingo Lodge. Ibis, herons, osprey and egrets hang out here. Most notable are the scarlet roseate spoonbills, thought to have inspired the village's name when early settlers mistook them for flamingos.

Good, but easy, hiking trails near Flamingo include the **Snake Bight,** through tropical hardwoods to a boardwalk over Florida Bay; **Rowdy Bend**, under Spanish moss and brilliant red bromeliads; **Christian Point**, winds past giant wild pine bromeliads attached to the trees; and **Bear Lake**, a trail formed by fill from the **Homestead Canal**.

Over the Loop Road: There is another wheeled way of penetrating Everglades National Park, but you must drive all the way back to Homestead and north on the Florida Turnpike, then west on **Tamiami Trail**, nearly 50 miles, to get there. The **Shark Valley** entrance station is across the street from the **Miccosukee Village and Culture Center**. In the summer, most of this freshwater slough is underwater. But in the winter, the park operates a tram ride through the sawgrass prairie (teeming with wildlife) and up to an observation tower. Alligators congregate in willows at the foot of the tower. They make a variety of sounds. A hiss is warning that they are annoyed and you should stay out of their way.

You can also walk or bike the tram route. The **Otter Cave Hammock Nature Trail** has a pamphlet to guide you. Tread softly and you may see otters munching on live frogs' legs in the trough beside the road. The splashes are probably garfish.

verglades
ational Park
anger in a
hortcut
rough the
wamp.

recently caught up with it, and about 200 full-time residents still get only fuzzy black-and-white pictures on their sets. The Sea World marine park chain that has branches in Orlando, Cleveland and San Diego established a **Shark Institute** here next door to the lovely **Lime Tree Bay Resort**. The facility is not open to the public, but many of the menacing lemon, tiger, bull, hammerhead and sawfish sharks on view at Sea World in Central Florida are graduates of the institute. The sharks were caught within a 5-mile radius of Long Key.

The most famous graduate of a training academy that made the next island, **Grassy Key**, prominent was the dolphin Flipper of the television series. **Hawk's Cay Resort**, which has held a four-star rating, is one of the few places in the Keys where guests can, for a fee, swim with resident dolphins. Grassy Key lies at the other end of Long Key Viaduct. The bridge skirts minuscule **Duck** and **Conch Keys** en route.

By now, the names and characteristics of each key begin to blur. There's **Key Colony Beach** and **Crawl Key**. You begin to feel as though you have finally left civilization behind. Then the metropolis of **Marathon** on **Key Vaca** leaps out to spoil that thought.

Not quite Seven Mile Bridge: With a colossal population of about 10,000, Marathon boasts no less than three shopping centers. It masquerades as a resort town, but comes across as an urban hamlet plastered together by blue-collar workers lonely for Pennsylvania.

Knight's Key is the gateway to one of the nation's first great engineering marvels, the **Seven Mile Bridge**. The span, actually 110 feet short of 7 miles, is laser straight except for a bend at **Pigeon Key**. It was the crowning achievement of Henry Morrison Flagler's 8-year battle against nature and the elements while building his Overseas Railroad. About 700 men were killed on the job, which concluded when Flagler, then 82, rode the first train into Key West on January 22, 1912 – that city's biggest celebration to date. By rail and steamer, the round-trip fare from Miami to Havana, Cuba, via Key West was $24.

The 1935 hurricane put the railroad out of commission. The state replaced it with a road using Flagler's bridges and foundations. One old mileage marker found on Big Pine Key has been roped off by road crews because of its historical value. The Seven Mile Bridge, a hair-raisingly narrow structure, was replaced by a shorter, modern bridge.

The magnificent ride over the Gulf of Mexico and Atlantic runs aground again in the vicinity of **Ohio Key**, which developers have renamed Sunshine Key. Continue to **Bahia Honda**, where the rickety old bridge that parallels a newer one provides a glimpse into the past. The recreation area has campsites, which should be reserved well in advance, and one of the best beaches in the Keys.

A big island with little deer: Bahia Honda, Spanish for "Deep Bay," marks the eastern boundary of the **National Key Deer Refuge**. Bridges across more blips of land lead to **Big Pine Key**, an island second in size only to Key Largo in the chain. This is the heart of deer country, as the signs warn. Follow these markers

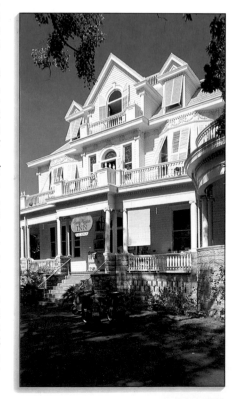

to the headquarters of the refuge on Watson Boulevard. Freshwater ponds and groves of Caribbean pines, nestled in the fossil coral and oölitic limestone that compose Big Pine, make you feel like you are back on the mainland. This key is so different from the others in the chain, some geologists believe it is part of the Appalachian Ridge forced up during a tumultuous period in the earth's infancy.

The star attraction here is a colony of diminutive deer, a subspecies of the Virginia white-tail. The animals grow to about 30 inches in height and up to 38 inches in length. Hunters and developers reduced the population to less than 50 by 1947, but efforts by the refuge have boosted numbers to several hundred.

About two-thirds of the deer live on Big Pine and **No Name Key**, although a few have been spotted on 14 neighboring islands. Rangers say the best times to see Key deer is in the early morning or late afternoon.

Overnight camping is prohibited on Big Pine, and housing subdivisions criss-

cross the refuge land. But near the end of State Road 94, **Pine Woods Nature Trail** leads through the hardwood Watson Hammock. South of the trail is an old rock quarry, the Blue Hole, brimming with fresh water. Here, alligators lurk and Key Deer drink.

An aquatic showcase: Before leaving Big Pine, avid snorkelers and divers should consider a boat trip to **Looe Key Reef**, said to be one of the world's most sensational aquatic showcases.

Further down the Overseas Highway, the **Torch Keys** are named for their flammable trees. Just off the **Little Torch Key** is a private island that houses the very secluded and very expensive **Little Palm Island** resort. Accessible by a ferry that departs from the Overseas Highway on Little Torch Key, Little Palm is made of 14 thatch-roof villas and caters to an elite clientele. The resort's restaurant, however, is open to the public.

Summerland offers some scenic side roads and **Cudjoe Key** some modern campsites for large trailers. **Sugar Loaf Key**, named for an Indian midden that looked like loaves of old-fashioned sugar, has a tall wooden tower, one of a pair built during World War I as boarding houses for bats. A local businessman imported bats in the hope they would swallow the island's mosquito problem – but once released from the tower, they never returned. The seas and keys to the north of Sugar Loaf are part of the **Great White Heron National Wildlife Refuge**.

The **Saddlebunch Keys** are little more than a series of mangrove outcroppings. **Big Coppit**, **Rockland** and **East Rockland** house the servicemen of the US Naval Air Station on **Boca Chica**, "Little Mouth" Key. **Stock Island**, once a center for cattle herds and pigpens, serves as a suburb to Key West and is the home of the **Tennessee Williams Fine Arts Center**.

Before crossing the next bridge, prepare yourself for the short hop into another, very different, world. You have literally reached the end of the road. Some even call it the end of the world. This is **Key West**.

Left, San Carlos Institute, Key West. **Right**, cruising the Keys.

KEY WEST

Key West was a town where you had to pick and choose. It was always a favorite of pirates.

—Thomas McGuane in
Ninety-two in the Shade

The gateway to Key West is as prosaic as any in Florida. US 1 deposits automobiles into a twisted intersection that forks into North and South Roosevelt Boulevards. The latter road rims the Atlantic Ocean, which washes the shore on the left, and passes pungent salt flats of bygone industry on the right, finally dribbling into an oblivion of cement block-houses. North Roosevelt runs smack into Searstown and the modern rubble of any resort city – Holiday Inn, Days Inn, Burger King and company.

But the character of the town inevitably changes, slowly at first, then suddenly. Tacky neon storefronts begin to alternate with dignified old homes bur-

ied under fragrant pink blooms of frangipani. Legions of cats scramble along narrow alleys that cry out to be explored. The American flavor of fast-food emporiums and clean white houses evaporates in an ambience that's not quite Bahamian, not quite Cuban, not quite nautical… just very Key West.

Eventually you wind up on Duval Street, which bisects Old Town. Here, bars, shops and homes – some restored, some still crumbling – merge in a collage of discordant color that somehow suits this city. The people who blend into this bizarre landscape are as incongruous as the colors. Among them are long-haired survivors of the hippie era, impeccably groomed gay couples, leather-faced fishermen, and jet-setters in color-coordinated tennis ensembles. Only in Key West could so much so different seem so right.

Island of Bones: The uniqueness of Key West derives in large part from its history as a haven for transients from the ends of the earth. Its proximity to the US mainland and the West Indies has intro-

Revelers toast the setting sun…

duced many cultural influences, but its relative isolation from both has left it to develop in its own special way.

Somehow, the Calusa Indians managed to get to this speck 100 miles from the Florida peninsula, 90 miles from Cuba, 66 miles north of the Tropic of Cancer. Traces of even earlier inhabitants have occasionally been uncovered. Journalist-historian Wright Langley once stumbled upon some human bones on US Navy property, reviving tales that a cannibalistic tribe had inhabited Key West – though most historians laugh off the stories.

But mid-18th century Spanish explorers said they found this place buried in human bones, a tale that may have led to its Spanish name of *Caya Hueso*, "Island of Bones." The name eventually was anglicized into Key West, although a handful of keys lie further west.

In addition to the Calusas, who had good reason for developing a hostile streak toward Europeans, equally savage pirates made the Keys a risky place to settle. In fact, a young Spanish caval-

ryman – granted Key West by his governor in 1815 – gladly sold it six years later for just $2,000 to an Alabama businessman, John Simonton. The United States government stepped in by 1822, after Simonton split his holdings with John Whitehead, Pardon C. Greene and John Fleming. Commodore David Porter added the first naval presence and systematically wiped out piracy. Construction of a naval base and lighthouse and incorporation of the city of Key West followed.

Cuban migrants brought cigar-making along with their rich culture, and Key West brands eventually became more prized than those from Havana.

Sponge fishermen also prospered. But the Key West economy was built on wrecking. Treacherous reefs, sand bars and unpredictable weather turned the surrounding waters into an "elephants' graveyard" for ships laden with treasures from the Caribbean, South America and Europe.

Lawmakers attempted to bring order to the ensuing plunder as Key West

became a center of salvage operations. Licensed boat captains posted a watch: when the words "Wreck ashore!" ripped through the town's balmy air, the race to the floundering boat was on. The first ship to arrive at the wreck was legally entitled to strip it – after rescuing any remaining passengers. The trade became so lucrative, and sinkings so frequent, that the courts eventually wised up to under-handed schemes. Cargo ship captains were conspiring with wrecking crews to waste their vessels deliberately, then split the booty.

Meanwhile, the US government poured millions into the economy. Fort Zachary Taylor's position was substantially strengthened with the addition of the Martello Towers and Fort Jefferson in the Dry Tortugas.

All this activity combined to boost population to 18,000 by 1888, making Key West Florida's largest city. It also became the richest city per capita in the United States, a distinction that lasted through the turn of the century. Completion of the Overseas Railroad in 1912

added another dimension to the booming economy – tourism.

Yet by 1930, Key West faced collapse. The stock market crash of 1929, coupled with the closing of the US Naval station and disease in the sponge beds, began a decline that climaxed with the destruction of the railroad in the 1935 hurricane. Labor troubles forced cigar makers to Tampa. The population declined. But the "Bubbas" – long-time residents who compose the core of Key West's native-born Conch population – stayed and put the pieces back together.

Ships, trains and trolleys: World War II provided a catalyst when the Navy reclaimed its island facilities. President Harry S. Truman established his "Little White House" on the base. The Cuban Missile Crisis and Bay of Pigs invasion during John F. Kennedy's presidency brought another brief wave of military money. Although not as visible as in the past, the Navy is still present in Key West, taking up almost one-quarter of the town. From the air and water, Navy

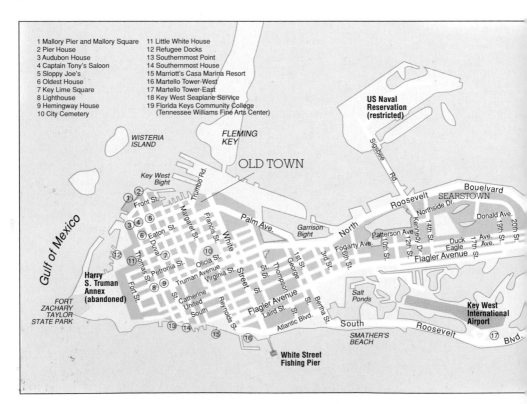

1 Mallory Pier and Mallory Square
2 Pier House
3 Audubon House
4 Captain Tony's Saloon
5 Sloppy Joe's
6 Oldest House
7 Key Lime Square
8 Lighthouse
9 Hemingway House
10 City Cemetery
11 Little White House
12 Refugee Docks
13 Southernmost Point
14 Southernmost House
15 Marriott's Casa Marina Resort
16 Martello Tower-West
17 Martello Tower-East
18 Key West Seaplane Service
19 Florida Keys Community College
   (Tennessee Williams Fine Arts Center)

berths, piers, runways, and radar towers can be seen. Tourism, shrimping and restoration now appear to be Key West's major businesses.

To follow a concise blueprint for experiencing Key West would be tantamount to replaying a completed chess match – interesting but unsatisfying. You'll want to pay homage at the Hemingway House, ride the Conch Train, and sip a margarita at Sloppy Joe's; but don't allow some pre-packaged itinerary to prevent you from straying into conversation with a crusty old Conch at the Half Shell Raw Bar. Don't rush off to make a dinner reservation if you find yourself slipping into song with a banjo player and accordionist at Mallory Pier. You are more likely to find the real Key West if you follow your adventurous inclinations instead of a tour guide.

First, you'll need a base. The island has the usual range of accommodations and then some. Many restored homes have opened their doors as guest houses, where you can watch Key West go by as you sip morning tea from a gingerbread balcony. The Spanish Renaissance-style **Marriott's Casa Marina** on Reynolds Street is another of Flagler's many monuments to luxury, also restored and catering to a new generation of big spenders under the Marriott banner. **The Pier House**, located at the northern tip of Duval Street, provides a more contemporary setting with two-story loft suites and balconies that overlook a private beach where topless sunbathing is permitted. Across the street from the Pier House is the **Ocean Key House**, another modern hotel with luxurious suites and a tropical atmosphere.

After you settle in, there are two good introductions to the scene. The venerable **Conch Train** and its newer clone, the **Old Town Trolley**, combing the streets on 1½-hour tours. These remarkable tours are very different from standard tram trips. Guides point out the city's warts and its treasures, from a "cat house where we've never seen any cats" to rookeries where winos congregate and deposit empty bottles in the gutter.

nest
emingway
th son,
mpy, at
ay in Key
est, 1928.

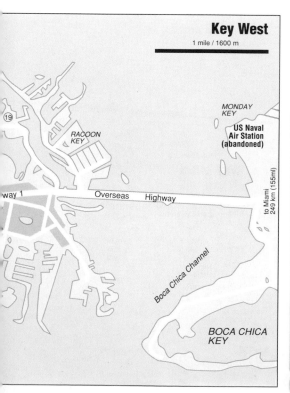

The other prerequisite for venturing out into the streets is the "**Key West Picture Show**," an award-winning, 40-minute film that captures the city's charm precisely by satirizing 1950s-style travelogues. The film features the late Reverend Furlow Weed and his wife playing the blues on horse conchs. Local saloon-keeper and former city mayor Captain Tony appears before the camera to explain one popular local pastime: "The closer to the equator, the greater the sex drive." The movie unreels at various intervals at the Conch General Store at Mallory Market.

Hemingway brawled here: Quench your thirst afterward at **Captain Tony's Saloon**, 428 Greene Street. The interior, wallpapered in business cards and newspaper clippings, will take you back to the days when the legendary Ernest Hemingway relaxed here with a drink or a fist fight after a hard day at the typewriter or fishing rod. This was the original Sloppy Joe's. Tony Tarracino, a former gambler, bootlegger and boat captain, owned the bar – considered the oldest in the state – for decades. He sold it in 1988 and a year later was elected mayor of Key West. Although Tarracino was good at cutting through bureaucratic silliness, his brash style did not sit well with the more conservative crowd and he was voted out of office at the end of his term.

The current **Sloppy Joe's** is a few steps away at the corner of Greene and Duval. Hemingway also patronized this establishment, as the writing on its facade unblushingly announces, when it was called the Midget Bar. Old photos and memorabilia recall the great writer's presence. The moth-eaten fish, mounted on the walls may or may not have been caught by him. Claims that certain artifacts belonged to Hemingway are as rampant and hard to substantiate in Key West as stories about where President George Washington slept in Washington, DC. Parachutes, which definitely have no Hemingway tie-in, hang from the ceiling and give the interior an Arabian tent aura. At night the music is loud: the crowd here likes it that way.

Pool House study where "Papa" Hemingway wrote.

212

You may as well make it a Hemingway day after the bar stops. Pay a visit to his home, now called the **Hemingway House**, on the corner of Whitehead and Olivia streets. He bought the Spanish colonial in 1931 and lived and worked there for about 10 years before moving to Cuba. In the second-floor study of the pool house out back, he wrote classics like *For Whom the Bell Tolls, A Farewell to Arms* and *The Snows of Kilimanjaro.*

Key West's popularity with creative geniuses pre-dates and post-dates Hemingway's presence. Pulitzer Prize-winning playwright Tennessee Williams, author of *The Glass Menagerie, A Streetcar Named Desire* and *Cat on a Hot Tin Roof,* lived here for 34 years until his death in 1983. He kept a low profile at a home near Duncan and Leon streets. Thomas McGuane, James Leo Herlihy, Gore Vidal and Carson McCullers all spent time inhaling the creative airs that apparently waft through the streets of Key West.

Today's generation most readily associates the city with the Bahamian-flavored ballads of pop star Jimmy Buffet and his Coral Reefer Band. After years of frequent visits, he now has a permanent Key West address and operates the **Margaritaville Cafe** on Duval Street. He is presently involved in efforts to save Florida's manatees.

John James Audubon usually heads the lists of painters associated with Key West. In actuality, the naturalist-artist spent only a few weeks here while studying and sketching Florida's countless species of birds. That tenuous connection with the city didn't stop entrepreneurs from renovating and re-opening as "Audubon House" the place where he spent those weeks. The building has been standing at Greene and Whitehead since 1830. It showcases period furnishings, including Chippendale antiques, most of them hauled off sinking ships by wreckers.

Conch House ramble: Conchs are not only shellfish and people. They are also houses. Fortunately for Florida, Key Westers have indulged in an infatuation for restoring vintage homes, a hobby

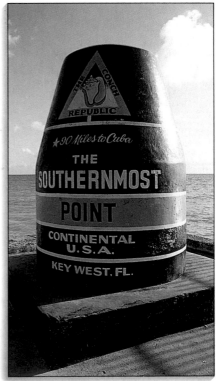

that has transformed the island into a live-in architectural museum.

There is no strict definition of a Conch House. Anything that looks like it belongs in Key West qualifies, particularly if it has gingerbread railings and expansive verandas. The styles recall Early American in New England, British Colonial in the Bahamas, the Spanish and French homes of New Orleans – often all in the same structure. Most are at least 100 years old.

Conch Houses were built in the 19th century, usually by ships' carpenters who had never designed homes before. Some of the best samples can be seen in the heart of Old Town. Start on Caroline Street where several of the old mansions have been modified into office suites. The **Captain George Carey House** at 410 is typical of Bahamian styles as is the building at 310. The **George A.T. Roberts House** at 313, with its blazing red poinciana, spacious double veranda and gingerbread trim, exemplifies Conch architecture. A building's history can also put it into the Conch House cat-

egory. The notorious **Red Door Inn** at the corner of William Street has become a legend because of the prostitution, drinking, gambling, even murder that occurred behind its red doors.

Wind up your ramble with a look at the colorful homes on Whitehead Street.

Gingerbread buffs should make it a point to take in a two-story house on Duval Street next to **La Terraza De Marti Restaurant** (which locals call "La-Te-Da"). Gingerbread is the ornamental wooden grillwork that became popular fence and veranda art in the Gay Nineties. The gingerbread here – bottles, hearts and spades – reputedly served as a surreptitious sign to sailors and other fun-seekers that they would find wine, women and gambling inside.

Sunset celebrations: Inanimate objects like homes and saloons get their real color here from the characters who people them. The Conchs, native-born, are low-key and unpretentious. Freshwater Conchs are usually a bit more flashy, but have lived here long enough to earn "bubba" status. Hippies here still paint

Conch House corner.

their homes with garish colors and pretend the '60s never ended. Transients find no more road to hitchhike down and stay awhile. Gays dress exquisitely and run many of the shops and restaurants. The total population is about 35,000, yet Key West seems to encompass more races, cultures and lifestyles than many metropolises.

For watching this wonderful world and mingling with it, there's no better place than **Sunset** – with a Capital S. The sun doesn't just set here. On the contrary, the shiny orange orb gets an extraordinary send-off every evening from an astonishing assortment of jugglers, fire-eaters, acrobats, para-sailors, bongo players, cookie peddlers, peg-legged pirates, even ordinary people.

The spectacle begins at the **Mallory Pier** shortly before the sun drops. The miniature Mardi Gras occasionally upstages even the main attraction. But a sunset that teases the sky with a pink streak before torching it aflame in reds and oranges, can elicit standing ovations from the assemblage.

Conservative visitors and families may wish to exercise discretion when attending Sunset, however. It's that time of day when the people here get mellow – some drink wine, some smoke pot. With its proximity to South America, Jamaica and Mexico, Florida is the major port of entry into the US for marijuana and other illegal narcotics. State narcotics agents have their hands full trying to police the vast coastline; some of the biggest drug busts in US history have been made in Florida.

Key West is still vulnerable to clever smugglers who float drugs past the law in many ingenious ways. Bales of marijuana sometimes literally wash up on the shores of the Florida Keys. Locals call it "square grouper." Once word gets out that a load has been dropped in the ocean, boats and beaches fill up with potential rescuers like in the wrecking days of old. A catch of "square grouper" can bring in infinitely more money than the edible kind.

Eat it raw: If you wish to toast the setting sun, you can do so aboard the

Lounging on Pier House Beach.

very houseboat patronized by the cast of the 1960s television series *Surfside 6*. Anchored at Mallory Pier, the houseboat has a large, autographed blow-up of the stars inside.

Some folks fan out from Mallory Pier to other parts of town after the sun takes its nightly plunge into the sea. Key West restaurants are known for their tropical atmosphere, and have recently acquired first rate reputations for their food to go along with their rather high prices. The **Buttery**, **Cafe Marquesa**, **Cafe des Artistes**, **Louie's Backyard**, and **Antonia's** (names are subject to occasional changes) are among the finest that feed you in elegant, old Key West settings. For those in search of fresh sushi or steak teriyaki, **Kyushu** on Truman Street is the place. For the money, the food at **The Pier House** is as good as any, and its seaside setting is very romantic.

In very informal surroundings, the **Half Shell Raw Bar** on the dock at the foot of Margaret Street lustily advises you to "Eat It Raw" and features oysters and other fresh, reasonably priced seafood. The delights of Cuba – *picadillo* (a ground beef dish), black bean soup, and *cafe con leche* (coffee with milk) can be sampled at **La Cacique** on Duval.

Bars, other than Captain Tony's and Sloppy Joe's, include **The Bull & Whistle** (complete with a bull's head crashing through a brick wall), **Havana Docks**, a mellow waterfront bistro; the **Copa**, a primarily gay disco; the **Green Parrot**, a boisterous locals' hangout; and **Coconuts**, a sophisticated grownups' bar with a panoramic view of the city atop the La Concha Hotel. (Again, the names and clientele may change.)

Grunt Bone Alley: The tourist who deems it his duty to race through a sightseeing quota will find no lack of attractions in Key West. **Mallory Square** is a standard starting point. It is the spot around which the city grew, and lately the spot around which its renaissance has revolved. You can stock up on brochures and tips at the **Hospitality House**, once a ticket office for passenger and freight services in the late 19th

The Iguana Man used to walk his pets on Duval Street.

century. **Waterfront House**, circa 1850, and **Harbor House**, 1892, are also here.

Twenty years ago, much of Old Town, and most of Mallory Square and Duval Street were barely standing. Locals had abandoned the decaying gambling halls, bawdy houses and tenements for modern concrete block structures (CBs) on the fringes of the island. Now a new infusion of entrepreneurial money has restored its charm and driven out some of its undesirable elements. You can spend days exploring **Pirates' Alley, Key Lime Square** and **Grunt Bone Alley**. You can wash clothes at the **Margaret Truman Launderette**.

For the record, popular attractions scattered around the city include the **Martello Towers**, part of the 19th-century effort to fortify the southern boundary of the United States. The East Martello Tower houses the **Key West Art and Historical Society Museum**. Nearby, **Fort Zachary Taylor** looms over the southwest tip of the island, another mid-1800s edifice destined to become an attraction. The **Oldest House**

attracts its share of visitors to 322 Duval Street, while the **Lighthouse** at Truman and Thomas Avenues dates to 1846 and houses a military museum.

The **Southernmost Point** at the end of Duval Street has lost its title to a spot on the Big Island of Hawaii. But it is still 375 miles south of Cairo, Egypt, and 755 miles south of Los Angeles. Chinese immigrant Jim Kee began selling shiny sea shells here in the late 1930s, and his descendants continue to do so. Nearby is the opulent, privately owned **Southernmost House**.

Even the **City Cemetery** bordered by Francis, Angela and Olivia streets has fascinating sights. Among them are a monument to men who died aboard the *USS Maine* in Havana in 1898, and a statue of a Key deer that marks the grave of a beloved pet. The cemetery has been the center of a controversy because of the local custom of recycling the graves. There's so little space, Key Westers for the past 60 years have shoveled up old skeletons and reburied them deeper to make room for newcomers. Officials

, candid
pitaph at
ity
emetery.

estimate that up to 100,000 bodies may be buried in just 15,000 spaces in the Solares Hill section of the cemetery.

An abandoned section of the **US Naval Base**, best visited aboard the Conch Train or Trolley, encompasses President Harry Truman's Little White House, President Kennedy's Bay of Pigs Invasion command post, and the refugee landing docks. Many of the 125,000 Cubans who fled their country in 1980 on anything that could float landed here. The **San Carlos Institute**, a museum, theater and cultural center dedicated to the Cuban contribution to Key West, recently opened in a magnificent Spanish-style building on Duval Street. It tells the history of Cuban exiles in Key West while also explaining the culture of the people.

Shoppers looking for souvenirs representative of the city can try **Key West Hand Print Fabrics**, 201 Simonton Street. There, Cuban workers apply acrylic paint in tropical patterns to the cloth, which you can buy as raw fabric or ready-made fashions from the racks. A block away, the **Key West Fragrance Factory** sells smells made on the premises.

Purists may find it all a bit too touristy, too commercial. But even the locals take the new look in stride as just another of the many phases in the city's unorthodox history. Whether shopping, sightseeing, sipping, supping, sunbathing, snorkeling or simply slumming, you'll find an alternative way of doing it in Key West.

The farther Keys: The Overseas Highway ends in Key West, but Florida doesn't. The breathtaking, cobalt blue seas to the west embrace islands even more surprising than Key West. Getting to them is in itself an adventure. Several seaplanes operating out of the lower keys provide beautiful bird's-eye trips.

Pilot Russ Sprague, who operates out of **Key West Seaplane Service** at Murray's Marina on Stock Island, takes passengers slow and low over the waters for a good look at the **Quicksands** – shifting sandbars that create gorgeous patterns in the surf. Nearby are a ring of islands called the **Marquesas**, considered the only atoll in the Atlantic Ocean (although Russ says they are technically in the Gulf of Mexico). You'll see **Rebecca Shoal**, the site where treasure-hunter Mel Fisher found the sunken Spanish ship *Nuestra Senora de Atocha*, which sank in these waters in 1622.

The most impressive sight lies at the end of the 35-minute flight in the **Tortugas**, 68 miles from Key West. From the air, it looks like a piece of the Lost City of Atlantis is rising straight out of the sea. The hexagonal fortress is the "Gibraltar of the Gulf" – **Fort Jefferson**. As the plane drops closer for splashdown, passengers can see that the fort actually covers most of the 16-acre **Garden Key**.

Construction commenced in 1846 and continued for 30 years without completion. Federal troops occupied the fort in 1861 to keep it from falling into Confederate hands during the Civil War, but it saw little action then or at any other time. After the war, it served as a prison. Inmates included four men linked to the assassination of Abraham Lincoln. The

The mascot of the Bull and Whistle Bar leaves via the wall.

most famous was an innocent victim of that crime, Dr Samuel A. Mudd. Obeying his physician's code, he set the broken leg of John Wilkes Booth, unaware that Booth had injured it after shooting Lincoln. Mudd was convicted of conspiracy and sentenced to a life of hard labor at Fort Jefferson. During a yellow fever epidemic that struck the Tortugas in 1867, he worked tirelessly to aid the stricken, earning an early pardon two years later.

The fort is now a national monument. Visitors can roam the ramparts and wonder what it must have been like to be imprisoned behind its 50-foot-high walls, cut off from the world by a moat as well as an ocean.

Outside, there are primitive camping facilities and a secluded sand beach. Take a picnic lunch and bathing suit. The snorkeling is excellent. Though victimized by indiscriminate hunting, the huge turtles – loggerheads and hawkbills – after which Ponce de León named the Tortugas, can still be seen cruising the waters. Further west is **Loggerhead**

Key, the end of Florida, with a 130-year-old lighthouse that is still being used today.

Homeward bound: Plan your trip to the Tortugas for April or early May, if possible, for another educational experience – if you don't mind sharing the island with armies of bird watchers wielding cameras.

East of Fort Jefferson is **Bush Key** where, for some inexplicable reason known only to Mother Nature, thousands of sooty terns come each year from the Caribbean, the west central Atlantic Ocean and as far away as West Africa. They zero in on Bush Key each spring to lay eggs in depressions in the warm sand. The parents take turns shading their single egg from the sun. Juvenile sooties fly 9,000 miles to West Africa, but manage to find their way back to tiny Bush Key when they are 4 years old. Other spectacular species that can be observed on Bush Key are brown noddy terns and the monstrous but graceful frigate birds which have wingspans of nearly 7 feet.

221

A drive uphill, north from Melbourne, along Florida's East Coast, is a pleasure trek that retraces the tourist migration routes that fed the rush to the Gold Coast playgrounds of Miami and Fort Lauderdale. Down the East Coast tens of thousands of Florida's first tourists poured in a steady flow along the Atlantic, leaving small oases every dozen miles or so. Eventually, they struck roots in the lower eastern portion of the state, a slice of Florida that for many years was virtually the only spot for tourists.

Yet, the Melbourne-to-Jacksonville strip of East Coast Florida has all the trademarks of tourism, all the strata of the eras of the good years and the bad years, all the topography of generations of visitors who came and made the state a mecca for leisure money. To retrace that route is to experience a trip back and forth through time. Depending on how you want to cover the 200 or so miles, you can experience Florida in terms of Yesterday, Today or Tomorrow.

Beginning with Melbourne and Cape Canaveral, the journey proceeds to the wildlife haven of Merritt Island, the old-fashioned town of Cocoa with its specialty shops and flower tubs, and then to New Smyrna Beach which, in spite of its name, is one of the oldest settlements in America. The pace quickens dramatically a little further north at Daytona Beach, which is famous for its ear-splitting, high-energy Speedway race-track. It slows to trotting pace in St Augustine, a town for narrow lanes, horse-drawn carriage rides and early American architecture, and eventually pulls up on the white sands of Amelia Island, 32 miles north of Jacksonville.

You have a choice of three land routes north from Melbourne – the old, rustic, weaving and sometimes frustrating A1A that snakes along the coast line, often within tantalizing sight of the shimmering Atlantic Ocean; a more traditional but rather random US 1 that also leads straight up the coast, sometimes bypassing some of the smaller towns but allowing travelers a continual view of Florida in all its sparkle and bangles; and finally the route of Tomorrow, Interstate 95, which ribbons along clean and untouched, fast and four-laned, leaving the motorist with quick and unclear visual impressions of a landscape that whizzes by in a sameness of trees, cars and interchanges.

Preceding pages: roadside rest stop. **Left**, a snake charmer at Daytona Bike Week.

THE SPACE COAST

Melbourne is an ideal place to start. It is surrounded, like the petals of a flower, by communities that between them have all the age and nostalgia of Old Florida, the shiny and startling newness of New Florida, and the brash technology of Future Florida.

While Melbourne as a community dates back to the 1970s, the land was long home for the first Floridians – Indians of the Ais and Timucuan tribes.

The first homesteader to make the Melbourne area his home was a surveyor commissioned after the Civil War to determine if the Florida Territory was suitable as a colony for thousands of newly freed slaves. His report was unfavorable, but his personal opinion was just the opposite – he settled in Florida, first in an area that is now downtown Miami, later in a place he called "Eau Gallie." He took the name from the French word *eau*, meaning "water," and the Chippewa Indian word *gallie*, meaning "rocky," which he chose for the ledges and foundations of natural coquina rock – a soft, whitish limestone made up of broken sea shells and corals and used as a building material throughout Florida.

By 1893, the Florida East Coast Railroad extended its southern tip to Eau Gallie. After that, growth was steady until the post-World War II construction of Patrick Air Force Base, now also home for a seaside missile display. In 1890, a second nearby community was born and named Melbourne; in 1969 Melbourne merged with Eau Gallie.

Today's Melbourne offers the standard amusements and distractions – at least seven public golf courses, fresh and salt-water fishing, museums, bicycle trails, a variety of parks and nature trails, even a zoo in an orange grove. **Houser's Zoo**, where you'll find more than 100 animal species, from a Kodiak bear to a Florida puma, is worth a browse.

The **Brevard Art Center and Museum** has a nice touch for visitors – a "please touch" gallery for the visually handicapped, and the local Chamber of Commerce offers a tour covering some 50 historical sites such as early churches, homes, hotels and trysting pathways favored by yesteryear's young loves.

The **Florida Institute of Technology** in Melbourne is the home of a botanical garden with more than 300 species of palms, ferns and other tropical foliage that flourish along a quiet stream. It's free and open from dawn to dusk.

The mixture of the modern and the natural continues throughout this section of East Coast Florida. A few miles north of Melbourne is **Rockledge**, one of the oldest winter resorts on the East Coast, first established in 1837 and named for the ledges of coquina rock which look out over the **Indian River.** This area is noted for old and beautiful residential homes.

Just north of **Cocoa Beach** on A1A is the city of **Cape Canaveral**, which includes **Port Canaveral**, a deep water port that gives Central Florida access to shipments of oil, cement, lumber and

eft, the launch pad at ennedy pace Center. ight, going r a swim.

fish. A bit more unusual is the occasional berthing there of atomic submarines, which dock while undergoing Polaris and Poseidon missile launch tests. Nearby are missile-tracking ships that accompany the nuclear subs.

Gateway to the stars: Midway between Cocoa and Cocoa Beach is **Merritt Island,** flanked by the **Banana River** on one side and the Indian River on the other. Here again is an odd blend of the old and the new. The island includes a well-kept air strip, facilities for private aircraft and the largest, most modern shopping mall in this part of Florida.

North and east of the malls and air strips is the **Merritt Island National Wildlife Refuge** that shares a common boundary with the **Kennedy Space Center's Spaceport USA**.

You can visit Spaceport USA via the NASA Parkway, State Road 405. At the main gate, visitors receive a pass that permits entry to the **Visitors' Center,** which is a veritable museum of America's space program.

The Visitors' Center is also the launching point for tours of the vast Kennedy complex. Air-conditioned buses transport you to the enormous **Vehicle Assembly Building,** one of the world's largest in volume, the space shuttle launch pads and to other sites of interest. For more details on the Kennedy Space Center, turn to our feature "On Finding Space at the Cape."

For Tomorrow fans, there are spaceships and rockets poking into the blue Florida sky. You can view 10-story high Titan missiles at close range at **Patrick Air Force Base**. Such displays appear at several points fronting directly on A1A. But Spaceport USA remains the biggest paean to flight and its spectacle is unmatched.

Because of the curvature of the Florida coastline, these launch centers project well out into the Atlantic. When such vehicles are launched here they roar down the **Eastern Test Range,** pass directly by local beaches while still at relatively low altitudes, and provide spectacular views of the Space Age all along the Melbourne area coastline.

The VAB looms over Kennedy Space Center and the Merritt Island Wildlife Refuge.

Appropriately, the Merritt Island refuge is one of the nation's premier sanctuaries of the creatures that taught man to fly. The refuge is a natural habitat for more than 250 species of birds, many in danger of extinction.

The freedom of the wildlife on Merritt Island makes an indelible impression on visitors, particularly since it sits right next to a man-made world of new and artificial flight.

Among the endangered species taking refuge here is perhaps the most exciting of all Florida birds – the southern bald eagle. Its large nests – some more than 10 feet thick and 6 feet in diameter – may be seen in the tall slash pines along the refuge's roads. In the past, between 15 and 20 pairs of bald eagles may have nested at Merritt Island; today, no more than five pairs are regularly nesting there.

Birdwatchers estimate that as many as 70,000 ducks use the refuge during the winter months. This winter tourist population includes some 23 species that migrate to the refuge from their northern nesting grounds each year. One native, the Florida mottled duck, also nests here.

Gone fishin': As on most of Florida's East Coast, offshore waters are famous for their abundance of trout, redfish, drum, crevelle jack, sailfish and snook. The beaches of the Space Coast provide fine offshore fishing for surf casting; indeed, record catches have been lured right from **Canaveral Pier**, a manmade promontory that reaches 825 feet into the Atlantic Ocean at Cocoa Beach. Deep-sea fishing provides a different breed of potential catches: grouper, flounder, mackerel and kings, among others. There are limits on the size and number of fresh and saltwater fish and on certain shellfish and crabs that you are allowed to catch.

One bizarre sea creature that you won't need a rod and reel to catch is the walking catfish. It is exactly what its name implies, using sturdy pectoral fins near the head to lift itself out of the water. They squirm snake-like over lawns and roads along the East Coast and Central

oin the
pace race.

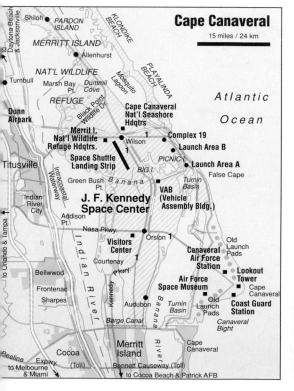

Florida. A native of Southeast Asia that escaped from fish farms near Boca Raton in the early 1960s, these walking catfish have gills that enable them to breathe on dry land.

There's one last feature to Melbourne that you might want to take in if you're there between June and August full moons. On the deserted beaches south of the bright lights and heavily populated cities, a phenomenal night spectacle takes place when giant sea turtles return to the beaches, scoop out their nests and lay thousands of ping-pong-ball-sized eggs. Three turtle species bury their eggs here. The most common is the loggerhead, averaging 200 to 300 pounds, but sometimes topping the scale at 500 pounds. It is one of the sea's oldest creatures, dating back as far as 10,000 years.

Occasionally the leatherback, which averages 700 pounds, and a few 130-pound green turtles come ashore too. But most of the turtles here are loggerheads, who spend most of their life out at sea and return to land only to lay their eggs under the cover of darkness. These turtles and their eggs are protected by federal law; they cannot be touched or hindered. But you *can* view their egg mounds, each containing perhaps as many as 100 eggs.

Note the tortuous paths in the sand made by the huge parent turtles. When their babies hatch, some 7 to 8 weeks later, they make the perilous trek toward the surf. Many never make it, falling prey to seagulls, raccoons, the hot sun and large fish in the water. Predators also destroy many nests.

Melbourne's northern neighbor, **Cocoa**, offers a calmer, more leisurely contrast to the hustle and bustle of the Kennedy Space Center. Cocoa boomed in population with the coming of the Space Age, yet the community manages to retain a certain picturesque charm.

The city was first named Indian River City when it was founded in 1882 because it sits on the west edge of that baylike river. But the US postal authorities said that name was too long for use as a postmark. When word arrived at **A grasshopper and its enemy.**

Willard Store that a new name was needed, someone suggested "Cocoa" – picked from the front of a box of Baker's Cocoa that had just been brought in with the freight. The name stuck.

The tranquility of old-fashioned **Cocoa Village** in downtown Cocoa remains. The streets are lined with flowering planters and specialty shops where visitors can view a potter at his wheel, a leathersmith making belts, antiques being restored, and artists at work.

Brahma bulls: West of Melbourne is the huge **Deseret Ranch**, acquired by the Church of Jesus Christ of Latter Day Saints during the 1950s. It encompasses 316,000 acres – that's 44 miles in one direction and 29 in the other. It's so big that *all* roads leading from Melbourne and its vicinity to Walt Disney World cross the ranch at some point.

Deseret Ranch's main products are beef cattle, timber and citrus. The ranch has about 2,000 acres of citrus trees and more than 5,000 head of Brahma cattle, animals particularly suited to Florida's climate because they are the only breed with sweat glands. They are also more resistant to many diseases that can decimate typical English breed herds.

Aside from all that cattle and citrus, Deseret is also home to 275 or so horses – and communities of deer, turkey, quail, panthers, bears, alligators and, no doubt, snakes. There are plans to construct a tourist center at Deseret Ranch. In the meantime, groups are welcome – with advance notice.

As you observe the acres of cattle in Florida, you may wonder why they are always followed by longlegged white birds with yellow bills. These cattle egret feed on grasshoppers and other insects stirred up as the cattle plod along.

Indian River country: As you continue northward from the Space Coast, the seaside again begins to look like early Florida. There are fewer condominiums and more houses nestled in dunes and shrouded in sea oats, palmetto bushes and scrub. On up US 1, through **Mims**, **Scottsmoor** and **Oak Hill**, the return route takes you along the **Canaveral National Seashore** on the right and the

A Cracker cowboy cools off his cattle.

Intracoastal Waterway to the left.

Before getting there, though, you first enter **New Smyrna Beach**, a small but charming community with a wide, flat and firm beach that invites motorists to leave the hot asphalt and concrete ribbons of man for a leisurely drive along some of the smoothest sand in the world.

New Smyrna Beach offers 8 miles of drive-on-it, park-on-it, sunbathe-on-it beaches. It's considered the world's safest beach because of tremendous rock ledges 25 to 40 miles offshore in the Atlantic that prevent dangerous ocean undercurrents which can pull an unwary wader out to sea.

New Smyrna Beach is one of the oldest settlements in America. Shell mounds around the city indicate that early Florida Indians lived there, generation after generation. Historic **Turtle Mound**, which overlooks both river and ocean, is the highest point on the coast for miles around.

Records show that the Indian village of Caparaca once stood on the site of what is now New Smyrna Beach, and

historians claim that in 1513 Ponce de León, buffeted by a storm off what is now Cape Canaveral, found refuge and fresh wood and water here before being attacked by Indians and forced to retreat back to his ship. Called Rio de la Cruz (River of the Cross) by the Spanish and later nicknamed "The Mosquitoes," for obvious reasons, the inlet was officially named **Ponce de León Inlet** in 1926.

The first colony of settlers came to the area in 1767. This group, led by Dr Andrew Turnbull, a Scottish physician, included 1,500 Greeks, Italians and Minorcans looking for a new land to raise fruit, indigo, maize, sugar cane, cotton and rice. Dr Turnbull named his colony New Smyrna, in honor of his wife's birthplace in Greece. The colony disbanded in 1777 because of a shortage of funds and political intrigues.

Yet, during the 10 years it existed, a system of irrigation and drainage canals was built and is still in use today. The ruins of coquina wells, foundations and indigo vats – still visible – indicate the wide scope of activity by the colonists. Check out the **Turnbull ruins** and the **Sugar Mill ruins**, built in the 1830s and torched by rampaging Seminole Indians a half-century later.

It is a lovely drive down A1A past luxury stilt houses to the windblown dunes and sea oats that mark the entrance to the Canaveral National Seashore. Beyond stretch 25 miles of primitive beach and shoreline uninhabited by man. On the way, stop at **Turtle Mound** where 600 years' worth of oyster shells were piled up by ancient Indians. More than 100 plant species have taken root here. It's an interesting climb to the top.

Curiosity-seekers may wish to ask directions to **Canova Street** before leaving New Smyrna. Here lies another of Florida's numerous oddities – a grave on an island in the middle of the street. It is the final resting place of the 16-year-old son of a pioneer citrus grower who died while hunting in 1860.

Detour back on A1A en route to Daytona for a look at Ponce's Inlet and its 175-foot, red brick lighthouse. It is a hot, hard climb to the top, but the trip is well worth it.

Left, catch of the day. **Right**, NASA in action: the Miami coast taken by satellite.

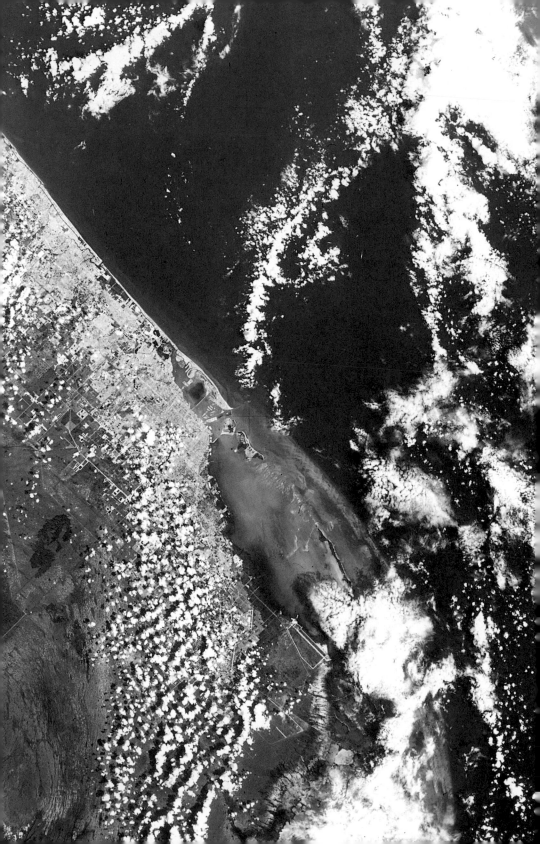

community. It's estimated that between the first week of March and Easter more than 500,000 students visit.

Aided by the theme parks near Orlando, Daytona seems to put out more of a welcome mat for the student, with cut-rate prices on many of the city's 16,000 hotel rooms, free beer parties and lots of friendly smiles.

During a typical peak Spring Break, one of the top disco spots along the beach's blocks-long boardwalk – aptly named **Top of the Boardwalk Discotheque** – may see as many as 700 to 800 students walk through the doors each night, despite a maximum capacity of only 250. The **Boardwalk** also offers a selection of amusement centers, arcades, and rides.

There are also places like **Finky's**, a Texas-theme club on Grand View Avenue near Seabreeze, and **701 South**, a popular lounge with live disc jockeys, laser shows and video screens. All contribute to Florida's pervasive carnival atmosphere. College students have found the bizarre streets of neon and glitter tacky enough for their spring tastes – and easier to reach than Fort Lauderdale further down the coast. Many hotels, however, require a damage deposit by student guests.

Rockefeller's retreat: A few miles north, you can visit what was once considered a "Millionaires' Colony." This is **Ormond Beach**. Its beginnings, however, were modest. No one is exactly sure who the first settlers here were. Some say, a bit romantically, that they may have been victims of shipwrecks which were prevalent along the coast in the 1600s.

In 1804 Spain offered grants of land to English colonists living in the Bahamas. Among those who accepted such grants was Captain James Ormond, who acquired a tract on the Halifax River. Another was Charles Bulow, whose plantation was destroyed in the Seminole Wars. Remnants of Bulow's sugar mill can be seen north of the city.

Climate was another factor in the settling of Ormond Beach. In 1873, the Corbin Lock Company of New Britain, Connecticut, sent representatives to Florida to establish a suitable health resort for its employees threatened with tuberculosis, which was then prevalent. They chose a tract on the west side of the Halifax and 12 families came and called the place New Britain. The name was changed to Ormond in 1880 when the community incorporated.

In the late 1800s, the establishment of the **Ormond Hotel**, the completion of a bridge over the river, and an extension of the Flagler East Coast Railroad brought millionaires with names like Vanderbilt, Astor and Gould. Some, such as John D. Rockefeller, Sr, built homes here. Rockefeller found the place suited his health and spent more than 20 winters here until he died in 1937 at the age of 97. His home, **The Casements**, is now a cultural center and museum. The old Ormond Hotel is facing the threat of demolition.

Besides their money and their names, the wealthy who visited Ormond Beach brought something else at the turn of the century – the automobile. Like Daytona and New Smyrna Beach, Ormond Beach

Sunday drive on Daytona Beach…

had its share of wide, hard ocean sand. It was ideal for driving your brand-new gas buggie and seeing how fast you could go on a flat, smooth surface.

A "measured mile" was created and speed tests were run. Soon new vehicles built specifically for speed were raced and tested by men with names like Chevrolet, Olds, Duryea, Ford, Old-fields, Winton and others. Records were broken beginning with the first recorded 57 miles per hour by R.E. Olds and Alexander Winton in 1902, and continuing until Sir Malcolm Campbell's 5-miles-a-minute record of 276.82 mph in 1935.

To celebrate these historic achievements, the Birthplace of Speed Association holds an annual Antique Car Meet every Thanksgiving. The Turkey Rod Run, featuring antique cars, is also held during this period. During the day, sprints are held on the beach for old-time gas-eaters. There's also a **Flea Market** where antique car hobbyists can buy, sell, and swap parts to fit their treasured vehicles, some of them are worth over $100,000 to a collector.

At Ormond Beach, motorists have a choice of routes north: either to pick up US 1 or A1A, or double back to I-95. The A1A passes through **Flagler County** and some of the less-traveled communities on the coast, where development has been slower, kinder and more individualized.

A1A will also take you through **Flagler Beach**, **Beverly Beach**, **Painters Hill** and a couple of state parks (there are three in the county altogether), including **Washington Oaks Garden Park**, which hosts a wide variety of flowers and plants. More importantly, A1A feeds right into **Marineland of Florida**, one of the oldest and serenest attractions in the state and a home for all manner of ocean dwellers. This attraction features two huge **oceanariums**, an electric eel pavilion and the **Aquarius Theatre**, with performing porpoises doing six shows a day. Visitors are encouraged to take photographs – there are even experts on hand to help you get the photo you want.

.were even pular back round 1920.

STREET IN ST. AUGUSTINE.

COPYRIGHTED 1882.

236

ST AUGUSTINE

A dozen or so miles north, you can turn the clock back 400 years at an archaeologist's delight called **St Augustine**.

Like many Florida cities, St Augustine lays claim to a title – the Nation's Oldest City. The rationale is this: St Augustine was the first permanent settlement by Europeans in what is now the continental US. Jamestown, Virginia, was established 42 years later. St Augustine was 55 years old by the time the first Pilgrims came to New England.

Tourists rule today. The city likes to show off its wrinkles and years, so consequently there are a half-dozen ways to sample its attractions. In addition to usual car, bus and foot tours, St Augustine also offers leisurely horse-drawn carriage rides to historic points of interest. Most carriage drivers offer a bit of narration on the city's history and key sights. Their drivers provide a flavorful report about all points past and passed,

and occasionally stop to allow riders to inspect on foot. There is also a sightseeing train that motors down the narrow one-way streets. Finally, there are *Victory II* cruises along the waterfront on a 75-minute tour of the city's edge and **Matanzas Bay**.

Throughout the city, bits of history beg for your attention. What better place to start than **The Fountain of Youth** itself, a memorial park on the site believed to be where Ponce de León first set foot on his fruitless, thirsty search for a magic elixir. Past a stone arch and a modest sign that advertises the fountain, you will find a natural spring bubbling in a coquina shelter presumably of Spanish design. Many visitors like to take a taste, just to see what all the legend's about and can buy a whole bottle of the stuff at a gift shop. But don't be disappointed if you come away without feeling younger.

Railway man Flagler's first compound of hotels, at the corner of Cordova and King, included the Alcazar, now the **Lightner Museum** and **City Hall** com-

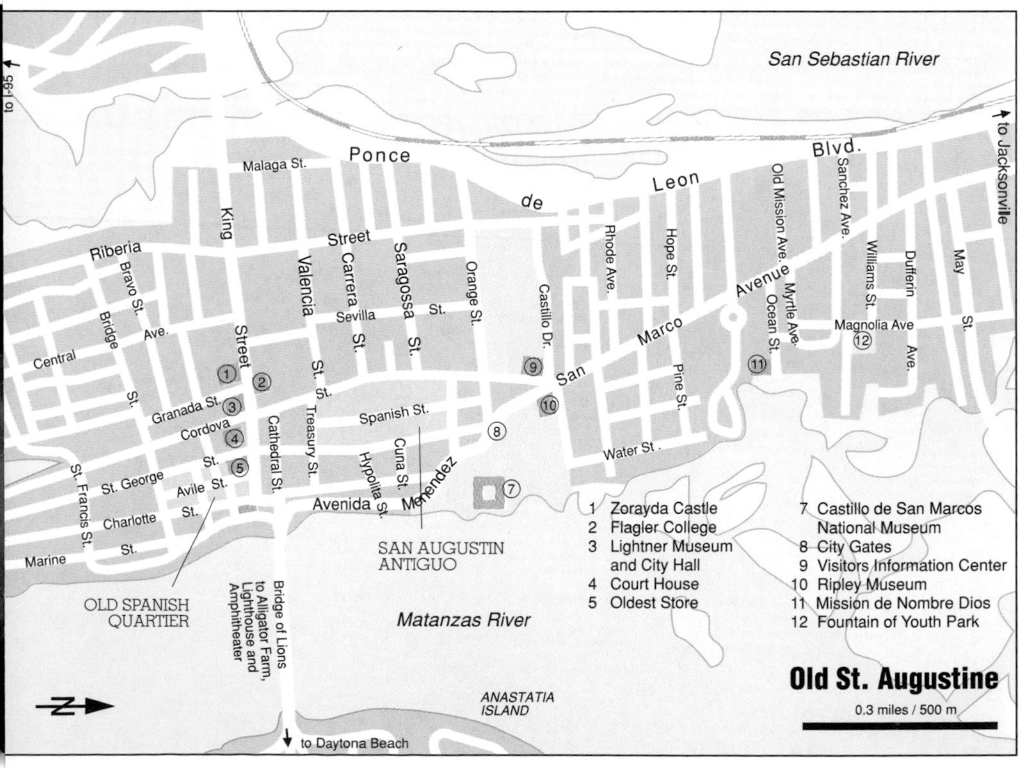

1 Zorayda Castle
2 Flagler College
3 Lightner Museum
   and City Hall
4 Court House
5 Oldest Store
7 Castillo de San Marcos
   National Museum
8 City Gates
9 Visitors Information Center
10 Ripley Museum
11 Mission de Nombre Dios
12 Fountain of Youth Park

Old St. Augustine

0.3 miles / 500 m

JACKSONVILLE

Our trip northward continues through more beach communities whose history reaches back to the earliest days of Florida's development. The **St Johns River**, one of the few rivers in the US to flow northward, leads inland toward **Fort Caroline**, located about 5 miles from the mouth of the river. This sanctuary was established by Huguenots (French Protestants) in 1562. Like its cousin forts at St Augustine, Caroline saw warfare, sorties and massacres. Early French and Spanish colonists were a militant lot who treated one another's forces as pirates and marauders. They felt no remorse about killing men, women and children.

Today, the original site of Fort Caroline no longer exists. Its meadow-like plain and part of the bluff on which it sat overlooking the St Johns River were washed away after the river channel was dredged deeper in 1880. To help visitors visualize the original scene, the fort's walls have been reconstructed on the river plain, according to 16th-century sketches by Jacques le Moyne, the colony's artist and mapmaker.

Jacksonville Beach has a 1,200-foot fishing pier that lances out into the Atlantic, and a **Flag Pavilion** that houses flags of all 50 states. **Mayport Naval Station**, home of giant US aircraft carriers, has at least one Navy ship open for public tours on weekends. The Mayport naval base also offers the old **St Johns Lighthouse**, a historical thorn that rises at the foot of Palmer Street inside the base's security fence. The Navy considers it a hazard to planes and would like it torn down, but it still stands as a landmark listed in the National Register of Historical Places.

Visitors to Jacksonville Beach can even go ghost-hunting. The 100-year-old **King House** in Mayport is said to play host to the restless spirits of some of its old seafaring residents.

Jacksonville, a bit farther inland on the St Johns River, is the largest city

French artist Le Moyne drew this picture of Fort Caroline in 1564.

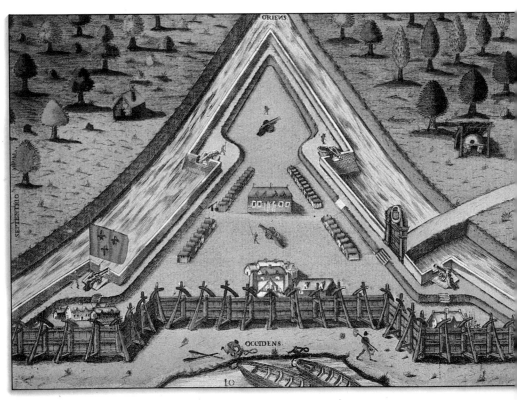

inland area in the US, covering 841 square miles and with a population of almost one million. It also boasts one of the tallest office buildings in Florida – the 37-story, 535-foot **Independent Life Insurance Company Building**.

The city spans both banks of the St Johns, and, as the local Chamber of Commerce is likely to point out, Jacksonville, unlike most of Florida, has seasons – all four of them. That's because the city is north of Florida's tropical zone. The seasons are mild, but noticeable. The city boasts more than 12,000 hotels rooms, and more than 1,000 restaurants. For football fans, Jacksonville has the 70,000-seat **Gator Bowl** stadium.

The largest city in the US: Surveyors laid out the town site in 1822 at a long-used river cattle crossing called Cow Ford by the British and Wacca Pilatka by the Indians. The city continued to grow, despite a fire in 1901 that burned down 2,400 buildings – half the town – and left 10,000 homeless.

Jacksonville prospered as the gate-way to Florida's first tourist region – the St Johns River, described in "The Panhandle" chapter. One famous resident of that era immortalized the state in classical music. Composer Frederick Delius lived in a run-down orange grove on the St Johns. He was enthralled by the impromptu music of black farm laborers. When he returned to his native England, Delius incorporated those rhythms into musical compositions like *Florida Suite*. You can visit his restored cottage at **Jacksonville University**.

Jacksonville Port is one of the Southeast's busiest. Among unexpected sights here are the rainbow colors of thousands of bright imported cars arriving from Japan, or the slow, patient decay of an old tugboat rich in its rotting colors, bobbing serenely in a backwater cove.

There is also a **Seaboard Coast Line Locomotive** on view, sitting in the parking lot of the **Prime Osborn Convention Center**. This 1919 steam engine remains as a third tribute to the railroading era.

Jacksonville Zoo is one of the South's

Work at Jacksonville's docks continues through the night.

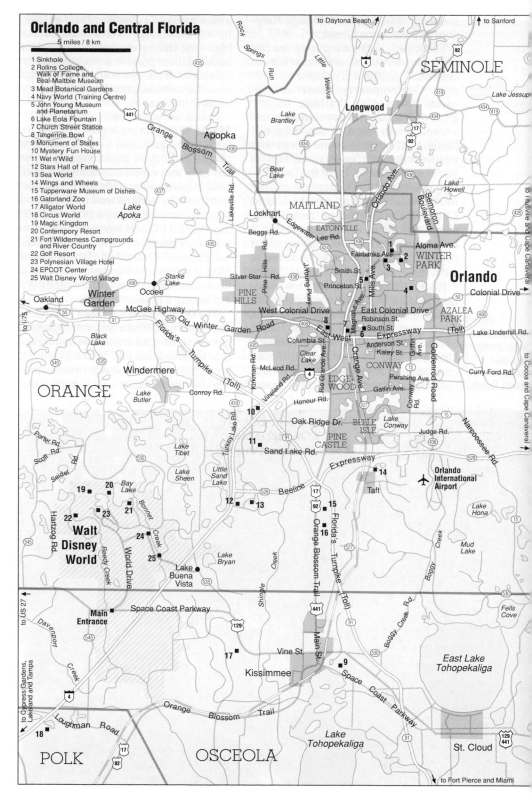

Orlando and Central Florida

5 miles / 8 km

1 Sinkhole
2 Rollins College,
  Walk of Fame and
  Beal-Maltbie Museum
3 Mead Botanical Gardens
4 Navy World (Training Centre)
5 John Young Museum
  and Planetarium
6 Lake Eola Fountain
7 Church Street Station
8 Tangerine Bowl
9 Monument of States
10 Mystery Fun House
11 Wet n'Wild
12 Stars Hall of Fame
13 Sea World
14 Wings and Wheels
15 Tupperware Museum of Dishes
16 Gatorland Zoo
17 Alligator World
18 Circus World
19 Magic Kingdom
20 Contempory Resort
21 Fort Wilderness Campgrounds
   and River Country
22 Golf Resort
23 Polynesian Village Hotel
24 EPCOT Center
25 Walt Disney World Village

to Daytona Beach   to Sanford

SEMINOLE

Longwood

Lake Jessup

Lake Brantley

Bear Lake

Lake Howell

MAITLAND

EATONVILLE

Lockhart

Beggs Rd.

Fairbanks Ave.

WINTER PARK

Aloma Ave.

Orlando

Colonial Drive

Apopka

Orange Blossom Trail

Lake Apoka

Ocoee

Starke Lake

Silver Star Rd.

PINE HILLS

Smith St.

Princeton St.

AZALEA PARK

Lake Underhill Rd.

Oakland

Winter Garden

McGee Highway

West Colonial Drive

East Colonial Drive

Robinson St.

East-West Expressway

Columbia St.

Anderson St.

Kaley St.

CONWAY

Pershing Ave.

Curry Ford Rd.

ORANGE

Black Lake

Florida's Turnpike (Toll)

Windermere

Lake Butler

Conroy Rd.

Clear Lake

McLeod Rd.

EDGE-WOOD

Honour Rd.

Gatlin Ave.

Lake Conway

Judge Rd.

Oak Ridge Dr.

BELLE ISLE

PINE CASTLE

Sand Lake Rd.

Lake Tibet

Lake Sheen

Little Sand Lake

Expressway

Beeline

Taft

Orlando International Airport

Lake Hona

Mud Lake

Bay Lake

Walt Disney World

Lake Bryan

Lake Buena Vista

Main Entrance

Space Coast Parkway

East Lake Tohopekaliga

Fells Cove

Kissimmee

Vine St.

Main St.

Space Coast Parkway

POLK

OSCEOLA

Lake Tohopekaliga

St. Cloud

to Fort Pierce and Miami

to Cypress Gardens, Lakeland and Tampa

to US 27

Davenport

Loughman Road

Orange Blossom Trail

252

erties at **Lake Buena Vista**. If you want to spend your vacation out on a limb, try the **Treehouses**. Lake Buena Vista also offers Vacation Villas, Fairway Cluster Villas and Club Lake Villas.

Otherwise, Interstate 4 between the Walt Disney World exit and Orlando is wall-to-wall with less expensive accommodations. Many have shuttle service to Disney World. Nearby, US 192 offers over 10,000 more units.

After exiting I-4, you'll find it's still a long drive to the gates of the World. Tune in to the Disney radio network for current Disney World information. Unless you're staying at a hotel within, continue through the gates into one of 12,000 parking spaces. Make a mental note of your section. Each is named after a Disney character, so just ask the kids if you forget. It's still a tram ride to the ticket windows where you'll find a variety of prices. The most economical provide passes to all attractions for several days. Then you can ride a monorail or ferryboat to Walt Disney's masterpiece – the **Magic Kingdom**.

When you enter and find Mickey Mouse etched in flowers in front of the railroad depot, put aside notions that what you are about to experience is for the sake of the children. Adult visitors outnumber youngsters four to one.

The depot is a time machine that transports you to **Main Street, USA**, a thoroughfare straight out of a Norman Rockwell painting. The shop facades of Federal and Victorian era architecture give it the ambience of an Eastern seaboard resort at the turn of the century.

Dinner at the castle: Merchandise in the maze of shops ranges from stuffed animals, records, books and souvenirs of Disney creations to a corner camera shop where you can buy anything from instamatics to professional Nikon equipment – and get ailing cameras fixed free. In keeping with the time warp, there's a **Main Street Cinema** (featuring silent film classics) and a barber shop where you can still get a hot lather shave and facial massage. Magic shops, candy stores, china shops, tobacco emporiums and more line a street that looks up toward the centerpiece of the Magic Kingdom – the **Cinderella Castle**.

It is breathtaking at first sight, a crown jewel of a creation that doesn't look real. Its gold-crested spires float 181 feet above a moat. The fairy tale architecture is a composite of European castles at Fontainebleau and Versailles and the châteaux of the Loire Valley. But the principal inspiration was a Bavarian castle built by mad King Ludwig. The attention to detail in the design commands study: gargoyles sculpted right to the top reaches that tourists never see; interior columns embellished with carved birds and mice from the animated *Cinderella* film classic. Mosaics of scenes from the movie adorn the walls. An Italian artist spent 18 months creating them from 500,000 individual Italian tiles made of gold leaf and distinctive colored glass.

A winding staircase in the black hall ascends to the Arthurian **King Stefan's Banquet Hall**. Meals are reasonably priced but you must make a reservation early in the day.

Close encounters: The paths to the six

Bay Lake in Disney's Kingdom.

themed lands of the Magic Kingdom radiate outward from the park in front of the castle like the spokes of a wheel. To maximize enjoyment and minimize encounters with the routinely huge crowds (9,000 people even showed up the day Hurricane David drenched the state), arrive when the gates open. Failing that, wait until after noon when traffic thins out. The beginning and end of the day are best for getting into attractions without a long wait. Midday is better for shopping and sightseeing – and avoiding the hot Florida sun.

You can save treadwear on your feet by touring the Magic Kingdom systematically, walking from Adventureland to Frontierland, Liberty Square, Fantasyland and Tomorrowland – or vice versa. There's more in these places than meets the eye, so pause to admire the details. Each world takes its theming seriously, right down to what employees call "generic landscaping." Notice the mesquite trees imported from the southwest US for the **Pecos Bill Cafe** in Frontierland. And the souvenirs. You can buy genuine Paul Revere silverware in **Liberty Square**, including service sets worth up to $13,000.

Enchanted birds: Enter **Adventureland** over a wooden bridge festooned with Tiki-type effigies. The immense tree that houses the **Swiss Family Robinson residence** is actually 200 tons of concrete and steel with a 90-foot wide spread of limbs sprouting 800,000 plastic leaves (all made by a single family in Mexico).

The **Enchanted Tiki Birds** pavilion, patterned upon architectural styles of the islands of Bali and Borneo, is the exotic roost for numerous singing tropical birds. Disney "imagineers" have brought them to life using a complex, computer-controlled system called Audio-Animatronics. It combines voices, music and sound with three-dimensional figures that move realistically.

The **Jungle Cruise** provides a vicarious trip for would-be Indiana Joneses down what may be a tributary of the Amazon River. The **Pirates of the Caribbean** boats you back to the days when buccaneers plundered the West Indies, including a trip through the middle of a cannon battle between an enormous pirate ship and a fort.

"Authentic dirt": It's only a short walk around a corner to the Old West – **Frontierland**. Here, full-size Mississippi stern wheelers and a realistic 2-acre sculpture of an Arizona desert scene stand out. The latter is the stage for the **Big Thunder Mountain Railroad** ride, which trundles past redstone buttes, canyons, and bubbling geysers at 30 miles an hour.

If everything looks dusty, don't fault maintenance. "We try to make things look authentically dirty," an operations official said. One new supervisor ordered the attractions cleaned up, but when superiors discovered her overzealous mistake, she was asked to return them to their original state.

The line for the **Country Bear Jamboree** moves excruciatingly slowly, so wait until it's short. It has Audio-Animatronic action with a barnful of bears who "sing" country music standards like "Tears Will be the Chaser for My Wine" and "All the Guys That Turn

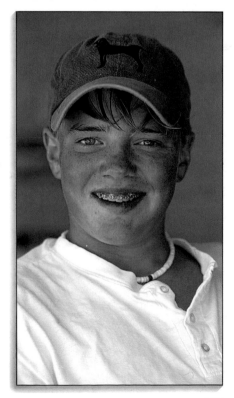

Me On Turn Me Down." Watch the facial expressions on the buffalo, moose and elk mounted on the wall.

American history: The most impressive use of Audio-Animatronics is **Liberty Square's Hall of Presidents** where "imagineers" have resurrected past presidents and cloned those still living. A 15-minute movie on a 120-degree screen chronicles the history of the American Constitution. Then a curtain rises on an eerie scene. Each "president" acknowledges his spotlighted introduction with a nod or wave. The illusion of life is maintained throughout a speech by Abraham Lincoln. His colleagues scratch their noses, chat, nervously tap their feet and even yawn in the background. The Lincoln figure alone is capable of 47 separate body actions and 15 head motions and expressions.

The architecture of Liberty Square also incorporates idiosyncrasies of early America. The window shutters have been tilted at angles so that they seem to be mounted on the leather hinges used in the 18th century and the "antique"

windows are warped and full of air bubbles. The **Diamond Horseshoe Revue** has a saloon with an old-fashioned variety show; be sure to reserve seats before 9.30am.

On a rise overlooking **Tom Sawyer Island** broods the **Haunted Mansion**. Its horrors far outclass those of any carnival rides with similar names. After an introductory scare in a room that "stretches," doom buggies carry you through corridors loaded with special effects. At one point, you see a party of transparent ghosts that you would swear are made from genuine ectoplasm.

Space riders: Fantasyland pays tribute to characters popularized in Walt Disney animated classics such as *Snow White, Cinderella, Dumbo, Peter Pan* and *Pinocchio*. World travelers will enjoy trying to place familiarly-costumed dolls from the hundreds that populate **It's a Small World**.

Spacy submarines styled on those dreamed up by Jules Verne highlight **20,000 Leagues Under the Sea**. Here, the Animatronic fish include a giant

A rocket ride above Tomorrowlan

squid that attempts to swallow your ship. Another slow-moving line.

Finally, there's **Tomorrowland**. Since its inception at Disneyland in the 1950s, many of its concepts have materialized; "Todayland" might be a more appropriate name. The structure that looks like an oversized tent with spires is **Space Mountain**. Disney's unique concept of keeping visitors entertained while standing in line stands out here. You enter through a cooled tunnel lined with diverting window displays until you arrive in the rarefied atmosphere of a distant planet where meteors and asteroids career overhead. Compact rockets take you on a roller-coaster ride in the dark. You can't see the hills and turns ahead, a situation that intensifies the thrills and illusions of hurtling through outer space. Expectant mothers and people with heart conditions are wisely advised not to board. Real astronauts and Jordan's King Hussein have been among distinguished space riders.

In the underground: A fascinating part of the park, off-limits to visitors, exists right under your feet. The Magic Kingdom is built above more than a mile of catacombs called **The Utilidor System**. This is the brains and brawn of the Kingdom. Disney World officials rarely provide glimpses into this private domain to preserve the illusion of fantasy above. Rest assured that thousands of people labor below to assure the amazing efficiency above.

Eventually, Walt Disney realized his Walt Disney World was just a few stages short of being a utopian city of the future. He resolved that the second phase of his Florida masterpiece would be just that – a planned community that would bring people together in an ideal environment. With an investment that grew to nearly $1 billion, the Disney corporation went ahead with the largest private construction projects in the US to date. Futuristic buildings of glass and metal rose above 600 acres of reclaimed swampland. In October, 1982, EPCOT **Center** – the "thinking man's theme park" – opened a new Disney era.

No sign of Mickey: EPCOT Center was a

EPCOT's monorail cruises past Spaceship Earth.

through the forest to tiny **Umatilla** and **Eustis** at the southern boundary. About 1,300 of Florida's 30,000 lakes speckle this county, aptly called **Lake**. Hikers can test their stamina on the forest's **Florida Hiking Trail**.

Just south is **Lake Apopka**, second largest in the state. The neighboring city of **Apopka** got its name from the Indian word for "Potato-eating place."

Lake Wales, at 250 feet above sea level, is one of the highest folds of earth in Florida. Even higher than Lake Wales is a 205-foot tower of marble and coquina atop **Iron Mountain**. Dutch immigrant Edward Bok, an early editor of the *Ladies Home Journal*, donated this **Singing Tower** to the state in 1929. He is buried at the foot of it. The tower's 53-bell carillon rings out concerts.

Spook Hill haunts Fifth Avenue in **Lake Wales**. Turn off your car motor at the bottom of the steep drive, put it into neutral, and your car will appear to roll back uphill. **Masterpiece Gardens** here has a 300,000-piece mosaic copy of *The Last Supper*. Another local religious spectacular is the **Black Hills Passion Play** at the amphitheater. Led by sturdy septuagenarian Josef Meier, it runs from February through March. The place to dine and sleep in the area is **Chalet Suzanne** at US 27 and 27A. Its rooms have Moroccan, Mexican, Italian and Indian furnishings.

US 27 south from Lake Wales leads to a city which is famous only for auto racing – **Sebring**. The city's population of 7,500 swells by tens of thousands annually in March during the 12 hours of the Sebring endurance test race.

Off US 27 west of Sebring, drive into the steamy jungles of **Highlands Hammock State Park**. It has excellent hiking trails through cypress swamps. Head west on SR 70 to **Arcadia** (more cowboys and big rodeos), then north on US 17 to **Bartow**. It marks the center of a controversial industry that has taken its toll on the environment, but bolstered the state's economy. Whether you turn east or west on State Road 60, you will pass lunar-like landscapes of sand mountains and craters filled with slime or stinking water. This is Bone Valley, the heart of the phosphate mining industry.

Florida produces 25 percent of the world's phosphate, which is a chemical byproduct of alluvial wastes washed into the sea in prehistoric times. These waste matters settled under the soft soil as the seas receded. Most phosphate is turned into agricultural fertilizers vital to food production.

Phosphate officials argue that the industry contributes $3 billion a year to the state's economy. But because of the industry's obvious effect on land and rivers, phosphate producers have a public relations problem. You can probably arrange a tour of mines and reclamation efforts through the **Florida Phosphate Council** office in Lakeland.

Draglines frequently dig up fossils of incredible Pleistocene era animals such as mammoths, saber-toothed tigers and giant sharks – hence the name Bone Valley. Some skeletal remains are on display at the **Bone Valley Exposition**.

Organic architecture: Lakeland, north of Bartow, is another blue-collar city. Of main interest to tourists is **Florida Southern College** at McDonald Street and Ingraham Avenue. Students study within the world's largest collection of buildings designed by Frank Lloyd Wright. He began showcasing his "organic architecture" here, considered futuristic at the time, with construction of the **Annie Pfeiffer Chapel** in 1938. Maps providing a self-guided tour of these functional works of art can be obtained at the administration building. Visit the esplanade between buildings and marvel at its colored-glass squares that provide a rainbow of sunshine.

Now that you have seen Central Florida, whet your appetite for one of the best feasts of southern home-cooking this side of Atlanta. Follow the signs on I-4 to Branch Forbes Road and **The Branch Ranch** restaurant. The Branch family converted their home into dining rooms in 1956 and have fed legions of fans ever since. Order a main course of fried chicken, prime rib, even lobster, then endless plates of okra, fried eggplant, squash and cornbread will pile up before you. You'll leave Central Florida with a happy stomach.

Right, inspecting a phosphate slime pit dig.

271

273

In the midst of a seemingly endless swath of North Florida pine forest, a billboard needs only three words to tell the contemporary story of this largely undiscovered and undeveloped region.

"Florida's Last Frontier," proclaims the sign, put there by a real-estate man anxious to sell lots to modern "pioneers." If the billboard gives the impression that the northern reaches of the Sunshine State are a little old-fashioned and move at a slower pace than the rest of Florida, perhaps it is correct. And if the sign means that some of the state's last hidden treasures – unsullied beaches, meandering rivers and inland wilderness – await discovery here, that is also true.

But if the billboard implies a place without a past, a clean slate ready for the first chalkings of civilization, then it is woefully misleading. For it was these piney woods that attracted Florida's first Spanish settlers, that resounded with the musketry of both international and civil warfare, that helped some men amass fabulous wealth but seldom allowed them to keep it.

No, this area is not one that lacks a past. If anything, it has too many pasts. Pensacola, for example, is now a thriving metropolis, but the city has been the booty of five different nations. There were places like Magnolia and Saint Joseph and New Port, once prosperous communities with fancy hotels and sedate mansions, now wiped off the face of the earth by fire or rain or disease. Madison's Southern charm and Gainesville's air of academia have roots dating back before the Civil War. Indeed, the heritage of this entire region is written in overnight success, in booms of lumber and cotton and citrus, followed by busts so total that little remains of the heady glory days.

And what of North Florida today, this last frontier? It is a land of contrasts, cosmopolitan in its big cities of Pensacola and Tallahasee, but overwhelmingly rural in the Panhandle that stretches between them. Like the rest of the state, it has its frenetic seaside communities. But there are fewer of them than elsewhere, and many more stretches of pristine beach, white and powdery as sugar, without a hint of a high-rise building.

Preceding pages: morning mist near the Suwannee River. **Left**, retirees out for a race.

THE PANHANDLE

At the western gateway to the state – more than 600 miles from the crowds and condominiums of fast-paced Miami – rests **Pensacola**, a coastal city that is a mixture of Old South charm, Spanish heritage and Navy bravado.

In many ways, it is the forgotten city of Florida. Tucked away in the far west corner of the state, Pensacola long has been shunned by snow-weary tourists migrating south on the interstate. Likewise, the state's more cosmopolitan residents have tended to ignore the city, tossing it off as South Alabama "Cracker Country."

What's more, the history books have all but ignored the city's claim to fame as the oldest settlement in America. Instead, the East Coast's St Augustine, the oldest continuous settlement, has garnered the glory and the tourists.

But never mind that others seem to have forgotten. Pensacola has not. The city has remembered its past and begun promoting its future in tourism. And well it might. There's no question it has the beaches, miles and miles of undeveloped coast where sand dunes – not condominiums – spiral high above blue seas. The northern tourist may not have discovered Pensacola's Santa Rosa Island yet, but Mississippians and Alabamans did long ago.

Pensacola also has history on its side. For the vacationer seeking more than sun, the city boasts dozens of blocks of history preserved in two districts near downtown, in museums, old battlesites and forts. And it isn't just in museum pieces that the city's history lives. It walks streets with names like Intendencia, Zaragoza and Cervantes, that somehow have survived in a grits-for-breakfast town. And it moves in the wind at St Michael's Cemetery, where tombstones bearing Spanish inscriptions date back to the 1700s.

Pensacola is the largest city in the Panhandle, with a metropolitan area population of more than 300,000. It offers good seafood restaurants, lively downtown, greyhound racing year round and stock-car racing during the summer tourist season. It is a city that moves at the pace of a slow southern drawl. But it is also a city of nightlife, with entertainment ranging from goodtime jazz to the more flashy pleasures of the famous **Trader Jon's**, where sailors from the nearby Naval Air Station drink and party surrounded by memorabilia of Navy history and famous pilots who came to Trader Jon's before them.

Make no mistake, Pensacola is a melting pot. It is a ragtag mixture of Spanish, French, British, American, Confederate and Navy influences that has been stirred for four centuries.

For the record, Pensacola was settled in 1559, six years before St Augustine. But alas, Don Tristan de Luna and the 1,500 colonists who ventured with him into Florida abandoned the settlement two years later, fed up with hurricanes, Creek Indians and each other.

So it was not until 1752 that Pensacola was established as a permanent settlement, though the Spaniards had tried

again in 1698 and 1722. Since its founding, Pensacola has flown the flags of five countries in **Plaza Ferdinand VII**, a downtown park named for the one-time king of Spain. You might say Pensacola became a volleyball, tossed back and forth between countries so many times that its government changed 17 times in 300 years.

Springtime in Seville: Each year in May, the city remembers its checkered history with the Fiesta of Five Flags, a celebration complete with parades, art shows, exhibits and contests, capped by a local citizens' re-enactment of de Luna's landing in 1559. The fiesta is a good time to visit Pensacola, not only because of the pageantry, but also because May brings beach weather to the Panhandle. The bulk of the festival takes place in the **Seville Square** area, where the colony was established in 1752 and, under order of King Ferdinand VI, named "Panzacola." The name, later modified, is said to be of Indian origin, meaning "long-haired people."

Today, the original square near Pensacola Bay is the centerpiece of a 37-block section of restored homes, specialty shops and old-time eateries that is Pensacola's crowning achievement in historic preservation. Several museums trace the city's history and booms. The square is a pleasant place to spend an afternoon roaming on foot.

Most vaunted of the area's several restored houses (all open for touring daily) is, of course, "the Oldest House." Many Florida cities have one. This structure, also known as the **Lavalle House,** is part of the **Pensacola Historic Village**, which features three museums, including the **T.T. Wentworth Jr Museum**, once the city hall. The exact construction date of Lavalle House is unknown, but historians consider it typical of the French Creole cottages of the 18th century. Much sturdier than modern homes, its wood frame has brick nogging in all the walls to which plaster was directly applied.

Other old houses have been turned into stores specializing in antiques or handmade quilts, or quaint restaurants

Aftermath of a 1906 hurricane that hit Pensacola Harbor.

serving deli sandwiches, wine and cheese or gourmet ice cream. The **Pensacola Art Center**, housed in an old jail, is in their midst.

Seville Quarter, *the* nightspot in town, is located on the fringe of the Seville Square area in a restored 19th-century building. The most famous inhabitant is **Rosie O'Grady's Goodtime Emporium**, a jazz joint where the bartenders sing and dance as well as serve. The atmosphere is beer-and-peanuts casual. Also in the Quarter are a disco, an easy-listening lounge featuring fruit drinks, an outside courtyard bar, an oyster bar and an aviators' pub as well as a restaurant.

"A vast, howling wilderness": Although most of the houses now in Seville Square's preservation district were built in post-Civil War days, the area has a history that began with the Revolutionary War. Then, the square was part of a British stockade. The English also occupied **Fort George**, the ruins of which still stand on Palafox Street. The British lost Pensacola in 1781 after a Spanish military leader named Bernardo de Galvez successfully commanded a month-long siege upon the fort. The victory not only returned the province to the Spaniards, but cut off British access to America and buoyed the hopes of colonists fighting for independence further north.

Four decades later, when the Americans – led by Andrew Jackson – marched into Pensacola to claim Florida as their own, the Spaniards may have pondered the wisdom of that assistance. Jackson, the first territorial governor of Florida, stomped about the city, struggling to convince the Spaniards to clean up streets and forts he found "filthy and disgusting." His prim wife Rachel was shocked by the vice she saw, and urged dancers and gamblers to "make the Sabbath the market day for thy soul."

"Oh, how shall I make you sensible of what a heathen land I am in?" she moaned in a letter to friends. "I feel as if I were in a vast, howling wilderness, far from my friends of the Lord."

The Jacksons stayed two months in Pensacola. Then they packed up and went home, leaving the job of governing the "heathen" city to a subordinate who later embezzled the town treasury.

Geronimo!: Seville Square isn't the only area of Pensacola where a hundred tales of the past lie buried, waiting to be found. Across the bay, **Fort Pickens**, a pentagonal-star stronghold with a bastion at each corner, took five years to build and accommodated as many as 600 men in battle. Here the ghosts of the Civil War mingle with that of a proud Indian chief.

In the opening days of the War Between the States, Fort Pickens on Santa Rosa Island went to war against **Fort Barrancas** on the mainland, just a few miles away. It was American against American, Rebel versus Yankee. Some historians believe the first shots of the tragic national conflict may have actually been fired here, not at Fort Sumter in South Carolina. In the end, the Union soldiers, manning the gunneries at Fort Pickens, triumphed over the Confederates at Barrancas, and the city of Pensacola fell into Union hands.

ld growth.

Both forts can be toured, and guides are available to answer questions. Pickens has 160 campsites. A mile and a half east, the **Dune Nature Trail** winds through spectacular sand ridges, towering slash pine and live oak laden with reindeer moss. Barrancas, built by the Spaniards and later fortified by the English, is located in the grounds of the Naval Air Station.

Although neither fort saw much action after the Civil War, Fort Pickens remained in the limelight through the 1880s. For two years, the fort was jail to Geronimo, the proud Apache chief who refused to give in to the white man. Soldiers chained Geronimo to the massive walls of the garrison from 1886 to 1888. On Sunday afternoons, it is said, Geronimo had to face the jeers of prosperous Pensacola residents, who came to Pickens to ogle the chief.

That was in the days of Pensacola's lumber boom, when the city was chopping and exporting trees with wild abandon. Without thinking of the day when the timber would be gone, the residents built big houses and made big money. Today, dozens of houses from that era still stand in a 50-block area called the **North Hill Preservation District**, near downtown. Thanks to preservationists who set out to save the decaying neighborhood, many of the homes have been restored, and others are in the process of being refurbished. They were built in Classic Revival, Queen Anne or Spanish Mission style. Visitors must content themselves with the view from outside, as most are private residences.

The same boom that produced the elaborate houses also brought the railroad to the the city through the work of a local man, W.D. Chipley. After linking Pensacola to eastern Florida by rail, Chipley turned to another job: promoting Pensacola. He dubbed the city "the Naples of Florida" and assured northerners that in "winter and summer, its healthfulness is marvelous, except during epidemics."

But a bust usually follows a boom. One day the trees were gone. The foreign ships left Pensacola's ports. And

Pensacola-based Blue Angels taxi for a take-off

the ship-building at the Pensacola Navy Yard shut down. Without the Navy and a new-fangled contraption called the airplane, Pensacola might have turned into a ghost town. Instead, it became home to America's first **Naval Air Station** in 1914. Today, it is billed as the world's largest, the "Annapolis of the Air." All Navy training for land and sea is headquartered at the base. The Navy is the city's biggest employer with 9,000 civilians on its payroll in addition to the 10,000 sailors stationed on base.

The fly boys: Located on the west side of town at **Sherman Field**, near Warrington, are the headquarters of the famous precision-flying team, the Blue Angels, who wing their way through two local shows each year. Fort Barrancas and the **National Museum of Aviation** are also on the base. Exhibits include 40 full-size aircraft, a Space Age Skylab module, and memorabilia from the exploits of "Pappy" Boyington and the Black Sheep Squadron.

From the base, it is just a jaunt across the bay to Pensacola's most natural attraction – its pristine beaches. On **Santa Rosa Island** off the coast of the city, the sand and sea are protected as part of the **Gulf Islands National Seashore**, and development is limited. From Pensacola Beach west to Fort Pickens, there's nothing but sand, scrub live oak and sea oaks for miles. Visitors can stop at park sites and unload for a day in the sun, or a picnic. There are also campsites for overnight stays and nature trails for exploring the area.

In the other direction on State Route 399, the resort city of Pensacola Beach mimics Miami along a crescent of natural coast packed with high-rise hotels. Further east, Route 399 again becomes a strip of concrete bordered only by sand and sea.

Pensacola is *the* military town in the Panhandle, but the US Air Force also has two bases to the east – **Eglin** and **Tyndall**. Eglin is the largest American air base in the world. It has an aircraft museum that is open daily.

Eglin also boasts the world's largest environmental test chamber, the

McKinley Climatic Laboratory. Here, snow can be produced and tropical monsoons and jungle or desert climes simulated. It is not usually open to the public.

The smaller base at Tyndall lies east of Panama City, providing basic and advanced flight training for Air Force personnel. Tyndall opened on the morning that the US entered World War II and counted actor Clark Gable, a gunnery student, among its first graduates.

A Garden of Eden: Interstate 10, a four-lane, limited-access superhighway, exits Pensacola and crosses the center of the Panhandle, putting motorists in Tallahassee in less than four hours. Most of the landscape is small farms and the ever-present pine tree, but there are places worth seeing on either side of the expressway.

The largest of Florida's four state forests is located northeast of Pensacola. **Blackwater River State Forest** is a 183,000-acre woodland with hiking, camping, boating and fishing. The **Red Ground Trail**, once a major trading corridor for the Indians, is now a popular hiking path, and an environmental center where visitors can learn about indigenous plants and animals.

East of Blackwater on US Highway 331 near the Florida-Alabama border is the state's highest point – 345 feet above sea level, but remember that most of Florida is as flat as a flyswatter. Follow the arrow to a crumbling church on **Britton Hill**.

Although Florida is full of rivers, the lack of much vertical contour in the land has contributed to its lack of waterfalls. So rare is the sight that the state has created a 154 acre recreation area in the pastoral surroundings of the 80-foot **Falling Waters**, just south of Chipley on State Road 77A.

An entirely different atmosphere oozes from the eerie surface of the **Dead Lakes**, a recreation area 4 miles north of Wewahitchka on State Road 71. A forest of barren cypress, oak and pine is drowned by the natural overflow of the Chipola River.

Midway along the interstate to Tallahassee is the **Florida Caverns**

Pigs poke...

State Park, north of Marianna. It is a labyrinth of limestone made by hard-shelled sea creatures centuries before the Ice Age, when all of Florida was submerged. The floor and ceiling are decorated by crystalline projections, some honed by the years into formations resembling animals, birds, fruit, flowers and human beings. One configuration even looks like a huge pipe organ. Chambers include the Waterfall Room, Cathedral Room and beautiful Wedding Room.

East of Marianna is **Torreya State Park**, now a retreat for campers and and anglers but once, according to local legend, the home of Adam and Eve. Local folks say this was the site of the biblical Garden of Eden, citing as evidence the nearby Apalachicola River and the rare tree from which the park takes its name.

The torreya tree also is known as gopher wood, which is said to be the substance Noah used to build his biblical ark. The tree grows naturally only on the banks of the Apalachicola, which is said to be the world's only "four-headed" river system – the one described in the Bible as being near the site of the downfall of Adam and Eve.

From Bagdad to Sumatra: Highway signs along the busy interstate point the way to small towns like Bagdad and Two Egg. Unfortunately, the names are more exotic than the places themselves.

Bagdad was once a prosperous lumber port where a company of the same name operated. Like the fabled Asian city, Florida's Bagdad lies between two rivers on a grassy peninsula.

Also in the same area, on US 90, is **Milton**, once known as Hard Scrabble and Scratch Ankle. Those names were warnings of its many briars, which caused painful ankles among those who had to scrabble their way through town. Most were smugglers trying to avoid the payment of tariffs at the official import-export station in Pensacola. On the last Thursday in March residents recall this bit of 1800s memorabilia at the Scratch Ankle Festival.

Closer to Tallahassee, visitors may

...and a granny plows.

see signs directing them to **Sumatra** and **Sopchoppy**. Sumatra owes its name to a variety of tobacco once cultivated in the area, a strain similar to that grown on the island of Sumatra in the Indonesian archipelago. Sopchoppy's name came from the Indian words for "long" and "twisted," certainly a precise description of the nearby Sopchoppy River.

The whitest sand: If you have time on your hands and a yen for magnificent scenery, the route to take from Pensacola is State 399 east along Santa Rosa Island, later picking up US 98. Driving pleasure isn't the only plus here. The route passes through territory chock full of untrammeled vacation spots that might cause you to stop for a day or for the rest of your vacation.

Beyond the condominiums and hotels of Pensacola Beach, you can revel in miles of billowing sand dunes topped by miniature magnolias. This stretch is the beginning of the **Miracle Strip**, a sweep of beach from Pensacola to Panama City largely undiscovered by tourists. It's also part of the **Gulf Islands National Seashore**, which stretches 150 miles westward from Pensacola to Gulfport, Mississippi. The strip's promoters claim the sands are the whitest in the world. On a sunny day, with the wind rippling patterns across miles of empty beach, it becomes hard to argue with them.

Communities along here ebb and wane from small to smaller. They include a bevy of beaches: Oriole, Woodlawn, Navarre, Grayton, Seagrove.

Fort Walton Beach is the first big coastal city you run into after you swing back to US 98. Its proximity to the military bases lends it a honky-tonk air. The town is filled with swaggering young recruits whose patronage has resulted in a strip of tacky bars, amusement parks and miniature golf courses. But the small military paychecks have also kept the beach attractions relatively inexpensive.

Fort Walton earned its slapdash military look early, as the site of the garrison after which it was named. The fort served as a safe haven during the Seminole Wars against the Indians. Its sands are rich in remnants from its early days as a home for the Pensacola, Apalachicola and Apalachee tribes.

Next on US 98 is **Destin**. Named for a sea captain, it calls itself the "World's Luckiest Fishing Village." The waters here change color, from pale green to cobalt blue, where Choctawhatchee Bay merges with the Gulf of Mexico. Its fishing reputation stems from its proximity to De Soto Canyon where marlin and sailfish test their strength and cunning against fishermen. Once a quiet resort, it is now marred by towering condominiums.

You can trade in those high-rises for a look at a gracious old Southern mansion that compliments the land just a mile north of Highway 98 in **Point Washington**. The white-columned home was built of heart-pine and cypress before the turn of the century by a local lumber baron. Located on Choctawhatchee Bay, it became a social center in the Panhandle. It has been restored and refurnished with antiques, among them a 200-year-old French

Florida beach sand sculpture.

284

grandfather clock and a 17th-century cherry bed. It is open to visitors.

Continue back to US 98, then turn off on the secondary road, State 283, that leads to State Road 30A. Near **Seagrove Beach**, you can park your car and hike through sand-dune valleys to the crystal Gulf waters and blinding beach sands. Pick a warm day in February or March, and you will have complete privacy. Only a few dune buggy tracks and bird-claw prints blemish the sands at this time of year.

After an afternoon of solitude, more gregarious travelers may wish to continue back to US 98 and venture east to **Panama City Beach**, another stretch of garish "Goony Golf" courses and souvenir emporiums. This southern Coney Island is quiet in the winter when frosty winds make the Panhandle cooler than peninsular parts of Florida. But in the summertime it comes to life.

The Redneck Riviera: So many Southerners from Georgia and Alabama own summer retreats or standing reservations at hotels along the Miracle Mile

that Panama City Beach has become the heart of what even the locals call the "Redneck Riviera." Here, country music saloons and a **Christian Music Hall** shaped like Noah's Ark mingle with a slew of beer guzzling bars and gaudy attractions. You can fly in a helicopter, ride on a dune buggy, surf on a sailboard or slide down water flumes. Penny arcades provide the latest in Japanese electronic wizardry. Round off your visit with a stop at **Zoo World**, or catch the sealion and dolphin shows at **Gulf World**.

In spite of the clutter, it's advisable to spend a night here rather than vacation in **Panama City**, on the mainland across St Andrews Bay, where fumes from the local paper mill are best avoided. The name may conjure up images of Latin architecture and Spanish revelry, but don't look for any. The founder merely noticed the fledgling community was on a direct line between Chicago and the real Panama City in the Canal Zone, so he borrowed the name. On the city's eastern outskirts is Tyndall Air Base.

Sand that looks like snow, Miracle Strip.

Several parks with more breathable air are within driving distance of Panama City. At the **Washington County Kennel Club**, greyhounds chase mechanical rabbits to the cheers of hopeful bettors. The club's season is from May to September.

The beachy atmosphere tapers off somewhat after Panama City as the coastline becomes more rugged. The towns here are more compact and their night life less effervescent, but their region is rich in both nature and history.

The first community of any size is **Port St Joe**. It's the kind of slow-moving place where the local disco shares its dance floor with a bowling alley. Today's sleepy pace belies a tempestuous yesteryear that saw the town spurt into existence almost overnight in the 1820s, only to be wiped out repeatedly by disease and other calamities. Port St Joe earned recognition as the site of Florida's first constitutional convention in 1838 and 1839. A museum now marks the spot.

Port St Joe was originally known as Saint Joseph, but the pious name belied the freewheeling character of the community, once considered the "richest and wickedest city in the Southeast." In those days, the town jumped to the rhythm of a major cotton-shipping port replete with wharves, warehouses, casinos, racetracks and sprawling mansions. That ended when yellow fever ravaged the town, killing three-quarters of the population within a year. A woodland fire did further damage, and a tidal wave administered the final blow, literally burying the city in sand.

Detour south then west on State 30E to sample the otherwordly magnificence of the **Cape San Blas** shoreline. Sunset is a particularly moody time to sit on the sand dunes and gaze out over the sullen Gulf of Mexico. But be sure to take insect repellent.

Southeast of Port St Joe is **St Vincent Island**, a 13,000-acre wildlife preserve of stunning beauty. St Vincent is for those who enjoy sand between their toes. And wildlife enthusiasts will find nirvana here. A plethora of native and **Stilts and sails near the Miracle Mile.**

transplanted animals, including sambar deer from India and loggerhead turtles, mingle with white-tailed deer and wild turkeys. Once a private hunting preserve, it is now owned by the federal government. The preserve can be reached only by boat.

Shucking oysters: About 25 miles east of Port St Joe is the old cotton port of **Apalachicola**, now a city whose name is synonymous with oysters. Apalachicola Bay provides Florida with 90 percent of its annual oyster harvest.

Here you can watch "farmers" harvest oysters by hand in waters close to shore. They use tongs – two crossed shovels joined at the lower end of the handles – to pincer their prey, which is cultivated in carefully selected water, neither too salty nor too fresh. Befriend an oyster farmer and he may teach you the technique.

Oyster shucking is another art. Scrape them from the half-shell, then eat them the way the natives do at the "raw bars."

Although the city's reputation revolves around oysters, mouth-watering mollusks are not Apalachicola's only contribution to mankind. One of the city's early physicians made the world more bearable by giving us manmade ice, refrigeration and air-conditioning.

While struggling to control malaria in the region in the late 1840s, Dr John Gorrie succeeded in building a machine that kept his patients' rooms cool. Gorrie did get a patent for the machine, but did not get credit for his work until long after his death in 1851. Now, a museum in his honor in Apalachicola displays a replica of the first ice machine. The original is in the Smithsonian Institution in Washington, DC. A statue of Dr Gorrie stands in the Statuary Hall of Fame in the US Capitol.

You'll make use of another memorial to the good doctor when you leave Apalachicola, taking the Gorrie Bridge east over Apalachicola Bay. Here you cross into the Eastern time zone (you've been in Central), so set your watch ahead an hour. At the end of the Gorrie Bridge, across the toll bridge to the right, is **St George Island**, where a state park with

Apalachicola blue crabs.

more than 9 miles of undeveloped beach boasts mountains of sand.

Another remnant of a long-gone boom era is **Carrabelle**, about 30 miles east along the coast. Once a prominent lumber port, it is now a tiny town with an economy based on commercial fishing. In fact, business from the vacation crowd is only a sideline along most of the waterfront in the eastern Panhandle. The seafood industry brings in the big bucks. From dozens of small ports as you drive down US 98, you will see shrimp boats sally forth into the Gulf of Mexico for days or weeks at sea, dropping their nets into the isolated sandy haunts of the delectable crustacean known in these parts as "Pink Gold."

Buying the vote with mullet: The most exciting of the inshore catches here may be mullet. Fishermen use long, narrow skiffs in their search, the better to pole shallow bayous often favored by mullet. Paying out nets in a half-circle, the mullet fishermen wait until a school blunders into the mesh, then close the circle around the frantic fish, and pull

the net in by hand. Numerous seaside industries in the Panhandle and other parts of Florida process and smoke mullet for export throughout the world.

Decades of back-slapping office seekers have made mullet the main course of the Panhandle political dinner. Candidates in other areas ply their potential constituents with any of a hundred vote-getting menus, but in North Florida, deep-fried mullet is the way to win votes. Politicians usually serve it with coleslaw or baked beans, grits and hush puppies – made from a batter of cornmeal mixed with eggs.

Beyond Carrabelle, the coastal drive dribbles away into even smaller settlements. A right turn on State 370 leads to more beaches, as well as that increasingly predominant denizen of the Florida coastline, the stilt house. The road deadends at **Alligator Point**.

Swing back to US 98, and take another detour at **Spring Creek**, off State Route 367. This is the first of the sleepy fishing villages dominating the Big Bend area of Florida, where the Panhandle arcs into the state's peninsula.

Necessity is one reason why commercial fishing looms so large in the economies of places like Apalachicola, Carrabelle and Spring Creek. Dense swamp and forest to the north make living from the land impossible. Indeed, Carrabelle lies near one of the most deserted areas of the state, **Tate's Hell Swamp**. Ironically, only 50 miles or so north is Torreya State Park, the place thought by some to have been the Garden of Eden.

An unusual place with an unusual name, Tate's Hell sprawls over most of Franklin County. Its inhospitable interior, a breeding ground for the deadly water moccasin, may have been a bog as long ago as 100 centuries, according to fossil discoveries. The swamp is owned by a lumber company that has identified trees deep within its recesses as more than 600 years old.

The strange name of this eerie enclave emanated from the legend of Old Man Tate, a hunter who vanished into its tangled depths almost a century ago. According to local lore, he entered the

A shrine in the sunshine

swamp in search of a panther that had been killing his livestock. It took him a week to find his way out, a terrifying ordeal during which he was fatally bitten by a snake. A Will McClean folk song tells the rest of the story:

When Tate was discovered, these words he did tell:
'My name is Old Tate boys, and I've just been to hell!'
These few spoken words were the last that he said;
His spirit it left him, Old Tate he was dead.

That, at least, is the legend. Invention or not, it resulted in a colorful name which also describes some pretty forbidding territory.

The swamp bleeds into another vast domain with remote nooks and crannies of its own, the **Apalachicola National Forest**. It covers parts of four counties, and extends to the fringes of Tallahassee Municipal Airport. The largest of the three national forests in Florida, the Apalachicola preserve has numerous recreational facilities.

The adventurous may wish to challenge the preserve's **Bradwell Bay Wilderness**. Though not actually a bay in the traditional sense, the low elevation of the Bradwell Bay terrain has left parts of it submerged and choked with underbrush. Federal law prohibits modern forestry techniques here, part of a national wilderness program designed to keep certain isolated regions in a natural state. Would-be explorers are welcome but forewarned of the formidable hiking conditions.

The lower end of the **Ochlockonee River** meanders through the Apalachicola National Forest, providing canoeists with pristine rowing through pine and cypress woodlands rife with wildlife. A canoe trail begins 20 miles west of Tallahasee and continues downriver for 67 miles to Ochlockonee River State Park, on US 319 south of Sopchoppy between Carrabelle and Spring Creek. The upper Ochlockonee River pours into Lake Talquin west of Tallahassee, 73 miles after commencing near Thomasville, Georgia.

A good catch.

tory here in full blue-and-gray regalia.

Beyond the national forest, US 90 continues through another string of small towns before reaching Jacksonville (*see* "*East Coast*") and crossing the **St Johns River**, a wide channel that marks the eastern boundary of the region covered in this section. The renowned French marine explorer, Jacques Cousteau, filmed a television special about the endangered manatees of the St Johns. The river courses backwards – that is, south to north. Below Jacksonville, it passes through the last of the enclaves that fell victim to the boom-and-bust cycle of North Florida. Today strung out along US 17, these settlements saw sudden wealth vanish as industry and immigrants moved further south.

Here, steamboats and citrus brought the early wealth. In the middle and late 19th century, the steamboats cruised the St Johns, ferrying wintering northerners to fine hotels and hunting clubs at places like Mandarin, Enterprise, Palatka and Green Cove Springs. The paddle-wheelers followed the same routes blazed centuries earlier on the river by French and Spanish explorers.

Citrus fruits, meanwhile, provided a stable income for growers in the area. Among famous residents was the author of *Uncle Tom's Cabin*, Harriet Beecher Stowe, whose home in Mandarin has succumbed to fire.

All that was before railroads put the steamboats out of business, a series of freezes killed the local citrus industry, and tourists and oranges headed south.

Now some old residences of the wealthy have been restored, mainly in **Green Cove Springs**. **Palatka** has traded in its reputation as a center of hostelries to become the "Bass Fishing Capital of the World."

The Palatka area also boasts its own Sasquatch or yeti-type creature. In minuscule **Bardin**, northwest of the town, residents talk of a hairy half-ape, half-man creature, about 7 feet tall, that stalks the woods around the village. They call it the Booger.

From Palatka, it's a pleasant drive west on State Route 20 through rural communities to **Gainesville,** home of the **University of Florida**, the state's largest center of learning. It dates back to 1854, when Florida achieved statehood and received a federal grant to establish two seminaries. East Florida Seminary later became the University of Florida, while West Florida Seminary was the precursor to Florida State University in Tallahassee.

The university area abounds with the restaurants, discos and taverns that are part of higher education today. To get a feel for some of the local flavor, stop in at **Lillian's Music Store** downtown on 1st Street. Scotch and soda have replaced sheet music at Lillian's which is now one of the town's most popular bars. Florida writer Harry Crews who lives in Gainesville, occasionally shows up at the bar as do professors, students, bankers, and plumbers. Those seeking intellectual stimulation can try the school's art gallery, which presents regular showings by faculty members and students, and the popular **Hippodrome** for theatrical performances.

The home of author Marjorie Kinnan Rawlings is in **Cross Creek**, southeast of Gainesville on State 325. This setting provided the inspiration for her Pulitzer Prize-winning *The Yearling*. She migrated in 1928 from her native New York, wrote of her experiences among country folk, and is buried a few miles away at **Island Grove**.

West of Cross Creek is **Micanopy**, another 19th-century vacation spot and citrus center that fell on hard times and is now being restored.

Further west, off US 41, is **Payne's Prairie**, a vast sea of grass. It once encompassed a large lake that served as an Indian homesite as far back as 7000 BC. A herd of buffalo once hunted to extinction here has been replaced with a new herd allowed to roam this state preserve. Guided tours are available.

One of Florida's many illustrious sinkholes can be toured on the northwestern outskirts of Gainesville. **The Devil's Millhopper** is particularly remarkable. It covers 5 acres, drops 100 feet, and is overgrown with exotic subtropical rainforest, including giant ferns and a splendid waterfall.

Right, Cross Creek crossing.

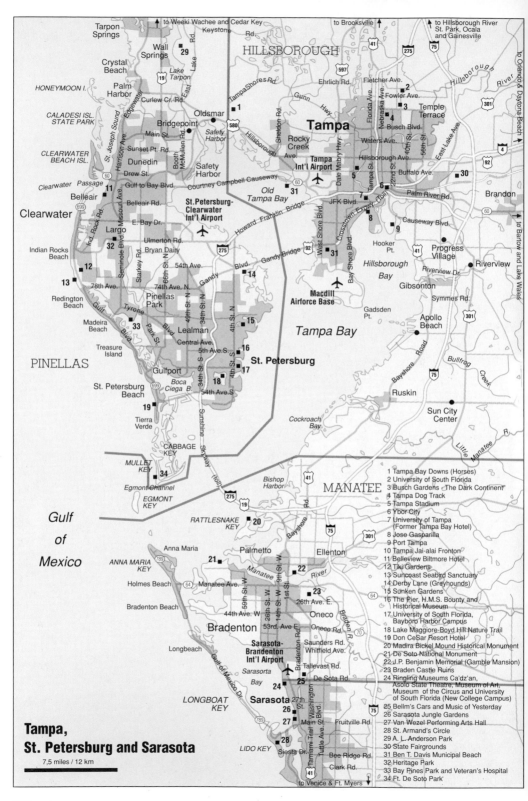

Tarpon Springs
Wall Springs • 29
Keystone Rd.
to Weeki Wachee and Cedar Key
to Brooksville
to Hillsborough River St. Park, Ocala and Gainesville

HILLSBOROUGH

Crystal Beach
HONEYMOON I.
Palm Harbor
CALADESI ISL. STATE PARK
CLEARWATER BEACH ISL.
Dunedin
Clearwater Passage
Belleair
Clearwater

Lake Tarpon
Curlew Cr. Rd.
Oldsmar • 1
Bridgepoint
Safety Harbor
Main St.
Sunset Pt. Rd.
Drew St.
Gulf to Bay Blvd.
Belleair Rd.
E. Bay Dr.
Ulmerton Rd.
Bryan Dairy
54th Ave.
74th Ave. N.
78th Ave.
Tyrone

Ehrlich Rd.
Fletcher Ave. • 2
Fowler Ave. • 3
Temple Terrace
Busch Blvd. • 4
Waters Ave.
Hillsborough Ave.
Buffalo Ave.
• 30
Brandon

Tampa
Rocky Creek Ave.
Tampa Int'l Airport
St. Petersburg-Clearwater Int'l Airport
Courtney Campbell Causeway
Old Tampa Bay • 31
Howard Franklin Bridge
Gandy Bridge
• 92
• 5
• 7
• 6
JFK Blvd.
• 8
• 9
Palm River Rd.
Causeway Blvd.
Hooker Pt.
Progress Village
Riverview Dr. • Riverview
Hillsborough Bay
Gibsonton

Indian Rocks Beach • 12
• 13
Redington Beach
Madeira Beach • 33
Treasure Island
PINELLAS
Largo • 32
Pinellas Park
Lealman
Central Ave.
5th Ave. S.
Gulfport
Boca Ciega B.
St. Petersburg Beach • 19
Tierra Verde
• 14
• 15
• 16
• 17
• 18
54th Ave. S.
St. Petersburg
Macdill Airforce Base
Gadsden Pt.
Tampa Bay
Symmes Rd.
Apollo Beach
Bullfrog Creek
Little Manatee R.

CABBAGE KEY
MULLET KEY • 34
Egmont Channel
EGMONT KEY
Gulf of Mexico

Bishop Harbor
Cockroach Bay
Ruskin
Sun City Center
• 75

RATTLESNAKE KEY • 20
ANNA MARIA KEY
Anna Maria
Holmes Beach
Bradenton Beach
Palmetto • 21
Manatee Ave.
Manatee River
• 22
Ellenton
• 23
26th Ave. E.
Oneco
Bradenton
44th Ave. W
53rd Ave. E
Longbeach
Saunders Rd.
Whitfield Ave.
Oneco Rd.
MANATEE
Sarasota-Brandenton Int'l Airport
Sarasorta Bay
• 24 • 25
Tallevast Rd.
De Sota Rd.
LONGBOAT KEY
Sarasota
• 26
• 27
27th St.
Main St.
Fruitville Rd.
Bee Ridge Rd.
Clark Rd.
LIDO KEY • 28
Siesta Dr.
to Venice & Ft. Myers

Tampa, St. Petersburg and Sarasota

7,5 miles / 12 km

1 Tampa Bay Downs (Horses)
2 University of South Florida
3 Busch Gardens "The Dark Continent"
4 Tampa Dog Track
5 Tampa Stadium
6 Ybor City
7 University of Tampa (Former Tampa Bay Hotel)
8 Jose Gasparilla
9 Port Tampa
10 Tampa Jai-alai Fronton
11 Belleview Biltmore Hotel
12 Tiki Gardens
13 Suncoast Seabird Sanctuary
14 Derby Lane (Greyhounds)
15 Sunken Gardens
16 The Pier, H.M.S. Bounty and Historical Museum
17 University of South Florida, Bayboro Harbor Campus
18 Lake Maggiore-Boyd Hill Nature Trail
19 Don CeSar Resort Hotel
20 Madira Bickel Mound Historical Monument
21 De Soto National Monument
22 J.P. Benjamin Memorial (Gamble Mansion)
23 Braden Castle Ruins
24 Ringling Museums Ca'dz'an, Asolo State Theatre, Museum of Art, Museum of the Circus and University of South Florida (New College Campus)
25 Bellm's Cars and Music of Yesterday
26 Sarasota Jungle Gardens
27 Van Wezel Performing Arts Hall
28 St. Armand's Circle
29 A. L. Anderson Park
30 State Fairgrounds
31 Ben T. Davis Municipal Beach
32 Heritage Park
33 Bay Pines Park and Veteran's Hospital
34 Ft. De Soto Park

The Gulf of Mexico caresses the fine, bleached sand of Florida's West Coast. Its warm waters undulate gently, or not at all, often flat as a sheet of plate glass on humid summer days. Shells of every color and shape are washed up on the sands to the endless delight of beachcombing vacationers.

However, this tranquility contradicts the clamor on the shores. Newcomers and developers have laid siege to this once placid part of Florida. From the metropolitan Tampa/St Petersburg nucleus, one of the fastest growing towns in America, north to New Port Richey and south to Fort Myers, the West Coast has begun to resemble the waterfront wall of windows characteristic of the Miami to Palm Beach strip on the East Coast: retirement farms and youth-oriented singles complexes, stilt houses and stucco mansions. With them have come professional sports, massive malls – and anything else anyone is looking for.

And like the rest of Florida, the West Coast is a place for indulging the imagination. St Petersburg delves into the surreal with the Dali Museum, containing the largest collection of Salvador Dali's work in the world, while the glittering world of the circus is celebrated in Sarasota and Venice, where the circus master John Ringling has left a legacy of theaters, circus museums, schools for the performing arts, and festivals. And when it comes to theme parks, Tampa's Busch Gardens, otherwise known as The Dark Continent, draws more tourists than any other theme park except Disney World and Sea World. Over 300 acres of land have been turned into a mini Africa, complete with big game, a jungle cruise and an imitation Foreign Legion outpost.

But the old West Coast lingers in the fishing villages around Cedar Key and spots south of Naples, and Hispanic color still enlivens Tampa's Ybor City, founded by a wealthy Cuban tobacco merchant in the late 19th century and now, with its specialty shops and museum, a tribute to Florida's once thriving tobacco industry. Art Deco, too, may still be encountered in downtown Tampa, proving this architectural renaissance is not confined to the sunny shores of Miami Beach.

Preceding pages: a nostalgic view of Tampa.

TAMPA

The aroma of fine cigars still flavors some of the old brick-lined alleys of **Tampa**. Yet there's youthful new vigor in the air as well. Emerald office towers soar above one side of the **Hillsborough River**. The imposing spires of the old Tampa Bay Hotel-turned-university grace the other side. But for all its obvious appeal, tourists usually rush through Tampa on the interstate en route from Suncoast beaches to Disney World and company, or come to spend only a day at Busch Gardens or an evening at an excellent restaurant. Tampa certainly deserves much closer attention.

Part of the problem is that the average tourist expects a sandy beach and the sea to be part of his Florida vacation package. Tampa proper can't provide that. A pretty but polluted **Tampa Bay** and the Pinellas County peninsula lie between the city and the Gulf of Mexico. The big, bird claw of a bay bustles with international freighter traffic, carrying 51 million tons of cargo annually. It has made Tampa the nation's seventh largest port. It exports phosphate from nearby mines, citrus from area groves, cattle from Florida ranches, seafood, even yachts. At the **Twiggs Street docks**, watch the banana boats unload and see the state's largest shrimp boat fleet bring in their catch at **Hooker's Point** at the end of Bermuda Avenue.

The blue-collar workers remain the backbone of the city. They roll out 3 million cigars a day from Ybor City factories, stir vats of Schlitz and Busch beer at two major breweries, grow strawberries, pilot tankers, and pack seafood. But the brisk market in office buildings underscores an influx of white-shirted attorneys, architects and entrepreneurs.

Tampa's population of nearly 300,000 is third only to Jacksonville (whose numbers are inflated by its unusual county-size boundaries) and Miami. But it's the center of a rapidly merging multi-city megalopolis of over 2 million people.

Spanish roots: The Spanish influence here is subtler, more elegant than that of the barrios of Miami's later Cuban influx. The deep Spanish roots date way back to the landing of Pánfilo de Narváez in 1528. Settlement began much later with the establishment of Fort Brooke in 1824, one of a series built to keep tabs on the Seminole Indians. But like the East Coast cities, Tampa developed when railroad tycoon Henry B. Plant extended his narrow-guage South Florida Railroad to the Hillsborough River in 1884.

In emulating the East Coast's Henry Flagler, Plant built the **Tampa Bay Hotel**. Its incongruous silver minarets topped by Islamic crescents still lend character to the city's skyline today. Plant added Oriental rickshaws to carry guests around the opulent grounds, wicker chairs on the cool verandas and imported antiques. The hotel now houses the administrative offices of the **University of Tampa** on Kennedy Boulevard. You can visit the **Henry Plant Museum** off the lobby. It contains his collection of late Victorian era furniture and art objects. In spite of the structure's

Left, Hillsborough Lodge, downtown Tampa. Right, two feet from the water.

Middle Eastern appearance, it's another tribute to Tampa's Spanish lineage, a model of the Alhambra in Granada.

The Cuban connection: About the time Plant was building his railroad and hotel, Vincente Martinez Ybor was moving his cigar factory away from labor problems in Key West. Today, **Ybor City** no longer pulses with the color and excitement of its Cuban heyday: when crowds gathered at cockfights in the alleys and to hear Cuban freedom fighter José Marti make fiery speeches to recruit rebels and contributions for his revolution against Spain; when Teddy Roosevelt rode into town on his horse, Texas, flanked by his dog, Cuba, and the Rough Riders, before galloping to glory on San Juan Hill near Santiago; when prostitutes plied their wares on "Last Chance Street" near the docks to soldiers awaiting transfer to the Spanish American War.

Still, street vendors peddle deviled crabs and Cuban coffee. Some perfectionists still roll fine tobacco into finer cigars. Ybor City has even received a facelift that brings back shouts of "Cuba Libre!" – if only from the local bars. The very building around which the enclave grew, Ybor's cigar factory, now serves as a centerpiece that spurs restoration of other classic buildings.

Take Interstate 4 to the Ybor City exit, then head south on 21st, west on 10th and south again to 13th Street. At this cigar-making site, built in 1886, hundreds of workers used to sit at long benches inside, tediously shaping prized cigars while a "reader" sat on a platform above entertaining them with selections from poetry, books and newspapers. It kept workers happy and production high. Italian and German immigrants joined the move to this "Cuba City" to cash in on its economic vitality.

Automation eventually put most of the cigar factories out of business. Entrepreneurs rescued Martinez' handsome building, restored its iron grillwork, oak interiors, and cleaned its red-brick exterior. They have added restaurants and shops and now call it **Ybor Square**, where you can still buy a good cigar or

Cigar-making at an Ybor City factory, *circa* 1910.

treasures from Tampa attics. You can lunch with local businessmen at the rustic **Rough Riders** restaurant under old photographs of Teddy and his men and you can still see *puros* (cigars) made by hand. Or stop in at the **Ybor City State Museum**, former site of the Fertila Bakery building, on 9th Avenue. The Museum complex includes three restored cigar workers' homes, historic photos and artifacts of the cigar industry, and offers a guided history lesson on Ybor City.

Seventh Avenue has more shops. Some sell lacy Spanish fabric. Connoisseurs consider the Cuban sandwich at the **Silver Ring Cafe** Tampa's best. Atmosphere and more Spanish food is the specialty of the landmark **Columbia Restaurant** at 22nd Street. Built in 1905 by Casimiro Hernandez, the 11-room, 1,600-seat structure is a Tampa tradition. There's a flamenco floor show, strolling violinists, and dishes like chicken and yellow rice and garbanzo bean soup.

Pirate invasions: Downtown Tampa's

gleaming new skyscrapers, including a $93 million office and **Hyatt Regency Hotel** complex, are the West Coast's biggest. Nearby, the low-slung **Franklin Street Mall** allows you to window-shop unmolested by automobile traffic. The facades of **Hayman Jewelry Co.**, **Adams' City Hatters** and **Butler Shoes** showcase Florida's ubiquitous 1930s Art Deco look. The restored **Tampa Theater** here unreels movie classics, foreign films and occasional live shows.

The Tampa Museum of Art behind **Curtis Hixon Convention Hall** presents changing art and culture exhibits. The **Museum of African-American Art** on Marion Street is one of only 10 museums in the US devoted primarily to African-American art. South of downtown area are the **Shops of Harbour Island**, one of Tampa's newest attractions. Crammed onto a triangular slice of land, Harbour Island is a well-designed, waterfront shopping and entertainment complex of boutiques, restaurants and bars.

You can watch University of Tampa

Left, street scene in modern Ybor City. **Right**, downtown Tampa.

students practice crew racing along Hillsborough River. South of downtown, Bayshore Boulevard offers a waterside drive from the foot of Platt Street Bridge. Joggers jam its sidewalk, speculatively called the world's longest. If the barge docked here resembles a pirate ship, that's because it is.

Tampa's Rites of Spring occur every February when its businessmen and bigwigs exchange their tailored suits, brougham shoes and briefcases for puffy-sleeved shirts, buckled boots, pistols and sabers – even nose rings and scars – and board the *José Gasparilla* which launches for the annual Gasparilla Invasion from the Tampa Yacht Club, and berths the rest of the year at the Platt Street Bridge at Bayshore Boulevard. The ship, commissioned in 1954, has three masts which tower 100 feet above the deck. With the aid of a few early morning beers, some pirates climb to their crows' nests. They raise 300 flags in an explosion of color, blast cannon salutes, and weigh anchor for the mouth of the Hillsborough River flanked by hundreds of smaller craft with their own swashbuckling crews.

Upon landing, Ye Mystic Krewe of Gasparilla swarms into the streets of Downtown Tampa where hundreds of thousands of spectators watch them lead a parade. The mayor surrenders the city and declares a holiday. Buccaneers fling gold doubloons and blank shells from their pistols to adoring throngs in an all-day procession.

The first Gasparilla Invasion was held in 1904. It grew out of the Gulf Coast's reputation as a haunt for bloodthirsty buccaneers, particularly a dubious character named José Gaspar who, believers say, plundered, tortured and raped his way up and down the coast. Although history books sometimes record how José led a mutiny aboard the Spanish ship, *Florida Blanca*, in 1785 before becoming a pirate, no records prove his existence. Gaspar was more likely the invention of a Marco Island fisherman named Johnny Gomez, about 1870. Gomez claimed to have sailed with Gaspar and the tales helped his booming business in buried treasure maps.

Busy February also means the annual staging of the Florida State Fair at its permanent exhibition sites off Interstate 4 east of Tampa. In addition to livestock, plant and horse competitions and commercial exhibits, it features an enormous Midway chock-a-block with thrill rides, carnival games and freak shows.

The world's largest wine cellar?: Gourmands will find Tampa's restaurants among the best in Florida. One dining must that has earned a full-page story in *Playboy* magazine is **Bern's Steak House**. Its claustrophobic baroque decor, likened to the interior of a funeral parlor by some, may not appeal to all, but the selection of beef and wines will. The quality steak is aged and hand-turned 5 to 8 weeks, fine gourmet points that are explained on a menu that gives the vital statistics of each cut and a choice of weights and thickness (from a *petit filet* to a 60-ounce sirloin that serves six). Fresh caviar is flown in regularly. Cress seeds, imported from London, add the right touch to salads.

But it's the wine list that makes Bern's

Ye Mystic Krewe aboard the *José Gasparilla*.

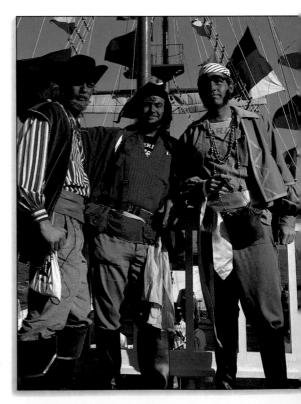

place so extraordinary. About half a million bottles, representing some 7,000 varieties of wine, fill the cellars. This collection is thought to be the largest on-hand stock of wines maintained by any restaurant in the world. An abridged version of the encyclopedic list stands on the table, but ask for a peek at the complete volume. You may have to brace yourself to lift it.

A more average meal in even odder surroundings may be eaten at **Crawdaddy's**. Don't be put off by the dirty washing on the clothesline, the chickens and barnyard smells, or the fact that the crooked building looks like it's about to tumble into Tampa Bay. Instead, feed on fried alligator and dance in the spacious disco.

From the windows of Crawdaddy's you can watch planes climb into usually clear skies from **Tampa International Airport**, a hub for traffic from Europe, the Caribbean, Mexico, South America and most of the US. This slick and extremely efficient facility has been voted the best airport in the nation by the Airline Passengers Association for the ease with which you can walk from stacked parking lots to ticket counters and on to shuttle cars that whisk you from the terminal's lobbies to gateside and back. At the southern point of the city, many of the country's combat pilots earn their wings at **MacDill Air Force Base**.

On Fowler Avenue in northeast Tampa, the **University of South Florida** serves 25,000 students on a campus that offers a planetarium and fine arts gallery for visitors. Its large arts faculty has become a leader in new visual forms.

On Busch Boulevard, the brewers of Budweiser beer have transformed the grounds around their plant into a miniature Africa alive with wild animals, snake charmers and tropical birds.

The African connection: The 300-acre theme park that has evolved around Busch Brewery and Gardens is billed as **The Dark Continent** – to the dismay of black residents who had hoped that unenlightened term had gone the way of segregated schools. The name stuck,

Sculpture at the Tampa Convention Center.

however, and the racial furor subsided. The attraction now entices more tourists than any other Florida theme park except Disney World and Sea World.

It all started simply as **Busch Gardens**, a patch southwest of the factory where families used to stare at flamingos, converse with parrots and drink free beer (limit three to a customer) at the **Hospitality House** after a tour of the brewery – where barrels of hops are turned into beer and squirted into bottles and cans traveling at breakneck speed on incredible conveyor belts.

The Busch family added an **Old Swiss House** restaurant, then some wild animals for people to watch while dining. Then someone who realized the Florida terrain could pass for an African plain brought in more animals, constructed a train and monorail to cruise the grounds, and soon discovered people would pay admission for a close look at zebras, giraffes, elephants and tigers who run free of zoo bars. Taking a cue from Walt Disney, Busch entered the theme park competition without looking back and

now encompasses over 300 acres. Its animal area became the **Serengeti Plain** and a pond in its midst was named **Lake Tanganyika**. They called the small animal farm **Nairobi** and a section with a theater and log flume **Stanleyville**.

Newer additions include sanitized versions of **Morocco**, the **Congo** and **Timbuktu**. A large hall that looks like a Foreign Legion outpost is the **Festhaus** and entertains the hot and hungry with an air-conditioned Octoberfest year round. Anyone expecting to visit Africa in Florida shouldn't quibble about finding a German oasis in Timbuktu.

There are also the inevitable thrill rides: the neck-twisting Python, the back-wrenching Scorpion, the Ubanga-banga bumper cars, the nauseating Mamba, and the African Queen jungle cruise which the park ballyhooes as having live animals, *not* plastic ones.

After a steamy day in the jungle, you can refresh yourself in the body flumes, lagoons and waterfalls of **Adventure Island** one mile north of Busch Gardens (for a separate admission fee).

High-flying Buccaneers collar a Cowboy.

Tampa panders to all people. The greyhounds match muscled strides at **Tampa Track**; horses do the same at **Tampa Bay Downs**. The Tampa Bay Buccaneers butt heads with other professional football teams at **Tampa Stadium** whenever the Tampa Bay Rowdies aren't getting their North American Soccer League kicks in the grass there. Strip joints beckon voyeurs on late-night **Dale Mabry Boulevard**.

Showtown, USA: Take US 41 south along Tampa Bay for a look at the industrial side of the state. Here, the stacks of chemical factories edge the water instead of palm trees. The road crosses a bridge over the **Alafia River** into **Gibsonton**. The **Giant's Fish Camp** is a clue to what you will find in this campy town. Fat men, bearded ladies, dwarves, the Alligator-Skinned Man, the Acrobatic Half Girl – you might see them all shopping for groceries.

The city's proximity to Sarasota, where John Ringling lived and assembled his fabulous circuses early this century, attracted them. Most of these "show people," as they prefer to be called, live here from November to May when they are not on the road.

The naked and the wild: North of Tampa, nature lovers of the *au naturel* kind will find one of the nation's oldest and largest nudist colonies – **Lake Como** in **Lutz** on US 41. The camp has made Tampa a leader in the anti-clothes movement and has spawned a trend for nudist bathing in the area. In the nearby town of **Port Richey**, and the unofficial clothes optional spots like **Beer Can Island** off **Davis Island** in Tampa Bay, family-style nude sunbathing and swimming is common. **Zephyrhills** boasts more than a bizarre name. It hosts the world parachuting championships. Six miles south of town, **Hillsborough River State Park** has 3,000 forested acres and a scary suspension bridge.

Further north on US 41, **Brooksville** is the hub of a natural wonderland. The 20-mile scenic **Dogwood Trail** takes you through **Chinsegut Hill National Wildlife Refuge** and **Withlacoochee State Forest**. The **Dade Battlefield State Historic Site** is at the north end of the forest, near **Bushnell**. It's a memorial to Major Francis L. Dade and his 100 men who were massacred here at the start of the Seminole Wars in 1835.

South of Brooksville, **Masaryktown** still celebrates Czechoslovakian Independence Day, the last Sunday of October, with native foods and dancing. Czechs settled here in 1925.

North of Zephyrhills on State Road 52, the city of **St Leo** is almost totally owned by the non-profit **Saint Leo College**, the **St Leo Abbey**, a Benedictine monastery and the **Holy Name Priory**. Nuns and monks regularly get elected to the city commission.

Three bridges connect Tampa to the Pinellas County resorts across the bay. The **Howard Frankland** (15,782 feet long) is the longest and most traveled because it's part of I-275. The excitement of the long ride over water dissolves, however, if your car breaks down midway. There are no emergency lanes. The **Gandy Bridge** is a more pleasant means of getting from Tampa to St Petersburg and back.

Gibsonton resident fondles his performing pet.

ST PETERSBURG

St Petersburg has always been the antithesis of Tampa. It's a slow-paced resort city with a reputation for catering to large numbers of fixed-income elderly. But with the booming changes sweeping the Suncoast, even sedate St Pete has begun shedding its old image. Downtown buildings are taking on new facades, while restaurants and lounges reach out for a younger, upwardly mobile crowd. The American Stage Company continues to offer live theater intermixed with foreign films at its Central Avenue stage and the summer afternoon band concerts in Williams Park are drawing an enthusiastic younger audience these days.

The opening of a **Bayboro Harbor** branch of the University of South Florida marked another milestone in Downtown St Petersburg's revitalization. The college kids have found the old hotels and boarding houses near campus economi-

cal and share them with the aged. The university library is named after the late owner of the Times Publishing Company, Nelson Poynter, a leader in the city's growth. Poynter's publications, housed in editorial offices on First Avenue South and 50th Street, include the nationally-respected, Pulitzer Prize-winning *St Petersburg Times*. The company has pioneered the use of eye-catching graphics and quality color photographic reproduction on newsprint while maintaining high journalistic standards in its editorial columns and news reports.

The loveliest and most eye-catching feature of Downtown is its **Bayfront**. The **Municipal Marina** offers a variety of sailboats at their moorings, many with exotic names like *Vanity's Fair* and *At World's End*, from ports around the world.

An inverted pyramid at the end of the **Pier** juts out into Tampa Bay from Second Avenue North. It encompasses a popular restaurant with romantic views, an observation deck on top and an array of shops and displays. The approach on the Pier offers a scenic stroll and a panorama of nature, from diving pelicans to jumping mullet, while seagulls cry overhead for a tossed or abandoned tidbit.

The classic lines of world-class competition yachts add class to docks at the **St Petersburg Yacht Club** each February. Champion helmsmen like Atlanta Braves owner Ted Turner and Americas Cup winner Dennis Conner come to town along with magnificent craft like *Tenacious, Williwaw* and the *Kialoa*. The occasion is the running of the Southern Ocean Racing Conference (SORC). The tradition began with a St Petersburg to Havana race in 1930.

That ended in 1959 when Fidel Castro took over Cuba. Since 1961, the sleek yachts have sliced through 370 miles of surf to Fort Lauderdale, then on to Nassau. Several weeks of short competitions, fine-tuning, testing and, of course, partying, precede the main event, then the yachts tack out to an area off **Pinellas Point** where a series of gunshots marks the start of each class.

Left, the pier on St Pete's Bayfront. **Below**, St Petersburg's Sunken Gardens.

Delightful Dali: During its current renaissance, St Petersburg has also received a sorely-needed cultural transfusion. In fact, a neat, spacious building adjacent to the USF Bayboro campus houses one of the world's largest collections of paintings by the late Spanish surrealist, Salvador Dali. The **Dali Museum**, opened in 1982, contains a total of 93 oils, 200 watercolors and drawings, and 1,000 prints by the artist. They are displayed on a rotating basis.

The collection was assembled over a 40-year period by a wealthy Cleveland, Ohio plastics machinery designer, A. Reynolds Morse, and his wife, Eleanor. Experts have estimated the total value of the art works at $35 million.

Guided tours through the collection – and the offbeat career of Dali – begin at regular intervals in the lobby. From the museum, it is a short drive north to St Petersburg's Bayfront.

While along the waterfront, keep an eye out for a small, brick building near the foot of Second Avenue North. It's a public restroom called affectionately by locals "**Little St Mary's.**" Legend has it that an architect for St Mary Our Lady of Grace Church a few blocks south of there used the same blueprints when commissioned by the city to design a public facility.

Next door, the **St Petersburg Historical Museum** contains Indian artifacts from the significant Weedon Island and Safety Harbor cultures. The **Museum of Fine Arts** on Beach Drive has European, Oriental and American art. Historical homes open for tours in the area are the **Grace S. Turner House, Lowe House** and **Haas Museum**, all in the 3,500 block of Second Avenue South. **Beach Drive** has taken on a continental look with expensive shops and the **Plaza Mall**. **Peter's Place** here is among the state's finest gourmet restaurants.

The **Al Lang Field** south of Beach Drive is the spring training home of the St Louis Cardinals. The **Bayfront Center** has hosted diverse entertainments – from the annual filming of the Ringling Brothers and Barnum and Bailey Circus television special to sold-

Meditating at the Dali Museum.

out performances by folk singer Lawrence Welk, and Broadway shows. Even Bob Dylan has played here.

North of the Pier, the impressive, sand-colored building on the horizon once catered to wealthy patrons. The **Vinoy Hotel** now caters to vagrants and vandals. Its windows are broken and the paint is cracking, but there has been talk of restoring it. West of the bayfront, green benches still line the streets of downtown as they have since 1907.

Mirror Lake is a shady place for pensive moods. A geyser-like fountain spouts at programmed intervals. On its northern edge, you'll hear the crackle and shush of shufflers at play at the world's largest shuffleboard club. Adjoining the courts is the **Shuffleboard Hall of Fame**. Here, such greats as Mae Hall and Lucy Perkins have been enshrined. The **Coliseum** on Fourth Avenue N. features ballroom dancing to the sounds of Big Band-era orchestras.

Free outdoor concerts often sound off at the **William's Park Bandshell**, a pigeon feeder's paradise. This bandshell

Subterranean delights.

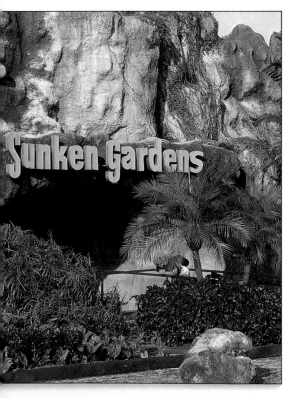

and all of downtown marches to the beat of All-American high school bands every March.

Of bands and boats: When invited to participate in St Petersburg's Festival of States, high school musicians throughout the country spend their winters selling oranges and hawking concert tickets to raise money for the trip south. They jam downtown hotels four to a room, warm up their tubas and trombones while dangling their feet in Tampa Bay, and participate in prestigious competitions for the Mayor's and Governor's Cup which highlight a week of festivities. More than 100 bands take part in a parade that closes the festival.

It was the extension of Peter Demens' Orange Belt Railroad into the Pinellas Peninsula that gave birth to St Petersburg. Demens, the Russian exile who named the city for his birthplace in 1888, shaped it with the aid of Detroiter John C. Williams. Its reputation as a health spa lured elderly Yankees early on. Hollywood director Robert Altman filmed his little-seen movie *Health* here.

Progressive residents have been trying to shake their city's image as a haven for the old and ill. Early this century, they dreamed up a "purity league" that demanded the city outlaw "shocking bathing suits" in hopes the publicity would draw young people wanting to see the suits. "Doc" Webb opened "The World's Largest Drugstore" – a forerunner of modern shopping complexes, that included a floor full of talking plastic mermaids and live dancing ducks – and held beauty contests on the premises.

Eventually, St Petersburg settled into a cluster of neighborhoods: **Snell Isle** with its winding streets and gaudy mansions; the **Northeast's** brick streets and Spanish-Mediterranean homes; the **pink streets** near Pinellas Point; and **the Jungle** (in jungles on **Boca Ciega Bay** that are so thick you can barely see the old estates through the vines and trees).

Other points of interest include **Sunken Gardens** on Fourth Street, a once water-logged sinkhole drained and landscaped by George Turner nearly a century ago. Tropical birds and exotic plants still make it one of the state's better garden attractions. The **Boyd Hill Nature Trail** skirts **Lake Maggiore** off Ninth Street.

Other fine parks are **Lake Seminole, Sawgrass** and **Bay Pines**. The latter, on the piney grounds of a Veterans' Administration Hospital, often plays host to rare and nesting bald eagles. Historic homes have been renovated and moved to **Heritage Park** at Walsingham and 125th Street in neighboring **Largo**.

The regal structure across from Pasadena Golf Course, once the Rolyat Hotel, now encompasses the classrooms of **Stetson Law School**.

On the southern fringes of the city, **Mullet Key** is the site of the area's finest park – **Fort De Soto**. The series of penny ante toll booths, thoroughly irritating and incomprehensible, should not deter you from a drive to this oasis of calm in a West Coast sea of development. You can scramble around the historic fort, watch huge tankers ease into Tampa Bay from the beach, and also pitch your tent here overnight.

The Bayway itself was once a magnificent drive across **Boca Ciega Bay**, with unobstructed views of sand, sea and fowl. That changed in the 1970s when developers crammed in condos.

Tierra Verde, on the way to Fort De Soto, is another island once lush with mangroves and wildlife. It is now lush with condos and homes. In fact it was so primitive a paradise, that at one time an eccentric chap by the name of Silas Dent built himself a palm frond hut and lived the life of "the happy hermit" here, existing on fish and fowl, playing his banjo and rowing across the channel to the nearby settlement of Pass-a-Grille in his Santa Claus suit, to the delight of local children. Dent became such a living legend that his death, at the age of 76 in 1952, warranted an obituary in the *New York Times*.

The Gulf beaches: The long, narrow islands clinging to the west coast of Pinellas County resisted mass intrusion by developers longer than the lower East Coast islands. However, thoughtless landowners and construction crews have made up for lost time over the past

few decades. Early settlers confined themselves to Pass-a-Grille, at the southern end of Long Key, now known as **St Petersburg Beach**, and north at **Sand Key** in the vicinity of **Indian Rocks Beach**. It's hard to imagine today, but flamingos, wild boars, sea turtles, deer and alligators were once more common sights in these islands than people. Today there are more than 40,000 full-time residents, a total which is swelled by tens of thousands of vacationers during the spring season.

Turn left when the Bayway ends to **Pass-a-Grille**. The pink palace in front of you is the **Don Cesar Hotel**. It's had its ups-and-downs since T.J. Rowe erected it in the 1920s. F. Scott Fitzgerald and his wife Zelda are said to have been among its illustrious guests. The army bought the building for use as a hospital during World War II, but it was restored to a hotel in 1973.

The Don marks the southern boundary of a wall of big beach hotels. South of it, Pass-a-Grille still retains some of its fishing village charm.

Below, the Don Cesar Resort Hotel. Right, smiles on a sunny day.

TO CLEARWATER AND BEYOND

North on Gulf Boulevard, an endless procession of hotels, condominiums, fast food restaurants, T-shirt shops and concrete are barely distinguishable from one another in what's left of the scenery. Property owners have inexplicably fought for high density zoning from here to Sand Key, burying the beauty so many come to Florida to find, then wondering why real estate values here don't match those in more sensibly planned communities like Longboat Key near Sarasota.

Fortunately, this strip still boasts some of the state's best beaches, but their sands are behind all those buildings so you will have to use "public access" paths to get to most of them.

Points of interest in St Petersburg Beach run from the calming, pristine beaches to the pleasantly eccentric "early diner" architecture of the **Pelican Diner** on the corner of Gulf Boulevard and A19A. To continue the drive up these beaches, turn north onto Blind Pass Road from A19A. It runs back into Gulf Boulevard and onto **Treasure Island** (which early settlers named after hearing of treasure chests buried here). No treasure has ever been found. **Sunset Beach** harbors an ever-increasing number of stilt houses facing the Gulf.

Otherwise, it is more of the same – buildings. The municipal beach here is an extraordinary wide piece of sand. A draw bridge connects Treasure Island with **Madeira Beach**, known locally as "Mad Beach. " Sailing out of **John's Pass Village** on Madeira Beach is the loud and lively **Europa FunKruz**. A cruise ship with dining, dancing and live entertainment, the highlight of the FunKruz experience is casino gambling. As soon as the ship sails into the International Waters of the Gulf of Mexico, casino doors fly open and the high-stake games begin. The ship departs twice daily for both morning and evening trips.

Bird Key, east of the span in John's Pass, is a roost for birds, but for an

Epiphany rites, St Nicholas Greek Orthodox Cathedral.

insight into what happens to them when they come up against the motors, fishing lines and deliberate cruelty of modern man – proceed north to the **Suncoast Seabird Sanctuary** in **Indian Shores.**

The Bird Man of Florida: Birds can't pay for hospital visits, but that hasn't stopped Ralph Heath from catering to them. He depends on contributions from birdlovers the world over to tend the sick and injured, a cause that has made him a celebrity on TV programs like ABC's *20/20* and in the old "Profile" ads for Dewars scotch. (Heath never drank Dewars.) In fact, word of his Suncoast Seabird Sanctuary has flown so far that Heath finds injured fowl actually flying or limping into his clinic of their own accord. He also boats in search of birds who may have gotten hung up in fishing lines and were mauled, accidentally or intentionally, by thoughtless humans. You can visit his fascinating sanctuary without charge, but have a generous heart when you pass one of the contribution boxes.

The Intracoastal Waterway butts against the edge of Gulf Boulevard as you enter **Indian Rocks Beach.** The Gulf is only yards away to the west, a reason why this sliver is called "The Narrows." The railroad once brought Tampans right to this beach resort, so many older families still own weekend retreats here. You can fish for shark from the **Big Indian Rocks Pier**.

Gulf Boulevard proceeds north past the big gulf-front homes of **Belleair Beach** to the tip of **Sand Key**. Once a desolate sand spur thick with Norfolk pines, its natural beauty has been all but obliterated by highrises.

Another sandy resort, one that is increasingly popular among travelers from Canada, Great Britain and Germany, basks in the sun that almost always shines on **Clearwater Beach** across the toll bridge from Sand Key. Its long, wide beach, blinding white in daylight, even has a few dunes. You'll find patches of sea oats shimmying in the gulf breezes, but don't pick or trample these endangered, protected plants.

At **Boatyard Village**, a recreated,

Clearwater Beach pier.

1890s-period fishing village nestled on a cove along Fairchild Drive, a collection of restaurants and arts and crafts shops resemble the simple life of days gone by. Special events and live entertainment take place on the streets and in the village playhouse regularly.

Condos and a cult: Across landscaped **Memorial Causeway**, Clearwater proper rests on a bit of bluff. It is the government seat of Pinellas, Florida's most densely-inhabited county. Clearwater evolved around Henry Plant's classic, wooden **Belleview Biltmore Hotel** which opened in 1897. It still stands, flanked by a few modern additions, on the bay behind two rolling golf courses. This colossal heart-pine structure is listed in the National Registry of Historic Places.

Another old hotel, the Fort Harrison, is no longer open to the public. Instead, it has become the "flag" headquarters of the controversial **Church of Scientology**. This California-based group, founded in the early 1950s by science-fiction writer L. Ron Hubbard, claims several million adherents throughout the world. Its foothold in otherwise conservative Clearwater has caused much concern among residents.

For an overall look at the city, try Gulf-port artist Steve Smith's aerial mural atop the city **Utilities Building** at Chestnut and Prospect. Smith has also painted a postcard mural that decorates the lobby of St Petersburg's main library. The Clearwater offices of the *St Petersburg Times* provide a look at the future, being powered by a windmill and layered solar panels on the roof.

A scenic drive along Bayshore winds up at quaint **Safety Harbor**. A small, interesting history and fine arts museum south of Main Street has been built here near a Timucuan Indian mound.

Scots and Greeks: Early Scottish immigrants established the community of **Dunedin** north of Clearwater. A squeal of bagpipes fills the air every March when a kilted and tartan-clad band kicks off the annual Highland Games festival.

Cross **Hurricane Pass** by boat from **Dunedin Beach** to **Caladesi Island State Park**. It is a pocket of tranquility away from the traffic and piledrivers on the mainland – 1,400 acres of cabbage palms, yucca plants and sand. Get an eagle's-eye view from the 60-foot observation tower.

You will have to grit your teeth and bear the drive north up US 19, by far one of Florida's most abominable boulevards. Mobile home parks, malls, country music parlors, condominiums, billboards, signal lights and traffic clash in an unnerving drive that gives one second thoughts about pushing onward. More pleasant, but also slow, is Alternate 19. Both highways emerge in another of those Florida incongruities, a city that would look more at home in Greece's Aegean Sea.

Tarpon Springs sprang up on the Anclote River around the turn of the century when Peter Demens brought in his railroad. With Key West's sponge beds dwindling, John Corcoris summoned his brothers and friends from the Aegean islands to test the beds around Tarpon Springs. They found them rich in sponges. Tarpon Springs soon stripped

Tarpon Springs shipbuilder.

the title of "Sponge Capital" away from Key West.

Corcoris pioneered the use of old, copper-helmeted diving suits to hunt for sponges in deeper waters. These early outfits, clumsy and poorly made, sometimes became shrouds for the brave young Greek divers who wore them. But the industry grew into a multi-million dollar business. It began to ebb in the 1940s when red tide disease ruined some of the beds. Later, the introduction of inexpensive, synthetic sponges virtually shut down the industry.

But that Greek heritage still drives this colorful city. Most visitors head straight for the historic sponge docks along **Dodecanese Boulevard**, perhaps more accurately called shrimp docks now. Spongers still man a few boats and you may spot some cleaning their catch on deck. Tourists can also board a boat for a demonstration of sponge-diving – although there are rumors about that the divers stuff a sponge inside their suit before diving to ensure that they will "bring one up."

You can buy genuine sponges from the sea here in a variety of forms – either wool sponges, wire sponges, finger sponges or loofahs for body massages. **Spongeorama** exhibits items and photos from earlier sponging days. Most of the historic **Sponge Exchange** itself, built in 1907 to provide a place for storage and auctions, has fallen to the tides of time and demolition experts.

The owners of the popular **Louis Pappas' Riverside** restaurant (delicious food in spite of the crowds and off-the-wall architecture) began demolishing the Exchange in 1981 to make way for another mall full of souvenir shops. Some members of the city's 20,000-strong Greek community, appalled at the prospect of losing this link with their past, got a court order to stop the wrecking ball in mid-flight. The State Legislature, meanwhile, deliberated belatedly whether to buy the Exchange, as a historical site. But the Pappas' had already battered a large portion of the storied walls into rubble before being stopped. People draped black cloth along the

Tarpon Springs Docks, 1930s.

boulevard in a gesture some said would put a curse on the place.

Curse or not, their restaurant is thriving. Big Greek salads, *mousaka, baklava* and other native dishes are served along with fresh seafood. Alternatively try some of the holes-in-the-walls in this part of town where the food is usually more delightful than the decor. **Zorba's** is the best place to go if you want to watch belly dancers.

In addition to sponge-diving, boat-building has always been big business in Tarpon Springs (as it is in most of Pinellas County). Small builders like **Peer Lovfald Marine** here concentrate on customized yachts, while shipbuilding giants like **Irwin Yachts**, **Gulfstar** and **Watkins Yachts** have larger assembly plants in some of the neighboring communities.

St Nicholas Greek Orthodox Cathedral on Pinellas Avenue in downtown Tarpon Springs dates to 1943. Its neo-Byzantine walls are chock full of icons, including a statue of the Blessed Mother that has been said to shed tears at times. The **Universalist Church** on Grand Boulevard has a collection of paintings by the late landscape artist, George Inness, Jr. Prime time in the city is the Feast of the Epiphany in January when the Greek Orthodox archbishop comes to town to bless local waters and toss a crucifix into **Spring Bayou**. Boys aged 16 to 18 dive into the chilly winter waters to retrieve it and earn extra blessings for themselves and their families. A dove, symbolic of the Holy Spirit, is released to begin a *glendi* with Greek food, music and dance.

Near Tarpon Springs on US 19, **Innisbrook**, one of the plushest resorts in the country, offers accommodations on package plans in the midst of three championship golf courses, tennis courts and rolling, wooded splendor. **A.L. Anderson Park** on **Lake Tarpon** is a pretty place for a picnic.

Mermaids of the spring: A collection of burgeoning new communities and snoozing old ones alternate the rest of the way up the West Coast. **New Port Richey**, which grew at a 75 percent clip

"Prehistoric" service station.

during the 1980s, sports the worse traits of rapid urbanization with its jammed highways and indiscriminate development. It also holds the *Guinness Book of World Records* mark for throwing the largest barbecue, a distinction the local Sertoma Club attempts to surpass annually at its Chasco Festival on the banks of the **Pithlachascotee River**.

The number of cars and convenience stores thin out as you cross into **Hernando County**. Since 1947, live mermaids have played in the waters of **Weeki Wachee Spring** here, on US 19. It is just beyond the 110-foot long, 48-foot tall concrete dinosaur that looms over Harold and Dana Hurst's Fina gas station. Named by Indians for the "winding waters" of its snaking river that flows to the Gulf, **Weeki Wachee** sprang from immeasurable depths. Navy frogman Newton Perry found its waters so clear he used them to stage underwater shows. He taught young women the techniques of breathing through hoses so they could remain far below the surface for long periods of time. Then he

dressed them in mermaid costumes and a famous attraction was born.

The Weeki Wachee mermaids perform strenuous acrobatics about 16 feet underwater, which you watch through plate glass windows. The park also offers a cruise down the river past a rain forest (where sprinklers provide the precipitation) and a pelican orphanage for 60 recovering patients from the Suncoast Seabird Sanctuary. Weeki Wachee also delights in those plastic sculptures so characteristic of old Florida, including King Neptune and family. The only beach in the vicinity is a small patch at **Pine Island Park** on the western tip of County Road 595. Crab catchers and fishermen usually prefer to try their luck from the pier at **Bayport Park**.

US 19 here becomes a more pleasant drive north. You may even be lucky enough to see your car's headlights reflected off the eyes of a deer late at night. The next town of any consequence, **Chassahowitzka**, marks the entrance to a national wildlife refuge of the same name. A remnant of the re-

gion's relocated sweets industry is the **Yulee Sugar Mill Historical Memorial. Homossassa** (Indian for "the place of pepper trees") **Springs** has been turned into another tourist attraction, but is not quite as commercialized as **Silver Springs**.

In **Crystal River**, you can swim with a herd of manatees, the docile but endangered mammals that resemble a cross between an elephant and a walrus. Some say the best way to attract them so you can pat their backs is by humming "The Star-Spangled Banner" into a snorkel. More than 100 springs keep **King's Bay** filled, while the **Crystal River State Archeological Site** marks the center of a huge ceremonial ground for Indians who lived here about 1,600 years ago. About 450 graves have been opened here and have yielded important relics of that era.

North of Crystal City, locks of the unfinished **Cross Florida Barge Canal** adjoin US 19. They are a symbol of one victory environmentalists can claim. Shippers have tried to engineer construction of a canal connecting the Gulf of Mexico to the Atlantic Ocean since 1818. Work finally began in the 1930s. It proceeded, with many interruptions, until conservationists, worried about damage to the Oklawaha River, convinced President Nixon to halt the canal construction in 1971. The state cabinet eventually voted to abandon the project five years later.

Head west on State Road 24 for the 25-mile drive to **Cedar Key**, a sleepy resort which served as one of the busiest ports and the largest city in the state only a century ago. Manufacturers made pencils from the cedar trees that gave this group of small islands their name. Even Florida's first big railroad line terminated here. A severe hurricane leveled the town in 1896 and it never regained its former importance. The **Cedar Key State Museum** documents the port's short-lived prominence.

Cedar Key remains a favorite destination of seafood lovers who flock to its small restaurants that serve up turtle steak and deviled crab with swamp cabbage salad. Thousands cross the scenic bridges to the island for a Sidewalk Art Festival in April and a Seafood Festival each October.

Towards the southern latitudes: The **Sunshine Skyway** staples the Pinellas peninsula to the southern stretches of the West Coast. Total tollbooth-to-tollbooth length is about 11 miles, with a central bridge more than 4 miles long and 250 feet above the water. The height enables oil tankers and fertilizer freighters to pass underneath en route from the Gulf to the Port of Tampa. But even those specifications, thought sufficient when the first span opened in 1954, have not been able to accommodate today's enormous ships. On a stormy, May 9 morning in 1980, a phosphate freighter rammed the southbound span of the Skyway. The metal grill roadbed – and a bus, cars, and a truck that had been crossing it – plunged into the bay, killing 35 people.

Now a beautiful, golden span stretches over the blue waters, past the remnants of the old bridge with its gaping maw. The new bridge features a main span supported by twin, fan-like arrangements of cables, and this unusual style of construction makes the Sunshine Skyway well worth its $1 toll each way, and ranks it as Florida's first suspension bridge. Nevertheless, the Skyway is likely to remain haunted by the accident and other incidents that have tarnished its history.

A Coast Guard cutter called the *Blackthorne* rammed another freighter near the bridge only months before it fell. The cutter sank and crewmen died. A memorial to the men of the *Blackthorne* can be visited in a park north of the bridge. The top of the Skyway has also been a favorite jumping-off spot for suicides.

Terra Ceia Island, immediately west of the Sunshine Skyway, is the site of the **Madira Bickel Mound Historic Memorial**, believed to have been occupied by primitive Indians from the time of the birth of Christ until the 17th century. There is a burial mound about 20 feet high that was used during the Weedon Island archaeological period from AD 700 to 1400.

Right, Weeki Wachee mermaid.

324

SARASOTA AND POINTS SOUTH

South of the Sunshine Skyway, signs point the way to the **J.P. Benjamin Memorial** in **Ellenton**. This white, frame Southern mansion has 18 pillars surrounding the front veranda and sides. It was built by Major Robert Gamble Jr. around 1845 (making it the oldest home on Florida's West Coast). The major once employed some 300 slaves on a 1,500-acre sugar plantation in the grounds. Gamble provided refuge here after the Civil War for the Secretary of State of the defeated Confederacy, Judah P. Benjamin. He later escaped to England. Don't be surprised that Florida has chosen to honor a war fugitive with a memorial: the birthday of Confederate President Jefferson Davis is celebrated as a state holiday.

Ellenton has also attracted a growing number of residents, permanent and seasonal, who subscribe to the Mennonite faith. These men with their distinctive hats and beards and women wearing old-fashioned bonnets and dresses have brought a flavor to the city usually associated with Pennsylvania Dutch country and the Amish areas of Ohio and Indiana.

US 41 continues south through **Palmetto** and crosses the **Manatee River** into **Bradenton**. The river is named for the sea mammal, but heavy boat traffic has decimated the manatee population here. During the high spring season, automobiles inch along US 41 in solid lines that often stretch all the way from the Skyway to **Fort Myers**. The opening of Interstate 75 has alleviated some of that traffic.

A national monument at the mouth of the Manatee commemorates the landing of Hernando de Soto in 1539. Modern-day conquistadors (actually local businessmen) re-enact the landing each March during a week of festivities in Bradenton. The helmets worn by de Soto and crew were forged in Germany from molds used during the days of the legitimate de Soto and the swords were forged from imported Toledo steel. A

contingent of prominent people from Spain regularly attend the show. The highlight is a pageant at the memorial that traces the exploits of the ruthless but courageous conquistadors.

Settlers didn't put down roots on the river until about 300 years after de Soto's arrival. Among them was a sugar planter, Joseph Braden, who gave the town his name. The ruins of **Braden Castle** are off State Road 64. The city fringes remain agricultural with tomato farms and packers, citrus groves and processors. At US 41 on 26th Avenue East, you can watch oranges and grapefruits bounce along conveyor belts while workers sort them into chutes for packing. Owner Bill Mixon ships more than 100,000 crates a year.

The "Greatest Show on Earth": You can reach **Sarasota** via US 41 South, but the island chain across **Sarasota Bay** provides a more pleasant approach. Take State Road 64 west from Bradenton to **Anna Maria Island**, then head south on Gulf Drive. You will pass through weathered **Bradenton Beach** and posh

Longboat Key, getting good peeks at azure Gulf waters all along the way. The drive runs smack into **St Armand's Circle**, a ring of expensive boutiques and restaurants named after its original, French owner. But the man for whom the intersecting boulevard is named, circus master John Ringling, left a more indelible imprint on Florida, from Venice to Gibsonton to Barnum City's Circus World. The theme of the Italian statuary on **Lido Key** is elephants.

The hub of Ringling's world lies back up US 41, past the lilac-colored, shell-shaped **Van Wezel Auditorium** and the **Sarasota Jungle Gardens** on Bayshore Road to glittering **C'ad'zan**, a museum of art and the circus, and the **Asolo State Theater**. Flush with a fortune from his "Greatest Show on Earth," and lucrative investments in oil, railroads and real estate, Ringling brought in artisans, stone, tapestries and art from around the world. The 30-room mansion, patterned after the Doges' Palace in Venice, Italy, was completed in 1926 as a gift to his wife, Mabel. *C'ad'zan* means "House of John" in Venetian. Tour the cavernous living room with its tapestries and Aeolian pipe organ, then walk through the landscaped grounds that are studded with fat banyan trees.

Ringling collected so much art he decided to erect a museum to put it in. He patterned the adjoining edifice after a 15th-century Florentine villa. It now contains one of the world's most important collections of works by the Flemish painter, Pierre Paul Rubens, in its large baroque art section. A magnificent bronze cast of Michaelangelo's *David* dominates the courtyard. A less imposing building houses the circus museum with memorabilia from Ringling's three-ring extravaganzas.

The Ringling influence transformed Sarasota into the cultural nerve center of Florida. A prime example of that function is the nationally-renowned **Asolo State Theater** company which performs an annual selection of plays in an 18th-century Italian theater. The interior was dismantled piece-by-piece at a castle in Asolo, Italy, then shipped

C'ad'zan, circus king Ringling's home.

here in 1950 and reassembled behind the art museum.

Special events also add to the excitement of the Ringling complex. An arts and crafts festival attracts hundreds of exhibitors and thousands of buyers from around the country each year. More unusual, but in keeping with Ringling's eccentricities, is a Medieval Fair held each March. The setting lends itself to performers who resurrect the days of King Arthur. Knights in armor joust on the bay. Cone-capped maidens frolic in the gardens. Craftsmen shear sheep, spin flax and carve flutes. Roving minstrels spin lusty ballads.

You will find a human chess match where live actors and athletes engage in axe-wielding, sword-swinging, mace-mashing combat with frightening reality.

The University of South Florida's **New College** campus north of the museum has several buildings designed by architect I.M. Pei. The school emphasizes the liberal and performing arts. Van Wezel offers operas, symphony and ballet. Writers, notably, the late

John D. MacDonald, have found inspiration here. MacDonald wrote the popular Travis McGee novels that have sold more than 23 million copies.

Nature lovers, too, will find inspiration at **Myakka River State Park** on Stater Road 72. It is a wildlife refuge as large as Disney World and kept as close as possible to a pristine state. You can tour it by car or bicycle over a scenic 7-mile road or aboard guided boat and train tours.

Other Sarasota sights include **Bellm's Car and Music of Yesterday**, and the **Marie Selby Botanical Gardens** on South Palm Drive. Golfers may be interested to learn that Scotland's Col. John Gillespie built the nation's first golf links here in 1886.

Clown town: Sarasota's circus legacy spilled over into **Venice**, which is 20 miles south of US 41. The Ringling Clown College was located here, where, after a 9-week course, about half the class graduated to professional clowndom. The circus also spent the winters here. Today, Venice's main

The Three Musketeers at Asolo State Theater.

claim to fame is as the Sharkstooth Capital of the World. Apparently the tiny, fossilized teeth wash up on Venice's beach in the millions, attracting collectors, the curious and the crowds to observe the phenomenon. On the second weekend of August, there is an annual festival to celebrate the teeth, where between 25 and 30,000 people visit with fossil exhibitors, stroll among the arts and crafts booths, and eat seafood galore – the highlight of the festival is a seafood competition between Venice's restaurants, with anywhere between 30 and 50 kitchens competing.

Venice was planned early in Florida's development and still boasts wide streets and parks. **Warm Mineral Springs** on US 41 and San Servando Avenue, 12 miles south of Venice, touts the therapeutic value of its 87° waters that contain sodium, sulfate, chloride and other natural chemicals. Warm Mineral Springs has in addition hosted important archaeological digs that have produced evidence of some of Florida's earliest residents.

Punta Gorda and **Port Charlotte**, still small, provide a change of pace from the rapid growth to the north and south. **Ponce de León Park** commemorates the landing place of the father of Florida, fatally wounded during an Indian attack. The old city dock has been transformed into a **Fisherman's Village** specialty mall.

Swarms of ghosts of pirates and Spanish explorers inhabit **Charlotte Harbor**. You can cross a toll bridge at **Placida** to **Gasparilla Island** where the notorious, but imaginary, José Gaspar was rumored to have ruled. **Boca Grande**, in midisland, is a retreat for the wealthy from up and down the West Coast. They pull into port in their yachts while cruising the Gulf.

Playground of a genius: You can double back to US 41 or Interstate 75 south to the **Fort Myers/Cape Coral** area, the fastest growing metropolis in the nation during the 1970s, when the combined population of the cities grew by 94.2 percent. It is still growing, the influx consisting mainly of Northeasterners

Sarasota: high school students show their skills.

330

who come to cash in on retirement lots purchased during their working years.

The population surge adds more meat to stories about the incredible foresight of inventor Thomas Edison who predicted in 1914 that "There is only one Fort Myers, and 90 million people are going to find it out." Edison, however, managed to beat the rush when he built a winter estate here in 1886 at the age of 39. Doctors warned him his health was failing and advised him Florida's climate might help. It did.

Edison lived until the age of 84 and produced some of his greatest post-light bulb inventions in Fort Myers. Edison perfected phonographs, motion pictures, the teletype and many of his other patented inventions in his Florida laboratory. He tried using bamboo that he found on the banks of the Caloosahatchee River as light bulb filaments and experimented with the vulcanization of rubber from goldenrod grown in his gardens here.

The **Edison Winter Home and Museum** sprawls across both sides of McGregor Boulevard (State Road 867) beautified by the royal palms planted by Edison. The home and guest house, among the first prefabricated buildings in the US, were constructed in Maine and brought to Fort Myers by four schooners. Tropical gardens engulf the homes. Native Florida palms and satin leaf figs, calabash trees from South America, cinnamon trees from India and Malaysia – some 6,000 species were collected by Edison at a cost of about $100,000.

Florida's first modern pool – built in 1900 with Edison's own Portland cement and reinforced with bamboo – has never cracked or leaked. In this paradisiacal setting he invented the future and entertained famous friends like next door neighbors Henry Ford and Harvey Firestone. Edison even offered to light up his new town with electrical installations, but the townspeople refused for fear the lights would keep their cattle awake at night.

Across the street, a museum contains photographs, personal items such as

SORC race entries sail past Fort Myers.

Edison's gold watch, a collection of automobiles, and a treasure house of inventions, including 170 phonographs with huge, handpainted speakers and, of course, dozens of light bulbs. A strip of tin foil 5 inches wide and 18 inches long – the world's first record – still plays "Mary had a Little Lamb." The laboratory in the back of the museum has been closed indefinitely because of concern about the stability of some of the aging chemicals inside. A banyan tree brought by Firestone from India in 1928 has grown into Florida's largest, with a circumference of 400 feet. Mrs Edison deeded all to the city in 1947 to be maintained as a shrine to her husband who died in 1928. A Pageant of Light tribute to the inventor illuminates the city each February.

Fort Myers is also the end of the line of **Shell Factory** billboards you have undoubtedly seen alongside highways during your Florida travels. It is a shell supermarket crammed with sea souvenirs. For an excursion into the Everglades without mounting a full-scale expedition, the **Everglades Jungle Cruise** takes you up the **Caloosahatchee River** to the edge of the vast wilderness on a 3-hour tour. The river was the main highway to Fort Myers in the days when the city still served as a stockade in the Seminole Wars fort network. Fort Myers is also the gateway to two islands where you can commune with nature within arms length of modern amenities.

A bounty of shells: Area residents long fought construction of a causeway linking **Sanibel** and **Captiva Islands** to the mainland. The case went all the way to the Supreme Court. But the bridge builders won and since 1963 thousands of cars have driven right onto these fragile showcases of nature. Uncontrolled development threatened to turn Sanibel and Captiva into two more uninteresting specks heavy with highrises, until 1974 when Sanibel seceded from **Lee County**, set up its own city government, put a near halt to further growth, and even managed to keep out highrises.

Thus, you will find air-conditioned homes and hotels, restaurants, a few shopping centers, even a playhouse. But

Sanibel also has the **J.N. "Ding" Darling National Wildlife Refuge**, named for the early environmentalist and newspaper cartoonist. A highlight of the 5-mile dike drive through the refuge is the sight of crimson-winged roseate spoonbills coming and going in the mornings and evenings in groups as regimented as air force squadrons. Their spatulate bills enable them to scoop up food from the shallow pools. That's the best way to differentiate them from flamingos. Anhingga "snake" birds, Louisiana herons, gulls, sanderlings, willet and vultures are among the hundreds of other birds that make the refuge home. Across the street, submerge yourself in nature at the **Sanibel-Captiva Conservation Foundation**.

Fortunately for the peace and well-being of the wildlife, these preserves are usually of secondary importance to tourists that descend on Sanibel. The island's reputation is built on its beaches which are usually so thick with shells you can't see the sand. Tides toss them up by the ton. And shelling is a science

Shell hunters indulge in "The Sanibel Stoop."

practiced by bent-over people afflicted with a local syndrome called the "Sanibel Stoop." Only Jeffreys Bay in Africa and the Sulu Islands in the Philippines are considered better for shelling. Of course, neither of those distant shores attracts the legions of collectors lured by Sanibel. In an attempt to restrict the practice and prevent Sanibel from becoming a shell of its former self, the city council allows only two live shells of each species to be taken per person. Early morning, and the hours after storms and heavy tides, are the best time to hit the beach armed with a wire mesh scoop and bucket. At those times you may find your feet sinking into the mounds of mollusk casings. You have now become a shunter (short for shell hunter).

Shunt for shells like the rare royal Florida miter, golden olive and spiny oyster, and you may find avid collectors offering their shirts for your finds. More common are the queen and horse conchs, murex, limpet, left-handed whelk, paper nautilus, cowrie, jewel boxes, jingles, tulips and lion's paw. A shelling checklist purchased on the islands will enable you to identify your finds.

A celibate commune: Cross the bridge over **Blind Pass** to Captiva. Here, according to stories, José Gaspar hid his loot and held young girls captive – hence the island's name. The hitch in the story is that Spaniards christened the island long before Gaspar's alleged reign. The **South Seas Plantation** at the north end features low-slung, Polynesian-style villas textured to the terrain, plus tennis courts, a marina and the whole works.

The next point of interest on US 41 south memorializes one of the state's most unusual pioneer settlements. Religious visionary Cyrus Reed Teed brought his followers from Chicago in 1894. He preached that the earth was a hollow sphere with the sun in the center and life covering the inner walls. A restored village at **Koreshan State Historic Site** in **Estero** demonstrates how Teed "proved" his theories and how his commune shared property and practiced celibacy. The movement never quite caught on, but the Koreshan newspaper,

Sanibel Island.

The American Eagle, and a magazine, *The Flaming Sword*, are still published by descendants of Teed's followers.

Gateway to Alligator Alley: The drive from Sanibel along State Road 901 through **Fort Myers Beach** and **Bonita Beach** is slow but scenic. It will get you to **Naples**, another of those sparkling, little Florida towns in the midst of a population explosion. It is being dissected into subdivisions filled with mobile homes, waterfront suburbs and condominium complexes.

Naples is laid out tidily with scrubbed avenues that end at excellent **Gulf beaches**. Train buffs will enjoy **Naples Depot's** restored old rooms and boxcars turned into shops. The legendary *Orange Blossom Special* once stopped here. Former Clevelanders may want to pay a nostalgic visit to the **Jungle Larry's Zoological Park and Caribbean Gardens** where Jungle Larry Tetzlaff and wife, Safari Jane, have set up winter quarters. Tetzlaff was a regular on the *Captain Penny* television show in that Ohio city.

At the **Old Marine Market Place** just off the US 41, a collection of old, tin fishing shacks have miraculously been transformed into a trendy enclave of art galleries and boutiques. The Market's **Merriman's Wharf** is a casual waterfront bistro popular with Naples locals. To the west of downtown, on Pine Ridge Road, is a spot sure to attract fluffy stuffed animal collectors. **Frannie's Teddy Bear Museum**, built by oil heiress and area resident Frances Pew Hayes, houses over 1,500 adorable bears.

Naples is also the gateway to the Everglades and a boundary of the Big Cypress Swamp. There is an excellent nature center on Merrimue Drive on the **Gordon River**. In Naples, US 41, also known as the "Tamiami Trail" (short for Tampa-Miami), curves west into the vast river of grass. Laid out by rugged laborers who weathered yellow fever in the 1920s, the road still crosses some rugged territory to Miccosukee Indian camps and the **Redlands** vegetable acreage before turning into Little Havana's Calle Ocho in Miami. The other, newer route across the swamp is the unswerving **Alligator Alley** toll road.

A popular annual event on Radio Road west of the Naples Airport on the waist-deep **Mile-O-Mud Track** has captured national attention – the World Championship Swamp Buggy Races. Souped-up hunting half-tracks roar from the starting line in a cloud of goop. The race course is flooded with water for two weeks before the race to assure it is in the worst possible shape. First run in 1949 to signal the opening of the Everglades hunting season, the track also hosts events like the traditional dunking of a "Mud Duchess."

Condo nests: Marco Island was another gorgeous Florida seascape caught in a tug-of-war between environmentalists and developers. The latter won. But they have pledged some concessions to nature. Some consider that the new developments are among the state's better planned communities. Developers have even erected artificial bald eagles' nests in the shadow of the condos in hopes of encouraging the birds to remain. Evidence, they say, that they will try to strike a balance between the needs of modern man and nature.

The quiet, old village of **Marco** at the north end of the island and **Goodland** in the southern tip still retain cottages and recall pleasant memories of an older Florida. Archaeological digs have uncovered carvings, tools, masks and weapons used by Calusa Indians who lived here as long ago as 500 BC.

Offshore and south of Marco Island, a labyrinth of mangrove splotches known as the **Ten Thousand Islands** beg to be explored by boat. Some consist of no more than a few trees. It is safer to take a guide, however, as expert navigators have been known to get lost in the tangle of islands. They melt into the sea at the western edge of **Everglades National Park**. **Collier-Seminole State Park**, 6,423 acres of virgin marshland marking the meeting of Big Cypress and the Everglades, lies just west of Marco Island. There is restricted canoeing, camping, and fishing in most of the park.

Beyond is **Everglades City**, a last outpost on the edge of a kingdom still ruled by wildlife.

Right, the good life at South Seas Plantation, Captiva.

INSIGHT GUIDES
TRaveL TIPS

FOR THOSE WITH MORE THAN A PASSING INTEREST IN TIME...

Before you put your name down for a Patek Philippe watch *fig. 1*, there are a few basic things you might like to know, without knowing exactly whom to ask. In addressing such issues as accuracy, reliability and value for money, we would like to demonstrate why the watch we will make for you will be quite unlike any other watch currently produced.

"Punctuality", Louis XVIII was fond of saying, "is the politeness of kings."

We believe that in the matter of punctuality, we can rise to the occasion by making you a mechanical timepiece that will keep its rendezvous with the Gregorian calendar at the end of every century, omitting the leap-years in 2100, 2200 and 2300 and recording them in 2000 and 2400 *fig. 2*. Nevertheless, such a watch does need the occasional adjustment. Every 3333 years and 122 days you should remember to set it forward one day to the true time of the celestial clock. We suspect, however, that you are simply content to observe the politeness of kings. Be assured, therefore, that when you order your watch, we will be exploring for you the physical—if not the metaphysical—limits of precision.

Does everything have to depend on how much?

Consider, if you will, the motives of collectors who set record prices at auction to acquire a Patek Philippe. They may be paying for rarity, for looks or for micromechanical ingenuity. But we believe that behind each $500,000-plus

bid is the conviction that a Patek Philippe, even if 50 years old or older, can be expected to work perfectly for future generations.

In case your ambitions to own a Patek Philippe are somewhat discouraged by the scale of the sacrifice involved, may we hasten to point out that the watch we will make for you today will certainly be a technical improvement on the Pateks bought at auction? In keeping with our tradition of inventing new mechanical solutions for greater reliability and better time-keeping, we will bring to your watch innovations *fig. 3* inconceivable to our watchmakers who created the supreme wristwatches of 50 years ago *fig. 4*. At the same time, we will of course do our utmost to avoid placing undue strain on your financial resources.

Can it really be mine?

May we turn your thoughts to the day you take delivery of your watch? Sealed within its case is your watchmaker's tribute to the mysterious process of time. He has decorated each wheel with a chamfer carved into its hub and polished into a shining circle. Delicate ribbing flows over the plates and bridges of gold and rare alloys. Millimetric surfaces are bevelled and burnished to exactitudes measured in microns. Rubies are transformed into jewels that triumph over friction. And after many months—or even years—of work, your watchmaker stamps a small badge into the mainbridge of your watch. The Geneva Seal—the highest possible attestation of fine watchmaking *fig. 5*.

Looks that speak of inner grace *fig. 6*.

When you order your watch, you will no doubt like its outward appearance to reflect the harmony and elegance of the movement within. You may therefore find it helpful to know that we are uniquely able to cater for any special decorative needs you might like to express. For example, our engravers will delight in conjuring a subtle play of light and shadow on the gold case-back of one of our rare pocket-watches *fig. 7*. If you bring us your favourite picture, our enamellers will reproduce it in a brilliant miniature of hair-breadth detail *fig. 8*. The perfect execution of a double hobnail pattern on the bezel of a wristwatch is the pride of our casemakers and the satisfaction of our designers, while our chainsmiths will weave for you a rich brocade in gold *figs. 9 & 10*. May we also recommend the artistry of our goldsmiths and the experience of our lapidaries in the selection and setting of the finest gemstones? *figs. 11 & 12*.

How to enjoy your watch before you own it.

As you will appreciate, the very nature of our watches imposes a limit on the number we can make available. (The four Calibre 89 time-pieces we are now making will take up to nine years to complete). We cannot therefore promise instant gratification, but while you look forward to the day on which you take delivery of your Patek Philippe *fig. 13*, you will have the pleasure of reflecting that time is a universal and everlasting commodity, freely available to be enjoyed by all.

Should you require information on any particular Patek Philippe watch, or even on watchmaking in general, we would be delighted to reply to your letter of enquiry. And if you send

fig. 1: The classic face of Patek Philippe.

fig. 4: Complicated wristwatches circa 1930 (left) and 1990. The golden age of watchmaking will always be with us.

fig. 6: Your pleasure in owning a Patek Philippe is the purpose of those who made it for you.

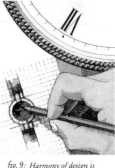

fig. 9: Harmony of design is executed in a work of simplicity and perfection in a lady's Calatrava wristwatch.

fig. 10: The chainsmith's hands impart strength and delicacy to a tracery of gold.

fig. 2: One of the 33 complica-tions of the Calibre 89 astronomical clock-watch is a satellite wheel that completes one revolution every 400 years.

fig. 5: The Geneva Seal is awarded only to watches which achieve the standards of horological purity laid down in the laws of Geneva. These rules define the supreme quality of watchmaking.

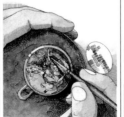

fig. 7: Arabesques come to life on a gold case-back.

fig. 11: Circles in gold: symbols of perfection in the making.

fig. 3: Recognized as the most advanced mechanical regulating device to date, Patek Philippe's Gyromax balance wheel demonstrates the equivalence of simplicity and precision.

fig. 8: An artist working six hours a day takes about four months to complete a miniature in enamel on the case of a pocket-watch.

fig. 12: The test of a master lapidary is his ability to express the splendour of precious gemstones.

PATEK PHILIPPE
GENEVE
fig. 13: The discreet sign of those who value their time.

your card marked "book catalogue" we shall post you a catalogue of our publications. Patek Philippe, 41 rue du Rhône, 1204 Geneva, Switzerland, Tel. +41 22/310 03 66.

Swatch. The others just watch.

seahorse/fall winter 94-95

TRAVEL TIPS

GETTING THERE

BY AIR

Most major US and international carriers serve Florida. Fare prices are competitive and often confusing, shop around before purchasing a ticket. A variety of discount fares and "package deals" which can significantly cut round-trip rates to and from Florida are also available.

Florida has a total of 32 airports serving commuters and general aviation. All of the state's major international airports – Miami, Fort Lauderdale, Orlando, and Tampa – are modern, efficient, safe and easy to get around.

The **Miami International Airport** (tel: 305/876-7077) is the state's largest in total passenger numbers and airlines. It is also a major jumping-off point for direct flights into the Caribbean and South America. Carriers that regularly fly into Miami include US Air, Delta, American, United, TWA, Continental, Northwest, British Airways, Air Canada, Iberia, Air France, Lufthansa, Avianca, Varig, Aer Lingus, KLM-Royal Dutch Airlines, Air Jamaica, Bahamas Air, BWIA, Icelandic, Aeromexico, CP Air, Japan Airlines, Aeroflot, Alitalia, and Aeroperu.

The **Fort Lauderdale/Hollywood Airport** (tel: 813/357-6100) is regularly served by US Air, Delta, TWA, United, American, KLM-Dutch Airlines, Air Canada, Bahamas Air, BWIA, Japan Airlines, Iberia, British Airways, SAS, Lufthansa, Olympic, and Swissair.

The **Tampa International Airport** (tel: 813/870-8700) is regularly served by Delta, US Air, American, TWA, Continental, United, Olympic, British Airways, and Northwest.

The **Orlando International Airport** (tel: 407/825-2001) is regularly served by Delta, US Air, American, United, Continental, TWA, Northwest, Olympic, Lufthansa, Avianca, Air France, Swissair, Sabena, Aer Lingus, Alitalia, British Airways, and Japan Airlines.

US Air, Delta and American offer regional, commuter service into some of Florida's smaller airports. They include **Key West, Palm Beach, Naples, Marathon, Gainesville, Jacksonville, Tallahassee, Daytona Beach, Melbourne, Sarasota, Fort Myers, Pensacola, Panama City**. Several other smaller, commuter airlines also offer regional service.

BY SEA

CRUISES

You can travel or leave Florida by cruise ship. You can also book one of many ships while in the state for cruises to a variety of exotic ports, particularly South American and Caribbean destinations.

There are seven major cruise ship ports in Florida, with **Miami** and **Port Everglades** leading with the most sailings. Minor ports include **St Petersburg, Madeira Beach, Treasure Island, Port Canaveral** and **Port Manatee**. The packages vary tremendously, with cruises that can last from one day to more than two weeks, and cruise-ship sizes also varying, as well as destination ports of call.

Although Florida offers year-round cruise departures into either the Atlantic, Caribbean or Gulf of Mexico, there are also seasonal – warm weather – cruises. Again, for a complete view of choices, check with a travel agency or look at the travel ads in any Sunday newspaper.

The Port of Miami is the largest cruise port in the world and welcomes well over 2 million passengers each year which represents 75 percent of all cruise passengers worldwide. It is just a five-minute ride from downtown with trolley service available. For general information telephone 305/371-7678.

CRUISE LINES

Admiral Cruises: 1220 Biscayne Blvd, Miami. Tel: 305/373-7501.
Carnival Cruise Lines: 3655 NW 87th Ave, Miami. Tel: 305/599-2200.
Commodore Cruise Lines: 800 Douglas Road, Coral Gables. Tel: 305/444-4600.
Costa Cruises: 80 SW 8th St, Miami. Tel: 305/358-7325.
Dolphine Cruise Lines: 1007 N American Way, Miami. Tel: 305/358-2111.
Emerald Seas: 1220 Biscayne Blvd, Miami. Tel: 305/373-7501.
Norwegian Cruise Line: 95 Merrick Way, Coral Gables. Tel: 305/447-9660.
Royal Viking Line: 95 Merrick Way, Coral Gables. Tel: 305/422-8000.
Sea Escape: 1080 Port Blvd, Miami. Tel: 305/379-0000.

MARINAS

Finally, you can come to Florida or cruise around it in your own vessel. Most marinas offer slips and facilities for waterway transients. The **Intracoastal Waterway** parallels the east and west coasts of the state. Write to the Dept of Natural Resources, Crown Bldg, Tallahassee 32304, for a copy of *Florida Boating*.

For those who sail into Miami on their own, there are over 50 marinas with 350 sq miles of protected

A Wise Man Never Thinks How Far He's Come. He Thinks How Far He Can Still Travel.

REMY XO BECAUSE LIFE IS WHAT YOU MAKE IT

American Express offers Travelers Cheques built for two.

Cheques *for Two*℠ from American Express are the Travelers Cheques that allow either of you to use them because both of you have signed them. And only one of you needs to be present to purchase them.

Cheques *for Two* are accepted anywhere regular American Express Travelers Cheques are, which is just about everywhere. So stop by your bank, AAA* or any American Express Travel Service Office and ask for Cheques *for Two*.

waters that can offer dock facilities for almost any size craft:

Biscayne Bay Marriott Hotel & Marina: 1633 N Bayshore Dr, Miami. Tel: 305/374-3900.

Causeway 79 Marina: 724 NE 79th St, Miami. Tel: 305/757-7671.

Crandon Park Marina: 4000 Crandon Park Blvd, Key Biscayne. Tel: 305/361-1281.

Mathesson Hammock Marina: 9610 Old Cutler Rd, Coral Gables. Tel: 305/665-5475.

Haulover Park Marina: 10500 Collins Ave, Miami Beach. Tel: 305/947-3525.

Dinner Key Marina: 3400 Pan American Dr, Coconut Grove. Tel: 305/579-6980.

Miamarina at Bayside: 401 Biscayne Blvd, Miami. Tel: 305/579-6955.

Rickenbacker Marina: 3301 Rickenbacker Cswy, Key Biscayne. Tel: 305/361-1900.

Maule Lake Marina: 17201 Biscayne Blvd, N Miami Beach. Tel: 305/945-0808.

Miami Beach Marina: 300 Alton Rd, Miami Beach. Tel: 305/673-6000.

BY RAIL

Amtrak offers slow, but leisurely, service to Florida from America's Midwest, Northeast and South – and connecting service from points west – to many Florida cities. Amtrak stations are located at Jacksonville, Kissimmee, Lakeland, Ocala, Orlando, Sanford, Sebring, Winter Haven, Winter Park, Tampa, Delray Beach, Deerfield Beach, Fort Lauderdale, Hollywood, Miami and West Palm Beach. For those who want to take their car along too, Amtrak offers Auto Train ferry-type service from Lorton, Virginia (near Washington, DC), to Sanford, near Orlando. For information on all rail service to Florida, call Amtrak's toll-free number: 1-800/872-7245.

BY ROAD

Greyhound provides service to Florida and throughout the state. (For information contact individual city Greyhound telephone listings.) Smaller operators with Florida routes include American Sightseeing, Arrow Line and Florida Tour Lines.

Gray Line offers a variety of sightseeing tours which are within Florida, while Greyhound, Trailways and Gulf Coast Motor Lines also have special travel services between Florida cities.

Many bus terminals, however, tend to be in "problem areas" of town, so exercise caution when traveling to and from stations and when venturing from the terminal on solitary walks.

TRAVEL ESSENTIALS

PASSPORTS & VISAS

For foreign visitors to Florida, a passport, a passport-size photograph, a visitor's visa, evidence that you intend to leave the United States after your visit is over, and (depending upon your country of origin) an international vaccination certificate will help smooth your entry into the United States and Florida at government customs booths. Canadian citizens and British subjects residing in Canada and Bermuda are normally exempted from these requirements when arriving from countries in the Western Hemisphere. Citizens of Mexico bearing Form 1-136 and coming from Canada or Mexico are also normally exempted from passport and visa requirements.

Obtain visas by mail, or by personal application at the US Embassy or consulate nearest your home. Evidence of intent to leave the United States may be in the form of a return ticket or any other documentation satisfactory to the embassy or consulate issuing the visa. UK citizens do not require a visa: UK subjects, however, do.

Vaccination certificate requirements vary, but proof of immunization against smallpox or cholera may be necessary.

MONEY MATTERS

Visitors to Florida may encounter problems exchanging foreign currency; the use of American dollar traveler's checks is advised. An increasing number of statewide banking corporations and community banks in Florida, including the Barnett, Southeast and Sun Bank chains, offer foreign exchange services, but this practice is not universal. Banks generally close on Saturday afternoons and Sundays. The increase in the number of foreign visitors has led some department store chains to offer foreign-currency exchange services.

WHAT TO WEAR

Light-colored, lightweight clothing is the norm in Florida. Most attractions permit shorts, swimsuits and sportswear, attire commonly seen even on city streets. Only posh Palm Beach has dared to differ and enforces stricter dress codes.

There is little need for formal wear, except at the

most sophisticated resorts (again, like those in Palm Beach). A sports coat with an open-neck sports shirt is the rule, rather than the exception, for men; and cocktail dresses or pants ensembles are acceptable in most instances for women. A light raincoat or umbrella may prove handy, particularly during the summer. A sweater or jacket should be packed in case of cold spells during the winter.

CUSTOMS

Residents of other countries visiting Florida have non-resident customs status. All articles brought into the United States, including gifts for other persons, must be declared to US Customs at the time you enter. Articles should be listed on the customs declaration form you receive while on board your plane or ship.

IMPORT REGULATIONS

No limit on the amount of money – American or foreign traveler's checks, money orders or negotiable instruments in bearer form – that you may bring into or take out of the United States. But you must file a report with US Customs at the time you arrive or depart for amounts exceeding $5,000 or the foreign currency equivalent.

Non-residents may bring into the United States, free of duty and internal revenue tax, not more than one quart (0.946 liters) of alcoholic beverages for personal use. Excess quantities are subject to duty and tax; Florida permits a tax exemption for up to one gallon. Foreign visitors may also bring in not more than 200 cigarettes (one carton), 100 cigars, or 3 pounds of smoking tobacco, or proportionate amounts of each. An additional quantity of 100 cigars may be brought in under gift exemption.

Special forms or declarations are also required to bring in firearms, prescription drugs, illegal drugs, food, animals, plants and alcoholic beverages. Some of those items are forbidden, or normally require a period of quarantine.

IMPORTING AUTOMOBILES

A non-resident may import an automobile free of duty for personal use and for the transportation of family and guests. The vehicle must be imported at the time of arrival. However, there is no time limit on the period that the vehicle may remain in the United States.

Motorists from countries which have ratified the Convention on Road Traffic of 1949 may drive in the United States for one year with their national license plates on their cars, but an International Distinguishing Sign must be displayed on the car to indicate the motorist's country of origin. Motorists from more than 120 countries with valid national driving licenses may drive in Florida.

LIQUOR LAWS

The legal drinking age in Florida is 21, except for active military personnel. Liquor is sold by the bottle at all retail stores; low taxes here keep prices lower than in many northern states. Retail stores may not sell liquor on Sundays until after 1pm. Public intoxication is not considered a criminal offense without an accompanying violation such as disorderly conduct, although police may detain intoxicated persons in jail for several hours.

GETTING ACQUAINTED

TIME ZONES

Most of Florida runs on Eastern Standard Time. The exception is the western Panhandle, west of the Apalachicola River, which is on Central Standard Time and an hour earlier. Set your clocks and watches an hour ahead for Daylight Savings Time, which begins in May and ends in October.

CLIMATE

In her book *Cross Creek*, Marjorie Rawlings said that Florida seasons "move in and out like nuns in soft clothing, making no rustle in their passing."

It is hard to tell spring from summer. And lacking the brilliant colors of a northern autumn, fall slips into winter without notice. Temperatures do drop in winter. Sometimes they even plunge, surprising tourists who brought their bikinis and little else. But snow and ice are so rare that a touch of either can cripple even northernmost Florida cities.

TEMPERATURE RANGES

January ranks as the coolest month (see chart). Nighttime lows range from an average of 41° in Tallahassee in the Panhandle to 66° in Key West. Occasional temperatures below these have brought frost and threatened Florida's fruit and vegetable crops. Afternoon highs in January climb to an average of 76° in Key West and 61° in nippy Apalachicola on the northern Gulf Coast. Due to the relatively mild winters, many South Florida homes are not equipped with heating systems, and erratic winter weather in recent years – including in 1977 the first snow flurries in Miami's recorded history – has caught residents quite unprepared.

In sharp contrast, June through September get quite hot, often combined with high humidity. Sea breezes along the coast and daily thunder showers can cool off Florida cities to temperatures more bearable than some northern cities in summer.

Average daytime highs during the dog days range from 86° to 91° with little variation from northern to southern regions. At night, temperatures "cool off" to between 70° and 80°, which usually necessitates the use of an air-conditioner for comfortable sleeping conditions.

RAINFALL

Florida's hottest months are also the rainiest. Thunderstorms occur with such regularity each day that you can set your watch by them. Southern parts of the state get rain almost daily during June and July. The Everglades soak up nearly 9 inches on average each June.

In contrast with other parts of the United States, there is little precipitation during November and December – only 2 inches of rain falls on average across the whole state.

Florida wears its nickname "The Sunshine State" so well that the *St Petersburg Evening Independent* has, since 1910, given its daily edition away free the day after any sunless day. The newspaper has only given away an average of 3.7 editions each year, and during one *Guiness Book of World Records* stretch, the newspaper's rooftop sun meter was activated 765 days in a row.

LIGHTNING

One of nature's most frightening – and one of Florida's most dangerous – phenomena is lightning. Unofficially dubbed the "lightning capital of the country," Florida records an average of 11 deaths and 25 injuries from lightning each year. Fort Myers

Average Monthly Temperatures*							
Month	Northwest Division	Northern Central	North Central Division	South Central Division	Southwest & Everglades Division	Lower East Coast	Florida Keys
Jan	52.7	55.7	59.7	61.9	64.7	66.6	70.7
Feb	54.7	57.5	60.9	63.1	65.6	67.2	71.6
Mar	60.2	62.7	65.6	67.2	69.1	70.5	74.6
Apr	67.9	69.5	71.3	72.3	73.2	74.4	78.1
May	73.7	75.5	75.5	76.9	77.1	77.3	80.9
Jun	79.8	80.0	80.3	80.4	80.5	83.2	83.5
Jul	81.1	81.4	81.5	82.7	82.0	81.8	84.6
Aug	81.1	81.4	81.7	81.9	82.4	82.2	84.7
Sep	77.0	79.0	80.0	80.5	81.5	81.1	83.2
Oct	69.5	71.5	73.8	75.0	76.9	77.3	79.6
Nov	59.4	62.6	65.9	67.7	70.5	71.8	75.1
Dec	53.6	56.7	60.8	63.0	65.9	67.7	71.5
Yr	67.7	69.4	71.5	72.6	74.1	74.9	78.2
Temperature, Degrees Fahrenheit							

Average Monthly Rainfall*							
Month	Northwest Division	Northern Central	North Central Division	South Central Division	Southwest & Everglades Division	Lower East Coast	Florida Keys
Jan	3.97	2.89	2.38	2.15	1.79	2.13	1.67
Feb	4.30	3.62	3.11	2.71	1.91	2.04	1.85
Mar	5.68	4.17	4.01	3.28	2.65	2.22	1.56
Apr	4.36	3.00	2.79	2.84	2.35	3.26	2.17
May	3.68	3.27	3.17	4.10	4.29	5.66	2.51
Jun	5.77	5.97	7.05	8.68	8.90	8.53	4.55
Jul	7.93	7.71	8.32	8.48	8.58	6.48	4.11
Aug	7.03	7.27	7.77	7.57	7.72	6.36	4.47
Sep	6.87	6.95	6.90	7.35	9.17	8.76	7.34
Oct	2.96	3.99	3.75	3.85	4.75	8.61	5.57
Nov	3.09	2.12	1.76	1.76	1.46	2.58	2.67
Dec	4.22	2.78	2.20	1.83	1.40	1.85	1.52
Yr	59.90	53.77	53.25	54.65	55.02	58.54	39.99
*Based on National Climatic Center records							

averages 100 lightning-packed days per year, Tampa has 90 and Miami 76.

Florida's dubious distinction has been attributed to the hot wet air close to the ground and unstable atmospheric conditions that exist mainly from May until September. The air near the ground gets hot, rises, then begins to cool. Droplets of water form menacing dark clouds. The air moves up and down so rapidly that it splits the water droplets in the clouds, causing an electrical spark to shoot out. The spark jumps from cloud to cloud or cloud to ground, passing through the air so quickly that a thunderclap occurs.

Lasting 1/1000th of a second, a bolt of lightning carries 30,000°F in a 1-inch channel and delivers a shock of 6,000 to 10,000 amps that can paralyze bodily functions. Nevertheless, two-thirds of those people hit by lightning in Florida have somehow survived.

The only way to avoid lightning is to take cover when you see dark clouds and bolts begin to approach. If you are riding in a car, stay inside until the storm passes. If you are at home, in a shopping center or inside any building, don't attempt to "make a run for it." Many lightning victims have been killed when entering or leaving their automobiles. Boaters should head for the nearest place they can tie up and evacuate the boat. If the lightning doesn't get you, waves churned up during the violent storms may.

TORNADOES

Florida's comparatively small **tornadoes** usually cause less damage and death than the awesome twisters that can develop in the Midwest and Northern United States. The many trailer parks that proliferate throughout the state are the most vulnerable.

HURRICANES

Much more damaging and definitely more dangerous is a weather phenomenon more common to Florida and other Gulf Coast states – the **hurricane**.

Seasonal: The hurricane season usually runs from June through October, although Hurricane Alice in 1955 formed off Florida's southeast coast in the month of January, an extremely unusual occurrence. The number of hurricanes that forms in a given year has ranged from as few as 2 to as many as 20, but most never swing into Florida. Still, the National Hurricane Center in Miami tracks each of the massive storms carefully with sophisticated radar detection equipment, satellites and reconnaisance planes – ready to issue evacuation orders if a hurricane appears headed for land or if resulting winds, rain and high waters threaten Florida or other coastal states.

Damage: Rarely a year goes by when some Caribbean or Gulf Coastal area from Florida to Mexico is not pounded by a hurricane or its side effects. In 1992 Hurricane Andrew caused massive destruction, but the death toll was low. In 1979, Hurricane David killed about 900 in the Dominican Republic, 16 in the United States and an estimated 1,100 more people throughout the Caribbean. The most intense storm of the decade, the "Labor Day Hurricane of 1935" belted the Florida Keys, destroying Henry Flagler's Overseas Railroad with winds estimated at up to 250 miles per hour.

Formation: A hurricane forms when winds rushes toward a low-pressure area and takes on a distinctive swirling motion. It begins as a tropical depression, and is classified a hurricane when winds reach 74 miles per hour. The size of storms can range from 60 miles in diameter to monsters more than 1,000 miles wide. Their patterns and routes remain very difficult to predict. Hurricanes thought to be on the wane have reformed into bigger storms. Others move out to sea away from land areas only to double back and come ashore.

Duration: The average life of a hurricane is 8 to 10 days. It begins to lose its punch and organization when it strays too far inland or over colder northern waters where tropical wind patterns are no longer able to feed it. Florida's eastern and southeastern seaboards are most vulnerable to hurricanes in August and early September, but patterns traditionally shift to the Caribbean later in September and in October, endangering the Keys, the West Coast and Panhandle.

Christening: Once named only for women, a practice thought to have begun when World War II servicemen in the Pacific named storms after their girlfriends, the National Weather Service adopted an equal rights policy in 1979 when it began alternating male names for every other hurricane.

Precautionary Measures: Florida residents are well versed on precautions that should be taken when a hurricane approaches. Newspapers and magazines publish special sections on the subject at the beginning of each season. Most coastal communities publish evacuation plans and routes. Many locals have adopted the hobby of tracking the path of each storm on special charts – available in newspapers, from radio and television stations, and even printed on the sides of grocery bags.

Needless to say, a tourist caught in Florida during an impending hurricane should drop plans to work on suntans or visit tourist attractions and follow National Weather Service advisories, television directives and common sense in riding the storm out.

HURRICANE DEVELOPMENTS

Tropical disturbance: This phase in a hurricane's development has no strong winds. But it may feature a weak counter-clockwise circulation of wind. Disturbances of this sort are common throughout the tropics in summer months.

Tropical depression: A small low pressure system

develops and the counter-clockwise rotation of air increases to speeds under 39 miles per hour.

Tropical storm: By now, the low pressure system has developed winds ranging from 39 to 73 miles per hour and can be accompanied by heavy rains.

Hurricane: The low pressure system has intensified to the point where strong winds of more than 74 miles per hour rotate in a counter-clockwise direction around an area of calm called the "eye." Storm tides may rise as much as 15 feet above normal and can surge as much as 6 feet in minutes.

STORM ADVISORIES

Hurricane watch: This signal means that the National Hurricane Center in Miami has determined a hurricane may threaten your immediate area within 24 hours. It is time to begin taking final precautions against a direct hit. Stay tuned to radio or television for the latest storm information.

Watch Precautions:
- Check car battery, water and oil and make sure your gas tank is full.
- Make sure you have new batteries for your radio and flashlight.
- Gather containers for storing clean drinking water. Fill drug prescriptions and make certain you have special medications like insulin on hand.
- Arrange for the safety of pets, because they will not be permitted into public shelters.
- Put together a survival kit consisting of non-perishable food (including a manual can opener), water (half a gallon per person per day), eating and cooking utensils, personal toilet articles and sanitary needs (like diapers and toothpaste), bedding (or sleeping bags), changes of clothing, portable cooler and ice, and a first aid kit.

HURRICANE WARNING

This is issued when the storm has reached winds of at least 74 miles per hour and high water and storm surges are expected in a specific area within 24 hours. Warnings will identify specific coastal areas where these conditions may occur. Be prepared to evacuate your home or hotel, even if the weather does not appear threatening when the warning is issued.

• Clear your yard of loose objects, lawn furniture, garbage cans, bicycles and any other objects which will harm you when they are hurled about during the hurricane.

• Secure your boat. Remember that most draw or swing bridges will be closed to boat traffic after an evacuation order is issued.

• Protect windows and take down awnings to secure your home. Also shut off gas valves, pull main electrical power switches, turn off main water pipes, take all important papers with you and leave your swimming pool full and super chlorinated.

• Complete the assembly of materials needed to take to a nearby shelter or anything else that you will need if you stay home.

• Prepare to evacuate if and when ordered. Most of Florida's coastal communities now have put together detailed evacuation procedure plans. Evacuation route signs are located along highways in many of these areas. Consult your local civil defense or hurricane emergency officials for details.

If your area does not have an evacuation plan, check the elevation of your property above mean sea level, study the storm surge history of your area and plan an evacuation route. Tornadoes may also be spawned by hurricanes, so follow news bulletins closely and be prepared to take immediate shelter. If your home is above or away from areas threatened by high tides, remain where you are so you do not inhibit evacuation of people from those areas.

During the storm: Stay indoors and do not travel once the hurricane begins buffeting your area. When the eye passes over you, there will be a temporary lull in wind and rain that may last up to half an hour or more. Do not mistake this for the end of the storm, although you may take the opportunity to make emergency repairs. Prepare for resumption of the storm, possibly with even greater force, from the opposite direction. Wait for word from the proper authorities before venturing out of shelter.

If ordered to evacuate: Follow instructions and designated routes as quickly as possible. Take blankets, a flashlight, extra clothing, medications, dietary foods (if needed), infant necessities and light-weight folding chairs. Leave behind alcoholic beverages, pets, weapons or extra food.

The storm surge: Ninety percent of all hurricane-related deaths are directly a result of the storm surge. It occurs when a massive dome of water that can be up to 50 miles wide sweeps across the coastline near an area where the eye of the hurricane comes ashore. It is caused by an extreme drop in barometric pressure and the force of high winds pushing on open waters. The hammering effect of breaking waves and the surge act like a giant steamroller crushing everything in their path.

After the storm passes: Drive with caution when ordered to return home. Debris may fill some streets and cause hazardous conditions. Roads in coastal areas may collapse if soil has been washed from beneath them. Avoid sightseeing as you may be mistaken for a looter. Steer clear of downed or dangling utility wires.

Seek medical attention if necessary at designated Red Cross disaster centers or hospitals. Stay tuned to radio stations about emergency medical, food, housing and other forms of assistance.

Re-enter your home with caution and make temporary repairs necessary to correct safety hazards and to minimize further damage. Open windows and doors to air out and dry the house and, in case of gas leaks, exercise caution when dealing with matches or fires. Report broken sewer or water mains to local utility departments.

Above all, do not take a hurricane lightly by inviting friends over for a "hurricane party." The deadly forces of wind, rain and tides that accompany a hurricane are no causes for celebration.

HOLIDAYS

During some of the holidays listed below, some or all state, local and federal agencies may be closed. Local banks and businesses also stop operations during these holidays.

January 1: New Year's Day
January 15: Martin Luther King's Birthday
Third Monday in February: President's Day
Last Monday in May: Memorial Day
July 4: Independence Day
First Monday in September: Labor Day
Second Monday in October: Columbus Day
November 11: Veterans Day
Fourth Thursday in November: Thanksgiving
December 25: Christmas

TIPPING

Service personnel expect tips in Florida. The accepted rate for baggage handlers in airports is about $1 per bag. For others, like taxi drivers and waitresses, 15 to 20 percent is the going rate depending on the level and quality of service rendered. Sometimes tips are included in restaurant bills when dining in groups. Generally, tipping is not required in cafeterias where you serve yourself, unless your tray is carried to your table for you.

Moderate hotel tipping is about 50 cents per bag or suitcase handled by bellboys or porters. A doorman should be tipped if he holds your car or performs other services. It is not necessary to tip chambermaids unless you stay several days. Florida hotels generally do not add a service charge to cover gratuities.

EMERGENCIES

HEALTH

SUNBURN

An early overdose of sun can ruin, in a few short hours, a vacation that involved months of planning and saving. One of the most common sights in Florida is that of the over-baked tourist, red as a beet, painfully trying to sit or walk without rubbing against anything. If you are set on getting a suntan, do so gradually. Begin with a sunscreen, containing PABA and marked with its numerical level of safeguard, and work up to less protective tanning lotions. The glare from Florida's azure seas and white sands increases the sun's intensity. Don't neglect to apply sunscreen on overcast days; the sun's ultraviolet rays still penetrate the cloud cover and the shade can lull you into staying outside too long.

INSECTS

People aren't the only living creatures attracted to sun and sand. Insects also prefer Florida's climate. Be prepared to itch, scratch, burn and curse while trying to swat or stomp on a variety of pests.

Entomologists call them bibinoid flies, but to Floridians they are simply known as **love bugs** – because you will usually find them "flying united" right into your hair, face or car's windshield.

Love bugs don't bite. They are too busy mating. But they can cause trouble during their May and September appearances in various parts of the state. In moist or wooded hammock areas, black clouds of love bugs occasionally hang over interstates and highways, slowing down traffic as they clog radiators and splatter windshields.

Florida is even more infamous for its swarms of **mosquitoes** that can take the joy out of watching summer sunsets. Most big cities have effective mosquito control programs that have effectively curtailed the pest's activities. But pack a bottle of insect repellent, especially when venturing into backwoods areas like the Everglades.

You should also tread carefully in the outdoors, particularly when barefoot. Grassy fields are prime locations for mounds of **fire ants**. These tiny red ants inflict a painful, burning sting and leave a reddish weal that turns into a chickenpox-like blister. The blister can become infected if scratched. Some persons are allergic to the sting of a fire ant, and can suffer chest constriction, wheezing, nausea or dizziness that requires prompt medical attention.

Visitors new to tropical or subtropical regions may be startled during their first confrontation with the local **cockroaches**. Often called palmetto bugs, they grow to sizes unheard of in colder climates, usually resembling miniature armored patrol cars as they dart under the carpet or disappear into cracks in the wall. They will eat book bindings, clothing, paper, garbage and virtually anything else, but they steer clear of people. Pest control services and regular house cleaning will aid in control, but rarely eradicate roaches.

Sand flies, appropriately called "no-see-ums" by the locals, are another nemesis of the sunset beach-goers. They are what you feel – but can't see – gnawing at your legs as you sink your toes into the sand. Insect repellent can help.

THOMAS COOK
MASTERCARD
TRAVELLERS CHEQUES...

...HOLIDAY ESSENTIALS

Travel money from the travel experts

THOMAS COOK MASTERCARD TRAVELLERS CHEQUES ARE
WIDELY AVAILABLE THROUGHOUT THE WORLD.

Don't be overcharged for overseas calls.

Save up to 70% on calls back to the U.S. with WorldPhone.®*

While traveling abroad, the last thing you need to worry about is being overcharged for international phone calls. Plan ahead and look into WorldPhone – the easy and affordable way for you to call the U.S. and country to country from a growing list of international locations.

Just dial 1-800-955-0925 to receive your free, handy, wallet-size WorldPhone Access Guide – your guide to saving as much as 70% on phone calls home.

When calling internationally, your WorldPhone Access Guide will allow you to:

- Avoid hotel surcharges and currency confusion
- Choose from four convenient billing options
- Talk with operators who speak your language
- Call from more than 90 countries
- Just dial and save – regardless of your long distance carrier back home

WorldPhone is easy. And there's nothing to join. So avoid overcharges when you're traveling overseas. Call for your free WorldPhone Access Guide today – before you travel.

Call 1-800-955-0925.

THE TOP 25 WORLDPHONE COUNTRY CODES.			
COUNTRY	**WORLDPHONE** **TOLL-FREE ACCESS #**	**COUNTRY**	**WORLDPHONE** **TOLL-FREE ACCESS #**
Australia (CC)♦		**Japan** (cont'd.)	
To call using		To call anywhere other	
OPTUS ■	008-5511-11	than the U.S.	0055
To call using		**Korea** (CC)	
TELSTRA ■	1-800-881-100	To call using KT ■	009-14
Belgium (CC)♦	0800-10012	To call using DACOM ■	0039-12
China (CC)	108-12	Phone Booths+	Red button 03,
(Available from most major cities)			then press*
For a Mandarin-speaking		Military Bases	550-2255
Operator	108-17	**Mexico** ▲	95-800-674-7000
Dominican Republic	1-800-	**Netherlands** (CC)♦	06-022-
	751-6624		91-22
El Salvador♦	195	**Panama**	108
France (CC)♦	19▼-00-19	Military Bases	2810-108
Germany (CC)	0130-0012	**Philippines** (CC)♦	
(Limited availability in eastern		To call using PLDT ■	105-14
Germany.)		To call PHILCOM ■	1026-12
Greece (CC)♦	00-800-1211	For a Tagalog-speaking	
Guatemala♦	189	Operator	108-15
Haiti (CC)+	001-800-444-1234	**Saudi Arabia** (CC)+	1-800-11
Hong Kong (CC)	800-1121	**Singapore**	8000-112-112
India (CC)	000-127	**Spain** (CC)	900-99-0014
(Available from most major cities)		**Switzerland** (CC)♦	155-0222
Israel (CC)	177-150-2727	**United Kingdom** (CC)	
Italy (CC)♦	172-1022	To call using BT ■	0800-89-0222
Japan♦		To call using	
To call to the U.S.		MERCURY ■	0500-89-0222
using KDD ■	0039-121		
To call to the U.S.			
using IDC ■	0066-55-121		

(CC) Country-to-country calling available. May not be available to/from all international locations. Certain restrictions apply.	+ Limited availability. ▼ Wait for second dial tone. ▲ Rate depends on call origin in Mexico.	■ International communications carrier. ♦ Public phones may require deposit of coin or phone card for dial tone.	

WORLD**P**HONE ℠
From MCI

Let it take you around the world.

RED TIDE

This form of "sea sickness" is caused by a microscopic organism called *gymnodinium brevis* (or "Jim Brevis"), always present in Gulf Coast waters in small quantities. It becomes deadly to fish and other marine life when its numbers multiply suddenly, for reasons still unknown to scientists even today. The coastal waters turn a brownish red color and thousands of dead fish wash ashore. After a few hours in the hot sun, they make beaches unbearable with their foul odor.

EMERGENCY PHONE NUMBERS

Telephone numbers for police, fire and ambulance in Florida are as numerous as the numbers of cities. The best policy in case of emergency is to dial the operator "0," state the nature of the emergency and clearly give your name and address. Better yet, telephone books in each city always list emergency numbers on a detachable yellow page near the front. Most of Florida emergency numbers use "911" as an all-purpose emergency number for fire and police and rescue ambulances.

CRIME

A rash of crimes committed against tourists in the early 1990s forced the Florida community to come up with effective safeguards to protect visitors from unwanted and dangerous attacks. One of the most important is that car rental agencies are now removing the special license plates which formerly earmarked hired cars, and replacing them with standard-issue plates, the sort used by residents. According to police, one of the tricks muggers have employed in the past is to bump a moving vehicle from behind, especially a car carrying tourists. When the bemused driver gets out to investigate, he or she is robbed at gunpoint.

Don't fall prey to this tactic: if you get bumped, proceed to the nearest well-lit and crowded spot, such as a gas station or convenience store, before stopping. Other tips: always park your car in a well-lit area, never in a shady back corner of a parking lot. When you first arrive in Florida, plot your route from the airport to your hotel in advance, with the aid of a map. (A spate of attacks in Miami occured because jet-lagged tourists disembarked from long flights, missed the highway signs for Miami Beach, and, only a couple of wrong turns later, found themselves in a violent part of town.) Better still, arrange to pick up your rented car from an agency near your hotel on the morning after you arrive rather than attempt to negotiate unfamiliar routes when very tired. Many car rental agencies will deliver to your hotel at no (or only a small extra) charge. Be sure to keep your car doors locked and windows closed while driving.

While in the street, use common sense and act like a New Yorker. In other words, don't carry around large sums of money or expensive video/camera equipment, don't make eye contact with unwelcome strangers. and don't travel alone at night.

COMMUNICATIONS

MEDIA

Newspapers: Award-winning daily newspapers roll off the presses in every area of the state. Color photography and artwork fill the newspapers; highly sophisticated, extremely expensive equipment are used to allow presentation of color photographs just hours after a news event occurs. There are more than 125 weeklies including the Spanish-language *El Imparcial* and *El Noticiero*. The *Miami Herald* also has a Spanish-language section.

Television: All major Florida cities have stations affiliated with major national networks, local stations and a vast offering of cable television hookups. Local newspapers provide daily and weekly information about television and radio programs.

POSTAL SERVICES

Post office hours vary in central, big-city branches and smaller cities and towns. Hotel or motel personnel will answer questions about opening hours of the post office nearest you. If you do not know where you will be staying in any particular town, you can receive mail simply by having it addressed to your name, care of General Delivery at the main post office in that town. But you must pick up such mail personally. Check with postal officials about current charges and the variety of mail delivery services available.

TELEGRAMS & TELEX

Western Union and International Telephone and Telegraph (ITT) will take telegram and telex messages by phone. You can check the local phone directory or you can call local information for the toll-free numbers of their offices.

TELEPHONE

Public telephones are located in hotel lobbies, drugstores, restaurants, garages, roadside kiosks, convenience stores and other locations throughout the state. The cost of making a local call is 25 cents at all pay telephones throughout the state. Long distance call rates decrease after 5pm, decrease further after 11pm, and are lower on weekends and holidays.

Getting Around

DRIVING IN FLORIDA

The automobile is the most popular means of getting to Florida. More than 20 million visitors enter the state by car annually, about twice as many as those entering by plane. One of the reasons for the reliance on the automobile is that it is practically a necessity to have a car once you arrive. Bus, train and taxi services within Florida are quite irregular, unreliable and slow to cover the state's vast distances.

Another reason for car-hopping is the excellence of interstate highway systems leading into Florida and within the state. The main north-south arteries which bring in droves of tourists from Ohio, New York, Michigan, Pennsylvania and other Northwest, Midwest and Southeastern states are Interstates 75 and 95. The latter thoroughfare ribbons its way down Florida's East Coast. Interstate 75 parallels the West Coast to Naples. Spurs from both interstates connect major cities with the expressway. The major expressway for travelers coming from the West is Interstate 10, which enters Florida near Pensacola, intersects Interstate 75 near Lake City and ends by melting into I-95 in Jacksonville.

The Florida Turnpike begins its southwest slash through the state's midsection from I-75 near Wildwood and peters out at Florida City south of Miami. Your toll depends on how much of the turnpike you use. The only other limited-access superhighway, Interstate 4, is Florida's "Fantasy Highway." This highway links Tampa to Daytona Beach with exits at Disney World, Circus World, Sea World, Stars Hall of Fame and other Central Florida attractions.

For easy driving, you can obtain excellent road maps by writing: Florida Dept of Commerce, Collins Bldg, Tallahassee 32304. Virtually all service stations also sell Florida maps, as well as detailed maps of the cities in which they are located. Another advantage of driving into Florida are the state's Welcome Stations which dispense information and free orange juice. The main station is located on Interstate 75 near Jennings. Others are at Havana on

US 27; Pensacola on US 90; near Yulee on US 17; at the junction of US 1,301 and 23 at Hilliard; and on County Road 688 off Interstate 275 near the St Petersburg-Clearwater International Airport.

PUBLIC TRANSPORT

Taxis are available in major tourism centers of the state, rare in smaller cities. They tend to be expensive, particularly for long rides and you usually have to phone in advance for pick up.

PRIVATE TRANSPORT

Visitors wishing to rent or lease an automobile after arriving in Florida will find offices of all US firms – including Hertz, Avis, Budget and National – in most Florida tourism centers, at international airports and even some smaller airports. Shop around for the best rates and features. Often, smaller local rental firms outside the airports offer less expensive, more desirable conditions than the large national companies. But be sure to check insurance coverage provisions with them before signing anything.

Most automobile rental agencies require you to be at least 21 years old (sometimes 25), to hold a valid driver's license and a major credit card, before permitting you to rent one of their cars. Some will take cash deposit, sometimes as high as $500, in lieu of a credit card. Foreign travelers may need to produce an international driver's license or a license from their own country. Liability is not automatically included in the terms of your lease, so advertised rates usually do not include additional fees for insurance. You should also check with your airline, bus or rail agent or travel agent for special package deals that provide rental cars at reduced rates.

Drivers must abide by Florida traffic laws. For a copy of "Florida Driver Information," write to the following address: Division of Tourism, Direct Mail Section, 107 W Gaines St, Tallahassee 32304.

Available rental vehicles range from modest economy cars to luxury convertibles and vans. For information contact the following companies:

Alamo: 1-800/327-9633
Avis: 1-800/331-1212
Budget: 1-800/527-0700
Dollar: 1-800/237-4584
Hertz: 1-800/824-9610
National: 1-800/328-4567

· HITCHHIKING

Hitchhiking is not advised and may prove to be hazardous in Florida. Picking up hitchhiking strangers is also potentially dangerous. Florida newspapers regularly recount stories of robbery, rape and even murder that began with an extended thumb.

If you choose to drive, you should also learn what areas of cities to avoid before starting out. Miami's Liberty City has most notoriously been the scene of criminal incidents involving motorists unfamiliar with the city. Ask questions of your rental clerk at the airport when you arrive or check with tourism offices before taking a drive.

WHERE TO STAY

Accommodations throughout the state range from modest, mom-and-pop motels to luxury resorts, historic bed and breakfast inns and youth hostels. Following is a general listing of reliable hotels, motels, inns and hostels. Reservations are usually required in advance and rates vary from the high season in winter months to the off season months of May-June and September-October. The state has a bed tax in addition to the sales tax which is added to the price of all hotel rooms. It varies from county to county and ranges between 1 and 2 percent.

Unfortunately, there is no official rating system for Florida accommodations. The following properties have been categorized as follows for a double room for one night in the winter season:

$ = Inexpensive: under $75
$$ = Moderate: $75–150
$$$ = Expensive: $150–and above
Rates on a weekly basis are lower.

ALACHUA

Days Inn: Rt 1 Box 225, I-75 and US 441, Alachua 32615. Tel: 904/462-3251. Modest but clean 60 rooms near the expressway with a restaurant and lounge on the property. $

ALTAMONT SPRINGS

Sundance Inn: I-4 and Hwy 436, Altamont Springs 32714. Tel: 407/862-8200. 150 rooms near the expressway in a suburban environment. Non-smoking rooms, restaurant and lounge, 24-hour food service, pool, pets allowed. $

APALACHICOLA

Gibson Inn: 100 Market St, Apalachicola 32320. Tel: 904/653-2191. A grand old inn listed on the National Register of Historic Places with 31 antique filled rooms, restaurant and lounge. $.

APOPKA

Budget Inn: 429 E Main St, Apopka 32703. Tel: 407/886-2092. 15 rooms in downtown with restaurants nearby. $

BAY HARBOR ISLANDS

Bay Harbor Inn: 9660 E Bay Harbor Dr, Bay Harbor Islands 33154, just north of Miami Beach. Tel: 305/868-4141. A comfortable and beautifully furnished inn with 36 rooms, two excellent restaurants, pool, boat docks, pets accepted. $$

BIG PINE KEY

Big Pine Motel: MM 30, Big Pine Key 33043. Tel: 305/872-9090. 32 rooms and five efficiency apartments with pool. $

BOCA RATON

Boca Raton Resort & Club: 501 E Camino Real, Boca Raton 33431. Tel: 407/395-3000. A plush and historic hotel with golf course, pools, tennis, and health spa. $$$

Friendship Inn: 1801 N Federal Hwy, Boca Raton 33432. Tel: 407/395-7500. 50 rooms located downtown on major highway. Restaurant, pool. $

Shore Edge Motel: 425 N Ocean Blvd, Boca Raton 33432. Tel: 407/395-7500. 16 motel rooms and efficiencies located on the beach near downtown, pool, restaurants nearby. $

BOYNTON BEACH

Golden Sands Inn: 520 SE 21 Ave, Boynton Beach 33435. Tel: 407/732-6075. 24 rooms in the downtown area not far from the beach, restaurant and room service. $

BRADENTON

Holiday Inn Riverfront: 100 Riverfront Dr, Bradenton 34205. Tel: 813/747-3727. A Mediterranean-style motor inn near the Manatee River. 153 rooms, pool, restaurant, lounge. $

CAPTIVA

South Seas Plantation Resort: South Seas Plantation Road, Captiva Island 33924. Tel: 813/472-5111. 600 rooms on the beach with four restaurants, two lounges, fishing, golf, tennis, pools, sailing school, children's programs and health club. $$$

CEDAR KEY

Island Place: First and C streets, Cedar Key 32625. Tel: 904/543-5307. 21 rooms on beach with 1 and 2-bdrm suites, pool, sauna, Jacuzzi, boat docks. $$

Historic Island Hotel: Main and B Streets, Cedar Key 32625. Tel: 904/543-5111. 10 rooms in the historic district with natural gourmet meals and Caribbean architecture. $$

CHATTAHOOCHEE

Morgan Motel: E US 90, Chattahoochee 32324. Tel: 904/663-4336. 20 rooms in downtown, restaurant, fishing, pets allowed. $

CLEARWATER BEACH

Belleview Lido Resort: 25 Belleview Rd, Clearwater Beach 34616. Tel: 813/442-6171. A large, historic inn on Clearwater Bay with 350 rooms, golf, tennis, pools, saunas, sailboats, fishing. $$$

Clearwater Beach Hotel: 500 Mandalay Ave, Clearwater Beach 35616. Tel: 813/441-2425. 156 rooms and efficiencies on the beach with pool, restaurant, room service, non-smoking rooms, pets allowed. $$

New Comfort Inn: 3580 Ulmerton Rd, Clearwater Beach 34616. Tel: 813/573-1171. A modest motor inn near the airport with 119 rooms, pool, restaurant, fitness center. $

Sheraton Sand Key Resort: 1160 Gulf Blvd, Clearwater Beach 34616. Tel: 813/595-1611. A 390-room resort with views of the Gulf, beach, pool, tennis, sailboats, restaurant, lounge. $$

CLEWISTON

Clewiston Inn Hotel: US 27 and Royal Palm Ave, Clewiston 33440. Tel: 813/983-8151. 60 motel rooms and efficiencies in downtown, restaurant, lounge, marina. $

COCOA

Cocoa Beach Oceanside Inn: 1 Hendry Ave, Cocoa Beach 32931. Tel: 407/784-3126. 40 rooms on the beach with fishing, pool, restaurant and shuttle service. $

Comfort Inn: 3901 N Atlantic Ave, Cocoa Beach 32931. Tel: 407/783-2221. 94 rooms on the beach with restaurant, lounge, pool, tennis and foreign language interpreters: French. $

CORAL GABLES

Biltmore Hotel: 1200 Anastasia Ave, Coral Gables 33134. Tel: 305/445-1926. A magnificent, historic hotel and resort with 275 rooms, enormous pool, fine restaurants, golf, tennis, health spa and lounge. $$$

Colannade Hotel: 180 Aragon Ave, Coral Gables 33134. Tel: 305/441-2600. A modern downtown hotel with 157 rooms, pool, shopping complex, restaurants, Jacuzzi, lounge and health club. $$$

Hotel Place St Michel: 162 Alcazar, Coral Gables 33134. Tel: 305/444-1666. 28 antique filled rooms in a historic small hotel located downtown with an elegant French restaurant, excellent service, lounge and foreign language interpreters: French and Spanish. $$

DAYTONA BEACH SHORES

Captain Quarters Inn: 3711 Atlantic Ave, Daytona Beach Shores 32127. Tel: 904/767-3119. A mid-rise hotel with antique furniture in 25 suites, full kitchens, pool, and cozy restaurant. $$

Daytona Beach Hilton: 2637 S Atlantic Ave, Daytona Beach Shores 32127. Tel: 904/767-7350. A towering hotel with 214 rooms overlooking the beach, pool, Jacuzzi, sauna, fitness center, playground. $$

Howard Johnson Hotel: 600 N Atlantic Ave, Daytona Beach Shores 32127. Tel: 904/255-4471. A remodeled Deco hotel with 324 rooms, kitchens available, pool, restaurant, lounge. $

DEERFIELD BEACH

Carriage House Resort: 250 S Ocean Blvd, Deerfield Beach 33441. Tel: 305/427-7670. This is a tidy and friendly beach motel with 30 rooms, pool, shuffleboard. $

EVERGLADES CITY

Rod & Gun Club: 200 Riverside Dr, Everglades City 33929. Tel: 813/695-2101. 25 cottage-style rooms in the heart of the Everglades fishing area with pool, tennis, fishing equipment rentals, restaurant. $

FERNANDINA BEACH

Bailey House: 28 S 7th St, Fernandina Beach 32034. Tel: 904/261-5390. A small and quaint Victorian guest house in the historic district with 4 rooms, no-smoking. $

FORT LAUDERDALE

Howard Johnson Motor Lodge: 700 N Atlantic Blvd, Fort Lauderdale 33304. Tel: 305/563-2451. 144 beachfront rooms with pool, lounge, 24-hour food service, shuttle service, foreign language interpreters: Spanish. $$

Pier 66 Resort: 2301 SW 17th St, Fort Lauderdale 33316. Tel: 305/525-6666. A landmark, high-rise hotel with 388 rooms, marina, pool, rooftop restaurant, tennis, health club, boat rentals, parasailing. $$$

Marriott's Harbour Beach Resort: 3030 Holiday Dr, Fort Lauderdale 33316. Tel: 305/525-4000. A 14-story oceanfront resort with 624 rooms, pool, cabanas, tennis, health club, restaurants, shopping, and windsurfing. $$$

Riverside Hotel: 620 E Las Olas Blvd, Fort Lauderdale 33316. Tel: 305/467-0671. Located in the beautiful downtown shopping district, this historic hotel has 117 antique furnished rooms, pool, volley ball, restaurants, lounge. $$

FORT MYERS

Cottage Court Apartment Motel: 3079 Cleveland Ave, Fort Myers 33901. Tel: 813/332-0301. A downtown motel with 27 rooms that offers weekly and monthly rentals, kitchens. $
Robert E. Lee Motor Best Western: 6611 US 41N, North Fort Myers 33903. Tel: 813/997-5511. 108 spacious rooms with views of the Caloosahatchee River, pool, dock, lounge. $
Sheraton Harbor Place: 2500 Edwards Dr, Fort Myers 33901. Tel: 813/337-0300. A modern high-rise hotel in the heart of downtown with 437 rooms, pool, tennis, boat docks, exercise room. $$

GAINESVILLE

Holiday Inn University Center: 1250 W University Ave, Gainesville 32601. Tel: 904/376-1661. 167 rooms in downtown near the University of Florida campus with rooftop pool, restaurant and lounge. $

HOMOSASSA SPRINGS

Riverside Inn: Box 258, Homosassa Springs 32687. Tel: 904/628-2472. A rustic inn with 76 rooms across from Monkey Island on the Homosassa River with marina, pool, tennis, boat docks, restaurant and bicycle rentals. $

INDIANTOWN

Seminole Country Inn: 15885 SW Warfield Blvd, Indiantown 34956. Tel: 407/597-3777. An old-fashioned, country inn with 28 rooms, whirlpool baths, restaurant with home-style cooking. $

ISLAMORADA

Cheeca Lodge: MM 82, Islamorada 33036. Tel: 305/245-3755. One of the most popular resorts in the Keys, this hotel has 203 rooms, tennis, golf, pools, fishing pier, restaurants, bars, private beach, snorkeling. $$$

JASPER

Jasper Hotel: 3 Main St, Jasper 32052. Tel: 904/792-1406. A 14-room inn in a quaint North Florida town with a big screened front porch and bathrooms down the hall. $

JACKSONVILLE

Comfort Suites Hotel: 833 Dix Ellis Trail, Jacksonville 32256. Tel: 904/739-1155. In the heart of the shopping and restaurant district, this 128-room hotel has full kitchens, pool, and health spa. $
House on Cherry Street: 1844 Cherry St, Jacksonville 32205. Tel: 904/384-1999. An antique filled river-side inn with 4 cozy rooms and hearty breakfasts. $
Marina Hotel at St Johns Place: 1515 Prudential Dr, Jacksonville 32205. Tel: 904/396-5100. A modern, 321-room resort hotel with tennis, pool, restaurant, shopping. $$

KEY LARGO

Holiday Inn Key Largo Resort: MM 100, Key Largo 33037. Tel: 305/451-2121. A modern and tropical resort with 132 rooms, pool, private beach, marina, restaurants, bars and spectacular ocean views. $$$
Sunset Cove Motel: MM 99, Key Largo 33037. Tel: 305/451-0705. A modest but pleasant motel that offers discounts to conservationists and senior citizens. 10 units with full kitchen facilities, water sports, boat ramps, sailboat rentals. $

KEY WEST

Curry Mansion: 511 Caroline St, Key West 33040. Tel: 305/294-5349. A grand Victorian-style mansion turned into a charming 15-room inn with pool and lush gardens. $$
Island City House: 411 Williams St, Key West 33040. Tel: 305/294-5702. Off the main strip, this tropical garden hotel has 24 suites with kitchens, pool, Jacuzzi. $$
Ocean Key House: Zero Duval St, Key West 33040. Tel: 305/296-7701. A plush, all-suite hotel with 100 rooms, Jacuzzis, water views, pool, restaurant, bars in the heart of downtown Key West. $$$
Pier House: One Duval St, Key West 33040. Tel: 305/296-4600. A luxury 142-room resort that feels like it's on a private island with pools, private beach, restaurant, bars, and cabanas. $$$
Southernmost Motel: 1319 Duval St, Key West 33040. Tel: 305/294-5539. A comfortable, motel with 127 rooms, pool, and full-service concierge. $$

KISSIMMEE

Beaumont House: 206 S Beaumont St, Kissimmee 32741. Tel: 407/846-7916. A small but beautiful 3-room bed and breakfast inn with antique and wicker furniture. $
Casa Rosa Inn: 4600 W Irlo Bronson Memorial Hwy, Kissimmee 34746. Tel: 407/396-2020. A simple, Spanish-motif inn with 54 rooms, pool, free movies. $

Comfort Inn Maingate: 7571 W Irlo Bronson Memorial Hwy, Kissimmee 32741. Tel: 407/396-7500. A comfortable, modest hotel close to Disney with 281 rooms, pool, restaurant, game room and shuttle service. $

Sheraton Lakeside Inn: 7769 W Irlo Bronson Memorial Hwy, Kissimmee 34746. Tel: 407/239-1919. A 15-story resort with 651 rooms, pool, miniature golf, tennis, restaurants, paddleboats. $

LAKE WHALES

Chalet Suzanne: HWY 27 and 17A 3 miles north of Lake Wales proper, 33859. Tel: 813/676-6011. A charming and whimsical collection of 30 antique decorated rooms, gourmet restaurant, private airstrip, pool, lake. $$

LAUDERDALE BY THE SEA

Tropic Seas Resort Motel: 4161 El Mar Dr, Lauderdale by the Sea 33308. Tel: 305/772-2555. A comfortable, 1950s motel on the beach with 16 rooms, pool, shuffleboard, barbecue facilities. $

MARATHON

Hawk's Cay Resort: MM 61, Marathon 33050. Tel: 305/743-7000. A rambling, Caribbean-style resort known to pamper its guests. 177 rooms, pool, tennis, restaurants, bars, boat rentals, scuba lessons, marina, and generous breakfast buffet. $$$

MIAMI

Everglades Hotel: 244 Biscayne Blvd, Miami 33132. Tel: 305/379-5461. A 380-room high-rise hotel in the heart of downtown Miami, pool, restaurants, close to downtown shopping. $$

Hotel Inter-Continental Miami: 100 Chopin Plaza, Miami 33131. Tel: 305/577-1000. A soaring, high-rise hotel with 644 rooms, gourmet restaurants, pool, skyline views, and jogging track in the heart of downtown Miami. $$$

Mayfair House: 3000 Florida Ave, Miami 33133. Tel: 305/441-0000. In the center of the Coconut Grove business district this super elegant 181-room hotel has uniquely designed suites with Japanese hot tubs, pool, gourmet restaurants, boutiques, and bars. $$$

Miami River Inn: 118 SW South River Dr, Miami 33130. Tel: 305/325-9227. A beautifully restored 40-room inn overlooking the Miami River in Little Havana with pool and Jacuzzi. $$

Hotel Mia: Miami International Airport, Miami 33159. Tel: 305/871-4100. A modern 259-room hotel located in the Miami airport with pool, restaurants and shopping. $$

MIAMI BEACH

Alexander Hotel: 5225 Collins Ave, Miami Beach 33140. Tel: 305/865-6500. A 16-story oceanfront hotel with 212 suites, kitchens, pools, cabanas, health club, gourmet restaurant. $$$

Cardozo Hotel: 1300 Ocean Dr, Miami Beach 33139. Tel: 305/534-2135. An oceanfront Art Deco hotel in the heart of the historic district with 56 beautifully decorated rooms. Fine restaurants and clubs nearby. $$

Hotel Cavalier: 1320 Ocean Dr, Miami Beach 33139. Tel: 305/531-6424. Another well-run Art Deco beauty with 46 rooms on the ocean. Fine restaurants and bars nearby. $$

Fontainebleau Hilton Resort: 4441 Collins Ave, Miami Beach 33140. Tel: 305/538-2000. An opulent 375-room 1950s hotel that underwent a massive renovation. Pool with waterfalls, tennis, cabanas, health club, restaurants, nightclubs, shopping, and children's activities. $$$

Miami Beach International Youth Hostel: 1423 Washington Ave, Miami Beach 33139. Tel: 305/534-2988. A popular and casual 120-bed youth hostel with dormitory-style rooms and kitchen facilities in the historic Art Deco District. Very inexpensive. $

NAPLES

Edgewater Beach Hotel: 1901 Gulfshore Blvd, Naples 33940. Tel: 813/262-6511. An all-suite Gulfront hotel with 124 rooms, beach, pool, exercise room, restaurant. $$$

Ritz Carlton: 280 Vanderbilt Beach Rd, Naples 33941. Tel: 813/598-3300. One of the more elegant hotels on the Gulf with 464 rooms, lavish public areas, pools, gourmet restaurants, tennis, golf, fitness center, sailing and children's activities. $$$

Vanderbilt Beach Motel: 9225 N Gulfshore Dr, Naples 33963. Tel: 813/597-3144. A pleasant motel right on the beach with 50 rooms and efficiencies and a pool. $$

NEW SMYRNA BEACH

Ocean Air Motel: 1161 N Dixie Freeway, New Smyrna Beach 32069. Tel: 904/428-5748. A modest but pleasant motel five minutes from the beach with 14 rooms, pool, picnic tables. $

Riviera Hotel: 103 Flagler Ave, New Smyrna Beach, 32069. Tel: 904/428-5858. A landmark hotel that overlooks the Intracoastal Waterway with 18 beautifully furnished rooms, pool, restaurant. $

OCALA

Seven Sisters Inn: 820 SE Fort King St, Ocala 32671. Tel: 904/867-1170. A Victorian mansion transformed into a charming inn with 7 rooms, period antiques, and gourmet breakfasts. $$

ORLANDO

Buena Vista Palace: 1900 Lake Buena Vista Dr, Lake Buena Vista 32830. Tel: 407/827-2727. A sprawling Disney property with 1,028 spacious suites, pools, lake, tennis, health club, restaurants, bars, game room. Ideal for large families. $$$

Days Inn Orlando: 7335 Sand Lake Dr, Orlando 32819. Tel: 407/351-1900. A clean and comfortable budget motel with 695 rooms, pools, lake, picnic areas, restaurants and video arcade. $

Normant Parry Inn: 211 N Lucern Circle E, Orlando 32801. Tel: 407/648-5188. Removed from the glittery Disney hotels, this is one of the finest historic inns in the state with 6 rooms, antique furnishings and wrap-around porch. Children welcome. $$

Orlando International Youth Hostel: 227 N Eola Dr, Orlando 32801. Tel: 407/843-8888. Sitting across from downtown's Lake Eola, this hostel is housed in a beautiful old house with 90 dormitory-style beds, kitchen facilities and park. Very inexpensive, children welcome. $

Sonesta Villa Resort: 10000 Turkey Lake Rd, Orlando 32819. Tel: 407/352-8051. A lakefront complex of comfortable apartments with 369 units, sand beach, pools, tennis, health club, restaurants and grocery deliveries. $$$

Walt Disney World Dolphin: 1500 Epcot Resort Blvd, Lake Buena Vista 32830. Tel: 407/934-4000. A modern Disney property adorned with dolphin sculptures and a 27-story pyramid. 225 rooms and suites, pools, tennis, health club, restaurants, bars, game room. $$$

PALM BEACH

Brazilian Court: 301 Australian Ave, Palm Beach 33480. Tel: 407/655-7740. An old tropical hotel with lush gardens, French doors and afternoon tea. 128 courtyard rooms, pool, restaurant, bar. $$$

The Breakers: One S Country Rd, Palm Beach 33480. Tel: 407/655-6611. One of the grand old hotels of the 1920s, this Florida oceanfront landmark has 526 luxurious rooms, pools, beach, croquet, tennis, golf, health club, restaurants, boutiques and nightclubs. $$$

PANAMA CITY BEACH

Miracle Mile Resort: 9450 S Thomas Dr, Panama City Beach 32407. Tel: 904/234-3484. A beachfront family-style resort with 632 units, pools, tennis, restaurants, bars. $

Marriott's Bay Point Resort: 100 Delwood Beach Resort, Panama City Beach 32407. Tel: 904/234-3307. An elegant resort with antique furnishings, Oriental rugs, and beautiful views. 400 rooms and suites, pools, golf, tennis, marina, sailboat rentals, restaurants and bars. $$

SANIBEL

Casa Ybel Resort: 2255 W Gulf Dr, Sanibel 33957. Tel: 813/472-3125. Contemporary one and two-bedroom condominium villas on the Gulf with 112 units, pool, tennis, sailing, biking, shuffleboard, restaurants. $$$

Sundial Beach & Tennis Resort: 1451 Middle Gulf Dr, Sanibel 33957. Tel: 813/472-4151. The largest all-suite hotel on the island with glorious Gulf views, 200 suites, kitchens, pools, private beach, tennis, sailing, restaurants, bars, children's activities. $$$

SARASOTA

Gulf Beach Resort Motel: 930 Ben Franklin Dr, Sarasota 34236. Tel: 813/388-2127. A casual motel that attracts lots of European families and others who return every year. 48 rooms, private gardens, kitchens, pool, shuffleboard, Gulf views. $$

Hyatt Sarasota: 1000 Blvd of the Arts, Sarasota 34236. Tel: 813/366-9000. A modern hotel in the heart of downtown with views of Sarasota Bay, 297 rooms, pool, sauna, health club, sailing, restaurants, bars. $$

Surf View Motel: 1121 Ben Franklin Dr, Sarasota 34236. Tel: 813/388-1818. A clean and comfortable motel right on the beach with 27 rooms, pool, and playground. $

ST AUGUSTINE

Casa Solana: 21 Aviles St, St Augustine 32084. Tel:904/824-3555. A small and gracious antique filled inn featuring four comfortable suites and homemade breakfasts. $$

Sheraton Palm Coast: 300 Club House Dr, St Augustine 32137. Tel: 904/445-3000. A nautical-style resort overlooking the Intracoastal Waterway with 154 rooms, private patios, pools, marina, tennis, health spa, restaurants, bars. $$$

St Francis Inn: 279 St George St, St Augustine 32084. Tel: 904/824-6068. An 18th-century mansion with a rich history reborn as a bed and breakfast inn. 11 rooms and suites with old-fashioned paddle fans, pool. $

ST PETERSBURG

Bayboro House: 1719 Beach Dr S E, St Petersburg 33701. Tel: 813/823-4955. A small but charming Victorian inn overlooking Tampa Bay with 3 cozy rooms, generous breakfasts, and an airy veranda. $

Colonial Gateway Resort Inn: 6300 Gulf Blvd, St Petersburg Beach 33706. Tel: 813/367-2711. A contemporary, family-oriented Gulf-front resort with 200 rooms – most with kitchens, beach bar, pool, restaurants, water sports.$$

Don CeSar Beach Resort: 3400 Gulf Blvd, St Petersburg Beach 33706. Tel: 813/360-1881. A shocking pink rococo resort built in the 1920s that sits smack on the beach. 277 luxurious rooms, pool, beach, tennis, fitness center, gourmet restaurants, sailing, windsurfing, scuba lessons. $$$

SEBRING

Santa Rosa Inn: 509 N Ridgewood Dr, Sebring 33870. Tel: 813/385-0641. A well-run, friendly historic hotel with 25 beautifully furnished rooms and suites, wicker filled sun porch, and home-cooked meals. $. Rates higher during the Sebring auto races.

TALLLAHASSEE

Governors Inn: 209 S Adams St, Tallahassee 32301. Tel: 904/681-6855. A southern-style inn in the heart of the Tallahassee historic district just one block from the Capitol. Featuring 40 cozy rooms, afternoon cocktails, and overnight shoe-shines. Children welcome. $$
Las Casas: 2801 N Monroe St, Tallahassee 32303. Tel: 904/386-8286. A comfortable hotel with the look of Old Spain with 112 rooms, a private courtyard, and pool. $$

TAMPA

Hyatt Regency Tampa: 211 N Tampa St, Tampa 33602. Tel: 813/225-1234. A modern high-rise hotel in the heart of downtown with 517 rooms, pool, restaurants, bars, exercise room. $$
Holiday Inn Busch Gardens: 2701 E Fowler Ave, Tampa 33612. Tel: 813/971-4710. A family-oriented motel with 399 rooms, free transportation to Busch Gardens, pool, sauna, restaurant, exercise room. $$
Tahitian Inn: 601 S Dale Mabry Hwy, Tampa 33609. Tel: 813/877-6721. A comfortable budget motel that caters to families. 79 rooms, pool. $

VERO BEACH

Guest Quarters Suite Hotel: 3500 Ocean Dr, Vero Beach 32963. Tel: 407/231-5666. A cozy, five-story hotel within walking distance of the downtown shopping district, with 55 one- and two-bedroom suites, pool, patios, restaurants. $$$

WEST PALM BEACH

Hibiscus House: 501 30th St, W Palm Beach 33407. Tel: 407/863-5633. A handsome 7-room inn with sun room, pool, deck. Kitchen available for use. $
Days Inn: 6255 W Okeechobee Rd, W Palm Beach 33409. Tel: 407/686-6000. A modern chain motel near the expressway with 154 rooms, pool, playground, 24-hour food service, pets allowed. $$

WINTER PARK

Park Plaza Hotel: 307 Park Ave, Winter Park 32789. Tel: 407/647-1071. A quiet and intimate bed and breakfast hotel built in the 1920s with 27 beautiful rooms and lots of southern charm. $$

CAMPING

FACILITIES

100,000 campsites at nearly 700 campgrounds sprinkled throughout Florida provide an ample choice of outdoors accommodations for the mobile traveler – from primitive areas marked off for tents and sleeping bags to elaborate facilities with utility hook-ups for home-on-wheels recreational vehicles (RVs), restaurants, heated pools, mini-golf courses and planned activities. There are even campgrounds that cater to nudists. Most state parks and forests offer at least primitive camping facilities. (*For details see Parks listings under Things to Do.*") But since state and national facilities usually offer the best rates in some of the best settings, reserve your space well in advance of your arrival to avoid disappointment. Most of these public camping facilities are booked solid during the busy late winter and early spring seasons.

PRIVATE CAMPGROUNDS

Private campgrounds have blossomed around many of the popular public and commercial attractions and usually have vacancies. Central Florida now appears to have the major share of these facilities (to accommodate the droves of people that descend on Walt Disney World each year). Within The World itself, Walt Disney offers 825 campsites at Fort Wilderness Resort. It's not even necessary to bring a tent or trailer, because upon arrival you can rent Fleetwood Travel Trailers complete with air-conditioning, carpeting, color TV, AM/FM radio, cookware and even linen. They sleep up to six people. The camping resort is located admist 650 acres of woods and winding streams on Bay Lake. River Country and Pioneer Hall are a short walk or tram ride from your campsite. For more information and reservations, write: Walt Disney World Central Reservations, PO Box 10100, Lake Buena Vista, Florida 32830. Or phone 407/824-2900, preferably between 5pm and 11pm in the Eastern Time zone. Information about special group rates can be obtained by writing: Fort Wilderness Resort, PO Box 40, Lake Buena Vista, Florida 32830.

Information: To obtain information about the numerous other private campgrounds near Disney World or in other parts of the state, write to the **Florida Campground Association**, 1638 N Plaza Drive, Tallahassee, Florida 32308-5323. The association publishes an annual *Florida Camping Directory and Map* that it will send you free of charge. The directory lists hundreds of campgrounds representing nearly 50,000 campsites in Florida divided by regions and with details about amenities. You can phone many of the parks for reservations via toll-free numbers listed in the brochure.

The association estimates that about 5 million people camped in Florida in 1990. About 3.9 million of those campers came from other states and another 100,000 from foreign countries. According to the association, one out of every 10 Florida tourists camps out.

CAMPING REGULATIONS AT PUBLIC FACILITIES

State parks rent sites for a small fee for periods up to 14 days. Fees are slightly higher in the Florida Keys. Reservations are accepted up to 60 days in advance of check-in and can only be made by calling the park where you plan to camp. The base fee covers a maximum of 4 people and a maximum of 8 people may stay at any site. At least one person 18 years or older, or a married person, must be present in each group. There is a small additional charge for extra cars and for electricity. Only Florida residents may obtain an annual camping permit (effective January 1 of each year). Only pets on handheld leashes are allowed in state park picnic areas. No pets are allowed in the campgrounds or on public beaches. For further information about camping at state parks, write: Florida Dept of Natural Resources, Bureau of Education and Information, Rm 616, Marjory Stoneman Douglas Bldg, 3900 Commonwealth Blvd, Tallahassee, Florida 32399-3000. Tel: 904/488-7326.

FOOD DIGEST

WHAT TO EAT

Unlike some states where regional cooking styles are embedded in the local psyche – Louisiana Cajun, Texas barbecue or nouvelle California cuisine – in Florida the range of foods includes diverse ingredients, flavors, and ethnic specialties. From old-fashioned Cracker catfish and hush puppies to Cuban rice and beans and the freshest of fresh seafood, the state is a hodgepodge of flavors.

Restaurants across the state also span the spectrum, from down-home cafeterias, fancy French, take-out Chinese, all-you-can-eat-shrimp, Kosher delicatessens, dinner show spectacles, Southern black, Caribbean spicy, fried eggs and grits, hearty Nicaraguan, Italian spaghetti houses, corner coffee stands, and oceanside Art Deco cafés.

Following is a list of some of Florida's best dining choices. Some of them are expensive and elegant, but most just offer good food and a friendly atmosphere. A general price range guide is:

$ = Inexpensive, an average meal costs under $10

$$ = Moderate, an average meal costs between $10–20

$$$ = Expensive, an average meal costs over $20.

BOCA RATON

La Vieille Maison: 770 E Palmetto Park Rd, Boca Raton. Tel: 407/391-6701. Housed in a historic building, this elegant French restaurant is one of the best in the state. Dishes include pompano in chardonnay sauce, citrus soufflés, and smoked salmon. Reservations. $$$

Tom's Place: 7251 N Federal Hwy, Boca Raton. Tel: 407/997-0920. Old-fashioned soul food in a very casual setting. Dishes include pork chop sandwiches, barbecue ribs, sweet potato pie. $

BRADENTON

Crab Trap: US 19 at Terra Ceia Bridge. Tel: 305 813/722-6255. Super fresh seafood in a rustic decor with alligator and wild pig also on the menu. $$

COCOA BEACH

Alma's Italian Restaurant: 306 N Orlando Ave, Orlando. Tel: 407/783-1981. A popular spot that is always crowded and noisy. It serves terrific Italian food like veal marsala, lasagna, antipasto, and eggplant Parmesan. $

Mango Tree: 118 N Atlantic Ave, Cocoa Beach. Tel: 407/799-0513. A romantic and tropical setting of fresh flowers, wicker furniture and white linen. Serves fine American cuisine and fresh seafood specialties. $$$

DAYTONA BEACH

Top of Daytona: 2625 S Atlantic Ave, Daytona Beach. Tel: 904/767-5791. A 29th-floor dinner club with a panoramic view of the city specializing in fine American cuisine like prime rib, veal and shrimp dishes. Reservations. $$

FLORIDA CITY

Alabama Jack's: 58000 Card Sound Rd, Florida City. Tel: 305/248-8741. Although badly damaged during Hurricane Andrew in 1992, Jack's is still standing and serving up homemade crab cakes, conch fritters and fried shrimp to the hundreds of faithful customers who have been coming here since 1953. $

FORT MYERS

Mucky Duck: 2500 Estero Blvd, Fort Myers Beach. Tel: 813/472-3434. A pleasant seafood house with fresh dishes that include grilled dolphin, bacon-wrapped shrimp and seafood salad. $$$
Sangeet of India: US 41 and Crystal Dr, Fort Myers. Tel: 813/278-0101. Serves up traditional saffron and curry Indian dishes. $$
Woody's Bar-B-Q: 13101 N Cleveland Ave, N Fort Myers. Tel: 813/997-1424. A very casual Old Florida favorite specializing in generous portions of barbecue pit beef, ribs, and chicken. $

FORT PIERCE

Mangrove Mattie's: 1640 Seaway Dr, Fort Pierce. Tel: 407/466-1044. A rustic spot overlooking the Fort Pierce Inlet that serves seafood dishes and make-your-own roast beef sandwiches. $

ISLAMORADA

Green Turtle Inn: MM 81.5, Islamorada. Tel: 305/664-9031. Since 1947, this comfortable old seafood house has been serving hearty turtle soup, conch salad, alligator steak, and Key lime pie. $$

JACKSONVILLE

Beach Road Chicken Diner: 4132 Atlantic Blvd, Jacksonville. Tel: 904/398-7980. An old-fashioned roadside diner that serves fried chicken and gravy, meat-loaf, and home-fried potatoes. Downhome and good. $
Crawdaddy's: 1643 Prudential Dr, Jacksonville. Tel: 904/396-3546. A riverfront fish house that serves up local and Cajun-style seafood dishes like jambalaya and all-you-can-eat catfish. $
Homestead: 1712 Beach Blvd, Jacksonville Beach. Tel: 904/249-5240. Another comfortable Old Florida kind of place that offers country cooking like fried chicken gizzards, chicken and dumplings, and strawberry shortcake. $
The Tree Steakhouse: 942 Arlington Rd, Jacksonville. Tel: 904/725-0066. A casual steak house that lets you choose your own piece of beef and then watch it sizzle on the charcoal grill. $$

JUPITER

Log Cabin Restaurant: 631 N A1A, Jupiter. Tel: 407/747-6877. A very casual old Florida roadhouse restaurant that offers all-American cooking like fried chicken, biscuits and gravy, and ribs. $

KEY LARGO

Crack'd Conch: MM 105, Key Largo. Tel: 305/451-0732. An old clapboard dining room with a screened porch that serves seafood specialties like fried alligator, conch chowder, grilled fish and over 80 brands of beer. $
Mrs Mac's Kitchen: MM 99, Key Largo. Tel: 305/451-3722. A very tacky but lots-of-fun locals' joint that serves meat-loaf on Monday, Mexican on Tuesday, Italian on Wednesday, and seafood Thursday through Saturday. Closed Sunday. $

KEY WEST

A & B Lobster House: 700 Front St, Key West. Tel: 305/294-2535. Casual seafood dining with a beautiful harbor view. $$
The Buttery: 1208 Simonton St, Key West. Tel: 305/294-0717. A well-mannered, elegant spot that takes pride in its very rich, fine foods – buttery steaks, creamy soups, and tripple-chocolate pies. Reservations. $$$
Cafe des Artistes: 1007 Simonton St, Key West. Tel: 305/294-7100. An intimate and elegant setting with classic French/tropical specialties like lobster in cognac sauce and shrimp in mango butter. Reservations. $$$
Dockside Raw Bar: Zero Duval St, Key West. Tel: 305/296-7701. A T-shirts and sandals kind of place that offers conch fritters, smoked fish, and frosty beers. $
El Sibony: 900 Catherine St, Key West. Tel: 305/296-4148. Traditional and generous Cuban dishes like roast pork and fried bananas served in a homey atmosphere.
Louie's Backyard: 700 Waddell Ave, Key West. Tel: 305/294-1061. Fine American and Caribbean cooking in a romantic, seaside setting with old Key West ambience. Reservations. $$$

MARATHON

Mile 7 Grill: MM 47, Marathon. Tel: 305/743-4481. Since 1954, this open-air diner at the northern end of the Seven Mile Bridge has been offering fish sandwiches, chili dogs, peanut butter pie to local fisherman and passing tourists. $

MARCO ISLAND

Island Cafe: 918 N Collier Blvd, Naples. Tel: 813/304-7578. A cozy and intimate café offering Continental and fine seafood specialties. $

MIAMI

Aux Palmistes: 6820 NE 2nd Ave, Little Haiti. Tel: 305/759-8527. Homestyle Haitian atmosphere and cooking with specialties including rice and peas, griot, lamb and goat. $
Bimini Grill: 620 NE 78th St, Miami. Tel: 305/758-9154. A very casual canal-front café specializing in Bahamian dishes like conch chowder and fritters. $

Cafe Abbracci: 318 Aragon Ave, Coral Gables. Tel: 305/441-0700. Part art gallery, part fine Italian restaurant. House specialties include gnocchi, linguine and clam sauce and rich pastries. $$

Chart House: 51 Chart House Dr, Coconut Grove. Tel: 305/856-9741. Friendly service in a beautiful marina setting. Huge salad bar and great grilled seafood. $$

El Inka: 1756 SW 8th St, Little Havana. Tel: 305/854-0243. Peruvian cuisine with four kinds of ceviche, marinated beef and fried sea bass. $$

Joe's Stone Crabs: 227 Biscayne St, South Miami Beach. Miami's most well-known restaurant. The stone crabs are delicious but the wait is always long. Closed in summer. $$$

Los Ranchos: 125 SW 107th Ave, Miami. Tel: 305/596-5353. Co-owned by the nephew of former Nicaraguan President Anastasio Somoza, this busy spot specializes in hearty Nicaraguan foods. $$

Thai Orchid: 9565 SW 72nd St, Miami. Tel: 305/279-8583. Fine Thai cuisine in a room decorated with orchids and Oriental art – garlic pork, snapper in ginger sauce, chicken curry. Reservations. $$

Versailles: 3555 SW 8th St, Little Havana. Tel: 305/444-4448. Delicious Cuban cooking in a wonderfully gaudy atmosphere. $

Yuca: 177 Giralda Ave, Coral Gables. Tel: 305/444-4448. Trendy, new wave Cuban cooking with terrific fried plantains, Cuban rice pudding, and conch-and-chorizo tamales. $$

MIAMI BEACH

A Mano: 1140 Ocean Dr, South Miami Beach. Tel: 305/531-6266. A very popular but very intimate Deco District favorite specializing in nouvelle tropical cuisine. Reservations. $$

Cafe Chauveron: 9561 E Bay Harbor Dr, Bay Harbor Islands, north of Miami Beach. Tel: 305/866-8779. Award-wining classic French cuisine. Excellent bouillabaisse and chateaubriand. Jackets required for men. Reservations. Closed during summer. $$$

Cafe Des Arts: 918 Ocean Dr, South Miami beach. Tel: 305/534-6267. French-provincial cuisine amid an art-filled Art Deco setting, indoor and outdoor seating. $$

Chef Allen's: 19088 NE 29th Ave, North Miami Beach. Tel: 305/935-2900. A sleek and modern Art Deco-design restaurant specializing in very fine nouvelle American cuisine like mesquite-grilled tuna, lamb medallions, and macadamia nut tortes. Reservations. $$$

Our Place: 830 Washington Ave, South Miami Beach. Tel: 305/ 674-1322. Small and casual with wholesome vegetarian and non-vegetarian meals. $

Puerto Sagua: 700 Collins Ave, South Miami beach. Tel: 305/673-1115. Large and loud, but hearty and good Cuban cooking. $

Unicorn Village: 3565 NE 207th St, North Miami Beach. Tel: 305/983-8829. A waterfront restaurant and market place offering natural foods. Salads, pastas, miso soup, pizza, terrific carrot cake. $$

NAPLES

Cafe La Playa: 9891 Gulfshore Dr, Naples. Tel: 813/597-3123. Indoor and patio dining with views of the Gulf. Fine French classics like vichyssoise, *pâté de fois gras*, and veal in Dijon sauce. $$

Villa Pescatore: 8929 N Tamiami Trail, Naples. Tel: 813/597-8119. A romantic linen-and-candlelight spot featuring· Northern Italian dishes like linguine with salmon and duck in sage sauce. $$$

NEW SMYRNA BEACH

Riverview Charlie's: 101 Flagler St, New Smyrna Beach. Tel: 904/428-1865. A seafood house with a view of the Intracoastal Waterway serving fresh local fish, steaks and chicken. $$.

The Skyline: 2004 N Dixie Hwy, Tel: 904/428-5325. A casual dining spot with an aeronautical decor beside the New Smyrna Airport and views of the take-offs and landings, offering New England chowder, homemade pastas, veal and steaks cut to your liking. $$

ORLANDO

Arabian Nights: 6225 W Irlo Bronson Memorial Hwy, Kissimmee. Tel: 407/239-9223. An elaborate dinner theater with an Arabian-style floor show of horses, live music and special effects. A choice of several four-course meals. $$$

Beeline Diner: 9801 International Dr, Orlando. Tel: 407/352-4000. A cozy, 1950s-style diner that's open 24 hours a day. Features thick sandwiches, griddle cakes, and a juke box with old songs. $

Brazil Carnival Dinner Show: 7432 Republic Dr, Orlando. Tel: 407/352-8666. A Brazilian carnival dinner show with dancers and live bands. A varied choice of dinners. $$$

The Bubble Room: 1351 South Orlando Ave, Maitland. Tel: 407/628-3331. Hearty portions of American foods – lamb chops, burgers, grilled fish – in a playful atmosphere of antiques and animated toys. $$

Fort Liberty: 5260 West Irlo Bronson Memorial Blvd, Kissimmee. Tel: 407/351-5151. A Wild West, cowboys and Indians dinner show restaurant. The food is all-American – fried chicken and corn on the cob, as is the shoot-'em-dead floor show. Reservations. $$$

Gary's Duck Inn: 3974 Orange Blossom Trail, Orlando. Tel: 407/843-0270. A silly name for a seafood restaurant but worth a try. Fresh Florida lobster, crab, shrimp and fish. Nautical decor. $$

Hard Rock Cafe: 5401 Kirkman Rd, Orlando. Tel: 407/363-7655. One of the international chain's many cafés serving greasy hamburgers, thick sandwiches and barbecue beef amid rock memorabilia. $

King Henry's Feast: 8984 International Dr, Orlando. Tel: 407/351-5151. A chicken and ribs dinner show with jugglers, mimes, magicians, singers and dancers in gaudy but fun King Henry VII setting. $$$

Le Coq Au Vin: 4800 South Orange Ave, Orlando. Tel: 407/851-6980. Considered the finest French restaurant in Central Florida with specialties including rainbow trout with champagne, roast duckling, and chicken liver pâté. $$$

Spaghetti House: 4951 Sunward Dr, Kissimmee. Tel: 407/351-3407. Over 120 pasta dishes with 30 different sauces in a sprawling Mediterranean-style decor. $

PALM BEACH

Chuck & Harold's: 207 Royal Poinciana Way, Palm Beach. Tel: 407/659-1440. As popular with locals as with tourists, this casual but classy spot offers fresh gazpacho, terrific steaks and salads, and tart Key lime pie. $$.

TooJay's: 313 Royal Poinciana Way, Palm Beach. Tel: 407/659-7232. A classic Jewish delicatessen with a bit of California style. Serves thick pastrami sandwiches, matzoh ball soup, potato pancakes, and rich chocolate cake. $

Charley's Crab: 456 Ocean Blvd, Palm Beach. Tel: 407/659-1500. Across the street from the beach, this elegant seafood house offers grilled fish, broiled lobster, steamed shrimp, and sumptuous salads. $$$

PANAMA CITY

Boar's Head: 17290 Front Beach Rd, Panama City beach. Tel: 904/234-6628. A rustic yet elegant restaurant and tavern that offers juicy prime rib, shrimp bisque, *escargot*, blackened fish dishes. $$

Capt. Anderson's: 5551 N Lagoon Dr, Panama city Beach. Tel: 904/234-2225. Greek and seafood specialties amid a rustic nautical decor. $·

PENSACOLA

McGuire's Irish Pub: 600 E Gregory St, Pensacola. Tel: 904/433-6789. A cozy, antique-filled Irish pub with thick sandwiches, lots of brands of beer, and spicy bowls of chili. $

Perry's Seafood House: 2140 Barrancas Ave, Pensacola. Tel: 904/434-2995. Housed in an old house built in 1858. Perry's offers fresh seasonal seafood caught by local fishermen. $

ST AUGUSTINE

Columbia: 98 St George St, St Augustine. Tel: 904/824-3341. Similar to the one in Tampa's Ybor City, this spot serves classic Spanish dishes like paella, *arroz con pollo*, and shrimp Marbella. $$

Raintree: 102 San Marco Ave, St Augustine. Tel: 904/824-7211. Housed in a beautifully restored old home, this restaurant offers a blend of fine cuisines including seafood, meats, and pastas with an impressive wine list. Free hotel pick-up available. Reservations. $$

Zaharias: 3945 A1A South, St Augustine. Tel: 904/471-4799. Greek and Italian specialties combined in a big, noisy buffet-style setting. $

ST PETERSBURG

Leverock's Seafood House: 54 Corey Ave, St Petersberg Beach. Tel: 813/376-5671. Inexpensive but good seafood specialties. $

Outback Steakhouse: 4088 Park Street N, St Petersberg. Tel: 813/348-4329. Grilled shrimp and massive steaks with a Down Under Australian attitude. $$

Hurricane Seafood Restaurant: 807 Gulf Way, St Petersburg Beach. Tel: 813/360-9558. A popular and inexpensive seafood house that serves blackened grouper, homemade crab cakes, steamed shrimp and grilled lobster. $

STUART

Mahony's Oyster Bar: 201 St Lucie Ave, Stuart. Tel: 407/286-9757. A nautical-style raw bar that serves fresh raw and steamed oysters, clams, and shrimp. Closed summer. $

The Inlet: 555 NE Ocean Blvd, Hutchinson Island. Tel: 407/225-3700. An intimate Continental restaurant serving creamy lobster bisque, oysters Rockefeller and steak Diane. Reservations. $$$

SANIBEL

Windows on the Water: 1451 Middle Gulf Dr, Sanibel. Tel: 813/472-4151. Fresh seafood dishes and a wonderful Gulf view. Reservations. $$$

McT's Shrimphouse: 1523 Periwinkle Way, Sanibel. Tel: 813/472-3161. A lively and informal tavern featuring fresh fish and all-you-can-eat shrimp and crabs. $$

SARASOTA

Bijou Cafe: 1287 1st St, Sarasota. Tel: 813/366-8111. A contemporary dining room that specializes in fine Continental dishes like rack of lamb, roast duck and poached fish. $$

Cafe L'Europe: An art-filled cafe offering light and elegant meals of fresh veal, seafood, and salads. $$

SIESTA KEY

Ophelia's on the Bay: 9105 Midnight Pass Rd, Siesta Key. Tel: 813/349-2212. A waterfront bistro specializing in gourmet dishes like mussel soup, seafood cioppino, and eggplant crêpes. $$

TALLAHASSEE

Anthony's: 1950 Thomasville Rd, Tallahassee. Tel: 904/224-1447. A favorite among locals offering classic Northern Italian cuisine. $$

Nicholson's Farmhouse: Follow signs from Hwy 27 to Hwy 12 toward Quincy. Tel: 904/539-5931. Although a little bit difficult to find, this informal country-style restaurant serves hearty meat and fish dishes cooked on an outdoor grill. $$

TAMPA

Bella Trattoria: 1413 S Howard Ave, Tampa. Tel: 813/254-3355. A loud, friendly and fine Italian restaurant with terrific angel-hair pasta, smoked salmon sauces, and truffle tortes. $$

Bern's Steak House: 1208 S Howard Ave, Tampa. Tel: 813/252-2421. Prime cuts of beef, organic vegetables, and over 7,000 bottles of wine. Reservations. $$$

Columbia: 2117 E 7th Ave, Ybor City. Tel: 813/248-4961. A neighborhood institution since 1908 serving fine Spanish foods with a Flamenco floor show. $$

Crawdaddy's: 2500 Rocky Point Dr, Tampa. Tel: 813/281-0470. A funky, locals' hangout that serves up fried alligator. $

Skippers Smoke House: 910 Skipper Rd, Tampa. Tel: 813/971-0666. Florida and Caribbean specialties like curried chicken, smoked oysters, gatortail, and shark in a rustic setting surrounded by trees. $$

TARPON SPRINGS

Louis Pappas' Riverside Restaurant: 10 W Dodecanese Blvd, Tarpon Springs. Tel: 813/937-5101. A waterfront landmark specializing in generous Greek meals. Reservations. $$

THINGS TO DO

TOURS & ATTRACTIONS

Adventure Island: 4500 Bougainvillea Ave, Tampa. East of Busch Gardens. Tel: 813/987-5600 (for information and ticket prices.) Water-oriented theme park on 22 acres. High drive platforms, water flumes, wave-making machines, restaurant, gift shop. Open daily March–December 10am–10pm; June–September 8am–9pm; until 6pm at other times.

Alligatorland Safari: Nine miles south of Kissimmee on US 192. Tel: 407/396-1012. Monkeys and alligators in a swamp setting reached by a long board walk. Open daily.

American Lighthouse Museum: 1011 N Third St, Jacksonville Beach 32250. Tel: 904/241-8845. Dedicated to recording the role American lighthouses served in history. Authentic scale models, rare photos and artifacts. Open Tuesday–Saturday 10am–5pm.

Art Deco Welcome Center: 1244 Ocean Dr, Miami Beach 33139. Tel: 305/672-2014. Housed in an historic Art Deco hotel, the welcome center offers a wealth of information on Miami Beach's Art Deco architecture. Open Monday–Friday 10am–6pm, Saturday 10am–2pm. Walking tours offered on Saturday mornings.

Audubon House: 205 Whitehead St, Key West 33040. Tel: 305/294-2116. Restored home of US Navy pilot John H. Geiger. The naturalist-artist John James Audubon lived here for several weeks in 1832 while sketching area birds. His original Double Elephant folio of *Birds of America* is on display along with other period antiques. Open 9:30am–5pm daily. Closed noon–1pm for lunch.

Bass Museum of Art: 2121 Park Ave, Miami Beach 33139. Tel: 305/673-7530. A permanent collection of Old Master paintings, sculpture, textiles furniture, and artifacts relating to South Florida. Open Tuesday–Saturday 10–5pm, Sunday 1–5pm.

Bellm's Cars and Music of Yesterday: 5500 N Tamiami Trail (US 41), Sarasota 33580. Tel: 813/355-6228 (for more information and current ticket prices.) More than 170 restored antique and classic cars and 1,200 music boxes from the Gay '90s and Roaring '20s. Also features a country store, livery stable, blacksmith shop, 250-piece antique arcade, high-wheeled bicycles and more. Open Monday–Saturday 8:30am–6:30pm; Sundays from 9:30am.

Birthplace of Speed Museum: 160 E Granada Blvd, Ormond Beach 32174. Tel: 904/672-5657. Ormond Beach has been called the birthplace of speed since the early 1900s, and the museum documents the role the area has played in the development of automobile racing. Open Tuesday–Saturday 1–5pm.

Brevard Art Center and Museum: 1463 N Highland Ave, Melbourne 32936. Tel: 407/242-0737. Both permanent and rotating exhibits of collections of national stature including American, European and Japanese art. Open Tuesday–Saturday 10am–5pm, Sunday noon–4pm.

Busch Gardens "The Dark Continent": 3000 Busch Blvd, Tampa. Tel: 813/987-5212. An African theme park full of wild animals, birds, reptiles, rides, restaurants and carnival games built around the Anheuser-Busch Brewery. Themed lands include the Serengeti Plain where more than 500 heads of big game roam free and can be inspected by train, monorail or cable car; Morocco, with a bazaar full of shops, belly dancers, snake charmers and magicians; Stanleyville, with trained animal shows, a jungle ride, flume ride, looping Python thrill ride and more; Timbuktu, trained dolphin shows, a continual Oktoberfest in the Festaus, and more rides; the Old Swiss House Restaurant; Hospitality House, with free beer; and daily brewery tours. The list of daily shows and events is subject to change. Open 9:30am–6pm daily; until 10pm June–Labor Day.

Castillo de San Marcos: One Castillo Dr E, St Augustine 32084. Tel: 904/829-6506. A massive fortress built by the Spanish in the 1600s. Constructed out of native shell stone, the fort is surrounded by a moat and outer defense works. Guided tours offered. Open 8:45am–4:45pm daily.

Central Florida Railroad Museum: 101 S Boyd St, Winter Garden 34787. Tel: 407/656-8749. Formerly a railroad depot, this museum includes historical telephones, locomotive bells and whistles, photographs, lanterns and railroad memorabilia. Open Sunday 2–5pm only.

Church Street Station: West Church St, Downtown Orlando 32801. Tel: 303/422-2434. A shopping and eating complex fashioned out of historic buildings. Attractions include Rosie O'Gradys Good Time Emporium, Phineas Phogg's Balloon Works (champagne flights over Central Florida), Apple Annie's Courtyard, Lili Marlene's Aviators' Pub, Rosie O'Grady's Flying Circus. Open 11am–2am daily.

Collier County Musuem: 3301 Tamiami Trail, Naples 33962. Tel: 813/643-5252. A permanent exhibit that traces the history of Collier County from prehistoric times to the present including a Seminole village, archaeological lab and steam locomotive. Open 10am–5pm daily.

Conch Tour Train: Key West 33040. Tel: 305/294-5161. Stations located at 501 Front St, 3850 N Roosevelt Blvd, and corner of Angela and Duval streets. A 14-mile, 1½-hour narrated tour through Key West, old and new, historic and contemporary. These tours are available 9:30am–4:30pm daily.

Coral Castle: 28655 S Federal Hwy, Homestead 33030. Tel: 305/284-6344. The unrequited love of an eccentric genius is reflected in this fairy tale mansion that conjures up images of Stonehenge in England. Includes rock furniture, a sundial and a 9-ton swinging gate. The late Edward Leedskalnin never revealed how he moved the massive coral rocks weighing up to 35 tons each. He claimed to know the secrets used to build the pyramids of Egypt. Open 9am–9pm daily.

Cypress Gardens: State Route 540, Winter Haven 33880. Tel: 813/324-2111. One of Florida's oldest and most venerable tourist attractions. Water skiers create pyramids and perform other amazing acrobatic feats, in Lake Eloise, a waterway flanked by acres of carefully-nurtured gardens. Magnificent moss-draped cypress giants live here. Cruise the Cypress River and lake in electric boats. View the Aquarama where Esther Williams filmed her underwater musical spectacles. A recent $5.5 million project has created 13 theme areas, including the New Southern Crossroads, a Living Forest, South Sea Island waterfalls, a fern forest, English courtyard, Japanese Garden, aviary and rose garden. Restaurants, two marine stadiums. Open 8am–6pm daily. Water ski performances at 10am, noon, 2 and 4pm.

Dolphin Research Center: US 1, Grassy Key, Florida Keys. Tel: 305/289-1121. Dolphin shows. This is the training center for the star of television's *Flipper*. Open 10am–5pm daily.

Dreher Park Zoo: 1301 Summit Blvd, West Palm Beach 33405. Tel: 407/533-0887. A 30-acre zoo featuring domestic and exotic animals in natural settings. Open 9am–5pm daily.

Edison Home: 2350 McGregor Blvd, Fort Myers 33901. Tel: 813/334-7419 (for ticket prices and more information.) The sprawling 14-acre estate of one of the world's greatest inventors. Home, guest house, gardens, laboratory and a museum with some of Thomas Alva Edison's personal light bulbs, gramophones, batteries, movie cameras and automobiles. Guided tours every 30 minutes. Souvenirs, refreshments. Open 9am–4pm Monday–Saturday; from 12:30pm Sunday. Closed at Christmas.

Elvis Presley Museum: 5770 Irlo Bronson Memorial Hwy, Kissimmee 34746. Tel: 407/396-8594. Over 150 personal items and memorabilia from the king of rock and roll including cars, costumes, jewelry and furniture. Open 10am–10pm daily.

Everglades Wonder Gardens: US 41, Bonita Spring 33923. Tel: 813/992-2591. The mammals, reptiles and birds of South Florida, including the rare Florida panther, endangered Everglades crocodiles, otters and alligators in their natural tropical setting. Continuous guided tours from 9am–5pm daily.

Fairchild Tropical Garden: 10901 Old Cutler Road, Miami 33156. Tel: 305/667-1651. A botanical garden with 83 acres of palms, cycads, a rain forest, vine pergola, sunken garden, palm glade, rare plant house. Hourly tram tours. Open 9.30am–4.30pm daily. Closed Christmas.

Florida Citrus Tower: US 27, Clermont 32711. Tel: 904/394-8585. Observation deck providing views of rolling citrus country and lakes. Carillon, large souvenir center, packing house, candy shop, restaurant, ice cream parlor. Open 8am–6pm daily.

Florida Sports Hall of Fame: 601 Hall of Fame Dr, Lake City 32055. Tel: 904/758-1310. The stories of more than 100 sports legends who lived or played sports in Florida. Open Monday–Saturday 9am–9pm, 10am–7pm Sunday.

Flying Tigers Warbird Air Museum: 231 N Hoagland Blvd, Kissimmee 34741. Tel: 407/933-1942. A World War II flying museum with restoration projects always underway. Open 9am–5pm daily.

Fort Myers Historical Museum: 2300 Peck St, Fort Myers 33901. Tel: 813/332-5955. Included in the museum are depictions of Calusa and Seminole Indian civilizations, as well as artifacts gathered from the region. Open Monday-Friday 9am–4:30pm, Sunday 1–5pm.

Fountain of Youth: 155 Magnolia Ave, St Augustine. Tel: 904/829-3168 (for admission charges and further information.) Built around Ponce de León's legendary search for a spring that would provide eternal youth. Sip from the fountain, see traces of ancient Indian burial mounds, gaze at a statue of the famed explorer, and tour a museum, Discovery Globe and planetarium. Open September–June 8am–5pm daily; June–Labor Day 8am–7:30pm. Closed Christmas. Planetarium shows hourly from 9am.

Frannie's Teddy Bear Museum: 2511 Pine Ridge Rd, Naples 33942. Tel: 813/598-2711. Some 2,000 bears from around the world are on display for teddy bear lovers. Open Wednesday–Saturday 10am–5pm, Sunday 1–5pm.

Fort Lauderdale Museum of Art: One E Las Olas Blvd, Fort Lauderdale 33301. Tel: 305/525-5500. Featuring American and European art from the 19th century to the present, pre-Columbian, West African, and Oceanic art. Open Tuesday–Saturday 10am–5pm, Sunday noon–5pm.

Gamble Plantation State Historic Site: 3708 Patten Ave, Ellenton 34222. Tel: 813/723-4536. An antebellum mansion located in Ellenton, a small town across the Manatee River from Bradenton. Built in 1850, the mansion was once the headquarters of a 3,500-acre sugar plantation. Open 9am–12pm and 1–5pm daily.

Gatorland Zoo: Hwy 441 North, Kissimmee 32741. Tel: 305/855-5496. Feed thousands of alligators and crocodiles. See Florida wildlife and birds. Take a swampwalk. Free tram. Covered walks. Open 8am–7pm daily in summer; otherwise until 6pm.

Gold Coast Railroad Museum: 12450 Coral Reef Drive, Miami. Tel: 305/253-0063. Steam into Florida's past aboard replicas of early Florida railroading. Visit the *Ferdinand Magellan*, the only Pullman ever built specifically for US presidents, used by Roosevelt, Truman, Eisenhower and Reagan. Open 10am–3pm Monday–Saturday; 10am–5pm Sunday. Train rides Saturday, Sunday and holidays.

Great Explorations: 1120 Fourth St, St Petersburg 33701. Tel: 813/821-8885. A hands-on museum that allows visitors to touch, move and interact with exhibits. Some of the more interesting include the Think Tank, Touch Tunnel and Body Shop. Open Monday–Saturday 10am–5pm, Sunday noon–5pm.

Gulfarium: US 98, Okaloosa Island, Fort Walton Beach 32548. Tel: 904/244-5169. Fish and scuba diving exhibitions. Trained porpoise and sea lion shows. Reef tank. Open 9am–6pm daily in summer; until 4pm in winter.

Hemingway House and Museum: 907 Whitehead St (US 1), Key West 33040. Tel: 305/294-1575 (for further information and admission fees.) A Spanish Colonial built in 1851. Ernest Hemingway purchased the building in 1931 and added a swimming pool. He lived here for about 10 years during a prolific writing period that included publication of *The Snows of Kilimanjaro*, *To Have and Have Not* and *Death in the Afternoon*. Open 9am–5pm daily.

Henry Flagler Museum: Coconut Row, Palm Beach 33480. Tel: 407/655-2833. Formerly the private home of the famed railroad magnate, Henry Flagler, including original furnishings, paintings, private railroad car, oriental rugs, and costumes from the early 1800s. Open Tuesday–Saturday 10am–5pm. Sunday noon–5pm.

Historic Pensacola Village: 205 E Zaragoza St, Pensacola 32501. Tel: 904/444-8905. A collection of museums housed in historic buildings left by early pioneers. Exhibits span over 200 years of area history. Open Monday–Saturday 10am–4pm.

Homosassa Springs: US 19, Homosassa Springs 32647. Tel: 904/628-2311. Walk under water in "Nature's Giant Fish Bowl." Cruise through tropical jungle waterways, hike on nature trails. Daily alligator and hippopotamus feedings. Located on a 55-ft deep spring at the source of the Homosassa River. Coffee shop, gift shops, orchid collection. Open 9am–5:30pm daily.

Jacksonville Art Museum: 4160 Boulevard Center Dr, Jacksonville 32207. Tel: 904/398-8336. Contemporary paintings, sculpture, drawings and historic artifacts. Open Tuesday–Friday 10am–4pm, Saturday–Sunday 1–5pm.

Jacksonville Zoological Park: 8605 Zoo Road off Heckscher Drive. Tel: 904/757-4463. Hundreds of animals, picnic facilities, children's rides, safari train. On the Trout River. Open 9am–5pm daily. Closed holidays.

Jungle Larry's Zoological Park and Caribbean Gardens: At 1590 Goodlette Road off US 41, Naples 33940. Tel: 813/262-4053 (for ticket prices and further information.) No tours are provided so you have to go on a self-guided tour. "Circus Africa" wild animal shows are held at 11:30am, 2pm and 4pm daily from November 1–May 1. Lions, tigers, elephants, snakes, birds and even more wildlife. Authentic souvenirs of Africa, India and Florida are available. The zoo is open 9:30am–5pm daily.

Jungle Queen Cruises: Located on State Route A1A, Fort Lauderdale Beach. Tel: 305/566-5533. Daily departures from Bahia Mar Yacht Center for 3-hour sightseeing cruises into the Everglades at 10am and 2pm. Evening cruises include barbecue and shrimp dinner at 7pm. Reservations are recommended.

Kennedy Space Center Tours and Seaport USA: Kennedy Space Center 32899. Tel: 407/452-2121. Begin at Spaceport USA on NASA Causeway 6 miles east of US 1 near Titusville. Two-hour narrated bus tours with stops at the enormous Vehicle Assembly Building (VAB), Mission Control, the Astronaut Training Facility and abandoned launch sites. Thirty rockets and more at the Air Force Museum near the south gate. Hall of History and more exhibits at Visitors' Center. Carousel Cafeteria. Tour itinerary and schedule may vary depending on launch schedule. Open 8am daily. Closed on launch days.

Key West Aquarium: One Whitehead St, Key West 33040. Tel: 305/296-2051. Hundreds of sea life specimens, shark pools, and tropical fish displays. Open 10am–6pm daily.

Key West Lighthouse Museum: 938 Whitehead St, Key West 33040. Tel: 305/294-0012. Florida's third oldest lighthouse built in 1847 now a museum and observation deck. Open 9:30am–5pm daily.

King Henry's Feast: 8949 International Drive, Orlando 32819. Tel: 305/351-5151. Unique dinner theater, with 3-hour show of fun, frivolity, food and drink in "olde English" manner, with knights in armor and serving maidens. Continuous entertainment and guest participation. Showtimes Sunday–Thursday 8pm; Friday & Saturday 6pm & 8:30pm.

Kingsley Plantation: 11676 Palmetto Ave, Jacksonville 32226. Tel: 904/251-3537. A restored, 18th-century cotton plantation with guided tours by the National Park Service. Open 9am–5pm daily.

Leu Botanical Gardens: 1730 N Forest Ave, Orlando 32803. Tel: 407/246-2620. Magnificent gardens of orchids, roses, azaleas and flowering trees, and a turn-of-the-century farmhouse in the heart of downtown Orlando. Open 9am–5pm daily.

Lightner Museum: St Augustine. Tel: 904/824-2874. One of the South's largest exhibits of antiques, collectibles and mechanical musical instruments. The exhibits are displayed on three floors of the former Alcazar Hotel, built in 1888. Open 9am–5pm daily except Christmas.

Lion Country Safari: Tel: 305/793-1084. Drive over miles of jungle trails that feature more than 1,000 roaming animals. Keep car windows rolled up. Safari boat rides, Everglades express train ride, petting and feeding area for small animals. Reptile park, dinosaur park, hiking trail and more. Restaurants, gift shops. Open 9:30am–5:30pm.

Lowe Art Museum: 1301 Sanford Dr, Coral Gables 33124. Tel: 305/284-3536. A diversified collection of permanent and rotating exhibits on the University of Miami campus. Open Tuesday–Saturday 10am–5pm, Sunday noon–5pm.

Lowrey Park Zoo: 7530 North Blvd, Tampa 33604. Tel: 813/932-0245. Wooden walkways wind through natural habitats including an Asian domain, primate area, manatee center, petting park, and aviary. Open 9:30am–5pm daily.

Margorie Kinnan Rawlings State Historic Site: Country Rd 325, Rt3, Hawthorne 32640. Tel: 904/466-3672. A rambling farmhouse, formerly the home of Pulitzer prize-winning author Marjorie Kinnan Rawlings. Her book, *Cross Creek*, recorded her impressions of the area. Guided tours available. Open Thursday–Monday 10–11:30am and 1–4:30pm.

Marie Selby Botanical Gardens: 800 S Palm Ave, Sarasota. Tel: 813/366-5730. Six acres of exotic plants. Greenhouse. Open 10am–5pm daily. Closed at Christmas.

Marineland: St Augustine 32084 on A1A south of St Augustine. Tel: 904/471-1111, St Augustine Chamber of Commerce. An entire village built around the granddaddy of all marine attractions. Huge oceanariums on the Atlantic Ocean side provide constant salt water environments, housing porpoises, manatees, electric eels, sharks, dolphins, barracudas. Eleven exhibits altogether. Aquarius Theater, newly-renovated and expanded. Shows at 9:30am, 11am, 12:30pm, 2pm, 3:30pm and 4:50pm. Restaurants, gift shops, motel. Park open 8am–6:30pm daily.

Mel Fisher Maritime Heritage Society Museum: 200 Green St, Key West 33040. Tel: 305/294-2633. Museum and maritime salvage center displays artifacts and treasures from the sunken *Atocha* and *Santa Margarita* Spanish ships. Open 9:30am–5pm daily.

Metro-Dade Cultural Center: 101 W Flagler St, Miami 33130. Tel: 305/375-1492. A downtown cultural complex that includes the **Center for the Fine Arts**, the **Historical Museum of Southern Florida** and the main branch of the **Public Library**. A good art and resource center that focuses on the South Florida area. Open daily 9:30am–5:30pm.

Metrozoo: 12400 SW 152 St Miami. Tel: 305/251-0400. Animals roam free over 295 acres. More than 3 miles of walkways, a monorail and petting zoo. Open 9:30am–5:30pm daily.

Miami Museum of Science and Space Transit Transit Planetarium: 3280 S Miami Ave, Miami 33129. Tel: 305/854-2222. More than 100 hands-on exhibits that let visitors explore the worlds of light, sound, electronics, electricity, biology, energy and the human body. The Planetarium is housed in a 65-ft dome that features a multi-media show of the universe. Open 10am–6pm daily.

Miami Seaquarium: 4400 Rickenbacker Causeway, Key Biscayne 33149. Tel: 305/361-5705. Killer Whale and "Flipper" dolphin shows. Pet sea lions, shark feedings, huge "living sea" aquarium. Monorail ride. Open 9am–6pm daily. Shows on the half hour beginning at 10am.

Miccosukee Indian Village: Mile Marker 70 Hwy 41, Miami 33144. Tel: 305/223-8380. A Miccosukee village in the heart of the Everglades features Indian arts, crafts, foods, cultural displays, alligator wrestling shows and airboat rides. Open 9am–5pm daily.

Mission of Nombre de Dios: San Marco Ave, St Augustine 32084. Tel: 904/824-2809. Believed to be the site of the first Christian mission in the nation started by Father Lopez de Mendoza Grajales about 1565. Prince of Peace Church, Shrine of Our Lady of La Leche, Mission Art Guild building. Illuminated, stainless steel cross marks site of the nation's first mass. Open 7am–8pm daily in summer; 8am–6pm daily in winter. Admission free, but donations are requested.

Monkey Jungle: 14805 SW 216th St, Miami 33170. Tel: 305/235-1611. The place "where humans are caged and monkeys run free." Safe caged walkways. "Amazonian rain forest." Exotic monkeys, gorillas, baboons, orangutans. Continuous shows. Open 9:30am–5pm daily.

Museum of African American Art: 1308 Marion St, Tampa 33602. Tel: 813/272-2466. One of the few museums in the US dedicated to African-American art. Included in the museum are pieces from over 50 of the most notable African-American artists of the 19th and 20th centuries. Open Tuesday–Saturday 10am–5pm, Sunday 1–5pm.

Museum of Discovery and Science: 401 SW 2nd St, Fort Lauderdale 33312. Tel: 305/467-6637. The largest science museum in South Florida featuring hands-on educational exhibits that include video games, an indoor citrus grove and bubble making experiments. Open Monday–Friday 10am–5pm, Saturday 10am–8:30pm, Sunday noon–5pm.

Museum of Fine Arts: 255 Beach Dr, St Petersburg 33701. Tel: 813/896-2667. Noted for its collection of French impressionist paintings, this museum also has outstanding holdings of ancient, Asian, pre-Columbian and American art. Open Tuesday–Saturday 10am–5pm, Sunday 1–5pm.

Museum of Florida History: 500 South Bronough St, Tallahassee 32399. Tel: 904/488-1484. Florida's history from prehistoric times to today including a 12-foot tall mastedon, Spanish treasures and war relics. Open Monday–Saturday 9am–4:30pm, Sunday noon–4:30pm.

Museum of Science and History: 1025 Museum Circle, Jacksonville 32207. Tel: 904/396-7062. Scientific, historical and anthropological exhibits. The museum includes a planetarium and a 1,200 gallon aquarium. Open Monday–Saturday 10am–5pm, Sunday 1–6pm.

Museum of Science and Industry: 4801 E Fowler Ave, Tampa 33605. Tel: 813/985-5531. Exhibits include the Gulf Coast Hurricane, a recreated 75 mph wind tunnel that you can lean into to sample Nature's seasonal fury. Also available are lots of hands-on exhibits and a working weather station. Open 10am–4:30pm daily.

Mystery Fun Houses: 5767 Major Blvd, Orlando, off I-4. Tel: 407/351-3355. Fifteen entertainment areas with magic floors, rolling barrels, laughing doors. Spectacular miniature golf.

National Museum of Naval Aviation: Building 3465, Naval Air Station, Pensacola 32508. Tel: 904/453-6289. One of the largest air and space museums in the world with exhibits from the dawn of flight to the exploration of space. Displayed are biplanes, blimps, spaceage aircraft, and aviation art. Open 9am–5pm daily except Christmas and Thanksgiving.

Norton Gallery of Art: 1451 S Olive Ave, West Palm Beach 33401. Tel: 407/832-5194. A museum with an outstanding permanent collection and a full schedule of rotating exhibits. Open Tuesday–Saturday 10am–5pm, Sunday 1–5pm.

Ocean World: 1701 SE 17th St Causeway, Fort Lauderdale. Tel: 305/525–6612. Porpoise shows, sharks, alligators and sea lions. Tour boat rides and a sky ride are available. Open 10am–6pm daily, but box office closes at 4:30pm. Continuous shows.

Oldest House Museum: 322 Duval St, Key West 33040. Tel: 305/294–9502. Built by sea captain Francis B. Atlington in 1829, it has been restored and refurnished with antiques, paintings, model ships and toys. Open 9am–5pm daily, except Wednesday.

Oldest House: 14 St Francis St, St Augustine 32084. Tel: 904/824–2872. First built in the early 18th century. Constructed of coquina from Anastasia Island. Full of antiques. Open 9am–5pm daily. Closed Christmas.

Oldest Store Museum: 4 Artillery Lane, St Augustine 32084. Tel: 904/829–9729. Modeled upon a turn-of-the-century general store. Antiques on sale and display. Open Monday–Saturday 9am–5pm; Sunday from noon. Closed Christmas.

Oldest Wooden Schoolhouse: 14 St George St, St Augustine 32804. Tel: 904/824-0192. Built by Spanish for use as a private home and later utilized as a school. Open 9am–5pm daily.

Orlando Museum of Art: 2416 N Mills Ave, Orlando 32803. Tel: 407/896-4231. Rotating and permanent exhibits of early American, European and pre-Columbian art. Open Tuesday–Saturday 9am–5pm, Sunday noon–5pm.

Paddlewheel Queen: 2950 NE 32nd Ave, Fort Lauderdale. Tel: 305/564-7659. Three-hour sightseeing cruises on the Intracoastal Waterway beginning at 2pm daily. Dinner cruises are scheduled at 7:30pm on Tuesday, Thursday, Friday and Saturday. Reservations needed.

Parrot Jungle: 11000 SW 57 Ave, Miami 33156. Tel: 305/666-7834. Free-flying macaws, marching flamingos in natural settings. Bird shows. Six shows daily in amphitheater at 1½-hour intervals. Open 9:30am–6pm daily.

Potter's Wax Museum: 17 King St, St Augustine 32084. Tel: 904/829-9056. One of the oldest and largest in United States. More than 240 wax sculptures of famous personalities from history and legend in period settings that include authentic antiques. Open 9am–8pm daily during summer; until 5pm otherwise. Closed Christmas.

Ringling Museums: PO Box 1839, Sarasota 33578. Off US 41. Tel: 813/355-5101. The Venetian-Gothic Ringling residence, **Ca'd'zan**, built by circus king John Ringling for his wife Mabel in 1925. Features colored glass windows; antiques, tapestries, marble floors. The estate also includes the Italian-style **Museum of Art** containing an impressive collection of Pierre Paul Rubens paintings, classical sculpture in a courtyard, contemporary collection and special exhibits. The adjoining **Asolo State Theater** presents annual repertory plays, films and operas. The interior was brought from Asolo, Italy, where it had served as a theater since 1798. The **Museum of the Circus** has antiques and memorabilia from Ringling's "Greatest Show on Earth." One price admission tickets. Open weekdays 9am–7pm; Saturday until 5pm; Sunday 11am–6pm.

Ripley's Believe It or Not Museum: 19 San Marco Ave, St Augustine 32084. Tel: 904/824-1606. Unusual collection of oddities, curiosities and art objects collected by Robert L. Ripley during his world travels. Three floors stocked with thousands of exhibits. Open 9am–9pm daily during summer; 9am–6pm at other times.

St Augustine Alligator Farm: On A1A South, St Augustine 32084. Tel: 904/824-3337. Billed as "the world's original alligator attraction." Established in 1893. Alligators and crocodiles piled high. Florida wildlife shows every hour, featuring reptiles. Gator wrestling. Open 9am–5pm daily.

St Augustine Sightseeing Trains: 170 San Marco Ave, St Augustine 32084. Tel: 904/829-6545. A 7-mile conducted tour of the nation's oldest city. Stop-off privileges at attractions. Regular tickets are good for a period of 24 hours.

St Nicholas Greek Orthodox Cathedral: 36 N Pinellas Ave, Tarpon Springs 34689. Tel: 813/937-3540. A replica of St Sophia's in Istanbul, this church is an excellent example of New Byzantine architecture and is a cornerstone of the Tarpon Springs Greek community. Hours 9am–5pm daily.

St Petersburg Historical Museum: 25 Second Ave, St Petersburg 33701. Tel: 813/894-1052. Thousands of pioneer artifacts and unusual exhibits are featured included coins, dolls, shells, and Chinese glassware. Open Monday–Saturday 10am–5pm, Sunday 1–5pm.

Salvadore Dali Museum: 1000 Third St, St Petersburg 33701. Tel: 813/823-3767. This museum houses the world's largest collection of the Spanish surrealist painter's works including 93 oils, 200 watercolors and drawings, and 1,000 graphics. Open Tuesday–Saturday 10am–5pm, Sunday–Monday noon–5pm.

Sarasota Jungle Gardens: 3701 Bayshore Road, off Myrtle Street, Sarasota. Tel: 813/355-5305. A 15-acre park containing more than 5,000 varieties of tropical plants – including orchids, flame vines and birds of paradise. Alligators, macaws, mynah birds, flamingos and swans share the grounds. Bird and reptile shows. Open 9am–5pm daily.

Sea World: 7007 Sea World Drive, Orlando 32821. Tel: 407/351-3600 (for more information and current admission charges.) World's largest marine life park starring Shamu the killer whale, dolphins, seals and other shows, marine exhibits and aquariums, water-ski show, Hawaiian and Japanese Villages. Walk through a tunnel surrounded by toothy creatures in **Shark Encounter**. More than 125 acres of attractions, stadiums, shops, restaurants. Also a 400-ft observation tower decorated as a giant Christmas tree in December. Deer park. Computerized indoor water fountain show. Open from 9am, until dark, daily.

Silver Springs: State Road 40 Silver Springs 32688. Tel: 904/236-2121. Veteran attraction built around the source of the Silver River and the largest spring in the state. It flows at a rate of 587 gallons per day. Water is a constant 73.4°F temperature. Swimming, picnicking, parks, glass-bottom boatrides, jungle cruise, reptile institute, antique car collection, deer park. The grounds abound with alligators, wild monkeys and waterfowl. One price admission. Restaurants, souvenir shops. Open 9am–6:30pm daily during summer; 9am–4:30pm rest of year.

Six Flags Atlantis: Bordering an 11-acre lake in Hollywood, Fort Lauderdale (at the intersection of I-95 and Stirling Road). Tel: 305/926-1000. Water theme park with wave-action pool, speed slides, rapids rides, diving platforms, coves and pools for children. Live performances at a land amphitheater. Restaurants, games arcades and shops. Boats and rafts for rental. Open daily at 10am (closing hours vary with seasons). One admission price.

South Florida Museum/Bishop Planetarium: 201 10th St W, Bradenton 34205. Tel: 813/746-4132. Devoted to Florida history, the museum houses one of the finest collections of Civil War artifacts and memorabilia in Florida. The planetarium contains a hemispheric dome that features viewing of the entire solar system. Hours: Tuesday–Saturday 10am–5pm, Sunday noon–5pm.

Spaceport USA: TWS Kennedy Space Center 32899. Tel: 407/452-2121. Daily bus tours plus IMAX Theater showing Space Shuttle launches and space activity on screen 5½-stories high. Free parking, free kennels and free admission to Spaceport USA. Open 9am daily. First bus tour starts at 9:45am and operates continuously until 2 hours before dark.

Spongeorama: 510 Dodecanese Blvd, Tarpon Springs 33589. Tel: 813/942-3771. Attraction revolving around the sponge-diving industry and Greek heritage. Sponge factory and museum. Displays, photographs. Film of sponge diving trip on the half-hour. Arts and crafts shops. Genuine sponges for sale.

Stephen Foster Center: US 41, White Springs 32096. Tel: 904/397-2733. Memorabilia, museum displays, dioramas, musical instruments, in memorial to the composer who immortalized the Suwannee River. Also a 97-bell Deagan carillon in a 200-ft tall tower that plays medleys of Foster's music at regular intervals. Entertainers, gift shops and a restaurant.

Park open 8am until sunset daily; museum and tower open 9am–5pm daily.

Swimming Hall of Fame: One Hall of Fame Dr, Fort Lauderdale 33316. Tel: 305/462-6536. A combination museum and aquatic center including four pools, an art gallery and Olympic Games memorabilia. Open daily 8am–4pm winter, 8am–8pm the rest of the year.

Tallahassee Museum of History and Natural Science: 3945 Museum Dr, Tallahassee 32304. Tel: 904/576-1636. Native Florida animals in their natural habitats including the endangered Florida panther and red wolf. Other exhibits include segments of historic buildings and farms. Open Monday–Saturday 9am–5pm, Sunday 12:30–5pm.

Tampa Museum of Art: 601 Doyle Carlton Dr, Tampa 33601. Tel: 813/223-8130. Seven galleries that feature changing exhibitions of ancient and contemporary art. Hands-on activities for children and adults. Open Tuesday–Saturday 10am–5pm, Sunday 1–5pm.

Theater of the Sea: US 1, Islamorada 33036. Tel: 305/664-2431. Dolphin shows, glass-bottom boat rides, shark pit. In attractive coral grotto. Open 9:30am–4pm daily.

Universal Studios Florida: 1000 Universal Studios Plaza, Orlando 32819. Tel: 407/363-8000. More than 40 rides, shows and movie sets in this working television and movie studio. Lots of special effects and participation for kids. Open daily 9am–closing times vary.

Vizcaya Museum and Gardens: 3251 South Miami Ave, Miami 33129. Tel: 305/579-2708. Private palace of 50 rooms built by James Deering in 1914. Italian Renaissance architecture and formal gardens overlooking Biscayne Bay. Guided or self-guiding tours. Collection of European decorative arts. Gift shop and café. Sound and light shows at 8pm Friday and Saturday. Open 10am–5pm except Christmas. Ticket window closes at 4:30pm.

Wakulla Springs and Lodge: Wakulla Springs 32305. Tel: 904/222-7279. Glass-bottom boat tours the crystal waters of the Wakulla River, a registered natural landmark. Jungle Boat tours. Swimming, picnicking, wildlife trails, souvenirs, accommodations. Open 9:30am–5pm daily in winter; until 5:30pm during summer months.

Walt Disney World: PO Box 10040, Lake Buena Vista 32830. Tel: 407/824-4321 or 407/824-4500 (for details and information.) (*See "Walt Disney World" in the Places section for detailed descriptions.*) Mickey Mouse's Vacation Kingdom opens at 9am daily. Closing times vary from 7pm during winter to midnight during summer and later on special holidays. Extended operating hours also during Christmas and New Year holidays. Write to: Box 78 for reservations. You can choose from several types of tickets and admissions packages at gate. The kingdom includes the River Country water-oriented theme park, Walt Disney World Village, Discovery Island, Disney-MGM Studios and much more.

Weeki Wachee Springs Mermaid Show: US 19 at Florida 50, Weeki Wachee 33512. Tel: 904/596-2062. Exotic bird show, wilderness river cruise, enchanted rain forest, nature trails and the unique underwater swimming show featuring beautiful mermaids who dance and perform to music in the spring. The mermaids can be viewed through an underwater amphitheater. The spring is the source of the Weeki Wachee River. Climactic mermaids dive to a depth of 117½ ft. Thirty-minute shows at regular intervals. Open 9am until dusk daily.

Wet 'N' Wild: 6200 International Drive, Orlando 32809. Tel: 407/351-1800. Surf lagoon, whitewater slideways, crazy water playground, puddle jumper pool, *kamikaze* water slide, picnicking, boating, beach activities. Open 9am–9pm daily during summer; 10am–5pm the rest of the year.

Wild Waters: State Route 40, next to Silver Springs 32688. Tel: 904/236-2121. Water theme park with flume rides, wave pool, frisbee court, water fort, wet miniature golf, picnic areas. Open late March–early June, 10am–5pm; from the first week in June to the first week in September, 10am–8pm.

Wrecker's Museum: 322 Duval St, Key West 33040. Tel: 305/294-9502. Housed in the former home of a sea captain and "wrecker," the museum features ship models, antiques, marine artifacts and documents. Open 10am–4pm daily.

Ybor Square: 1901 N 13th St, Tampa 33605. Tel: 813/247-4497. A former cigar factory which has been turned into a shopping center and historic district including several antique shops and Cuban restaurants. Open Monday–Saturday 9:30am–5:30pm, Sunday noon–5:30pm.

Zorayda Castle: 85 King St, St Augustine 32084. Tel: 904/824-3097. A huge architectural reproduction of the Alhambra, Spain's most famous castle in old Granada. Within the walls of this replica are displays of how the Moorish kings lived, entertained and ruled Spain. Treasures from around the world on display as well. Open 9am–5:30pm daily.

NATIONAL FORESTS

Apalachicola: Extending west from Tallahassee to the Apalachicola River, its 557,000 acres of pine hardwood forest, swamps, rivers, sinkholes and springs make it the largest of Florida's three national forests. Encompasses the Silver Lake Recreation Area with tent camping, trailer sites, swimming and picnicking for a small fee, south of Florida 20 on Florida 260. Hitchcock, Wright and Camel Lake areas also offer recreational facilities. Contact: Apalachicola Ranger Station, Sumatra Star Route, Box 9, Tallahassee 32304. Wilma Ranger Station is located 20 miles southwest of Hosford, Florida on Hwy 65.

Ocala: Situated east of the city of Ocala between the Oklawaha and St Johns River; the "Big Scrub" covers 366,000 acres of sand, longleaf and slash pine, cypress and hardwoods. Tubing, canoeing, and cave-diving are extremely popular at Juniper Springs, 24 miles east of Ocala on State Hwy 40. Write: Juniper Springs Recreation Area, Route 2, Box 701, Silver Springs, Florida 32688, or tel: 904/625-2520.

Alexander Springs Recreation Area, 16 miles north of Eustis, east of Florida 19. More tubing, swimming, camping and picnicking. Contact: Alexander Springs Recreation Area, PO Box 11, Altoona, Florida 32702. For general information on the park contact: Lake George Ranger District, Post Office Bldg, PO Box 1206, Ocala 32670. The Lake Bryant Ranger Station is 18 miles east of Ocala on Florida 40 and Pittman Ranger Station is 11 miles north of Eustis on State Road 19.

Osceola: East of Lake City on US Hwy 90, comprises 157,000 acres. Controlled hunting of deer, quail and dove is permitted; bass, bream and perch fishing is also popular. Ocean Pond, 15 miles east of Lake City and 3 miles north of US 90, has good swimming, fishing and camping. Contact Route 7, Box 95, Lake City, 32055. The Olustee Guard Station is 3 miles east of Olustee on US 90.

NATIONAL PARKS & PRESERVES

Biscayne National Underwater Park: Over 180,000 acres – 96 percent underwater – of beautiful natural reefs to explore at the northern tip of the Florida Keys. Most of the reefs are located about 10 miles offshore so a boat is necessary to reach them, but there are several concessionaires available at the park's visitor centers for the short trip. Whether you are snorkeling or scuba diving, Biscayne National offers good views of tropical fish, coral, and many forms of sea life. Fishing and guided tours are also available. Park headquarters are at the Convoy Point Information Station, North Canal Drive, Homestead. For information write the Ranger's Station, PO Box 1369, Homestead, Florida 33090; or tel: 305/247-2044.

Everglades National Park: Florida's biggest National Park, it covers most of Florida's southern tip. You can camp, fish, hunt, hike, boat, canoe and observe its wide range of fascinating wildlife concentrated over more than 1.4 million acres of pinelands, cypress forest, marshes and mangroves. (*See* "The Everglades" *chapter for further information*.) Boat tours into the park and the Ten Thousand Islands can be arranged. Write to Everglades National Park Boat Tours, Box 119 Everglades City 33929; or tel: 813/695-2591. Reservations for the lodge or campsites can be made by writing to Everglades Park Catering, Flamingo Lodge, Flamingo 33030; or tel: 813/695-3101.

Big Cypress National Preserve: Established in 1974 on 570,000 acres, or about 40 percent of the Big Cypress Swamp; offers nature trails, camping, hunting, trapping and fishing. (*See* "The Everglades" *chapter*.) Write to: S.R. Box 110, Ochopee, Florida 33943; or tel: 813/695-2000.

Canaveral: More than 67,000 acres of dunes and beach due south of New Smyrna Beach to Cape Canaveral. Headquarters are 7 miles east of Titusville on Florida 402. Most portions accessible only by foot. Swimming, surfing and picnicking at Playalinda Beach, 12 miles east of Titusville on Florida 406 or at Apollo Park, 10 miles south of New Smyrna Beach on A1A. No camping. Contact: PO Box 6447, Titusville, Florida 33090; or tel: 407/867-0634.

Gulf Islands: 150 miles of pristine coastline stretching from Destin in the Panhandle to Gulfport, Mississippi. Encompasses the ruins of Fort Pickens in Pensacola Beach, where Indian warrior Geronimo was imprisoned. Beach, swimming, picnic and concession facilities at the Santa Rosa area on Florida 399. Also includes historic sites at the Naval Air Station. More recreational facilities at Perdido Key on Florida 292 and Okaloosa, east of Fort Walton Beach. Contact: Superintendant, PO Box 100, Gulf Breeze 32561.

A BIRDWATCHER'S EXTRA

Visitors have always marveled at Florida's prolific bird population. Even master naturalist John James Audubon came here more than 100 years ago to sketch Florida's colorful fowl. The birds in our montage on pages 184–185 and the photographers who captured them are:

1 an osprey (Paul Zach)
2 a little blue heron (José Azel)
3 a snowy egret-detail (Ron Jett)
4 a purple gallinule (Paul Zach)
5 a snowy egret (José Azel)
6 American flamingos (Joe Viesti)
7 burrowing owl (Ron Jett)
8 a brown pelican (Tom Servais)

CULTURE PLUS

MUSIC/THEATER/DANCE

Asolo Center for the Performing Arts: 5555 N Tamiami Trail, Sarasota. Tel: 813/351-7115. Nationally prominent multi-purpose theater.

Broward Center For the Performing Arts: 201 SW 5th Ave, Fort Lauderdale. Tel: 305/522-5334. A 2,700-seat waterfront theater that features major cultural events.

Caldwell Theater Company: 7783 N Federal Hwy, Boca Raton. Tel: 407/241-7432. A professional regional theater.

Carr Performing Arts Center: 401 Livingston St, Orlando. Tel: 407/849-2070. A year-round community auditorium that hosts regional and national music, theater, dance.

Coconut Grove Playhouse: 3500 Main Hwy, Coconut Grove (Miami). Tel: 305/442-2662. A cozy, restored theater that features Broadway-bound plays and musical acts.

Colony Theater: 1040 Lincoln Rd, Miami Beach. Tel: 305/674-1026. This former movie house turned cozy theater in the Art Deco District hosts offbeat musical and stage performances.

Florida Philharmonic Orchestra: Tel: 305/561-2997. Florida's only fully professional orchestra with performances in Palm Beach, Broward and Dade Counties.

Florida Theater Performing Arts Center: 128 E Forsythe St, Jacksonville. Tel: 904/355-5661. Features nationally prominent entertainers and touring Broadway plays.

Florida West Coast Symphony Center: 709 N Tamiami Trail, Sarasota. Tel: 813/953-4252. A collection of classical music companies that perform at several West Coast locations.

Greater Miami Opera: 1200 Coral Way, Miami. Tel: 305/854-7890. Miami's resident opera company that features internationally prominent and regional singers.

Gusman Center for the Performing Arts: 174 E Flagler St, Miami. Tel: 305/372-0925. An ornate, historic theater that offers drama, dance and music productions.

Jackie Gleason Theater of the Performing Arts: 1700 Washington Ave, Miami Beach. Tel: 305/673-8300. An ultra-modern 1,800-seat theater that hosts Broadway plays.

Jacksonville Symphony Orchestra: Tel: 904/354-5479. A variety of classical music performances throughout the Jacksonville area.

Miami Arena: 721 NW 1st Ave, Miami. Tel: 305/530-4444. A huge, modern downtown arena that hosts concerts and sporting events.

Miami City Ballet: Tel: 305/532-7713. Latin-flavored classical ballet company with hints of jazz and modern dance. Various South Florida locations.

Minorca Playhouse: Tel: 305/446-1116. 323 Minorca Ave, Coral Gables. A small but pleasant theater that serves as home to several theater companies.

Naples Philharmonic Center for the Arts: 5833 Pelican Bay Blvd, Naples. Tel: 813/597-1111. Two theater complex offering concerts and plays.

New World Symphony: Tel: 305/673-3330. First-rate repertoire of classical music performed at various Miami area theaters.

Northwest Florida Ballet: 101 SE Chicago St, Fort Walton Beach. Tel: 904/664-7787. Regional dance company that performs throughout the Panhandle.

Orlando Arena: 600 West Amelia St, Orlando. Tel: 407/849-2020. One of the main venues for evening events and concerts in the Orlando area.

Parker Playhouse: 808 NE 8th St, Fort Lauderdale. Tel: 305/764-0700. Broadway plays, musical events and dance troupes.

Pensacola Little Theater: 186 N Palafox St, Pensacola. Tel: 904/432-8621. Presents regional plays and musical performances.

Pensacola Symphony Orchestra: Tel: 904/435-2533. A regional company that performs at several area locations.

Players of Sarasota: US 41 and 9th St, Sarasota. Tel: 813/488-1115. A community theater that hosts comedy acts, dramas and thrillers.

Royal Poinciana Playhouse: 70 Royal Poinciana Way. Tel: 407/659-3310. A well-respected regional theater company.

Ruth Eckard Hall: 1111 McMullen Booth Rd, Clearwater. Tel: 813/791-7400. National pop, jazz, classical, ballet and dramatic acts.

Sarasota Opera: 61 N Pineapple Ave, Sarasota. Tel: 813/953-7030. A regional opera company that performs in its own historic theater.

Sunrise Musical Theater; 5555 NW 95th Ave, Sunrise (west of Fort Lauderdale). Tel: 305/741-7300. A modern entertainment center that features internationally prominent musicians, comedians, and theater acts.

Surfside Playhouse: Brevard Ave and S 5th Ave, Cocoa Beach. Tel: 407/783-3127. A community theater featuring first-rate performances.

Tallahassee Symphony Orchestra: Florida State University. Tel: 904/224-0461. A regional symphony that performs on the university campus.

Tampa Bay Performing Arts Center; 1010 N MacInnes Place, Tampa. Tel: 813/221-1045. One of the largest performing arts centers in the state hosting classical and popular entertainment.

Tampa Theater: 711 Franklin St, Tampa. Tel: 813/223-8981. A restored 1926 movie theater that features concerts, foreign films and special events.

Teatro de Bellas Artes: 2173 SW 8th St, Little Havana (Miami). Tel: 305/325-0515. A Spanish-language theater that offers live dramas, comedies and musical events.

Tennessee Williams Fine Arts Center: 5901 Junior College Rd, Key West. Tel: 305/294-6232. A 490-seat theater that presents plays, dance, classical and jazz concerts.

Venice Little Theater: Tampa and Nokomis Aves, Venice. Tel: 813/488-1115. A community theater featuring musicals, dramas and comedies.

ANNUAL CULTURAL EVENTS

JANUARY

FORT LAUDERDALE
Florida Renaissance Festival. Tel: 305/978-8610. A medieval fair with jousting, classical music and art. Late January.

FORT MYERS
Riverview Art Festival. Tel: 813/433-5040. An outdoor arts and crafts festival. Early January.
Lee Sidewalk Arts and Crafts Show. Tel: 813/334-6626. Late January.
German-American Social Club Festival. Tel: 813/939-5050. German music, foods and dancing. Late January.

HOLLYWOOD
Canadafest. Tel: 305/921-3404. A celebration of Canada culture for the many Canadians who frequent this area each winter. Mid-January.

KEY BISCAYNE
Key Biscayne Art Festival. Tel: 305/361-5207. Late January.

KEY LARGO
Railroad Days. Tel: 305/852-1620. A celebration of railroad memorabilia. Mid-January.

MIAMI
Taste of the Grove Food and Music Festival. Tel: 305/442-2001. An outdoor food festival featuring dozens of area restaurants, music and entertainment. Mid-January.
Miami River Blues Festival. Tel: 305/374-1198. A riverfront blues festival. Late January.

MIAMI BEACH
Art Deco Weekend. Tel: 305/672-2014. A celebration of Miami Beach's Art Deco architecture with a street fair, music and art show. Early January.

PENSACOLA
Snowfest. Tel: 904/434-1234. A make-believe winterfest with snow. Late January.

SARASOTA
Sarasota Bay Festival of Arts and Crafts. Tel: 813/365-2032. Outdoor arts and crafts. Late January.

SEBASTIAN
Sebastian Seafood & Citrus Festival. Tel: 407/589-5969. Mid-January.

TARPON SPRINGS
Festival of the Epiphany. Tel: 813/937-3540. The Greek Orthodox Church's celebration of Christ's baptism. January 6.

VENICE
Venice Art Show. Tel: 813/488-7768. Late January.

WEST PALM BEACH
Palm Beach Seafood Festival. Tel: 407/832-6397. Fish, shrimp, lobster! Mid-January.

South Florida Fair. Tel: 407/793-0333. A regional fair with livestock, rides, music, entertainment. Late January.

WINTER HAVEN
Florida Citrus Festival & Polk County Fair. Tel: 813/293-3175. Agriculture, food, music and entertainment. Late January.

FEBRUARY

CRYSTAL RIVER
Florida Manatee Festival. Tel: 904/795-3149. An arts, crafts, music and foods tribute to the endangered mammal. Late February.

DAYTONA
Native American Indian Festival. Tel: 904/673-4701. Indian arts, crafts, music and foods. Mid-February.

FORT LAUDERDALE
Taste of Fort Lauderdale. Tel: 305/485-3481. Late February.

Las Olas Art Festival. Tel: 305/525-5500. Street arts, crafts, music and food. Late February.

FORT MYERS
Edison Festival of Lights. Tel: 813/334-2550. An annual tribute to one-time Fort Myers resident inventor Thomas Edison. Early February.

HOLLYWOOD
Seminole Tribe Fair. Tel: 305/961-9574. Native Indian arts, crafts, music and foods. Mid-February.

LABELLE
Labelle Swamp Cabbage Festival. Tel:813/675-2541. A music and festivities tribute to swamp cabbage, otherwise known as hearts of palm. Late February.

LAKE CITY
Olustee Battle Festival. Tel: 904/758-1312. A re-enactment of and tribute to the Civil War battle. Mid-February.

LAKELAND
Florida Sunshine Square Dance Festival. Tel: 813/499-8100. Square dancing and old-fashioned fun. Early February.

LAKEPORT
Lakeport Sour Orange Festival. Tel: 813/946-0040. Foods, music and entertainment in celebration of the all mighty orange. Mid-February.

MIAMI
Coconut Grove Arts Festival. Tel: 305/447-0401. The largest art festival in the state. Mid-February.

Miami Film Festival. Tel: 305/377-3456. Foreign, American and Florida films. Mid-February.

MOUNT DORA
Mount Dora Arts Festival. Tel: 904/383-2165. Outdoor arts and crafts. Early February.

PENSACOLA
Mardi Gras Parades. Tel: 904/434-1234. Not as big as in New Orleans, but fun. Late February.

PLANT CITY
Florida Strawberry Festival. Tel: 813/752-9194. A tribute to strawberries with music, foods and entertainment. Late February.

TAMPA
Florida State Fair. Tel: 813/621-7821. The big daddy of Florida fairs featuring livestock, agriculture, art, crafts, rides, food and entertainment. Early February.

Gasparilla Pirate Festival. Tel: 813/223-1111. A pirate invasion takes over downtown with music, foods and entertainment. Early February.

Fiesta Day. Tel: 813/247-3545. Tampa's historic Ybor City celebrates its heritage. Mid-February.

VENICE
Italian-American Festival. Tel: 813/497-2883. Late February.

WINTER HAVEN
Florida Citrus Festival. Tel: 813/293-3175. Another arts and music tribute to Florida's great crop. Mid-February.

MARCH

COCOA BEACH
Port Canaveral Seafood Festival. Tel: 407/459-2200. Another tribute to fish, shrimp and lobster. Late March.

FORT LAUDERDALE
Downtown Festival of the Arts. Tel: 305/761-5360. Outdoor arts and crafts. Late March.

FORT MYERS
Cracker Festival. Tel: 813/656-1237. A tribute to the Florida natives. Early March.

MIAMI
Carnaval Miami/Calle Ocho. Tel: 305/644-8888. A week-long Hispanic heritage festival. Early March.

Dade County Youth Fair. Tel: 305/821-1130. Rides, music, games, food and fun for kids and adults. Mid-March

SARASOTA
Medieval Fair. Tel: 813/355-5101. Jousting, dramas, music and renaissance entertainment. Early March.

TALLAHASSEE
Natural Bridge Re-Enactment. Tel: 904/922-6007. A tribute to the Civil War battle. Early March.

TAMPA
Tampa Greek Festival. Tel: 813/972-2000. A tribute to the substantial Greek population in the area. Mid-March.

APRIL

CRESCENT CITY
St Johns River Catfish Festival. Tel: 904/698-1644. Music and crafts tribute to catfish as king. Early April.

FERNANDINA
Amelia Island Shrimp Festival. Tel:904/277-0717. Shrimp: boiled, fried, sautéed, and some music and entertainment. Late April.

FORT LAUDERDALE
Fort Lauderdale Seafood Festival. Tel: 305/463-4431. Fish fries, steamed shrimp, music and entertainment. Mid-April.

South Florida Black Film Festival. Tel: 305/390-3838. African-American films. Late April.

FORT MYERS
Indian Exposition and Pow Pow. Tel: 813/992-2184. Native Indian arts, crafts, food and music. Early April.

Israeli Independence Day. Tel: 813/481-4449. Celebrations for the country's independence. Late April.

GAINESVILLE
Spring Arts Festival. Tel: 904/372-1976. Late April.

JACKSONVILLE
Jacksonville Landing Annual Folk Festival. Tel: 904/353-1188. Folk music, art and crafts. Early April.

Riverfest. Tel: 904/630-0837. Riverfront music, arts, and entertainment. Mid-April.

Country Music Festival. Tel: 904/630-0837. All American country music. Late April.

KEY WEST
Conch Republic Celebrations. Tel: 305/294-4440. Key West once again tries to secede from the state. Late April/early May.

NEW SMYRNA
New Smyrna Jazz Festival. Tel: 904/428-5741. Music and foods. Late April.

PENSACOLA
Pensacola Jazz Festival. Tel: 904/434-1234. Outdoor music and foods. Mid-April.

ST AUGUSTINE
Blessing of the Fleet. Tel: 904/829-5681. Fishing boats get their blessing for the season. Early April.

Minorcan Day. Tel: 904/692-1032. Minorcan celebrations. Mid-April.

Queen Isabella's Birthday. Tel: 904/825-5033. Yes, a tribute to the Spanish queen. Late April.

WALDO
Railroad Antique and Craft Fair. Tel: 904/468-1001. A railroad lover's delight. Late April.

MAY

COCOA BEACH
Memorial Day Reggae Festival. Tel:407/783-7549. Jamaican music loud and vibrant. Late May.

FORT WALTON BEACH
Billy Bowlegs Festival. Tel: 904/267-1216. A celebration in honor of a pirate who once ruled the area. Early May.

LIVE OAK
Suwannee Gospel Jubilee. Tel: 904/364-1683. Totally devoted to gospel music. Mid-May.

MONTICELLO
Watermelon Festival. Tel:904/997-5552. Another outdoor tribute to the great watermelon. Late May.

OPA-LOCKA
Arabian Nights Festival. Tel: 305/953-2821. Street celebrations in honor of the city's Arabian-style architecture. Mid-May.

PALATKA
Palatka Blue Crab Festival. Tel: 904/325-4406. Music and entertainment and plenty of crabs. Late May.

PENSACOLA
Pensacola Lobster Fest. Tel: 904/434-1234. Outdoor celebrations in honor of the ugly crustacean. Late May.

SIESTA KEY
Sandsculpture Contest. Tel: 813/951-5848. A serious contest for sandcastle aficionados. Early May.

WHITE SPRINGS
Florida Folk Festival. Tel:904/397-2192. Folk music, crafts and entertainment. Late May.

ZELLWOOD
Zellwood Spring Corn Festival. Tel: 407/886-0014. Spring celebrations and corn-eating competitions. Late May.

JUNE

CHIEFLAND
Chiefland Watermelon Festival. Tel: 904/493-1849. Yes, there's even a watermelon pit spitting contest here. Mid-June.

MIAMI
Miami/Bahamas Goombay Festival. Tel: 305/372-9966. Coconut Grove's enormous street party in honor of its Bahamian heritage. Early June.

TREASURE ISLAND
Pirate Days and Invasion. Tel: 813/360-0811. A silly tribute to ruthless pirates. Late June/July.

JULY

GAINESVILLE
Fanfares & Fireworks. Tel: 904/392-5551. Independence Day fireworks celebrations. Early July.

KEY WEST
Hemingway Days. Tel: 305/294-4440. A rowdy tribute to Ernest Hemingway and his work. Late July.

MARATHON
Starspangled Event. Tel: 305/743-5417. Waterfront Independence Day fireworks and party. Early July.

MIAMI
Columbian-American Festival. Tel: 305/770-0995. Miami's tribute to its South American neighbor. Late July.

NAPLES
Seminole Indian Days. Tel: 813/774-8476. Native Indian music, foods, arts and crafts. Mid-July.

TALLAHASSEE
Summer Swamp Stomp. Tel: 904/576-1636. Old Florida celebrations of food and music. Mid-July.

TAMPA
Pirate Days and Invasions. Tel: 813/360-0811. Another tribute to pirate history. Early July.

AUGUST

DELRAY BEACH
Bon Festival. Tel: 407/495-0233. Japanese gardens, trees and culture. Mid-August,

MIAMI
Jamaican Awareness Reggae Festival. Tel: 305/891-2944. The biggest reggae fest in the state in the brutal summer heat. Early August.

WAUSAU
Wausau Possum Festival. Tel: 904/638-1017. A small town tribute to the little critter. Early August.

SEPTEMBER

CARYVILLE
Worm Fiddler's Day. Tel: 904/548-5571. The lure of earthworms is honored for a day. Early September.

DADE City
Pioneer Florida Day. Tel: 904/567-0262. Celebrations honoring Florida's early settlers. Early September.

JUPITER
Shakespeare by the Sea Festival. Tel: 407/627-4127. Outdoor theater celebrations. Early September.

MIAMI
Festival Miami. Tel: 305/284-3941. Three weeks of performing and visual arts. Mid-September.

OAK HILL
Oak Hill Mullet Festival. Tel: 904/345-3198. Fish, fish, fish and entertainment. Late September.

ORLANDO
Puerto Rican Parade and Festival. Tel: 407/679-3584. Festive celebrations of the island culture. Early September.

PENSACOLA
Pensacola Seafood Festival. Tel: 904/932-2259. Another tribute to the fare of the sea. Mid-September.

OCTOBER

CAPE CORAL
Octoberfest. Tel: 813/772-4897. German foods, music and fun. Mid-October.

FORT MYERS
Fort Myers Hispanic Heritage Festival. Tel: 813/335-2332. Celebrations of Hispanic history. Late October.

JENSEN BEACH
Leif Erikson Day. Tel: 407/335-7273. A tribute to the great Viking. Early October.

KEY WEST
Fantasy Fest. Tel: 305/296-1817. Wild and crazy Halloween celebrations that last all week. Late October.

LAND O LAKES
Flapjack Festival. Tel: 813/996-5522. Simple, wholesome Florida fun honoring the breakfast flapjack. Early October.

MIAMI
Columbus Day Regatta. Tel: 305/858-1733. A sailing race and celebration. Mid-October.

Banyan Art Festival. Tel: 305/444-7270. Arts and crafts in Coconut Grove. Late October.

NAPLES
Florida State Chili Championship. Tel: 813/349-3101. Country music, entertainment and dozens of chili recipes to taste. Early October.

Octoberfest. Tel: 813/262-4177. More German celebrations. Mid-October.

NICEVILLE
Boggy Bayou Mullet Festival. Tel: 904/678-1615. Small town fun in honor of a fish. Mid-October.

SAN ANTONIO
Rattlesnakes. Festival. Tel:567-3769. Old Florida fun, but not for the squeamish. Mid-October.

NOVEMBER

APALACHICOLA
Florida Seafood Festival. Tel: 904/653-8051. One of the biggest seafood festivals in the state. Early November.

JENSEN BEACH
Pineapple Festival. Tel: 407/334-3444. A celebration of pineapple wine, jelly, jams, ice-cream, and the natural thing. Mid-November.

LAKELAND
Fall Fun Fest Square Dance. Tel: 813/499-8100. Old-fashioned square dances and contests. Mid-November.

ORLANDO
Light Up Orlando. Tel: 407/648-4010. Street celebrations of fireworks and music. Mid-November.

Christmas Parade. Tel: 407/896-0474. Although there's no snow, Christmas celebrations evoke the spirit. Late November.

STUART
Christmas Southern Style. Tel: 407/286-2848. Tropical Christmas celebrations. Late November.

WEST PALM BEACH
Renaissance Festival. Tel: 407/832-1988. Medieval games and parties. Early November.

DECEMBER

BUSHNELL
Dade Battlefield Commemorative Day. Tel: 904/793-4781. Re-enactments in honor of a historic battle. Late December.

LAKE BUENA VISTA
Walt Disney World's Very Merry Christmas Parade. Tel: 407/824-4321. The grand Disney version of a merry Christmas. Mid-December.

MIAMI
Holiday Spirit of Vizcaya Gardens. Tel: 305/579-2808. Christmas festivities at a Mediterranean mansion. Mid-December.

Orange Bowl Festival. Tel: 305/371-4600. Holiday celebrations and a New Year's Eve parade. Late December.

ST AUGUSTINE
International Christmas Celebration. Tel: 904/461-2033. Festivities of music, light and entertainment. Early December.

ST PETERSBURG
Lighted Boat Parade. Tel: 813/821-4069. A nautical-style Christmas parade. Mid-December.

SHOPPING

WHAT TO BUY

If you are into kitsch – plastic flamingo ashtrays, canned sunshine, orange perfume – you will find Florida a veritable treasure house. From roadside shacks to massive, futuristic malls, stores carry a healthy supply of traditional souvenirs. Don't be surprised if your souvenir picture plate has a sticker on the bottom that says "Made in Taiwan." And then, of course, there are the homegrown souvenirs like oranges, tangerines, limes, kumquats and grapefruits that can be shipped home for a small fee.

But if you look a little harder, Florida also has an array of quality goods to take home from a trip. There are shops worth seeking out that sell designer clothing at factory prices, primitive Haitian art, Art Deco and old Florida antiques, Native Indian crafts, and sand-polished shells that forever smell of the sea.

Hours vary, but most shopping centers are open seven days a week. Following "Clothing Sizes", is a city by city listing of some of the best shopping finds.

CLOTHING SIZES

This tables gives a comparison of American, Continental and British clothing sizes. It is always best to try on any article before buying it, however, as sizes can vary.

Women's Dresses/Suits

American	Continental	British
6	38/34N	8/30
8	40/36N	10/32
10	42/38N	12/34
12	44/40N	14/36
14	46/42N	16/38
16	48/44N	18/40

Women's Shoes

American	Continental	British
4½	36	3
5½	37	4
6½	38	5
7½	39	6
8½	40	7
9½	41	8
10½	42	9

Men's Suits

American	Continental	British
34	44	34
—	46	36
38	48	38
—	50	40
42	52	42
—	54	44
46	56	46

Men's Shirts

American	Continental	British
14	36	14
14½	37	14½
15	38	15
15½	39	15½
16	40	16
16½	41	16½
17	42	17

Men's Shoes

American	Continental	British
6½	—	6
7½	40	7
8½	41	8
9½	42	9
10½	43	10
11½	44	11

COCOA BEACH

Ron Jon Surf Shop: 4151 N Atlantic Ave, Cocoa Beach. Tel: 407/799-8888. An local institution and a beach bum's dream, Ron Jon sells bathing suits, surfboards, goggles, scuba equipment, suntan lotion, and lots of water toys. Open daily 9am–11pm.

FORT LAUDERDALE

The Swap Shop: 3501 W Sunrise Blvd, Fort Lauderdale. Tel: 305/791-9729. Billed as the world's largest indoor/outdoor flea market with over 2,000 vendors selling used and new merchandise. Open 5am–6:30pm daily.

FORT MYERS

The Shell Factory: 2787 N Tamiami Trail, N Fort Myers. Tel: 813/995-2141. The world's largest collection of shells and coral in natural forms, and transformed into jewelry, lamps, and baskets. Open 9am–6pm daily.

KEY WEST

Key West Aloe: 524 Front St, Key West. Tel: 305/294-5592. A factory and gift shop that sells hundreds of perfumes, suncreens and skin care products made from the native aloe plant. Open 9am–8pm daily.
Key West Hand Print Fabrics: 201 Simonton St, Key West. Tel: 305/294-9535. Watch as workers make brightly colored, hand-printed cotton and silk fabrics that are sold by the yard and as casual clothing. Open 10am–6pm daily.
Fast Buck Freddie's: 500 Duval St, Key West. Tel: 305/294-2007. A Key West institution, Freddie's is a department store that specializes in the bizarre – sequined bikinis, battery-operated alligators that bite, and fish-shaped shoes. Open 10am–6pm daily.
Haitian Art Company: 600 Frances St, Key West. Tel:305/296-8932. One of the largest collections of paintings, sculptures, steel and papier-mâché art from Haiti in the US. Open 10am–6pm daily.

MIAMI

Bayside Marketplace: 401 Biscayne Blvd. Tel:305577-3344. A waterfront shopping and entertainment complex in downtown Miami with over 150 specialty shops. Open Monday–Saturday 10am–10pm, Sunday noon–8pm.
Mayfair Shops: 3390 Mary St, Coconut Grove. Tel: 305/448-1700. An architectural beauty with dozens of high fashion boutiques. Open Monday–Saturday 10am–8pm, Sunday noon–6pm.
Miccosukee Indian Village: Tamiami Trail about 25 miles west of downtown Miami. Tel: 305/223-8380. Miccosukee arts and crafts: patchwork clothing, moccasins, beaded jewelry, paintings, wood carvings. Open 9am–5pm daily.

MIAMI BEACH

Bal Harbour Shops: 9700 Collins Ave, Bal Harbour just north of Miami Beach. Tel: 305/866-0311. A beautiful and elegant shopping center with over 50 up-scale boutiques including Neiman Marcus, Gucci, Fendi, Armani, and Ann Taylor. Open Monday–Saturday 10am–6pm, Sunday noon–5pm.
Lincoln Road Mall: Between Washington Avenue and Alton Road, Miami Beach. A five-block long outdoor mall of art galleries, boutiques, jewelry stores, vintage clothing, and Art Deco antiques.

MICANOPY

Micanopy: About 11 miles south of Gainesville on US 441, this small Northern Florida town has become an antique mecca. Along Main Street are dozens of antique shops that specialize in old Florida treasures – furniture, stained glass, silver, art, jewelry and quilts. Each fall about 200 dealers gather for a major antique show.

ORLANDO

Belz Factory Outlet Mall: 5401 West Oakridge Road. Tel: 407/352-9600. The second most-visited "attraction" in Orlando after Disney World, Belz is a bargain bonanza. This large, indoor mall is made up of four buildings that house almost 100 stores. One of the best places in Florida to shop for designer clothes – Anne Klein, London Fog, Christian Dior and many more – and just about every brand of blue jeans, sneakers and casual wear at discounts of up to 75 percent off retail prices. Open Monday–Saturday 10am–9pm, Sunday 10am–6pm.
Flea World: Highway 17-92 just north of Orlando. Tel: 407/646-1792. Flea World calls itself America's largest flea market, and with about 1,000 dealers spreading their wares over 100 acres of land, it may very well be. With garage-sale clean outs, discounted merchandise, and Florida antiques, Flea World is a favorite weekend diversion for the locals of central Florida. Open Friday–Sunday 8pm–5pm.
Mercado Mediterranean Village: 8445 International Dr, Orlando. Tel: 407/345-9337. More than 60 specialty shops along a series of brick streets with an atmosphere of a Mediterranean village. Arts, crafts, pottery, jewelry, clothing, leather goods. Open 10am–10pm.
Orange World: 5395 West Irlo Bronson Memorial Highway, Kissimmee. Tel: 407/396-1306. You can't miss the building – shaped like a gigantic orange – and inside is an assortment of fresh-picked fruits, citrus candies and orange blossom honey. All available to be shipped to friends and family back home. Open 8am–11pm daily.

PALM BEACH

Worth Avenue: Downtown Palm Beach. One of the world's most famous shopping streets with more than 200 very elegant and very expensive shops. Most shops open Monday–Saturday 10am–6pm.

PINNELLAS PARK

Sports Fans Collectibles: 4406 Park Blvd. Tel: 813/546-1678. In the heart of spring-training territory, this is the place to pick up antique baseball cards, autographed bats and balls, and offbeat sports treasures. Open Monday–Saturday 10am–6pm.

ST AUGUSTINE

St Augustine Outlet Center: SR 16 off of I-95. Tel: 904/824-8854. One of North Florida's largest factory outlet centers with more than 100 designer shops offering goods at up to 70 percent off retail prices. Open Monday–Saturday 9am–9pm, Sunday 10am–6pm.

SPORTS

FISHING

The Industry: Besides being one of the major sources of protein, eating enjoyment and a source of recreation, fishing is also a major commercial endeavor. Florida's commercial fleets stalk more than 60 kinds of food fish, including non-edible varieties for oil and fertilizer, a half-dozen kinds of shellfish and even sponges. Only the Game and Fresh Water Fish Commission can issue commercial fishing licenses. Fishermen who take non-game fish using nets, trap or trotlines with more than 25 hooks must possess a commercial license as well as regular sport fishing licenses. The Game and Fresh Water Fish Commission has strict rules on the use of wire traps, slat baskets, minnow seines, cast nets, shad haul nets, pound nets, gill nets and hoop nets. The total harvest from the sea continues to grow, totaling more than 175 million pounds of fish and shellfish annually.

Recreation: No license is needed for saltwater fishing and there is no closed season on any game fish. Florida's 8,000 miles of tidal coastline are home to more than 600 varieties of saltwater fish. Try a variety of methods for catching them: deep sea fishing, surf casting, bridge and pier fishing and tidal water fishing. Grouper, amberjack, marlin, pompano, sea trout, mackerel, red snapper, snook, redfish, sailfish, bonefish, kingfish and dolphin lurk in the deepest waters. In the late spring and summer, tarpon wait to challenge deep sea fishermen off Tampa Bay, Marathon, Boca Grande pass and Bahia Honda Channel. The Keys, the lower East Coast and upper Gulf regions are the homes of blue marlin.

Florida's 30,000 lakes and untold miles of rivers and streams also provide outstanding freshwater fishing. Non-resident freshwater fishing licenses are inexpensive and residents' licenses even cheaper. There has been growing pressure by conservation groups for the state to instigate a saltwater fishing license. For information about all fishing licenses, and about any limits on fish, salt or fresh, or any closed seasons on certain species, call the Florida Marine Patrol, tel: 1-800/342-5376, or write for the *Florida Fishing Handbook*, to the Florida Game and Fresh Water Fish Commission, 620 S Meridian St, Tallahassee FL 32399-1600, tel: 904/488-1960. The fee for a saltwater fishing license is about $30 for non-residents. A non-resident freshwater license good for 10 days costs about $15; a resident freshwater license costs about $12 per year.

Military personnel who live in Florida are not required to purchase fishing licenses, but must produce their military leave orders upon the order of wildlife officers. Residents fishing in the county in which they live with not more than three poles or lines are also not required to produce a license.

HUNTING

Game: Hunting enthusiasts will find a profusion of game in Florida's vast forests, swamps and grasslands. Deer, turkey, wild hogs, rabbits, bear, turtles, frogs, birds, raccoon, possums and fox are popular game. Open seasons vary, and each June the Florida Game and Fresh Water Fish Commission announces the dates and hours of the fall hunting seasons across the state. The daily bag limit for species changes frequently, depending on the annual review of state resources, and is also announced by the commission. **Licences**: A yearly hunting license costs about $11 for Florida residents and $150 for non-residents. Non-residents can also get a 10-day hunting license for $25. For a free copy of the annual *Florida Hunting Handbook* write the Game Commission at 620 Meridian St., Tallahassee FL 32399-1600, or call 904/488-4676.

GOLF

Florida is without a doubt one of the top golfing states in the country – one out of every 10 golf games played in the US takes place in Florida, and no other state has more courses. With over 1,000 golf courses spread across the state to choose from, you are never too far from a chance to tee off. Although many of the courses are private, there are still enough public courses for out-of-towners who don't have a friend at a local country club. And don't think that just because Florida is a flat state, its golf courses lack challenge and rolling hill beauty. In fact, many of Florida's courses were designed by golf experts who have created beautiful man-made undulations, hills and rolls amid the greens.

Greens fees vary from over $75 per person at the more exclusive, private courses to less than $20 per person at the public courses. At many, the fees are higher in winter months when Northerners flock to the state for a game. For information on location of courses, fees and regulations throughout the state write for a free copy of *The Official Florida Golf Guide*, to the Florida Division of Tourism, 107 W Gaines St., Tallahassee FL 32399. Or call the Florida Sports Foundation, tel: 904/488-8347.

TENNIS

As a major sponsor of international tennis matches, Florida attracts players from throughout the world. Many hotels have their own courts, along with tennis instructors who offer lessons. Several state, county and city parks also offer courts that are available to the public for free or a small fee. For information on more than 7,000 clay, grass and hard courts in the state contact the Florida Tennis Association, 801 NE 167th St, Suite 301, North Miami Beach FL 33162, tel: 305/652-2866.

JOGGING/RUNNING

Sweat-drenched and sunburned, joggers and runners are very much a part of the vast Florida landscape. Hundreds of miles of designated pathways are dedicated to the sport, and the flat and very regular road systems lend themselves to those who are willing to brave the traffic. If you are from a colder climate, take it easy the first time you are out running in Florida; the humidity and heat can easily dehydrate a non-acclimatized runner. If you want to exercise your hill skills you will have to find a high bridge in order to feel the challenge of an uphill run.

A few major and many minor races take place throughout the state, mostly in winter months. For information on local running clubs, races and paths, write to the Florida Athletics Congress, 1330 NW 6th St, Gainesville FL 32601. Tel: 904/378-6805. For information about the various events in the South Florida area contact the 1,500-member Miami Runners Club, 7900 SW 40th St, Miami FL 33155, tel: 305/227-1500.

SPECTATOR SPORTS

BASEBALL

As the official spring training grounds of at least 17 of the 26 major league teams, Florida from February through March is the place to watch your favorite players warm up for their summer games. Following is a listing of teams and stadiums that regularly conduct spring training sessions.

Atlanta Braves: Municipal Stadium, West Palm Beach. Tel: 407/863-6100.
Baltimore Orioles: Miami Stadium, Miami. Tel: 305/633-9857.

Boston Red Sox: Chain O'Lakes Park, Winter Haven. Tel: 813/293-3900.
Chicago White Sox: Ed Smith Stadium, Sarasota. Tel: 813/752-3388.
Cincinnati Reds: Plant City Stadium, Plant City. Tel: 813/752-3388.
Detroit Tigers: Marchant Stadium, Lakeland. Tel: 813/686-8075.
Houston Astros: Osceola County Stadium, Kissimmee. Tel: 407/933-5500.
Los Angeles Dodgers: Holman Stadium, Vero Beach. Tel: 407/569-4900.
Minnesota Twins: Tinker Field, Orlando. Tel: 407/849-6346.
Montreal Expos: Municipal Stadium, West Palm Beach. Tel: 407/684-6801.
New York Mets: St Lucie County Sports Complex, Port St Lucie. Tel: 407/879-7378.
Philadelphia Phillies: Jack Russell Stadium, Clearwater. Tel: 813/442-8496.
St Louis Cardinals: Al Lang Field, St Petersberg. Tel: 813/896-4641.
Texas Rangers: Charlotte County Stadium, Port Charlotte. Tel: 813/625-9500.
Toronto Blue Jays: Grant Field, Dunedin. Tel: 813/733-0429.

PARI-MUTEULS

THOROUGHBREED HORSE RACING

January-March: **Gulfstream Park**, 901 S Federal Hwy, Hallandale. Tel: 305/944-1242.
April-June: **Hialeah Park**, 102 E 21st St, Hialeah. Tel: 305/885-8000.
November-January: **Calder Race Track**, 21001 NW 27th Ave, Miami. Tel: 305/620-2569.
December-April: **Tampa Bay Downs**, 12505 Racetrack Rd, Tampa. Tel: 813/855-4401.

HARNESS RACING

November-May: **Pompano Park**, 1800 SW 3rd St, Pompano Beach. Tel: 305/972-7849.

JAI-ALAI FRONTONS

January-June: **Tampa Fronton**. Tel: 813/855-4401.
January-July: **Fort Pierce Jai-Alai**. Tel: 407/464-7500.
January-July: **Palm Beach Jai-Alai**. Tel: 407/842-3274.
January-December: **Orlando Jai-Alai**. Tel: 407/339-6221.
January-March/June-September: **Ocala Jai-Alai**. Tel: 904/591-2345.
February-July: **Daytona Beach Jai-Alai**. Tel: 904/255-0222.
September-January: **Melbourne Jai-Alai**. Tel: 407/259-9800.

November-April: **Dania Jai-Alai**. Tel: 305/949-2424.

November-September: **Miami Jai-Alai**. Tel: 305/633-6400.

GREYHOUND RACING

Bonita Springs Kennel Club: 28341 Old 41 Rd, Bonita Springs. Tel: 813/992-2411.
Daytona Beach Kennel Club: 2201 Volusia Ave, Daytona Beach. Tel: 904/252-6484.
Flagler Kennel Club: 401 NW 38th Ct, Miami. Tel: 305/649-3000. June-September.
Orange Park Kennel Club: HWY 17, Jacksonville. Tel: 904/646-0001. November-March.
Palm Beach Kennel Club: 1111 N Congress Ave, West Palm Beach. Tel: 407/683-2222. December-May/June-September.
Pensacola Greyhound Park: 951 Dogtrack Rd, Pensacola. Tel: 904/455-8595. January-December.
St Petersburg Kennel Club: 10490 Gandy Blvd, St Petersberg. Tel: 813/576-1831. January-May.
Sarasota Kennel Club: 5400 Bradenton Rd, Sarasota. Tel: 813/355-7744. May-September.
Washington County Kennel Club: Hwy 79, Ebro. Tel: 904/234-3943. March-September.

ANNUAL SPORTING EVENTS

JANUARY

DAYTONA BEACH
World Cup Figure Skating. Tel: 904/255-1314. Early January.

FORT MYERS
Mid-Florida Golf Festival. Tel: 813/369-2121. Mid-January.

ISLAMORADA
Presidential Sailfish Tournament. Tel: 305/664-4651. Late January.

MIAMI
Blockbuster Bowl Football. Tel: 305/371-4600. Early January.

PALM BEACH
Polo Season. Tel: 407/793-1440. Early January.

FEBRUARY

DAYTONA BEACH
Speed Weeks – three weeks of racing that culminate with the famous Daytona 500. Tel: 904/254-2700.

ISLAMORADA
Islamorada Sport Fishing Festival. Tel: 305/664-2321. Mid-February.

KISSIMMEE
Silver Spurs Rodeo. Tel: 407/847-5118. Late February.

MIAMI
Toyota Grand Prix of Miami. Tel: 305/379-7223. Late January.

Doral Ryder Open Golf Tournament. Tel: 305/447-4653. Late January.

MIAMI BEACH
Miami Beach International Boat Show. Tel: 305/531-8410. Mid-February.

NAPLES
Annual PGA Tour Golf Event. Tel: 813/353-7767. Early January.

MARCH

DAYTONA BEACH
Classics Day Vintage Motorcyle Races and Supersport AMA Road Races. Tel: 904/254-2700. Early March.

HALLANDALE
Florida Derby. Horse racing. Tel: 305/457-6225. Late March.

KEY BISCAYNE
Lipton International Players Championship. Tennis. Tel: 305/446-2200. Mid-March.

NAPLES
Naples Swamp Buggie Races. Tel: 813/774-2701. Early March.

TAMPA
Winter Equestrian Festival. Tel: 813/623-5801. Late March.

APRIL

COCOA BEACH
Dr Pepper Easter Surfing Festival. Tel: 407/783-7549. Early April.

KEY WEST
Round The Clock Shark Tournament. Tel: 305/292-1961. Early April.

MARATHON
Seven-Mile Bridge Run. Tel: 305/743-8513. Late April.

MOUNT DORA
Mount Dora Sailing Regatta. Tel: 904/343-2376. Late April.

PANAMA CITY BEACH
Gulf Coast Offshore Powerboat Races. Tel: 904/233-6503. Late April.

WEST PALM BEACH
PGA Seniors Championship Golf. Tel: 407/622-4653. Mid-April.

MAY

KEY WEST
Key West Fishing Tournament. Tel: 305/294-2780. Mid-May.

FLAGLER BEACH
Flagler Beach Fishing Regatta. Tel: 904/439-2814. Late May.

JUNE

DAYTONA
Annual Firecracker 5K and 10 Mile Beach Run. Tel: 904/255-1279. Late June.

HOMOSASSA
Citrus 95 Homosassa Ramblin River Raft Race. Tel: 904/795-9595. Early June.

JACKSONVILLE
Pier Fishing Tournament. Tel: 904/246-6001. Late June.

PANAMA CITY BEACH
Annual Ladies Billfish Tournament. Tel: 904/233-6503. Late June.

JULY

DESTIN
Destin Shark Fishing Tournament. Tel: 904/651-7131. Early July.

NAPLES
Port of the Islands Annual Shark Tournament. Tel: 813/394-3101. Late July.

PENSACOLA
International Billfish Tournament. Tel: 904/444-7696. Early July.

SANFORD
Central Florida Soap Box Derby. Tel: 407/330-5600. Mid-July.

AUGUST

DESTIN
King Mackeral Tournament. Tel: 904/651-7131. Early August.

SEPTEMBER

Marathon
Marathon Lobster Rodeo Contest. Tel: 305/743-5422. Late September.

OKEECHOBEE
Labor Day Rodeo and Parade. Tel: 813/677-2604. Early September.

SANFORD
Power Boat Racing. Tel: 407/323-1910. Late September.

SARASOTA
Triathalon. Tel: 813/383-22284. Late September.

OCTOBER

DESTIN
Destin Fishing Rodeo. Tel:904/651-7131. Early October.

FORT LAUDERDALE
Fort Lauderdale International Boat Show. Tel: 305/764-7642. Late October.

HALLANDALE
Breeders Cup. Horse racing. Tel: 305/454-7000. Late October.

KISSIMMEE
Kissimmee Boating Jamboree. Tel: 407/847-2033. Late October.

MARATHON
Annual Bonefish Tournament. Tel: 305/743-5422. Early October.

MOUNT DORA
Mount Dora Bicycle Festival. Tel: 904/383-2165. Mid-October.

NAPLES
World Championship Swamp Buggy Races. Tel: 813/774-2701. Late October.

OKEECHOBEE
Airboat Races and Festival. Tel: 813/763-6464. Mid-October.

NOVEMBER

KEY WEST
Key West Offshore Sailfish Tournament. Tel: 305/296-7586. Early November.

MIAMI
Miami Air Show. 305/422-7649. Early November.

NEW SMYRNA BEACH
New Smyrna Beach Aviation Festival. Tel: 904/423-5057. Mid-November.

ST PETERSURG
St Petersburg Boat Show. Tel: 813/892-5798. Late November.

DECEMBER

KISSIMMEE
Kissimmee Warbird Weekend. Tel: 407/847-7477. Late December.

SANFORD
Central Florida Sailfest. Tel: 407/425-0585. Early December.

SARASOTA
Sandy Claws Beach Run. Tel: 813/951-5572. Early December.

USEFUL ADDRESSES

AIRLINES

Airlines with Florida service:

Aer Lingus-Irish Airlines:	Tel:	1-800/223-6537
Aerolineas Argentinas:		1-800/327-0276
Aeromexico:		1-800/237-6639
Air Canada:		1-800/776-3000
Air Jamaica:		1-800/523-5585
Alitalia Airlines:		1-800/223-5730
American Airlines:		1-800/443-7300
British Airways:		1-800/247-9297
Delta Air Lines:		1-800/638-7333
Iberia Air Lines of Spain:		1-800/221-9741
Japan Air Lines:		1-800/525-3663
KLM-Royal Dutch Airlines:		1-800/556-7777
Lan-Chile Airlines:		1-800/255-5526
Northwest Orient:		1-800/447-4747
Sabena Belgian:		1-800/645-3790
Scandinavian Airlines:		1-800/221-2350
Swissair:		1-800/221-4750
TAP Air Portugal:		1-800/221-7370
Trans World Airlines:		1-800/221-2000
USAir:		1-800/428-4322
United Airlines:		1-800/521-4041
Varig Brazilian Airlines:		1-800/468-2744
Viasa Venezuelan International:		1-800/432-9070

CHAMBERS OF COMMERCE

This list also includes addresses of convention and visitors' bureaux.

Alachua Chamber of Commerce, PO Box 387, Alachua, FL 32615. Tel: 904/462-3333

Alachua County Tourist Development Council, PO Drawer CC, Gainesville, FL 32602.
Tel: 904/374-5210

Amelia Island Chamber of Commerce, PO Box 472, Fernandina Beach, FL 32034.
Tel: 904/261-3248

Anna Maria Island Chamber of Commerce, 503 Manatee Ave, Suite A, Holmes Beach, FL 34217.
Tel: 813/778-1541

Apalachicola Bay Chamber of Commerce, 128 Market St, Apalachicola, FL 32320.
Tel: 904/653-9419

Apopka Area Chamber of Commerce, 180 E Main St, Apopka, FL 32703. Tel: 407/886-1441

Auburndale Chamber of Commerce, 111 E Park St, Auburndale, FL 33823. Tel: 813/967-3400

Avon Park Chamber of Commerce, PO Box 1330, Avon Park, FL 33825. Tel: 813/453-3350

Baker County Chamber of Commerce, 20 E Macclenny Ave, Macclenny, FL 32063.
Tel: 904/259-6433

Bartow Chamber of Commerce, PO Box 956, Bartow, FL 33830. Tel: 813/533-7125

Bay County Chamber of Commerce, PO Box 1850, Panama City, FL 32402. Tel: 904/785-5206

Belleview-South Marion Chamber of Commerce, 5301 SE Abshier Blvd, Belleview, FL 32620.
Tel: 904/245-2178

Belle Glade Chamber of Commerce, 540 S Main St, Belle Glade, FL 33430. Tel: 407/996-2745

Bonita Springs Chamber of Commerce, PO Box 1240, Bonita Springs, FL 33959.
Tel: 813/992-2943

Brandon Chamber of Commerce, 408 W Brandon Boulevard, Brandon, FL 33511. Tel: 813/689-1221

Brevard County Tourist Development Council, 2235 North Courtenay Parkway, Merritt Island, FL 32953. Tel: 407/453-2211

Calhoun County Chamber of Commerce, 314 E Central Ave, Blountstown, FL 32424.
Tel: 904/674-4519

Cedar Key Area Chamber of Commerce, Second St, Cedar Key, FL 32625. Tel: 904/543-5600

Chamber of Commerce of South Brevard, 1005 E Strawbridge Ave, Melbourne, FL 32901.
Tel: 407/724-5400

Chamber of Commerce of the Palm Beaches, 501 N Flagler Drive, West Palm Beach, 33401.
Tel: 407/833-3711

Chamber of SW Florida, PO Box CC, Fort Myers, FL 33902. Tel: 813/334-1133

Chamber of SW Florida-Cape Coral, 2051 Cape Coral Parkway, Cape Coral, FL 33904.
Tel: 813/542-3721

Charlotte County Chamber of Commerce, 2702 Tamiami Trail, Port Charlotte, FL 33952.
Tel: 813/627-2222

Citrus County Chamber of Commerce, 208 W Main St, Inverness, FL 32650. Tel: 904/726-2801

Citrus County Commission and Tourist Development Council, 110 N Apopka St, Inverness, FL 32650. Tel: 904/726-8500

Clay County Chamber of Commerce, PO Box 1441, Orange Park, FL 32607-1441. Tel: 904/264-2651

Clermont Area Chamber of Commerce, PO Box 417, Clermont, FL 32711. Tel: 904/394-4191

Clewiston Chamber of Commerce, PO Box 275, Clewiston, 33440. Tel: 813/983-7979

Cocoa Beach Area Chamber of Commerce, 400 Fortenberry Road, Merrit Island, FL 32952.
Tel: 407/459-2200

Coconut Grove Chamber of Commerce, 2820 McFarlane Road, Coconut Grove, 33133.
Tel: 305/444-7270

Columbia County Chamber of Commerce, PO Box 566, Lake City, FL 32056. Tel: 904/752-3690

Coral Springs Chamber of Commerce, 7305 W Sample Road, #110, Coral Springs, 33065. Tel: 305/752-4242

Crestview Area Chamber of Commerce, 502 S Main St, Crestview, FL 32536. Tel: 904/682-3212

Crystal River Chamber of Commerce, 28 N US Hwy, 19, Crystal River, FL 32629. Tel: 904/795-3149

Dade City Chamber of Commerce, 402 E Meridian Ave, Dade City, FL 33525. Tel: 904/567-3769

Dania Chamber of Commerce, PO Box 838, Dania, 33004. Tel: 305/927-3377

Davie-Cooper City Chamber of Commerce, 4185 SW 64 Ave, Davie, 33314. Tel: 305/581-0790

Daytona Beach Shores Chamber of Commerce, 3048 S Atlantic Ave, Daytona Beach, FL 32018-6102. Tel: 904/761-7163

DeBary Area Chamber of Commerce, PO Box One, DeBary, FL 32713. Tel: 407/668-4614

DeLand Area Chamber of Commerce, PO Box 629, DeLand, FL 32721-0629. Tel: 904/734-4331

Deltona Area Chamber of Commerce, PO Box 5152, Deltona, FL 32728. Tel: 407/574-5522

DeSoto County Chamber of Commerce, PO Box 149, Arcadia, FL 33821. Tel: 813/494-4033

Destin Chamber of Commerce, PO Box Eight, Destin, Fl 32541. Tel: 904/837-6241

Destination Daytona, PO Box 2775, Daytona Beach, FL 32015. Tel: 904/255-0981

Dunnellon Area Chamber of Commerce, PO Box 868, Dunnellon, FL 32630. Tel: 904/489-2320

East Orange Chamber of Commerce, PO Box 677027, Union Park Branch, Orlando, FL 32867-7027. Tel: 407/277-5951

Englewood Area Chamber of Commerce, 601 S Indiana Ave, Englewood, FL 34223. Tel: 813/474-5511

Eustis Chamber of Commerce, PO Box 1210, Eustis, FL 32727-1210. Tel: 904/357-3434

Everglades Area Chamber of Commerce, PO Box 130, Everglades City, FL 33929. Tel: 813/695-3941

Flagler County Chamber of Commerce, Star Route 18-N, Bunnell, FL 32010. Tel: 904/437-0106

Fort Meade Chamber of Commerce, PO Box 91, Fort Meade, FL 33841. Tel: 813/285-8253

Fort Myers Beach Chamber of Commerce, PO Box 6109, Fort Myers, FL 33932. Tel: 813/463-6451

Frostproof Chamber of Commerce, PO Box 968, Frostproof, FL 33843. Tel: 813/635-9112

Gadsden County Chamber of Commerce, PO Box 389, Quincy, FL 32351. Tel: 904/627-9231

Gainesville Area Chamber of Commerce, Inc., PO Box 1187, Gainesville, FL 32602. Tel: 904/336-7100

Gilchrist County Chamber of Commerce, PO Box 186, Trenton, FL 32693. Tel: 904/463-6327

Glades County Chamber of Commerce, PO Box 490, Moore Haven, FL 33471. Tel: 813/946-0440

Greater Boca Raton Chamber of Commerce, 1800 N Dixie Hwy, Boca Raton, FL 33432. Tel: 407/395-4433

Greater Boynton Chamber of Commerce, 639 E Ocean Ave, #108, Boynton Beach, FL 33435. Tel: 407/732-9501

Greater Clearwater Chamber of Commerce, PO Box 2457, Clearwater, FL 33517. Tel: 813/461-0011

Greater Deerfield Beach Chamber of Commerce, 1601 E Hillsboro Blvd, Deerfield Beach, FL 33441. Tel: 305/427-1050

Greater Delray Beach Chamber of Commerce, 64 SE Fifth Ave, Delray Beach, FL 33483. Tel: 407/278-0424

Greater Dunedin Chamber of Commerce, 301 Main St, Dunedin, FL 34698. Tel: 813/733-3197

Greater Fort Lauderdale Chamber of Commerce, PO Box 14516, Fort Lauderdale, FL 33302. Tel: 305/462-6000

Greater Fort Lauderdale Convention & Visitors' Bureau, 512 NE 3rd Ave, Fort Lauderdale 33301. Tel: 305/462-6000

Greater Fort Walton Beach Chamber of Commerce, PO Drawer 640, Fort Walton Beach, FL 32549. Tel: 904/244-8191

Greater Gulf Breeze Chamber of Commerce, 913 Gulf Breeze Pkwy, Suite 17, Gulf Breeze, FL 32561. Tel: 904/932-7888

Greater Hollywood Chamber of Commerce, PO 2345, Hollywood, FL 33022. Tel: 305/985-4000

Greater Homestead-Florida City Chamber of Commerce, 650 US Hwy One, Homestead, FL 33030. Tel: 305/247-2332

Greater Key West Chamber of Commerce, 402 Wall St, Key West, FL 33040. Tel: 305/294-2587

Greater LaBelle Chamber of Commerce, PO Box 456, LaBelle, FL 33935. Tel: 813/675-0125

Greater Lake Placid Chamber of Commerce, PO Box 187, Lake Placid, FL 33852. Tel: 813/465-4331

Greater Lake Worth Chamber of Commerce, 1702 Lake Worth Road, Lake Worth, FL 33460. Tel: 407/582-4401

Greater Largo Chamber of Commerce, 395 First Ave, SW Largo, FL 34640. Tel: 813/584-2321

Greater Miami Convention & Visitors' Bureau, 701 Brickell Ave, Miami 3313. Tel: 305/539-3000

Greater Mulberry Chamber of Commerce, PO Box 254, Mulberry, FL 33860. Tel: 813/425-1215

Greater Orange City Area Chamber of Commerce, 520 N Volusia Ave, Orange City, FL 32763. Tel: 904/775-2793

Greater Orlando Chamber of Commerce, PO Box 1234, Orlando, FL 32802. Tel: 407/425-1234

Greater Palm Harbor Area Chamber of Commerce, 1000 US 19 North, Suite 300, Palm Harbor, FL 34684. Tel: 813/785-5205

Greater Pine Island Chamber of Commerce, PO Box 525, Matlacha, FL 33909. Tel: 813/283-0888

Greater Pinellas Park Chamber of Commerce, 5851 Park Blvd, Pinellas Park, FL 34665. Tel: 813/544-4777

Greater Plant City Chamber of Commerce, PO Drawer CC, Plant City, FL 33566. Tel: 813/754-3707

Greater Riverview Chamber of Commerce, PO Box 18, Riverview, FL 33569. Tel: 813/677-26074

Greater Sanford Chamber of Commerce, PO Drawer CC, Sanford, FL 32772-0868. Tel: 407/322-2212

Greater Sebring Chamber of Commerce, 309 South Circle, Sebring, FL 33870. Tel: 813/385-8448

Greater Seminole Area Chamber of Commerce, PO Box 3337, Seminole, FL 34642. Tel: 813/392-3245

Greater Seminole County Chamber of Commerce, PO Box 784, Altamonte Springs, FL 32715-0784. Tel: 407/834-4404

Greater Tampa Chamber of Commerce, PO Box 420 Tampa, FL 33601. Tel: 813/228-7777

Greater Tarpon Springs Chamber of Commerce, 210 S Pinellas Ave, #120, Tarpon Springs, FL 34689. Tel: 813/937-6109

Groveland/Mascotte Chamber of Commerce, PO Box 115, Groveland, FL 32736. Tel: 904/429-3678

Gulf Beaches Chamber of Commerce, PO Box 273, Indian Rocks Beach, FL 34635. Tel: 813/391-7373

Haines City Chamber of Commerce, PO Box 986, Haines City, FL 33844. Tel: 813/422-3751

Halifax Area Chamber of Commerce, PO Box 2775, Daytona Beach, FL 32015. Tel: 904/255-0981

Hamilton County Chamber of Commerce, PO Drawer P, Jasper, FL 32052. Tel: 904/792-1300

Hardee County Chamber of Commerce, PO Box 683, Wauchula, FL 33873. Tel: 813/773-6967

Hawthorne Area Chamber of Commerce, PO Box 125, Hawthorne, FL 32640. Tel: 904/481-2433

Hernando County Chamber of Commerce, 101 E Fort Dade Ave, Brooksville, FL 34601. Tel: 904/796-2420

High Springs Chamber of Commerce, PO Box 863, High Springs, FL 32643. Tel: 904/454-3120

Hobe Sound Chamber of Commerce, PO Box 1507, Hobe Sound, FL 33455. Tel: 407/546-4724

Holly Hill Chamber of Commerce, PO Box 615, Holly Hill, FL 32017. Tel: 904/255-7311

Holmes County Chamber of Commerce, PO Box 1977, Bonifay, FL 32425. Tel: 904/547-4682

Homosassa Springs Area Chamber of Commerce, PO Box 1098, Homosassa Springs, FL 32647. Tel: 904/628-2666

Immokalee Chamber of Commerce, 907 Roberts Ave, Immokalee, FL 33934. Tel: 813/657-3237

Jacksonville Chamber of Commerce Beaches Development Department, 413 Pablo Ave, Jacksonville Beach, FL 32250. Tel: 904/249-3868

Jackson County Chamber of Commerce, PO Box 130, Marianna, FL 32446. Tel: 904/482-8061

Jacksonville and its Beaches Convention & Visitors' Bureau, 6 E Bay St, Suite 200, Jacksonville, FL 32202. Tel: 904/353-0736

Jacksonville Chamber of Commerce, 3 Independent Drive, Jacksonville, FL 32201. Tel: 904/353-0300

Jensen Beach Chamber of Commerce, 1910 NE Jensen Beach Blvd, Jensen Beach, FL 34957. Tel: 407/334-3444

Kissimmee-Osceola County Chamber of Commerce, 320 E Monument Ave, Kissimmee, FL 32741. Tel: 407/847-3174

Kissimmee/St Cloud Convention & Visitors' Bureau, PO Box 2007, Kissimmee, FL 32742-2007. Tel: 407/847-5000

Lake Alfred Chamber of Commerce, PO Box 956, Lake Alfred, FL 33850. Tel: 813/956-1334

Lake City-Columbia County Chamber of Commerce, 15 E Orange St, PO Box 566, Lake City, FL 32056-0566. Tel: 904/752-3690

Lake County Tourist Development Council, 315 W Main St, Tavares, FL 32778. Tel: 904/343-9850

Lake Wales Area Chamber of Commerce, 340 W Central Ave, Lake Wales, FL 33859-0191. Tel: 813/676-3445

Lakeland Area Chamber of Commerce, 35 Lake Morton Drive, Lakeland, FL 33802. Tel: 813/688-8551

Land O' Lakes Chamber of Commerce, PO Box 98, Land O'Lakes, FL 34639. Tel: 813/949-1582

Lee County Visitor & Convention Bureau, 2180 W First St, Fort Myers, FL 33901. Tel: 813/335-2631

Leesburg Area Chamber of Commerce, PO Box 269, Leesburg, FL 32749. Tel: 904/787-2131

Lehigh Acres Chamber of Commerce, Inc., PO Box 757, Lehigh Acres, FL 33970-0757. Tel: 813/369-3322

Liberty County Chamber of Commerce, PO Box 523, Bristol, FL 32321. Tel: 904/643-2359

Longboat Key Chamber of Commerce, 5360 Gulf of Mexico Dr, Longboat Key, FL 34228. Tel: 813/383-2466

Longwood-Winter Springs Area Chamber of Commerce, PO Box 520963, Longwood, FL 32752-0963. Tel: 407/831-9991

Madeira Beach Chamber of Commerce, 501 150th Ave, Madeira Beach, FL 33708. Tel: 813/391-7373

Madison County Chamber of Commerce, 105 North Range, Madison, FL 32340. Tel: 904/973-2788

Maitland-South Seminole Chamber of Commerce, 110 N Maitland Ave, Maitland, FL 32751. Tel: 407/644-0741

Manatee Chamber of Commerce, 222 10th St West, Bradenton, FL 34205. Tel: 813/748-3411

Manatee County Convention & Visitors' Bureau, PO Box 788, Bradenton, FL 34206-0788. Tel: 813/746-5989

Marco Island Area Chamber of Commerce, PO Box 913, Marco Island, FL 33969. Tel: 813/394-7549

Mayo-Lafayette Chamber of Commerce, PO Box 416, Mayo, FL 32066. Tel: 904/294-2705

Miami Beach Chamber of Commerce, 1920 Meridan Ave, Miami Beach, FL 33139. Tel: 305/672-1270.

Monroe County Tourist Development Council, PO Box 866, Key West, FL 33041. Tel: 305/296-2228

Monticello-Jefferson County Chamber of Commerce, 420 W Washington St, Monticello, FL 32344. Tel: 904/997-5552

Mount Dora Chamber of Commerce, PO Box 196, Mount Dora, FL 32757. Tel: 904/383-2165

Naples Area Chamber of Commerce, 3620 N Tamiami Trail, Naples, FL 33940. Tel: 813/262-6141

Navarre Beach Chamber of Commerce, PO Box 5336, Navarre, FL 32569-5336. Tel: 904/939-3267

New Smyrna Beach-Edgewater-Oak Hill Chamber of Commerce, PO Box 129, New Smyrna Beach, FL 32070. Tel: 904/426-5401

Newberry Area Chamber of Commerce, PO Box 1004, Newberry, FL 32669. Tel: 904/472-4121

North Fort Myers Chamber of Commerce, 13180 N Cleveland Ave, Suite 115, North Fort Myers, FL 33903. Tel: 813/997-9111

North Tampa Chamber of Commerce, PO Box 271629, Tampa, FL 33688. Tel: 813/960-9344

Ocala-Marion County Chamber of Commerce, PO Box 1210, Ocala, FL 32678. Tel: 904/629-8051

Okeechobee County Chamber of Commerce, 55 S Parrot Ave, Okeechobee, FL 34972. Tel: 813/763-6464

Oldsmar Chamber of Commerce, PO Box 521, Oldsmar, FL 34677. Tel: 813/855-4233

Orlando/Orange County Convention & Visitors' Bureau, 7208 Sand Lake Rd, Orlando, FL 32819. Tel: 407/363-5872

Ormond Beach Chamber of Commerce, PO Box 874, Ormond Beach, FL 32074. Tel: 904/677-3454

Palm Bay Area Chamber of Commerce, 4100 Dixie Hwy NE, Palm Bay, FL 32905. Tel: 407/723-0801

Palm Beach County Convention & Visitors' Bureau, 1555 Palm Beach Lakes Blvd, #204, West Palm Beach, FL 33401. Tel: 407/471-3995

Palm City Chamber of Commerce, PO Box 530, Palm City, FL 33490. Tel: 407/286-8121

Panama City Beach Convention & Visitors' Bureau, PO Box 9473, Panama City Beach, FL 32407. Tel: 904/234-6575

Pensacola Chamber of Commerce, PO Box 550, Pensacola, FL 32593. Tel: 904/438-4081

Pensacola Convention & Visitors' Information Center, 1401 E Gregory St, Pensacola, FL 32501. Tel: 904/434-1234

Perry-Taylor County Chamber of Commerce, PO Box 892, Perry, FL 32347. Tel: 904/584-5366

Pinellas County Tourist Development Council, 4625 E Bay Drive, Suite 109A, Clearwater, FL 34624. Tel: 813/530-6452

Polk County Tourism Development Council, PO Box 1909, Bartow, FL 33830. Tel: 813/533-1161

Ponce de León Area Chamber of Commerce, PO Box 36, Ponce de León, FL 32455. Tel: 904/836-4747

Port Orange-South Daytona Chamber of Commerce, 3431 Ridgewood Ave, Port Orange, FL 32019. Tel: 904/761-1601

Port St Joe-Gulf County Chamber of Commerce, PO Box 964, Port St Joe, FL 32456. Tel: 904/227-1223

Port St Lucie Chamber of Commerce, 1626 SE Port St Lucie Blvd, Port St Lucie, FL 33452. Tel: 407/335-4422

Putnam County Chamber of Commerce, PO Box 550, Palatka, FL 32078. Tel: 904/328-1503

Safety Harbor Chamber of Commerce, 200 Main St, Safety Harbor, FL 34695. Tel: 813/726-2890

Sanibel-Captiva Island Chamber of Commerce, PO Box 166, Sanibel, FL 33957. Tel: 813/472-3232

Santa Rosa County Chamber of Commerce, 501 Stewart St SW, Milton, FL 32570. Tel: 904/623-2339

Sarasota Convention & Visitors' Bureau, 655 N Tamiami Trail, Sarasota, FL 34236. Tel: 813/957-1877

Sarasota County Chamber of Commerce, PO Box 308, Sarasota, FL 34230. Tel: 813/955-8187

Sebastian River Area Chamber of Commerce, PO Box 780385, Sebastian, FL 332978-0385. Tel: 407/589-5969

Siesta Key Chamber of Commerce, 5263 Ocean Blvd, Sarasota, FL 34242. Tel: 813/349-3800

South Hillsborough County Chamber of Commerce, 315 S Tamiami Trail, Ruskin, FL 33570. Tel: 813/645-3808

St Augustine-St Johns Chamber of Commerce, PO Drawer O, St Augustine, FL 32085. Tel: 904/829-5681

St Cloud Area Chamber of Commerce, PO Box 5, St Cloud, FL 32769. Tel: 407/892-3671

St Lucie County Chamber of Commerce, 2300 Virginia Ave, Fort Pierce, FL 34982. Tel: 407/468-1535

St Petersburg Area Chamber of Commerce, PO Box 1371, St Petersburg, FL 33731. Tel: 813/821-4069

St Petersburg Beach Chamber of Commerce, 6990 Gulf Blvd, St Petersburg, FL 33706. Tel: 813/360-6957

Starke-Bradford County Chamber of Commerce, PO Box 576, Starke, FL 32091. Tel: 904/964-5278

Stuart-Martin County Chamber of Commerce, 1650 S Kanner Hwy, Stuart, FL 33494. Tel: 407/287-1088

Sumter County Chamber of Commerce, PO Box 550, Bushnell, FL 33513. Tel: 904/793-3099

Sun City Center Chamber of Commerce, 1651 Sun City Center Plaza, Sun City, FL 33570. Tel: 813/634-5111

Suwannee County Chamber of Commerce, PO Box C, Live Oak, FL 32060. Tel: 904/362-3071

Tallahassee Convention & Visitors' Bureau, PO Box 1639, Tallahassee, FL 32302.
Tel: 904/224-8116

Tampa/Hillsborough Convention & Visitors' Association, 111 Madison St, Tampa, FL 33602.
Tel: 813/223-1111

Tavares Chamber of Commerce, PO Box 697, Tavares, FL 32778. Tel: 904/343-2531

Titusville Chamber of Commerce, 2000 S Washington Ave, Titusville, FL 327800. Tel: 407/267-3036

Treasure Island Chamber of Commerce, 152–108 Ave, Treasure Island, FL 33706. Tel: 813/367-4529

Umatilla Chamber of Commerce, PO Box 300, Umatilla, FL 32784. Tel: 904/669-3511

Venice Area Chamber of Commerce, 257 N Tamiami Trail, Venice, FL 34285. Tel: 813/488-2236

Vero Beach-Indian River County Chamber of Commerce, 1216 21st St, Vero Beach, FL 32960.
Tel: 407/567-3491

Walton County Chamber of Commerce, Chautauqua Bldg, Circle Drive, Defuniak Springs, FL 32422.
Tel: 904/267-3511

Washington County Chamber of Commerce, PO Box 457, Chipley, FL 32428. Tel: 904/636-4157

West Hernando Chamber of Commerce, 2563 Commercial Way, Spring Hill, FL 34606.
Tel: 904/683-3700

West Nassau Chamber of Commerce, PO Box 98, Callahan, FL 32011. Tel: 904/879-1441

West Orange Chamber of Commerce, PO Box 522, Winter Garden, FL 32787. Tel: 407/656-1304

West Pasco Chamber of Commerce, 407 W Main St, New Port Richey, FL 34652. Tel: 813/842-7651

West Pasco Chamber of Commerce-Hudson Office, 13740 Old Dixie Hwy, Hudson, FL 34667.
Tel: 813/868-9395

West Tampa Chamber of Commerce, 3005 W Columbus Drive, Tampa, FL 33607.
Tel: 813/879-2866

Winter Haven Area Chamber of Commerce, PO Drawer 1420, Winter Haven, FL 33882-1420.
Tel: 813/293-2138

Winter Park Chamber of Commerce, PO Box 280, Winter Park, FL 32790. Tel: 407/644-8281

Ybor City Chamber of Commerce, PO Box 5055, Tampa, FL 33675-5055. Tel: 813/248-3712

Zephyrhills Chamber of Commerce, 691 Fifth Ave, Zephyrhills, FL 34248. Tel: 813/782-1913

FURTHER READING

HISTORICAL/POLITICAL/CULTURAL

Allman, T.D. *Miami – City of the Future*, Atlantic Monthly Press, 1987.

Andrews, Evangeline W., and Andrews, Charles McLean (editors). *Jonathan Dickinson's Journal; or God's Protecting Providence*. New Haven: Yale University Press, 1945.

Apple, Max. *Propheteers*. Harper & Row, 1987.

Barbour, George, M. *Florida for Tourists, Invalids and Settlers, 1882*. Floridiana Facsimile Reprint Series, Gainesville: University of Florida Press, 1964.

Bartram, William. *Travels of William Bartram*. Edited by Mark Van Doren. New York: Dover Publications, 1951.

Bennett, Charles E. *Laudonniere and Fort Caroline: History and Documents*. Gainesville: University of Florida Press, 1964.

Boyd, Mark F., Smith, Hale G., and Grifin, John W. *Here They Once Stood: The Tragic End of the Apalachee Missions*. Gainesville: University of Florida Press, 1951.

Brevard, Caroline. *A History of Florida*. Edited by James A. Robertson. Two volumes. DeLand: Florida State Historical Society, 1924–25.

Brinton, Daniel G. *A Guide-Book of Florida and the South for Tourists, Invalids and Emigrants*. Philadelphia: G. Maclean, 1869.

Campbell, A Stuart. *The Cigar Industry of Tampa*. Gainesville: University of Florida Press, 1939.

Chandler, David Leon. *Henry Flagler – The Astonishing Life and Times of the Visionary Robbery Baron Who Founded Florida*. MacMillan, 1986.

Coe, Charles H. *Red Patriots: The Story of the Seminoles*. Cincinnati: The Editor Publishing Co., 1868.

Davis, William Watson. *The Civil War and Reconstruction in Florida*. New York: Columbia University Press, 1913.

Didion, Joan. *Miami*. Simon and Schuster, 1987.

Dodson, Pat. (editor) *Journey through the Old Everglades: The Log of the Minnehaba*. Tampa: Trend House, 1973.

Douglas, Marjory Stoneman. *The Everglades: River of Grass*. New York: Rinehart, 1947.

Douglas, Marjory Stoneman. *Florida: the Long Frontier*. New York: Harper & Row, 1967.

Douglas, Marjory Stoneman. *Hurricane*. New York: Rinehart & Co., 1958.

Lyon, Eugene. *The Search for the Atocha*. New York: Harper & Row, 1979.

MacCauley, Clay. *The Seminole Indians of Florida*. Smithsonian Institution Bureau of American Ethnology, Fifth Annual Report, 1883, 1884. Washington, DC, 1887.

Mahon, John K. *The Second Seminole War*. Gainesville: University of Florida Press, 1968.

Maloney, Walter C. *A Sketch of the History of Key West, Florida, 1876*. Edited by Thelma Peters. Floridiana Facsimile and Reprint Series, Gainesville: University of Florida Press, 1968.

Matschat, Cecile. *Suwannee River: Strange Green Land*. New York: Farrar and Rinehart, 1938.

McReynolds, Edwin C. *The Seminoles*. Norman: University of Oklahoma Press, 1957.

Motte, Jacob Rhett. *Journey Into Wilderness: An Army Surgeon's Account of Life in Camp and Field During the Creek and Seminole Wars, 1836–1838*. Edited by James F. Sunderman. Gainesville: University of Florida Press, 1953.

Neill, Wilfred T. *The Story of Florida's Seminole Indians*. St Petersburg: Great Outdoors Publishing Co., 1964.

Neyland, Leedell W. *Twelve Black Floridians*. Tallahassee: Florida A & M University Foundation, Inc., 1970.

Ober, Frederick A. *"Rambler," Guide to Florida, 1875*. Edited by Rembert W. Patrick. Floridiana Facsimile and Reprint Series, Gainesville: University of Florida Press, 1964.

Olsen, Stanley J. *Fossil Mammals of Florida*. Florida Geological Survey. Special Publication #6. Tallahassee: Florida Geological Survey, 1959.

Pettengill, George W. *The Story of Florida Railroads 1834–1903*. The Railway and Locomotive Historical Society, Bulletin No. 86. Boston: Railway and Locomotive Historical Society, 1952.

Rose, Rufus E. *The Swamp and Overflowed Lands of Florida: The Disston Contract and Sale*. Tallahassee: 1916.

Rothchild, John. *Up for Grabs*. Viking, 1985.

Shofner, Jerrel H. *Nor Is It Over Yet: Florida in the Era of Reconstructions, 1863–1877*. Gainesville: University Presses of Florida, 1974.

Simpson, George S. "Extinct Land Mammals of Florida." Florida Geological Survey, 20th Annual Report. Tallahassee: 1929.

Townshend, F. Trench. *Wild Life in Florida, With a Visit to Cuba*. London: Hurst and Blackett, 1875.

Will, Lawrence E. *A Cracker History of Lake Okeechobee*. St Petersburg: Great Outdoors Publishing Co., 1965.

Will, Lawrence E. *A Dredgement of Cape Sable*. St Petersburg: Great Outdoors Publishing Co., 1967.

THE SPACE PROGRAM & CAPE CANAVERAL

Armstrong, Neil. *First on the Moon: The Astronauts' Own Story*. Little, 1970.

Branley, Franklyn M. *Columbia and Beyond: The Story of the Space Shuttle*. Philomel, 1979.

Carr, Harriet. *Cape Canaveral, Cape of Storms and Wild Cane Fields*. St Petersburg: Valkyrie Press, 1974.

Kennedy Space Center Story. John F. Kennedy Space Center, Cape Canaveral: NASA, undated.

US News and World Report. *US on the Moon*. New York: Macmillan, 1970.

Verne, Jules. *From the Earth to the Moon*. Available in a variety of hardcover and paperback editions since it was first published in 1865.

Wolfe, Tom. *The Right Stuff*. Bantam, 1980.

FICTION & WRITERS OF FICTION

Bigelow, Gordon E. *Frontier Eden: The Literary Career of Marjory Kinnan Rawlings*. Gainesville: University of Florida Press, 1966.

Frederiksen, Alan Ryle. *Red Roe Run*. Green Key Press, 1983.

Hemingway, Ernest. *Islands in the Stream*. New York: Charles Scribner's Sons, 1970.

Hemingway, Ernest. *To Have and Have Not*. New York: Charles Scribner's Sons, 1937. While many of Hemingway's novels and short stories were written during the 10 years he lived at Key West, this one is set in a town at Florida's southern tip.

Hemingway, Ernest. *Collected Letters (1918–1961)*. New York: Charles Scribner's Sons, 1981.

Hirschfeld, Burt. *Key West*. Corgi. A steamy, seamy novel written by an esteemed paperback king.

Hurston, Zora Neale. *Their Eyes Were Watching God*. Philadelphia: Lippincott, 1936. A novel about the devastating 1928 hurricane by one of the state's leading black authors.

Kaufelt, David A. *American Tropic*. Poseidon Press, 1986.

MacDonald, John D. *Condominium*. Lippincott, 1977. This fine novel deals with the effects of a hurricane on a shoddily-constructed condominium complex.

MacDonald, John D. *The Travis McGee Series*. Hardcover, Lippincott; paperback, Fawcett. Various publication dates. *The Deep Blue Goodby* (1979), *The Dreadful Lemon Sky* (1975), *Dress Her in Indigo* (1971), *The Empty Copper Sea* (1978), *The Long Lavender Look* (1972), *and A Tan and Sandy Silence* (1979) are only a few of the titles by Florida's most prolific novelist, about his detective, McGee.

McGuane, Thomas. *Ninety-two in the Shade*. New York: Farrar, Straus and Girous, 1973. The sea and the seedy side of Key West play an integral role in this superb tale of treachery.

McLendon, James. *Papa Hemingway in Key West.* Miami: E.A. Seemann, 1972.

Norman, Geoffrey. *Midnight Water.* Dutton, 1983.

Pratt, Theodore. *The Barefoot Mailman.* New York: Duell, Sloan and Pearce, 1943.

Rawlings, Marjorie Kinna. *Cross Creek.* New York: Charles Scribner's Sons, 1942. The tales here reek of Deep South rural Florida and are probably more fact than fiction.

Rawlings, Marjorie Kinna. *The Yearling.* New York: Charles Scribner's Sons, 1939. The Pulitzer prize-winning story of a boy and his young deer.

Slaughter, Frank. Various novels, publishers and dates. Try *Storm Haven* (1953), *Fort Everglades, East Side General* (1952), *The Golden Isle* and *In a Dark Garden* (1946); novels with a Florida backdrop from another of the state's prolific tale-spinners.

Wilder, Robert. *Flamingo Road.* New York: Grosset and Dunlap, 1942. Happenings in Truro, the Peyton Place of Florida.

Williams, Tennessee. *Memoirs.* New York: Doubleday, 1975. The dean of American playwrights tells about his life in Key West and elsewhere.

Williams, Tennessee. Various plays. Many of William's plays convey the mood of a steamy night in the South. Try *Three by Tennessee: Sweet Bird of Youth, The Rose Tattoo* and *Night of the Iguana.* Signet Classics: New American Library, 1976.

GUIDES, REFERENCES, SPECIAL INTERESTS

Brookfield, Charles M. and Griswold, Oliver. *They All Called It Tropical: True Tales of the Romantic Everglades, Cape Sable and the Florida Keys.* Miami: Historical Association of southern Florida and Banyan Books, 1977. Reprint of 1949 edition.

Brown, Robin C. *Florida's Fossils – Guide to Location, Indentification and Enjoyment.* Pineapple Press, 1988.

Craighead, Frank C. *Orchids and Other Air Plants of the Everglades National Park.* Coral Gables: University of Miami Press, 1963.

Craighead, Frank C. *The Trees of South Florida, Vol. One, The Natural Environments and Their Succession.* Coral Gables: University of Miami Press, 1971.

Densmore, Francis. *Seminole Music.* Smithsonian Institution Bureau of American Ethnology, Bulletin 161. Washington: US Government Printing Office, 1956.

DeWire, Elinor. *Guide to Florida Lighthouses.* Pineapple Press, 1987.

Fichter, George S. *Birds of Florida.* Miami: E.A. Seemann Publishing, 1971. The definitive guide to Florida's feathered inhabitants.

Fleming, Glenn; Genelle, Pierre; and Long, Robert W. *Wild Flowers of Florida.* Miami: Banyan Books, 1976.

Fletcher, Leslie. *Florida's Fantastic Fauna and Flora.* Beau Lac, 1977.

Gantz, Charlotte Orr. *A Naturalist in Southern Florida.* Coral Gables: University of Miami Press, 1971.

George, Jean Craighead. *Everglades Wildguide.* Washington: US Government Printing Office, 1972.

Hiller, Herbert. *Guide to the Small and Historic Lodgings of Florida.* Pineapple Press, 1988.

Hoffmeister, John Edward. *Land From the Sea: The Geologic Story of South Florida.* Coral Gables: University of Miami Press, 1974.

Hudson, L. Frank, and Prescott, Gordon R. *Lost Treasures of Florida's Gulf Coast.* St Petersburg: Great Outdoors, 1973.

Key West Women's Club. *The Key West Cookbook.* New York: Farrar, Straus and Giroux, 1949.

Koukoulis, Andrew. *Poisonous Snakes of Florida.* Silver Springs: International Graphics, 1972.

Lakela, Olga, and Long, Robert W. *Ferns of Florida.* Miami: Banyan Books, 1976.

Lewis, Gordon. *Florida Fishing: Fresh and Salt Water.* St Petersburg: Great Outdoors, 1957.

Luer, Carlyle A. *The Native Orchids of Florida.* New York: The New York Botanical Garden, 1972.

Marks, H.S., and Riggs, Gene B. *Rivers of Florida.* Southern Printing, 1974.

Marsh, Richard. *Key West Ghosts.* Pocket Poetry, 1976.

Matschat, Cecile H. *Suwannee River: Strange Green Land.* Gainesville: University of Florida Press, 1980.

McLean, Will. *Florida Sand, Original Songs and Stories of Florida.* Orlando: Curry's Printing Co., 1969.

Morris, Allen. *Florida Place Names.* Coral Gables: University of Miami Press, 1974. The fascinating stories behind the dozens of names of Florida cities, countries, rivers, etcetera.

Morris, Allen. *The Florida Handbook.* Tallahassee: Peninsula Publishing Co. Published bienially since 1947. A standard Florida reference book.

Morris, Alton C. (collector/editor) *Folksongs of Florida.* Gainesville: University of Florida Press, 1950.

Morton, Julia. *Plants Poisonous to People in Florida and Other Warm Areas.* Miami: Fairchild Tropical Gardens, 1971, 1977.

Read, W.A. *Florida Place Names of Indian Origin and Seminole Personal Names.* Gordon Printing, 1977.

Rouse, Irving. *A Survey of Indian River Archaeology, Florida.* Yale University: Publications in Anthropology, No. 44, 1977. Reprint of 1951 edition.

Stachowicz, Jim. *Diver's Guide to Florida and the Florida Keys.* Miami: Windward Publishing, 1976. A good guide to underwater Florida.

Stevenson, George B. *Trees of Everglades National Park and the Florida Keys.* Miami: Banyan Books (distributor), 1969.

Tebeau, Charlton W. *Man in the Everglades National Park*. Coral Gables: University of Miami Press, 1969.

Truesdell, William G. *Guide to the Wilderness Waterway of the Everglades National Park*. Coral Gables: University of Miami Press, 1969.

Ward, Bill. *Miami Herald Outdoor Guide*. Published annually by the Miami Herald.

Warnke, James R. *Balustrades and Gingerbread: Key West's Handcrafted Homes and Buildings*. Miami: Banyan Books, 1978.

Williams, Joy. *The Florida Keys – a history and guide*. Random House, 1987.

Woodall's Florida Campground Directory. Highland Park III: Woodall Publishing Co. Revised annually.

DAILY NEWSPAPERS

Boca Raton News, 33 SE Third St, 33432.
Bradenton Herald, 102 Manatee Ave W, 33505
Brooksville Sun-Journal, 703 Lamar Ave, 34601
Cape Coral Daily Breeze, PO Box 846, 33904
Charlotte Harbor Sun, 23170 Harborview Road, 33980
Clearwater Sun, 301 S Myrtle Ave, 33515
Daytona Beach News-Journal, 901 Sixth St, 32015
Deland Sun News, 111 S Alabama, 32724
Deland News-Sentinel, 101 N New River Drive, Fort Lauderdale 33302
Delray Beach News, 34 SE Second Ave, 33432
Deltona Voulusian, PO Box 5339, 32728
Fort Lauderdale News, 200 E Las Olas Blvd, 33301
Fort Myers News-Press, 2442 Anderson Ave, 33901-3987
Fort Pierce News-Tribune, PO Box 69, 33454
Fort Walton Beach Playground Daily News, PO Box 2949, 32548
Gainesville Sun, Drawer A, 32602
Homestead South Dade News Leader, PO Box 339, 33090
Inverness Citrus County Chronicle, 130 Heights Ave, 32652
Jacksonville Florida Times Union, One Riverside Ave, 32201
Key West Citizen, PO Box 1800, 33040
Lake City Reporter, PO Box 1709, 32056
Lakeland Ledger, PO Box 408, 33802
Lake Wales Highlander, PO Box 872, 33853
Leesburg Commercial, Drawer 7, 32749-0600
Marianna Jackson County Floridian, PO Box 520, 32446
Melbourne Florida Today, PO Box 363000, 32936
Miami Herald, One Herald Plaza, 33132-1693
Naples Daily News, 1075 Central Ave, 33940
New Smyrna Beach News & Observer, Drawer B, 32069
Ocala Star-Banner, PO Box 490, 32678-0490
Orange Park Clay Today, PO Box 1209, 32067-1209
Orlando Sentinel, 633 N Orange Ave, 32801-1349
Palatka Daily News, PO Box 777, 32078-0777

Palm Beach Daily News, 265 Royal Poinciana Way, 33480
Panama City News-Herald, PO Box 1940, 32402-1940
Pensacola News-Journal, PO Box 12710, 32574
Punta Gorda Charlotte Herald-News, 114 W Olympia Ave, 33951-1808
Sanford Herald, 300 N French Ave, 32771
Sarasota Herald-Tribune, PO Box 1719, 33578-1719
St Augustine Record, Drawer 1630, 32085
St Petersburg Times, PO Box 1121, 33731
Stuart News, PO Box 9009, 34995
Tallahassee Democrat, PO Box 990, Tallahassee 32302-0990
Tampa Tribune, PO Box 191, 33601-0191
Vero Beach Press-Journal, PO Box 1268, 32961-1268
West Palm Beach Post, Drawer T, 33402

MUSIC

Try listening to some local music while reading *Insight Guide: Florida*, or on your car stereo while driving the state's byways and highways. The following music does not profess to be a comprehensive guide to melodies about the Sunshine State. It does, however, provide a sampling of music for a variety of tastes – including classical, jazz, Bahamian-flavored ballads, classic American folksongs, and hard Southern rock and roll – all in some way connected with Florida.

Buffet, Jimmy, A-1-A MCA 37027.
– *Changes in Latitudes, Changes in Attitudes*. MCA AB-990.
– *Coconut Telegraph*. MCA 5169.
– *Havana Daydreamin'*. MCA 37023.
– *Living and Dying in Three-Quarter Time*. MCA 37025.
– *Son of a Son of a Sailor*. MCA 37024.
– *White Sport Coat and Pink Crutaseans*. MCA 37026.
– *You Had to Be There*. MCA AK2-1008.
"Woman Goin' Crazy on Caroline Street," "Ringling, Ringling," and "Banana Republics," are some of the titles of songs composed by Buffet, who got his start playing bars in Key West. He now divides his time between Florida and Colorado. His Florida concerts are usually sell-outs.

Charles, Ray, Best. At. 1543.
– *Genius* (12–59). At. 1312.
– *Great*. At. 1259.
– *Greatest*. At. 8054.
– *Live*. (Double album). At. 2-503.
Born in the small Florida town of Greenville near the Georgia border, Charles went blind at an early age after a futile attempt to save his brother from drowning. He grew up here and began piano training at the Florida School for the Deaf and Blind in St Augustine, before leaving the state to set out

to become a legend. The trauma of those early days in Florida is still evident in the soulful stylings of Charles' compositions and interpretations.

Delius, Frederick
Florida Suite, Dance Rhapsody #2, Over the Hills and Far Away. The Beecham Royal Philharmonic, Seraphim 5-60212.

Florida even has its own resident composer, Delius, who moved to a small farm on the banks of the St Johns. The songs and melodies sung by plantation slaves are evident in his suites. Also try *Summer Night on the River, Song Before Summer, In A Summer Garden*, etc. Barbirolli, Halle Orchestra, Angel S-36588; and *Walk To the Paradise Garden* (1910), *Song of Summer*. Barbirolli, Angel S-36415.

Foster, Stephen
Old Folks at Home and other songs.
– The Florida Concert Society, Request 10035.
– Mormon Tabernacle Choir, Columbia MS-7149.
– Rogers Orchestra and Choir, London 44050.
– Gregg Smith Singers with the New York Vocal Arts Ensemble, Turn. 34609.

Although Foster never set foot in Florida, the state has adopted him as a favorite son for his use of the famous refrain "Way down upon the S'wanee River" in his "Old Folks at Home." "The Camptown Races," "Jeannie With the Light Brown Hair," "Oh! Susanna," and "My Old Kentucky Home" are only a few of his classics.

Lynyrd Skynyrd
– *Bullets*, MCA 37070.
– *First and Last*. MCA 37071.
– *Nuthin' Fancy*. MCA 37069.
– *One From the Road*. (Double album), MCA 8011.
– *Pronounced Leh-nerd*. MCA 3019.
– *Second Helping*. MCA 3020.
– *Street Survivors*. MCA 3029.

They were the pioneers of deep-fried southern rock and roll until most of the band members died in a plane crash. But you would never know they were gone if you drive through Florida listening to stereo FM stations (which play their classic "Free Bird" as often as they play contemporary hits).

Molly Hatchet
– *Beatin' The Odds*. Epic FE-36572.
– *Flirtin' With*. Epic JE-35110.

Practitioners of the art of southern rock and roll. Many of the band members hail from Jacksonville and other Florida cities.

ART/PHOTO CREDITS

Photography by

Page 99, 105	Greg Anderson
16/17, 48, 61, 68, 80/81, 82, 83, 91, 92, 93, 94, 120, 121, 122, 127, 129, 142, 144, 145, 146, 147, 149, 151, 152, 154, 158, 159, 161, 165, 175, 178, 180, 192, 196, 205, 206, 213R, 264, 265, 304, 309, 315	Tony Arruza
77, 101, 157, 182, 186, 187, 204	José Azel
26, 27, 30, 32, 34, 35, 240	Charles E. Bennett
224	Russell Bronson
56, 58, 65, 106, 107, 195, 200, 243, 258, 259, 262, 290, 295, 313	Pat Canova
134/135, 155, 166, 190, 191, 208/209, 296	John Coley
31	Fredrick Dau
59, 64, 66, 67, 69, 70, 74, 75, 76, 102, 103, 150, 181, 183, 193, 207, 229, 239, 241, 257, 267, 268, 269, 271, 274, 276, 282, 283, 285, 287, 289, 292, 297, 300/301, 307L, 310, 311, 312, 314, 318, 319, 320, 330, 336	Ricardo Ferro
24, 36, 43, 44	Florida Division of Tourism
62	Bill Held
211R	John F. Kennedy Library, Boston
46	Henry Morrison Flagler Museum
41	Historical Association of Southern Florida
28	Historical Society of St Augustine
Cover, 7, 12/13, 18/19, 78/79, 96/97, 104/105, 130/131, 162, 164, 179, 197, 203, 222, 255, 260, 317	Catherine Karnow
108, 109	Don Kincaid
38	Library of Congress
14/15, 51, 52/53, 54/55, 71, 73, 84, 85, 86, 87, 88/89, 90, 95, 123, 125, 136, 173, 189, 213L, 214, 220/221, 225, 230, 232, 250, 266, 277, 279, 288, 305, 307R, 322, 323, 325, 326, 327, 333	Bud Lee
20, 316	Leonard Lueras
140/141	Walter R. Marks
50	Miami Herald
238	George Millener
110/111, 113, 114, 115, 116, 117, 231	Courtesy of NASA
176	Palm Beach County Historical Society
118/119, 124, 262, 263	Sea World
228, 293	Ron Smith
22/23, 37, 40, 45, 72, 234/235, 236	State Library of Florida
315	Rolf Steinberg
168	Ken Steinhoff
42, 278, 306	J. Manning Strozier Library
39	Courtesy of US Treasury
323	Bruce Walker
169, 171, 177, 216	C.J. Walker
244/245, 246, 248, 251, 254, 256, 261	Walt Disney Productions
280, 281	Bob Widner
172, 226, 328, 332, 335	Baron Wolman
47, 60, 100, 112, 132/133, 153, 163, 202, 212, 218, 219, 227R, 299, 308, 331	Paul Zach
92, 215, 253	Joseph F. Viesti
Illustrations	Klaus Geisler
Visual Consultant	V. Barl

INDEX